The Street Is Ours

The streets of Rio de Janeiro have long been characterized as exuberant and exotic places for social commerce, political expression, and the production and dissemination of culture. *The Street Is Ours* examines the changing uses and meanings of Rio de Janeiro's streets and argues that the automobile, by literally occupying much of the street's space and by introducing death and injury on a new scale, significantly transformed the public commons. Once viewed as a natural resource and a place of equitable access, deep meaning, and diverse functions, the street became a space of exclusion that prioritized automotive movement. Taking an environmental approach, Shawn William Miller surveys the costs and failures of this spatial transformation and demonstrates how Rio's citizens have resisted the automobile's intrusions and, in some cases, reversed the long trend of closing the street against its potential utilities.

Shawn William Miller is Associate Professor of History at Brigham Young University. He is an environmental historian and the author of *An Environmental History of Latin America* (Cambridge, 2007) and *Fruitless Trees: Portuguese Conservation and Brazil's Colonial Timber* (2000).

CAMBRIDGE LATIN AMERICAN STUDIES

General Editors
KRIS LANE, Tulane University
MATTHEW RESTALL, Pennsylvania State University

Editor Emeritus
HERBERT S. KLEIN
Gouverneur Morris Emeritus Professor of History, Columbia University,
and Hoover Research Fellow, Stanford University

Other Books in the Series

(Continued after the Index)

The Street Is Ours

Community, the Car, and the Nature of Public Space in Rio de Janeiro

SHAWN WILLIAM MILLER

Brigham Young University, Utah

CAMBRIDGE
UNIVERSITY PRESS

CAMBRIDGE
UNIVERSITY PRESS

University Printing House, Cambridge CB2 8BS, United Kingdom

One Liberty Plaza, 20th Floor, New York, NY 10006, USA

477 Williamstown Road, Port Melbourne, VIC 3207, Australia

314-321, 3rd Floor, Plot 3, Splendor Forum, Jasola District Centre, New Delhi - 110025, India

79 Anson Road, #06-04/06, Singapore 079906

Cambridge University Press is part of the University of Cambridge.

It furthers the University's mission by disseminating knowledge in the pursuit of education, learning and research at the highest international levels of excellence.

www.cambridge.org
Information on this title: www.cambridge.org/9781108447119
DOI: 10.1017/9781108551397

First published 2018
First paperback edition 2020

A catalogue record for this publication is available from the British Library

Library of Congress Cataloging in Publication data
NAMES: Miller, Shawn William, 1964–
TITLE: The street is ours : community, the car, and the nature of public
space in Rio De Janeiro / Shawn William Miller, Brigham Young University, Utah.
DESCRIPTION: Cambridge, United Kingdom ; New York, NY : Cambridge
University Press, 2018. | Series: Cambridge Latin American studies ; 111 | Includes
bibliographical references and index.
IDENTIFIERS: LCCN 2018009339 | ISBN 9781108426978 (hbk : alk. paper)
SUBJECTS: LCSH: Public spaces – Brazil – Rio de Janeiro. | Streets – Social aspects –
Brazil – Rio de Janeiro. | Community life – Brazil – Rio de Janeiro. | Sociology, Urban –
Brazil – Rio de Janeiro. | Rio de Janeiro (Brazil) – Social conditions.
CLASSIFICATION: LCC HT129.B7 M55 2018 | DDC 307.760981/53–dc23
LC record available at https://lccn.loc.gov/2018009339

ISBN 978-1-108-42697-8 Hardback
ISBN 978-1-108-44711-9 Paperback

A natureza, como a história, não se faz brincando.
(Nature, like history, follows no frivolous course.)

Joaquim Maria Machado de Assis, *Dom Casmurro* (São Paulo: Companhia de Melhoramentos, 1968), 206.

Contents

Maps and Figures

Acknowledgments

While it is often a lonely pursuit, we accrue many debts in the course of writing history: gifts of ideas, hospitality, financial support, and time, all freely given. I first thank all those who have been willing to debate or give a hearing to my working ideas: over frequent lunches with colleagues – Chris Hodson, Don Harreld, Jeff Shumway, Karen Carter, and Kendall Brown; in conference sessions – Alida Metcalf, Bill Summerhill, Brodwyn Fischer, Chris Ebert, Donald Worster, Edmund Russell, Emily Wakild, Ernesto Capello, Fares El Dahdah, Francisco Vidal Luna, Gijs Mom, Jeffrey Needell, Lise Sedrez, Myrna Santiago, Paul Josephson, Sandra Chaney, Thomas Zeller, and Zephyr Frank; and in correspondence – Christopher Wells and Joel Wolfe. I particularly thank those who have read and commented upon various elements and versions of the manuscript and its preliminary research – Christopher Neumaier, Evan Ward, Helmuth Trischler, Kendall Brown, Rex Nielson, and anonymous reviewers whose feedback has been invaluable. Herb Klein, my graduate advisor, I thank for extensive and constructive comments on the manuscript, and for continued support and encouragement. My father, Bill Miller, with thirty years as an autobody man and as an artist who has built Model T hotrods, could answer my every technical question about the nature and function of the automobile. Cacey Farnsworth, who has now begun historical work of his own, I owe for an exceptional year as my research assistant. I also thank all those whose scholarship has informed my own, whom I have credited specifically in the notes and bibliography.

I appreciate the persistent financial support from the Department of History, the College of Family, Home, and Social Sciences, Latin American Studies, and the Kennedy Center for International Studies at Brigham Young University, as well as the travel funds from the Rachel Carson Center in Munich and the Center for Latin American Studies at

Stanford University. I am also entirely indebted to the dedicated staffs of the archives I have consulted; there are too many individuals to name, most working out of sight of reading rooms, and we as researchers collectively owe much to those who have given a lifetime of accruing work that makes the writing of history at all possible. I must specifically thank Sátiro Nunes at the Arquivo Nacional and Barbara Tenenbaum at the Library of Congress for their particular efforts on my behalf. Critical to this book's research has been the monumental project of digitizing Brazil's diverse and vast collection of periodicals, administered and published online by the Fundação da Biblioteca Nacional in Rio. Without it, many of the questions I have asked about the meanings and utilities of Rio's streets would have gone largely unanswered. I applaud this ongoing endeavor, which strives to make our modern archives not just ordered repositories but elegant tools for disseminating the human record and deepening our understanding of the human past.

To the Cariocas I have been privileged to call friends over the years, I am greatly indebted. The Amelia and Manoel Bezerra family in Copacabana merits my family's particular gratitude for friendship and lively dinners extending back decades. My introduction to Brazil in the 1980s was very much at the level of the street, a youth peddling his religious convictions door to door in the sprawling *bairros* of Campo Grande and Jacarepaguá and in the dense corridor running from São Christóvão to Duque de Caxias. I remain deeply attracted to the city, its streets, squares, and hills, and to the people who inhabit them. The two, of course, remain inseparable in my mind. Carioca hospitality, in the street and in the house, exceeds its own celebrated reputation, and Rio's citizens have been to me exemplars of what community means and what community does.

And my thanks, finally, to companions in travel: Esmé, Lindy, Sadie, Hannah, Miles, and Kelly.

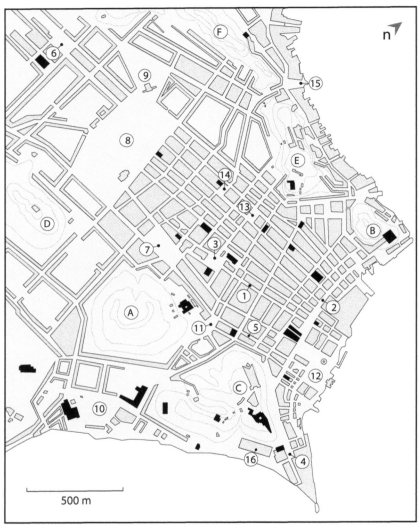

Map 1 Central Rio de Janeiro, 1867. Based on "Nova Planta da Cidade do Rio de Janeiro" (Rio de Janeiro: E. & H. Laemmert, 1867), Division of Maps, Library of Congress, Washington, DC. Religious edifices in black.

Key

1. Rua do Ouvidor (street)
2. Rua Direita (street)
3. Praça de São Francisco de Paula (square)
4. Largo da Misericórdia (square)
5. Rua da Assembléia (street)
6. Rocio Pequeno (square, later Praça Onze de Junho)
7. Praça da Constituição (square, formerly Rocio Grande)
8. Campo da Aclamação (square)
9. Estação Dom Pedro II (train station)
10. Passeio Público (park)
11. Largo da Carioca (square)
12. Largo do Paço (square)
13. Largo do Capim (square)
14. Largo de São Domingos (square)
15. Praça Municipal (square)
16. Santa Casa da Misericórdia (hospital)
A. Morro de Santo Antônio (hill)
B. Morro de São Bento (hill)
C. Morro do Castelo (hill)
D. Morro do Senado (hill)
E. Morro da Conceição (hill)
F. Morro do Livramento (hill)

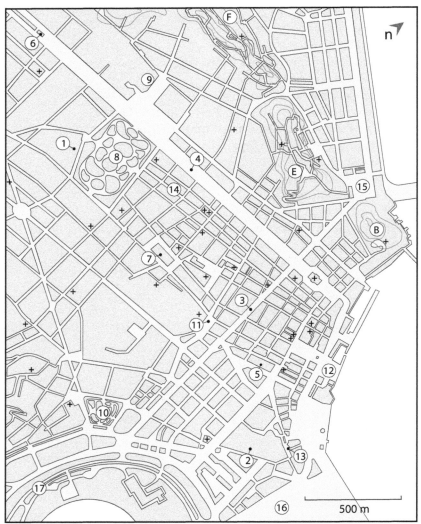

Map 2 Central Rio de Janeiro, c. 1965. Based on *Atlas da evolução urbana da cidade do Rio de Janeiro, ensaio: 1565–1965* (Rio de Janeiro: Instituto Histórico e Geográfico Brasileiro, 1965), 26. Religious edifices represented with +.

Key

1. Assistência Médica Central (first-aid clinic)
2. Santa Casa da Misericórdia (hospital)
3. Avenida Rio Branco (formerly Central)
4. Avenida Vargas
5. Garagem Menezes Cortes (parking structure)
6. Praça Onze de Junho (square)
7. Praça Tiradentes (square)
8. Praça da República (square)
9. Estação Dom Pedro II (train station)
10. Passeio Público (park)
11. Largo da Carioca (square)
12. Praça Quinze de Novembro (square)
13. Largo da Misericórdia (square)
14. SAARA Pedestrian Shopping District
15. Praça Mauá (square)
16. Santos Dumont Airport
17. Aterro do Flamengo (highway)
B. Morro de São Bento (hill)
E. Morro da Conceição (hill)
F. Morro do Livramento (hill)

INTRODUCTION

A Common Space to Enjoy

Ilha de Paquetá

The downtrodden do not feel entirely abandoned by the gods if before their eyes one street opens onto another.

João do Rio[1]

The streets of Paquetá Island have followed a radical, alternate pathway to the present. The island lies tranquil at the heart of Rio de Janeiro's great inner bay. Although slight in size, a shapely, verdant slip less than 3 kilometers in length, it is the largest urbanized space in the city not connected to the national automotive network, an urban landscape without cars. The bay's encircling shoreline hosts the congested centers of Rio de Janeiro, Duque de Caxias, Mauá, São Gonçalo, and Niterói, whose noise never quite seems to reach Paquetá's gentle shores. The island has been an oasis from the city, a garden that "emerges out of the midst of the sea like an immense bouquet of flowers," as one Frenchwoman described it in the mid-nineteenth century.[2] A place of inspiration for artists, the isle was also a resort for amorous encounters, a reputation that was reinforced by King João VI who called it the Island of Loves and who made many a discrete visit without his estranged queen. Not surprisingly, Brazil's first romantic novel, *A Moreninha*, which offers a love story as pure as nature and childhood, took Paquetá as its setting. For much of the twentieth century, Paquetá remained a popular destination for lovers who slept,

---

[1] João do Rio, *A alma encantadora das ruas* (Rio de Janeiro: Prefeitura da Cidade do Rio de Janeiro, 1995), 4.

[2] Adèle Toussaint-Samson, *A Parisian in Brazil: The Travel Account of a Frenchwoman in Nineteenth-Century Rio de Janeiro* (Wilmington, DE: Scholarly Resource Books, 2001), 51.

I

according to one popular song, in each other's arms through the most radiant of sunrises, and for beach-going families who enjoyed the island's glassy waters and its golden sands interspersed with weathered granite rocks that have all the appearance of raw loaves of bread rising.[3]

Despite its seclusion, modernity pressed itself on Paquetá after the turn of the twentieth century. The island's most famous artist, Pedro Bruno, born on the island that inspired his painting and poetry, resisted his home's modernization with a certain horror. When the city introduced electricity in 1922, he sobbed privately to a friend, "they have killed my island." Bruno also opposed the construction of apartment buildings, the introduction of swifter ferries, and, most vociferously, the growing number of automobiles – all without success. Still, the island's Artistic League, which Bruno had founded, tried obstinately to protect the island's natural beauties, preventing the capture of birds, the paving of streets, and the felling of trees, a number of which grew with prominent roots in the very centers of the streets.[4]

Locals had introduced automobiles to the island early in the century. By the 1940s the car's multiplication caused many accidents and some deaths among neighbors and visitors. Bruno continued to fulminate against the car until his death in 1949, but Paquetá's streetscapes had come to be dominated by automobiles. Then, in September of 1950, a truck leaped onto a Paquetá sidewalk and ran down a father, a mother, and their infant child, sending all three to the hospital with severe injuries. The driver fled, but with nowhere to run, the police jailed him, and the local papers vilified his conduct. Capitalizing on the tragedy, the Artistic League persuaded Rio's mayor to sign Decree 10,643, which banished all automotive vehicles from the island. Garages, even in private residences, were prohibited outright, and the decree limited wheeled transportation to one ambulance, two utility trucks, and horse-drawn carriages. Newspapers praised the mayor for his bold act: "[T]he graceful island was destined to suffer the same fate as the beauties and attractions

---

[3] For the novel, see Joaquim Manuel de Macedo, *A Moreninha*, first published in 1844 and twice adapted for film. Macedo actually never specifies the novel's setting as Paquetá, always referring to it as "*Ilha de* _____," but no reader has doubted the reference. For the song, listen to João de Barro and Alberto Ribeiro Nuno Roland, "Fim de semana em Paquetá," first recorded in 1947, but frequently interpreted.

[4] W. Guarnieri, "O namorado de Paquetá," *Revista da Semana*, Apr. 2, 1949, 28, 52. According to Coaracy, the island's kerosene lamps prior to electrification were also not lit on nights around the full moon, presumably to save fuel or simply because they were unneeded.

that used to surround our city – it too would have succumbed to the stupidity of utilitarianism." Even the Touring Club of Brazil, long a defender of the automobile's right to the public street, commended the mayor.[5] The car-free law did have local challengers. The island's parish priest imported a motor scooter so he could, he claimed, give last rites in a timely manner to his dying parishioners, but this encouraged a number of young men to ferry in their own motorcycles, many without mufflers, so he desisted in his ecclesiastical exemption, and all the motors were again exiled.[6]

The mayor decreed one of the rare spaces in the contemporary, urban world where no cars go. Today, to disembark from the island's ferry is to enter a world substantially alien to the modern eye, ear, and psyche. Some would say it is to step back a century in time, but the present is never entirely like the past. Granted, horse-drawn carts will greet you, but rather than the graceful, low-slung carriages of the nineteenth century, today's horses pull inelegant carts sporting recycled Michelin tires. The island's most striking sensation, the deafening quiet, takes time to comprehend and appreciate. Here, in a densely inhabited place of streets, homes, and shops, human voices, laughter, and the song of birds, not the internal combustion engine, are the dominant sonic presence.

Increasingly polluted beaches and reports of crime have diminished the island's cachet as a destination, and the number of visitors has declined in recent decades. Still, due to the emergence of *favelas* on the island's hills from the 1960s, residents today fill the streets with more bodies than had visitors in the past. Despite familiar socio-economic tensions, community thrives. Measured in conversations heard, the building of community is on obvious and audible display, especially at the island's center. Adults and children, of all classes, utilize the street to gather, recreate, and gossip, and informal groups dot the streetscape to share the day's news. Church congregations meet in the street's open air, and religious and civil festivals, as well as less formal celebrations, can happen spontaneously, without the need for permits, police, or traffic control. Even movement is an opportunity for community: on bicycles of every vintage, pedaling fathers steady trusting sons who stand confidently on frames; schoolgirls, three to a bike,

---

[5] Decreto 10,643, Nov. 22, 1950, *Legislação do Distrito Federal* [LEX], 1950, 133; "Proibido o trânsito de veículos motorizados em Paquetá," *Diário de Notícias*, Nov. 23, 1950; "Toda a família atropelada," *A Manhã*, Sep. 30, 1950, 3; "A graça natural de Paquetá," *Diário da Noite*, Nov. 23, 1950, 2; see also Vivaldo Coaracy, *Paquetá: imágens de ontem e hoje* (Rio de Janeiro: José Olympio, 1965).

[6] "Paquetá: o paraíso proibido," *Quatro Rodas*, Aug. 1963, 118.

pool rides in smartly pressed uniforms; and young men pause to place elderly women on their rear racks to take them to the market. In streets where the desire for stasis can hold its own against the demand for head-way, life moves slowly enough for meaningful exchanges to materialize, and as such, Paquetá is a rare remnant of the pre-automotive street, a present that holds the possibility of nostalgia for the kind of public spaces that most of us have never experienced.

In the rest of the city of Rio de Janeiro, the private automobile, already in the second quarter of the century, came to occupy and dominate the city's public spaces: all the streets, most of the squares, and, often, many of its sidewalks. The car even took to some of the city's beaches to race at full speed. Only those streets and pathways leading into the *favelas*, too steep or too narrow for the car to pass, or those in the most distant suburbs, remained unaffected. The streets' mechanical occupation had profound impacts on the life and community of the city. In previous centuries, the street as urban commons had embraced an almost limitless number of human activities, individuals of every category engaged in intimate gossip and popular festivities, petty crime and gross acts of state repression. A common space that had been available for child's play and impassioned protest, carnival parades and funeral processions, honest peddling and artful pickpocketing, civic celebrations and public executions, the street saw many of its habitual activities progressively diminished and some-times altogether displaced by the linear function of mechanical movement.[7] There are a number of factors that explain the changes in the use of public spaces, but the automobile's collective presence directly occupied the common ground on which residents had lived and worked. Over the course of the twentieth century, we ask: What role did the automobile play in the street's transformation from a meaningful place for sociality, commerce, and leisure to a space of darting and daily death? How did a place formerly perceived as architecture become a space largely experienced as engineering? And how did a place to be become increas-ingly a space between? The street was not a void that the automobile, after millennia, finally came to fill; the car displaced cultural practices that were old, new, and in continuous formation. The private automobile's presence

---

[7] Angela Jain and Massimo Moraglio, "Struggling for the Use of Urban Streets: Preliminary (Historical) Comparison between European and Indian Cities." *International Journal of the Commons* 8, no. 2 (Aug. 2014): 525, argue for this transformation in both Europe and India, although at different times. In fact, the transformation is common to most modern cities where the car has multiplied. In a sense, we argue that for Brazil, the timing, while behind that of the US and Europe, was closer to them than to India.

on public spaces has been so ubiquitous for so long that we find it difficult to conceive of the street without it; we have become acclimatized to its presence and power. Peter Norton, referring to the car's historical role in North American streets, asserts that "only when we can see the prevailing social construction of the street from the perspective of its own time can we also see the car as the intruder. Until we do, not only will we fail to understand the violent revolution in street use . . ., we will not even see it."[8] Hence, only after defining Rio's streets before the car can we begin to comprehend the automobile as both a violent revolution and a revolution in the use of violence. The car's impact fell broadly on the city; however, for the sake of brevity and due to the nature of the sources, we largely limit our attentions and specific claims to the city's historic center, which took the brunt of the car's impact.[9]

Urban public space has held a place of prominence in Brazil's culture. The Portuguese had a special designation for it, *logradouro*, a singular (as

---

[8] Peter Norton, *Fighting Traffic: The Dawn of the Motor Age in the American City* (Cambridge, MA: MIT Press, 2008), 2.

[9] The literature on automobiles and their influence on urban highways and expanding suburbs is extensive. The car's impact on existing city streets and street life has received less attention. Andrew Brown-May, *Melbourne Street Life: The Itinerary of Our Days* (Kew, Australia: Australian Scholarly Publishing, 1998), which was among the first studies, noted (xix) that the street has "rarely been observed in a scholarly way as a special element of urban space." That has begun to change in the last decade. Norton's *Fighting Traffic* and Clay McShane's *Down the Asphalt Path: The Automobile and the American City* (New York, NY: Columbia University Press, 1994), both make excellent, in-depth analyses of the early stages in US cities; Brian Ladd's *Autophobia: Love and Hate in the Automotive Age* (Chicago, IL: University of Chicago Press, 2008), chapter 3, offers some useful views from Europe; as does Kurt Möser, "The Dark Side of 'Automobilism,' 1900–30: Violence, War and the Motor Car." *Journal of Transport History* 24, no. 2 (2003): 238–58, who argues, as do I, that the automobile was a tool of class violence. Most recently, Christopher W. Wells, *Car Country: An Environmental History* (Seattle, WA: University of Washington Press, 2012) provides a comprehensive survey of the environmental impact of the car in the US across a century, in both cities and the countryside, and Gijs Mom, *Atlantic Automobilism: Emergence and Persistence of the Car, 1895–1940* (Oxford: Berghahn Books, 2014), takes the most global and comprehensive view to date with a noted technical sophistication. For a comparison of the process between an early change in Europe and more recent developments in India's cities, see Jain and Moraglio. "Struggling for the Use of Urban Streets," 513–30. For the declared lack of work done on Latin America's city streets, see Anton Rosenthal, "Spectacle, Fear, and Protest: A Guide to the History of Urban Public Space in Latin America," *Social Science History* 24, no. 1 (Spring 2000): 49. Since then, Marco Antônio Cornacioni Sávio's two histories of transit and automobiles in São Paulo, *A modernidade sobre rodas : tecnologia automotiva, cultura e sociedade* (São Paulo: EDUC, 2002) and *A cidade e as máquinas: Bondes e automóveis nos promórdios do metrópole pualista, 1900–1930* (São Paulo: Annablume, 2010), make some insightful inroads for Brazil.

opposed to plural[10]) term that encompassed altogether every street (*rua*), square (*praça*), alley (*beco*), lane (*viela* or *ruela*), wharf (*cais*), public garden (*jardin*), and beach (*praia*). All were understood as one, contiguous space. The *logradouro* was large and diverse, encompassing spaces whose labels have no direct English translation: *largo* – a small, irregular square; *ladeira* – a steep street often with steps carved into living rock; *campo* and *rocio* – undeveloped squares or spaces sometimes used as common pastures; *travessa* – a narrow street connecting two others; and *boqueirão* – a street running down to a river or port.[11] The sheer multiplicity of categories evidences public space's cultural significance. The *logradouro*, then, embraced essentially all of the city's unbuilt spaces. And the utility of one was rather similar to another as far as spatial dimensions allowed. Some recent studies of the plaza in Latin America have established its cultural, historical importance,[12] but before the arrival of wheeled vehicles in any numbers, the entire *logradouro,* the streets, beaches, and wharves, were understood and used very much like squares. As it was for the Romans, a square was just a broader street.

Above all, public spaces were understood as commons, spaces that residents could, within limits, put to their preferred use. *Logradouro* is a compound of the verb "*lograr*," which means to enjoy or take a benefit from, and "*douro*," which is the suffix for place, the same as "-tory" in say "laboratory" in English. The *logradouro*, by its very definition, was a common space to enjoy. Citizens were protected in their rights to access public spaces, to buy and sell, work and play, sing and protest. The spaces that today most resemble the spirit of the former *logradouro* are the city's famed beaches, whose continuity as commons form the last refuge of an authentic, although rather limited, form of outdoor public life. Certainly, the street was a space notorious for illegal and violent activities as well; the *logradouro* was simply too large to effectively patrol; hence gambling, prostitution, theft, brawling, and drunkenness were common ways of taking the best advantage of the street, too.

---

[10] The term is also used in the plural, but this usage was less common in the nineteenth century, when public spaces were typically referred to in the collective, than in the twentieth century, when they are fragmented by the automobile's impositions.

[11] In Portugal, the term *calçada* (or more typically its diminutive, *calçadinha*) referred to any paved street, a term picked up in Brazil to designate the paved sidewalks.

[12] James R. Curtis, "Praças, Place, and Public Life in Urban Brazil," *Geographical Review*, 90 (2000):477–84. Setha M. Low, *On the Plaza: The Politics of Public Space and Culture* (Austin, TX: University of Texas Press, 2000), 31.

Physically, the *logradouro* was a public space bounded by buildings. Modern dictionaries define the street as a thoroughfare, but the earliest Portuguese dictionaries defined "street" first as "a space between the houses of cities."[13] The street (*rua*) was strongly distinguished from the road (*estrada*) whose main purpose was movement and which was always, by definition, located outside city walls. More than in any physical description, however, the street's meaning is best expressed in how people have used and represented it, what sociologist and theorist Henri Lefebvre refers to as spatial practice. Just as sitting gives meaning to a chair, what citizens did in the street reveals their conceptions of the city's public spaces. And changing uses implied changing meanings, even among those who resisted the changes.

Moreover, Lefebvre argues for a capitalist evolution of human spaces, a process in which spaces are transformed, by their use, from a state of nature to an expression of culture. For Lefebvre, raw space is nature's domain, the absolute volume that exists before civilization makes its presence felt. When humans arrive on nature's raw ground, they begin to produce their spaces by constructing various kinds of containers, be they fences, walls, or rooms. Humans convert a raw natural resource into cultural space by hemming it inside manmade lines. A street is a street for no other reason than its being limited by human bounds. Initially, many human spaces, such as streets, do not have private owners. They resist becoming part of a capitalist order, thus forming a commons in which private rights and exclusions cannot be claimed. Many such spaces, including forests, waters, pastures, and even tilled farms, survived in a condition of community ownership for centuries. Lefebvre argues, however, that most such spaces eventually become dominated – that is, they come to be owned or controlled by particular individuals or classes, often with profit or spatial separation between classes as primary goals. This spells the end of any remaining commons. Technologies can empower groups with the tools for spatial domination – cheap barbed wire enclosing grazing lands, pumps draining common fens, or guns displacing the indigenous – but Lefebvre limits himself to one example, naming the car as the technology and the limited access motorway as the characteristic example of a modern dominated space.[14]

[13] António de Morais Silva, *Diccionário de lingua portuguesa* (1813); Raphael Bluteau, *Vocabulário Portuguez & Latino* (1728); both these works have become available online at the Universidade de São Paulo digital library, "Brasiliana USP": www.brasiliana.usp.br.

[14] Henri Lefebvre, *The Production of Space* (Cambridge, MA: Blackwell, 1991), 26, 38–40, 164–65.

Rio's streets follow Lefebvre's evolutions, but in a delayed, overlapping, and fractured process. Rio's citizens, while they built blocks and walls, did not build streets. Nor did they perceive their streets as special, cultural productions. The street, despite its heavy use, was understood as a remnant of nature, an unimproved space of raw soil, rank vegetation, and unregulated animal life. This was the street's historical character. City officials did not begin to produce (nor even officially name, for that matter) the city's streets until after about 1850. Thereafter, however, they commenced increasingly ambitious campaigns to pave, drain, curb, and beautify the city's public spaces. Only with asphalt's advance was nature expelled from the street, to paraphrase Lewis Mumford.[15] Still, the street remained an open commons and continued to be used largely as it had before its modernizing upgrades. With or without mud on citizens' feet, street life continued to evolve and diversify in remarkable ways. Finally, however, by the second decade of the twentieth century, elites, employing the technology of the automobile, came to dominate public spaces, effectively enclosing much of the street against many of its former uses, a conquest that only intensified in succeeding decades.

My interest in the street is largely environmental, by which I mean I see the street as a natural resource, a common public good over which users compete. Most of the historical commons have today been transformed into the private property systems preferred by modern states. In a recent historical synthesis of the commons, Derek Wall observes that "across continents, colonialism and marketization helped to eliminate usufruct rights and exclude people." The story, he asserts, "is near universal." He demonstrates that through multiple forms of enclosure, commons, whose spaces and resources had been available to the many, became exclusive private property. Rural commons in particular have largely disappeared.[16]

The common street, on the other hand, has resisted privatization. In fact, urban streets have significantly expanded in the last couple centuries. Hence, as Brazil's former slaves and rural workers migrated to cities, away from the increasingly enclosed forests, mangroves, fields, and fisheries that had provided livelihoods and represented a certain economic and spatial freedom,[17] rural commons were replaced in their function by

---

[15] Lewis Mumford, *The Culture of Cities* (New York, NY: Harcourt, Brace and Company, 1938), 253.
[16] Derek Wall, *The Commons in History* (Cambridge, MA: Massachusetts Institute of Technology, 2014), 84.
[17] For the specific case of the mangroves, which served as commons for tanners, fisherman, firewood gatherers, lime producers, and potters, see Shawn W. Miller, "Stilt-root

urban commons that provided similar livelihoods and offered similar freedoms. João do Rio, the newspaper reporter who took the city's name as his own, described Rio's streets as "the most egalitarian, the most socialist, and the most leveling of all the works of man."[18]

However, commons can become enclosed selectively against certain groups and activities even while they legally remain public spaces. Amy Chazkel has insightfully examined this process in Rio in the context of the official repression of a popular form of gambling, the lottery known as the *jogo do bicho* (animal game). She asserts that the "idea of enclosure relates to the shifting balance of control over shared resources between the state, private industry, and different sectors of the population." Enclosure and its consequences for the poor, under this definition, did not require privatization. Rather than a simple land grab, enclosure is more broadly the attempt to exclude – from common resources and spaces – those individuals who are deemed wasteful, ineffective, immoral, or low-priority users of said resources and spaces. Under such bans, the excluded become "trespassers," as Chazkel describes them, even on spaces that remain common.[19] Lottery ticket sellers have survived enclosure, Chazkel points out, by continuing to trespass on both the commons and the laws, by finding space in which to continue their now illegal street employment. This, in fact, has been the common response to attempts to enclose the street against certain groups, activities, and occupations. For much of the nineteenth century, the city tried to abolish and regulate – through laws, exclusive concessions, and police enforcement – peddling, carnival dancing, religious processions, prostitution, pasturing animals, singing and drumming, keeping dogs, setting up markets, washing horses, and laundering clothing, among many other activities, but by most accounts officials saw little or temporary success, at best.[20] If space remained on the city's hundreds of streets, individuals found ways to subvert, sidestep, and adapt to the city's ever-changing regulations and police actions. Law was not without consequences, but it was often aspirational, evidenced by the very frequency of its repetition to solve the same old problems. Due to the

Subsistence: Colonial Mangrove Conservation and Brazil's Free Poor." *Hispanic American Historical Review* 83, no. 2 (May 2003): 223–53.

[18] João do Rio, *A alma encantadora das ruas*, 4.

[19] Amy Chazkel, *Laws of Chance: Brazil's Clandestine Lottery and the Making of Urban Public Life* (Durham, NC: Duke University Press, 2011), 167, 268.

[20] Maria Odila Leite da Silva Dias, *Quotidiano e poder em São Paulo no século XIX – Ana Gertrudes de Jesus* (São Paulo: Brasiliense, 1984), 48–51, 57–58, examines these failures in the city of São Paulo.

streets' abundance and extent, and often due to police ambivalence and complicity, enforcement of street regulations could be fitful and fickle, as it would be for motorists later.

Chazkel sees urban public spaces as a "metaphorical commons" in which different groups struggle for the political and economic space to move and make a living, and she correctly characterizes this space as something abstract.[21] Even when street activities were deemed undesirable and outlawed, these prohibited abstract "spaces" had the chance of being filled if the physical space in which one might engage in them remained. Abstract political and social spaces are related to actual spaces, but my main interest is in the physical space itself, something that can be measured in cubic units. The automobile introduced to the street a more strictly environmental form of spatial competition, a direct and formidable occupier of physical spaces that more than most competitors had the power to exclude. While motorists and their backers did not initially target any particular street activity, the car's very physical reality threatened many existing street users. In fact, it began to challenge, diminish, and sometimes displace traditional street activities well before officials passed the legislation that gave official priority to the car's presence. In time, officials would find in the automobile a potent ally in enclosing the street against undesirable users, but it had shown an aptitude for pushiness even before its official promotion began.

The street has been unique as a common because rather than contributing specific extractable resources, its primary offering has been physical space, one that permits and facilitates human presence, activities, and production. Hence, the street offered a resource of manifold utility, one that in its unpaved, potholed, and poorly drained examples was often as raw and undeveloped as nature itself, although by definition heavily trampled. But even well trampled, space was eminently and instantly renewable, which also makes it unique among natural resources. Fish can be fished out of fisheries, and minerals depleted from mines, but unbuilt space, while consumed, remained fully intact for the next user. The urban commons were difficult to exhaust, and in some situations, like annual carnival celebrations or more ordinary street life such as the daily afternoon promenades, the more completely the street's space was being consumed, the merrier.

We have come to comprehend how the automobile's need for motion has reshaped urban, suburban, and even wild landscapes, but we have yet

---

[21] Chazkel, *Laws of Chance*, 9–10.

to come to terms with its direct occupation of existing human spaces. What made the car exceptionally effective in the process of street enclosure were two new and unusual characteristics of its street presence. First, the automobile became the mechanism of its own enforcement. Rather than having to rely on the police, which had repeatedly proven ineffectual in eliminating undesirable street users and behaviors, the automobile enforced its own territorial claims with the terror of velocity. To contest street space was no longer simply to risk police repression; in the new context of fast cars, it meant risking personal injury or an impersonal death. Already by the second decade of the twentieth century, auto-pedestrian accidents were a recognized epidemic, and each year hundreds were duly reported in the city's daily papers. Although young children and minors (who made up the majority of the car's initial victims in Rio) failed to fully understand the automobile's hazards, adults, while expressing anger and passive forms of resistance toward the car, changed, with some exceptions, their street behaviors in the face of obvious risks.

Second, even without the threat of violence, the car substantially damaged the street's spatial renewability because most automobiles in Rio, especially after the 1920s, had no private spaces to which to withdraw. Pre-automotive street vehicles – carriages, wagons, trams, and streetcars – when not using the street, exited the public domain to be housed in private homes, warehouses, and stables, leaving the commons for the next users. The street was not a place for storing private property, a rule consistently enforced before the car. By stark contrast, most automobiles, whether driven or parked, the largest objects of personal property humans have possessed, lived their entire existences on the public domain. They had extraordinary powers of movement, but they refused to leave. By the 1920s, despite continuing laws against it, the city relented, and free parking almost anywhere on the public domain became the norm. By the early 1930s, free parking was sanctioned by law.

Motorists and their cars came to collectively occupy much of the *logradouro*, and the space the automobile captured was not abstract. Even a stationary car consumes an astonishing amount of space and thus is not a benign object without consequences. Some early models occupied as much space as turn-of-the-century streetcars that carried 100 passengers. A single, parked passenger car consumed more squared space than the average Brazilian living room, as much ground as a standing elephant. Multiply that spatial requirement by tens of thousands and you begin to see the car's footprint in Rio de Janeiro by the end of the first quarter of the century. One major urban study has found that regardless of traffic, once

parked cars come to occupy just 9 percent of a street's space, achieved in
many of Rio's downtown streets by the 1920s, residents begin to abandon
the street's former uses, feeling that the street is no longer "theirs."[22]
By mid-century, parked cars occupied in excess of 50 percent of the
street's frontage in Rio's daytime downtown streets, and as much in
some nighttime suburbs. Once in motion, the car consumed many multi-
ples of its static spatial area, depending on its speed: a car going 40 mph
effectively occupied a space many times its actual size; hundreds of cars
doing 40 mph displaced all competitors from the street bed. On the public
spaces that cars collectively occupied, a burgeoning, permanent presence
that could be measured in square kilometers, they inevitably displaced, in
those spaces, all utilities but automotive movement and storage. Those
who could survive at the margins might continue to resist, but many users
and uses simply had to make way.[23]

Resources are used for production, and while this study is not interested in any particular street product, it is interested in the broad set of
realities and possibilities associated with that space. Streets produced
some of the most characteristic expressions of the culture, which included
a remarkable capacity for repartee, outpourings of collective religiosity,
spontaneous protests, elite promenading, and the mundanity of mass
loitering. New styles of music and dance for example, of which Rio was
particularly noteworthy, were not just shared on the streets; they were
invented there.[24] One might even argue that the longer availability of the
street in Rio, particularly in the *favelas* and poor suburbs, as a place for
play has produced the world's greatest soccer players. Some blame Brazil's
recent struggles in the international arena on the loss of public spaces –
a significant loss in a nation that does not offer athletic programs or
athletic fields in its educational institutions – for it was in these once

---

[22] Christopher Alexander, Sara Ishikawa, and Murray Silverstein, *A Pattern Language: Towns, Buildings, Construction* (New York, NY: Oxford University Press, 1977), 121–23.

[23] This process has repeated itself everywhere the car has entered the city. In India, Jain and Moraglio note than "on the one hand streets are shared spaces, open to everyone; on the other hand, they produce exclusion and segregation or even barriers for those who cannot attain a certain speed;" see Jain and Moraglio, "Struggling for the Use of Urban Streets," 518.

[24] John Charles Chasteen, "The Prehistory of Samba: Carnival Dancing in Rio de Janeiro, 1840–1917," *Journal of Latin American Studies* 28 (Feb. 1996), 29–47. For contempor- ary uses of urban space for hip-hop dissemination in São Paulo, see Marília Pontes Sposito, "A sociabilidade juvenil e a rua: Novos conflitos e ação coletiva na cidade," *Tempo Social* 5, nos. 1–2 (1993): 161–78.

available spaces that young players were able to perfect their skills.[25] The street's spatial practices had always been fluid and culturally fecund, and hence the street's former dominant place in Rio's cultural creativity. In 1908, João do Rio recognized and praised the streets as the primary shapers of the city's cultural identity, the space on which Rio's characteristic music, dance, poetry, piety, misery, playfulness, crimes, banter, and even its food and drink, were fashioned and disseminated in the vernacular of its everyday users, who were largely poor.[26]

Rio's founders, like the founders of other American cities, did not give streets official names at their creation. However, local residents gave their streets popular names, from the beginning and without exception. Streets were not named for the purpose of urban navigation but because they were evocative to the people who used them. Street naming customs had many motives, and streets were named in honor of saints, dignitaries, and the significant buildings they fronted, but many were known by the uses associated with the space. Hence, Rio encompassed Soap Street, Hay Square, Pig Slaughter Street, Ballgame Street, Barber's Alley, Flea Market Street, Music Street, Canoe Alley, Rock Salt Street, Fisherman's Street, Goldsmith's Street, and Tinsmith's Street. Some names expressed how one might physically use or experience the space: Alley of the Elbows, Proposition Alley, Street of Sighs, Breezy Street, Alley of the Flies, Slack Jaw Square, Scoundrel Alley, Slippery Lane, and Break-Ass Alley, the last describing how equines fell on their haunches descending a steep street.[27]

The traditional street had potent cultural meanings. Claude Lévi-Strauss, considered by some the father of modern anthropology, arrived in Rio in 1935 to begin his ethnographic work. On Rio's colonial streets, he wandered around hoping to see the city's indigenous past, a landscape formerly dotted with scores of native villages. But time had erased the

---

[25] Luis Roberto Porto, "A pelada é uma coisa," *Jornal do Brasil*, Sep. 23, 1965, in *Cadernos do Jornal do Brasil do IV Centenário*, 218, describes the former ubiquity of street soccer. Ewan MacKenna, "Brazil's Powerhouse Program Is Left Dilapidated by Years of Neglect," *New York Times*, Jun. 2, 2016, SP15.

[26] João do Rio, *A alma encantadora das ruas*, 4.

[27] All but two of these names are found on the "Nova Planta da Cidade do Rio de Janeiro" (Rio de Janeiro: E. & H. Laemmert, 1867), Division of Maps, Library of Congress, Washington, DC, and in order, in their original spellings, are Sabão, Capim, Mattaporcos, Jogo da Bolla, Barbeiros, Adellos, Múzica, Canoas, Pedra do Sal, Pescadores, Ourives, and Latoeiros, and experientially, Cotovello, Propósito, Suspiros, Sem Saída, Fresca, Mosqueira, Pasmado, Velhacos, Escorrega, and Caminho do Quebra Bunda. Slack Jaw Square (Praça do Pasmado) and Scoundrel Alley (Becco dos Velhacos) were referred to by Olavo Bilac in 1908. Break-Ass (Quebra Bunda) also refers to a disease of horses that destroys the hind legs.

marks that might make historical reimagining possible. What offered itself
to his senses was a modern, bustling city. Lévi-Strauss asked himself:
What is it around me, what is the master spatial token or sign that
indicates I am in Brazil? His first unequivocal impression, which comes
to him while exploring Rio's remaining narrow streets, he admitted might
be considered trivial, but he stated it emphatically: "I am in a room." He
characterized the street as an outdoor chamber, something that distinguished Rio's streets from those in cities he knew in northern Europe.
Rio's surviving colonial streets, still in 1935, served as a common room,
a space with floor and walls, and he noted that in Rio, "the street is not
only a space through which one passes; it is a place that is lived in."[28] João
Pinheiro Chagas in 1897 also noted the difference of Rio's streets from
those of his home in Lisbon: "The street is narrow: a corridor, a room."[29]

Residents indeed expressed their conception of streets as a series of
rooms in naming practices. They understood streets not as linear thoroughfares but as a series of distinct places, thus many linear streets that
today have one name previously had a succession of different names over
their length, as can still be seen in attenuated form in London and
elsewhere.[30] In the twentieth century, many former street names that
expressed utility were eliminated because they were thought to betray
a lack of sophistication and polish.[31] Officials also disliked the multiplicity of names, rejecting all but one. However, even when official names
were imposed, the original names, which retained past meanings and
former associations in all their multiplicity, remained in preferred use.
US Ambassador Hugh Gibson noted that residents into the 1930s still
used the popular and multiple colonial street names despite the installation of new signage that displayed the official, linear nomenclature.[32]

If the street's meanings are no longer reflected in official street names,
meaning is still shaped by use. The historian Richard White distills
Lefebvre's complex spatial theories – how space is constructed and what
spatial practice means – into a single contemporary answer: movement,

---

[28] Claude Lévi-Strauss, *Tristes Tropiques* (Paris: Librairie Plon, 1955), 78.
[29] João Pinheiro Chagas, *De bond: Alguns aspectos da civilização brasileira* (Lisbon:
Livraria Moderna, 1897), 46.
[30] Nireu Cavalcanti, *O Rio de Janeiro Setecentista: A vida e a construção da cidade da
invasão francesa ate a chegada da corte* (Rio de Janeiro: Jorge Zahar Editor, 2004), 265.
[31] For official changes in Rio's street and square names, and the addition of new streets,
from 1863 to 1883, see "Denominações dos logradouros públicos," c. 1883, manuscript
index, AGCRJ 120, 32–3-4.
[32] Hugh Gibson, *Rio* (Garden City, NY: Doubleday, 1937), 53.

the transposition of bodies and goods from one place to another, gives meaning to modern spaces. Movement has become the dominant utility.[33] Richard Sennett, a sociologist, agrees and has argued that since movement, especially rapid movement, has become the primary function of the street, our public spaces have become meaningless, "even maddening." Planners, he notes, take no thought that someone might actually want to remain or pause in these spaces, or do something other than get somewhere else, and he mocks an anonymous planner who referred to public spaces as "the traffic-flow-support-nexus." Under such a perspective, "one ceased to believe one's surroundings have any meaning save as a means toward the end of one's own motion." Sennett rues that a single meaning is no meaning at all, and he works from the assumption that things were not always so, that the street, in the past, had alternative, dominant utilities.[34]

Drawings, paintings, and illustrations from Rio's nineteenth century, even photographs to about 1910, demonstrate emphatically that the street was not a place strictly set aside for motion but functioned also as a place of stasis. In fact, motionlessness is more commonly depicted than movement. The street's space is a place where the majority are going nowhere: citizens pause to converse, stand in doorways and at windows, lean against walls, and sit on the very pavements. However, by 1917, it was no longer legal in Rio to even stop and converse on the downtown sidewalks, although many still did. The essence of modernity asks of space not how large or even how far, but how long – space becomes subservient to time.[35] Marx asserted that industrial capital and new modes of transportation strove to "annihilate space with time."[36] Once space becomes largely abstracted, converted from its reality as a three-dimensional volume to a two-dimensional line, its full reality ceases to exist. For example, in an automotive speed limit, expressed in linear units per unit of time, the cubic volume of real space disappears in the expression.

---

[33] Richard White, "What Is Spatial History?" The Spatial History Project, Stanford University, Spatial History Lab site, working paper submitted 1 February 2010, paragraphs 8, 16, 17, www.stanford.edu/group/spatialhistory/cgi-bin/site/pub.php?id=29 (accessed Feb. 25, 2013).

[34] Richard Sennett, *The Fall of Public Man* (New York, NY: W. W. Norton, 1992), 14, 15.

[35] Richard White, *Railroaded: The Transcontinentals and the Making of Modern America* (New York, NY: W. W. Norton, 2011), 146.

[36] Karl Marx, *Outlines of the Critique of Political Economy*, translated by M. Nicolaus (London: Penguin 1973), 538–39.

The street's space was essential to humans for more than cultural utility. Ecologically, the street was a habitat, a place of production and a medium for exchange, but more fundamentally a place for human bodies to be, a medium for existence. The spatial reality of our bodies is so obvious that we habitually ignore the implications. David Smith makes the point starkly: "[H]uman beings have no choice but to occupy a space: they just do."[37] Above all, the street made room. As the commons have disappeared, one's right to occupy a space has increasingly been secured by the ownership of that space. In rural areas, a body, unless it was that of the landholder, had no inherent right to be any place. Rural spaces were private, and one could be removed at the landlord's whim. In Brazil, due to slavery, even the medieval tradition of a landlord's obligation to provide peasants a space to live, had broken down in some measure.[38] To be poor, without real property, meant to be in a tenuous and dependent spatial condition, and Brazil's peasant often had to beg for the right to simply be somewhere.[39]

This was also true of most of a city's built space. Other than a few public buildings, such as prisons, parliaments, and public markets, and the status of the church as a private space for all, most of the city's built environment was controlled by landlords. One's spatial existence or placement in the city was frequently contingent on the goodwill of the propertied class, or on offering the holder some form of payment. The right to one's tenement apartment was secured by paying rent; the right to linger in a tavern or occupy a seat in the theater was secured by the purchase of beer or admission. Otherwise, outside the peripheral walls of one's owned home, one's very presence was subject to the will of another, dependent and provisional.

The significant urban exception, of course, was the city street, a genuine commons which all citizens had full right to occupy with no one's permission or leave. Nobody owned the street, and everyone belonged. In Rio de Janeiro, because of its tropical location, street life was a perpetual rather than a seasonal affair, the diurnal habitat of a very large proportion of the

---

[37] David M. Smith, *Geography and Social Justice* (Oxford: Blackwell, 1994), 151. Or, in more social scientific language, Edward W. Soja writes "there are no aspatial social processes"; see his *Thirdspace: Journeys to Los Angeles and Other Real and Imagined Places* (Oxford: Basil Blackwell, 1996), 46.

[38] Stuart B. Schwartz, *Slaves, Peasants, and Rebels: Reconsidering Brazilian Slavery* (Urbana, IL: University of Illinois Press, 1992), 65–69.

[39] Rural commons in Brazil were themselves contested, and one's right to be anywhere largely depended on dependency. Shawn W. Miller, "Stilt-root Subsistence," 223–53.

population. This was particularly important for the poor, for laborers, and for slaves who spent much of their daily existence in the streets. It was critical for the thousands observed sleeping in Rio's flophouses at the turn of the century, individuals – men, women, and even children – who rented nocturnal sleeping spaces on stiflingly crowded tenement floors, but who woke up homeless each morning to enter the street, the only place they belonged.[40] Likewise, non-residents and foreign non-citizens had as much right to bodily occupy street space as residents and nationals. Even slaves found a legal place in the street. A master might forbid a slave from entering the street, but if he or she exited the house against the master's will, the street embraced the slave's presence anyway. There were laws, regulations, and informal rules about how the street could be used, and legal and social penalties for infringement, which is true of all commons, but in no other space were individuals so protected in their essential requirement to simply be and occupy space. Maria Wissenbach suggests that for the large servile class of dependents and slaves, the street not only represented freedom, but in a seeming contradiction, public space offered them their only real privacy, where they could retreat from the eyes of their masters in whose private houses they lived.[41]

Despite the human body's uncontested spatiality, few legal systems considered the issue.[42] Spatial rights found no place in constitutions and bills of rights. The Brazilian Constitution of 1824 and the US Constitution protected private spaces from unlawful violation. They protected property. Liberal charters promised life, liberty, and sometimes equality, but the kind of happiness that might derive from making a place for oneself in the world would have to be pursued privately and materially. Some legal founding documents did guarantee citizens the right of peaceable assembly – "to associate and assemble freely," as stated in Brazil's 1891 constitution[43] – but they did not pledge to provide the space in which assembly could actually happen. In fact, cities and states strove to control the political use of public spaces, to prevent or regulate assembly, to

---

[40] João do Rio, *A alma encantadora das ruas*, 119–23.
[41] Maria Cristina Cortez Wissenbach, "Da escravidão a liberdade: dimensões de uma privacidade possível," in *História da Vida Privada no Brasil*, vol. 3, edited by Nicolau Sevcenko (São Paulo: Companhia das Letras, 1998), 130.
[42] Don Mitchell, *The Right to the City: Social Justice and the Fight for Public Space* (New York, NY: The Guilford Press, 2003), 33, raises but does not develop the issue of a right to occupy space in a capitalist society.
[43] Section 2, article 72, paragraph 8, *Constituição da República dos Estados Unidos do Brasil*, February 24, 1891, Palácio do Planalto, Presidência do Senado, www.planalto .gov.br/ccivil_03/Constituicao/Constituicao91.htm (accessed Jul. 1, 2015).

maintain order, often using sedition and riot acts to justify this infringement of an essential corollary of the constitutional right to free speech.[44]

Despite such restrictions, Rio's citizens took to the streets to protest
political changes, increased taxes, rising food costs, hiked transit fares,
and even mandatory vaccinations. When angry, they occupied public
spaces with body and voice because there was room to assemble. In the
popular Brazilian Portuguese of the past, there were more than ninety
words, some of African origin, that referred to crowd behavior in the city
street, connoting commotion, conflict, tumult, and protest. Among some
wonderful and often obscene examples: *água suja, bababi, bafafá, bololó,
cu de boi, cu de gato, embrulhada, frevo, motim, pega-pega, porqueira,
quebra-quebra, safarrascada,* and *turudundum.* In the decades since the
automobile, governments have appealed to traffic's necessary movement
as the primary excuse to control public spaces and exclude or limit peaceable assembly. The citizens of Rio have continued to occupy the streets
when the political need arises, but most of the terms for collective street
behavior, which described a more diverse political urban ecology, have
been forgotten due to the street's cultural and political impoverishment.[45]

Still, there were those who resisted the car, despite its potency as
a symbol of modernity and despite the political power of motorists who
in Brazil remained a small, privileged minority for the entire century.
Cariocas, as the city's residents call themselves, never ceded the streets'
spaces entirely to the automobile and found various means to defy the
machine's onslaught, both in spirit and in body. It was a losing battle for
much of the twentieth century, but many never gave up on the idea that
"the street belongs to everyone," or that "the street is ours," a popular
assertion that preceded the car but that had become a militant "national
philosophy" by 1920.[46] After many decades, this story comes not full but

---

[44] For an overview of the democratic struggles over public spaces, see Lisa Keller,
The Triumph of Order: Public Space and Democracy in New York and London
(New York, NY: Columbia University Press, 2009), chapter 1. Mexico City, as a rare
case, strongly protects the street for spontaneous political assembly: "Protests Test
Patience of Mexico City Drivers," *New York Times,* Aug. 1, 2010.

[45] *Novo Dicionário Aurélio da Língua Portuguesa,* 3rd edn. (Editora Positivo, 2004). For
popular protest in Rio, see Marco Morel, "Papéis incendiários, gritos e gestos: a cena
pública e a construção nacional nos anos 1820–1830," *Topoi: Revista da História* 4
(Mar. 2002): 39–58; and Jane Santucci, *Cidade rebelde: As revoltas populares no Rio de
Janeiro no início do século XX* (Rio de Janeiro: Casa da Palavra, 2008).

[46] Gregório Garcia Seabra Júnior, *Accidentes de automóveis: Delictos profissionaes dos
automobilistas, doctrina, jurisprudência, legislação* (Rio de Janeiro: Leite Ribeiro &
Maurillo, 1918), 306.

partial circle. During the last half century, Rio's citizens have taken various steps, radical and incremental, official and unsanctioned, toward reclaiming some of their streets, to again make a place for non-automotive utilities and the prospect of a more diverse civic life.

Scholarly work on public spaces has been criticized for being a "literature of loss." This view asserts that the changes in the street in the last century should be seen as merely transformation, not degradation, and that we should not let nostalgia gild our perceptions of the past.[47] Admittedly, not all street change has been negative; some of the horrors and annoyances of the traditional street – mud and dust, rabid dogs, raw sewage, human slavery, to name a few – are happily gone. We have no qualms about identifying them as distinct advances. On the other hand, since the car's arrival, cities and streets have suffered some notably negative consequences, the maiming and death of residents being only the most egregious. If we value our cities as human ecologies, as places for civic life, community construction, equitable access, free expression, and safety from harm, then the automobile's impacts on public spaces have been acutely deleterious and cannot be construed as neutral. Nor should they be described as inevitable.

Brazilians, when I share that I am studying the history of Rio's streets, immediately understand the intent and potential scope of my work. Theirs is still very much a street culture that persists in a few small physical patches, such as Paquetá, but more importantly, that survives in their consciousness. They suffer from a collective street nostalgia, and no culture suffers and enjoys nostalgia (*saudade*) more deeply than Brazilians.[48] When I tell North Americans that I am working on the history of the street, it often takes some explaining. Some wonder at what there is to say about such a utilitarian, infrastructural object, as if I were writing about airport runways. Most modern people have no direct memory of the traditional street, nor have they visited those rare places that have rejected cars, such as Paquetá and Venice, or parcels of Seville and Havana. Still, many of us suffer from what Renato Rosaldo refers to as imperialist nostalgia, "where people mourn the passing of what they

---

[47] Michael Brill, "Transformation, Nostalgia, and Illusion in Public Life and Public Place," in *Public Places and Spaces*, edited by Irwin Altman and Ervin H. Zube (New York, NY: Plenum Press, 1989), 7–8.

[48] Some say that there is no English translation for *saudade*, but "nostalgia" can serve the purpose. In Portuguese, *saudade* has a stronger association with people from whom one is separated rather than just from former places and times, and it's a term used far more frequently than among English speakers.

themselves have transformed," who praise innovation and modernity and yet at the same time "yearn for more stable worlds."[49] Complicit in the street's automotive transformation, we may look fondly back to an idealized street that never existed, as it is often depicted in film, in the illustrations in children's books, and in its attempted re-creation in amusement parks and shopping malls. While looking backward, this work is above all "nostalgic for the future," to borrow a phrase from the theorist Timothy Morton, who expresses a practical hope for not some imagined past but an incrementally better future.[50]

Jo Guldi and David Armitage have invited historians to consider their roles in contemporary issues, arguing that the writing of history is not an opportunity to use the club of hindsight to beat up past actors but rather a dialogue with the dead about what it means to live well as humans. History, they assert, "can draw a map that includes not only pictures of the fantasy world of capitalistic success [or] the world burning in climate change apocalypse, but also realistic alternative pathways to a world that we actually want to inhabit." In examining history's actual pathways, in unearthing how in fact we got to now, we may, they believe, "open up new ways of thinking and escape old nightmares."[51] The modern street represents a significant and deeply worn corridor to our present, but it has become a space of limited cultural utility or meaning. History has certainly bequeathed to us greater nightmares than the congestion and dangers of the automotive street, but if the streets of Rio de Janeiro, or any city, were returned to their former status as multi-use commons, what social, economic, and political openings might they present to our increasingly urban civilizations?

---

[49] Renato Rosaldo, "Imperialist Nostalgia," *Representations* 26, Special Issue: Memory and Counter-Memory (Spring 1989): 107–08.

[50] Timothy Morton, *Ecology without Nature: Rethinking Environmental Aesthetics* (Cambridge, MA: Harvard University Press, 2007), 162.

[51] Jo Guldi and David Armitage, *The History Manifesto* (Cambridge, UK: Cambridge University Press, 2014), 69. See also David Harlan, *The Degradation of American History* (Chicago, IL: University of Chicago Press, 1997), 206.

Systems Circulatory before the Wheel

Rua do Ouvidor

There is no pleasure greater than to hear in the street ... two neighbors conversing.

Lima Barreto, 1915[1]

Ah, my dear old Ouvidor Street! ... How I envy you! Now, in the quietude of your retirement and in the placid and smiling tranquility of your reminiscences, one forgets your iniquities and remembers only past glories.

Fon Fon, 1910[2]

Place yourself figuratively in the shoes of Henriqueta, an unmarried woman and resident of Rio de Janeiro. I say figuratively because Henriqueta, who was born free in Angola in about 1825, is a slave in Brazil in 1870 and, hence, does not wear shoes. In nineteenth-century Rio, which had more free persons of African descent than it did slaves, the unshod condition of one's feet, more than the color of one's skin, was the chief indicator of slave status. In the second quarter of the century, slaves made up almost half of the city's population. By 1872, that proportion had fallen to 18 percent; however, there were still 48,938 slaves enumerated in the city, maybe as many as had ever lived there.[3] Without shoes, Henriqueta and those who shared her status knew Rio de Janeiro's streets, the squares and the alleys, the cobbles and the mud, more intimately, with

---

[1] Lima Barreto, "Os outros," *Careta*, Dec. 11, 1915.
[2] A letter from Avenida Central ("friend and sister") to Rua do Ouvidor ("colleague and neighbor"), *Fon Fon*, Mar. 5, 1910.
[3] Herbert S. Klein, "The Colored Freedmen in Brazilian Slave Society," *Journal of Social History* 3 (Fall 1969): table 1, 36.

the soles of their feet, than did the shod and the free. Without freedom, the street, a space that embraced all with little discrimination, offered Henriqueta and others of her status a rare space where they might escape, if only momentarily, the patriarchal gaze.

Except for slim details gleaned from the documentation of her sale to a new master in 1869, we know nothing of Henriqueta's life. However, there were scores of similar transactions every month, and constant uprooting appears to have been a common part of slave reality, especially after the transatlantic trade ended in 1850. Henriqueta's sale required her to relocate to the heart of the city, into a new parish only about a kilometer from her former residence, but in the small geographies that made up a person's place and bounds in the nineteenth-century city, it was a move to a new, unfamiliar community. She certainly left behind neighbors and friends. And because her sale took place before the proclamation of the Slave Family Protection Decree later that year, which recognized for the first time a slave's legal right to kin, she may have left behind children. She also moved from a part of the city where female slaves, serving as maids, cooks, and laundresses, made up a majority, to the rough and tumble downtown where male slaves outnumbered females two to one. Hence, a mere kilometer in Rio de Janeiro was a social and personal disruption, a sundering of acquaintance and kin.[4]

Unshod her whole life, Henriqueta's calloused feet were prepared for the sharp, irregular cobblestones that were common to the city center's streets. Locals referred to the city's crude paving as *pé de moleque* after a popular, lumpy candy much like peanut brittle, but that can be literally translated as "slave boy's foot," another association of slave soles with the early Rio street. We do not know Henriqueta's particular assignments, and it is possible she spent much of the rest of her life cloistered in domestic duties, her contact with the street restricted to quick trips to Mass and views glimpsed out of the windows of her master's home.[5] But for many of her status and gender, entering the street was a common, daily

---

[4] Zephyr Frank and Whitney Berry. "The Slave Market in Rio de Janeiro circa 1869: Context, Movement and Social Experience," *Journal of Latin American Geography* 9, no. 3 (2010): 85, 87–89, 97. In this pioneering study of the spatial implications of slave transactions, the authors report that many children under the age of fifteen were sold in single transactions. The details of Henriqueta's sale can be found at the Spatial History Project, Stanford University, www.stanford.edu/group/spatialhistory/media/images/publi cation/Slave_Transactions_Rio_1869_1.txt (accessed Apr. 25, 2013).

[5] Frank and Berry note that some female slaves were put out to rent only under "the condition that they not be allowed to go about in the street" ("The Slave Market in Rio de Janeiro circa 1869," 86).

task, and female domestic slaves could spend much of their day running errands, laundering clothing in the local fountain, peddling goods, and engaging in other remunerative work, right on the streets. In a short period, Henriqueta's feet would have acquired an almost prehensile sense of her new streets' contours, the joints between the cobbles, the missing stones, the smooth flagstone pavers that fronted fancy shops, the compacted dirt and sand of unpaved lanes, the puddles, the mud, the prickly vegetation, and the dried blood and fish scales from yesterday's market that clung to the soles. That a slave's head and neck were often burdened with water, groceries, laundry, or saleable wares, pressing the feet all the more firmly onto the street's irregular surfaces and declivities, accelerated the tactile education.

Henriqueta's new neighborhood included two of Rio's most frequented public spaces: Rua do Ouvidor, the city's main street of high fashion and, in season, carnival dancing, and Rua Direita, the city's chief commercial space that fronted the port and main square. The two streets intersected. Machado de Assis, Rio's most perceptive narrator, described the notoriously narrow Rua do Ouvidor, despite its reputation as an "interminable alley excessively lit," as the generative heart of the city. If the entire city were destroyed, but Ouvidor preserved, he wrote, it would, like Noah's entourage saved from the flood, be the seed from which the city could fully regenerate itself. He gloried in its characterization as a place for loafers and loiterers, its slender confines forcing a familiar intimacy on all who went there. He accused those who wanted it widened of ignorance of confinement's social beauties, a place where a man in one shop could shake the hand of a friend in a café across the street without losing his balance. "Streets that offer us easy passage," he asserted, "hold little charm, neither do they inspire in us the desire to stop and see what there is to experience." He observed that with a will, one could walk Ouvidor's entire length in three minutes, but the trip, he asserted, generally took three hours; and one could gain more in interest and information by idling at the corners than by moving through with purpose. Brazilians were considered lazy by outsiders, but foreigners, he suggested, failed to understand that a deliberate sluggishness produced the street goods most prized by locals: interaction, news, entertainment, and community. It was also the place in which to mingle with and appreciate the opposite sex: Ouvidor was heavily frequented by women, at least by the second half of the century. To transit a street like Ouvidor expeditiously was to fail to understand what the street was for and why you came there in the first place.[6] Ouvidor represented community in its broadest, civic sense, a place to share with all those – many of them strangers – who made claim on the city as home, from the emperor to the slave. All belonged, even if not all were offered the same kind of welcome.

In 1850, Ouvidor was lined with jewelers, shoemakers, various workshops, and twenty-five newspaper and magazine presses.[7] By the later part of the century, the number of presses increased, and many shops were occupied by foreign keepers and French fashions. Beginning at the street's western extremity on São Francisco de Paula Square, residents made slow progress indeed in the busy late afternoon, a haptic encounter, literally rubbing shoulders with other women and men – rich and poor, black and white, slave and free, sellers and buyers, deliverers and receivers. There were indeed many loafers, but for those who moved, movement was haphazard, "all crossing each other's paths in every direction."[8] As narrow as it was, Ouvidor was not viewed as having merely a linear function. It was space experienced as volume, meters cubed, rather than a line. People made all sorts of connections: intimate chatter was incessant, and in walking, eyes met eyes, fastening and releasing on a succession of faces strange and familiar. On Ouvidor, you could buy one of many newspapers, but if you wanted the latest news, you listened to the enveloping conversations, those spreading pure gossip, matchmakers announcing prominent weddings, and ship captains sharing news from Europe and prices in Africa. The smells of natural bodies and manmade perfumes mingled with the scents of restaurant kitchens, roasting nuts, leaking gaslights, toasting coffee beans, smoldering tobacco, and the soil of potted flowers. As you progressed toward the port, there were fewer suits, cigarettes, and polished boots, each progressively supplanted by baggy pants, cheap pipes, and unshod feet. The fragrances became increasingly organic: salted cod and fresh beef attracting flies; popping corn and nutty candies drawing children; kerosene, hay, the manure of mules, pigs, and dogs; and the bouquet of caustic soap emanating from the public fountain.[9] This

---

[6] Joaquim Maria Machado de Assis, "A Semana," *Gazeta de Notícias*, May 21, 1893, 1. Miécio Táti, *O mundo de Machado de Assis* (Rio de Janeiro: Secretaria Municipal de Cultura, 1991), 14, 19 (footnote 3), 21; João Pinheiro Chagas, *De bond: alguns aspectos da civilização brasileira* (Lisbon: Livraria Moderna, 1897), 42–49, evidences in some detail the numerical place of women of all sorts on Rio's most fashionable street.

[7] Delso Renault, *O Rio antigo nos anúncios dos journais* (Rio de Janeiro: Jose Olympio, 1969), 233–34.

[8] Chagas, *De bond*, 22.

[9] Jorge Americano, *São Paulo naquele tempo, 1895–1915* (São Paulo: Saraiva,1957), 190–92, draws some of these scents from his olfactory memory.

was not a corridor. It was a living entity, a space in which the life of the city happened. João Pinheiro Chagas, a political exile who later became Portugal's first prime minister, found Rio's downtown streets in the late 1890s narrow, dirty, stifling, and poorly paved, offering the most uncomfortable transit. However, the street's failure as an efficient passage failed to bother him much "because the life of the streets makes me forget the street."[10]

Much of Ouvidor's diversity and focused life derived from the sheer number of its users. There was also safety in the absence of wheeled vehicles. For some time, Ouvidor, due to its narrow confines and burgeoning crowds, had been declared vehicle-free, at least from 9 AM to 10 PM.[11] On Ouvidor, "nada de rodas," nothing to do with wheels: no carriages, no horse carts, and no streetcars. In one popular anecdote, a man "very well gloved" in a smart carriage, smiling with confident authority, turned his driver up Ouvidor only to be abruptly ordered back by a low-ranking policeman. The notable insisted, stating, "[T]his carriage will pass because it belongs to the palace," to which the policeman responded, "[E]ven if it belongs to Susana de Castro," the city's most famous consort and a favorite of men of the royal family, "it shall not pass. No wheels on Ouvidor. I keep my orders."[12]

As Ouvidor opened onto the relatively broad Rua Direita, users did compete for space with the occasional wheeled vehicle, including mule-drawn streetcars running on narrow rails, a new addition to the streets from the late 1860s. But even these modern conveyances were notoriously slow, moving no faster than a brisk walker. The scene might still have been similar to that painted by Johan Moritz Rugendas, who depicted the street on a busy day, a bustling gathering spot of hundreds of individuals. He placed the spectacle of transpositional movement in the background, where it appears that a royal figure in a carriage arrives at the Nossa Senhora do Carmo church. But in the foreground resides the mundane, characterized not by movement but by stasis, scores of slave carters, female vendors, merchants, priests, gentlemen, ladies, muleteers, cabbies, and policeman, barely any of whom are engaged in transpositional movement. They take their places on the commons, where they belong and where they

[10] Chagas, *De bond*, 26.
[11] Rules against wheels on Ouvidor go back apparently to the 1840s, which is hard to document, but they were frequently reiterated, as in Decreto 29, Dec. 24, 1894, AGCRJ, 58-1-14, *folha* 52.
[12] Luiz Edmundo, *O Rio de Janeiro do meu tempo*, 2nd edn., vol. 1 (Rio de Janeiro: Conquista, 1957), 85–86.

FIGURE 1.1 Rua Direita and the nature of the *logradouro*, c. 1825. The street as commons permitted, even invited, a multitude of activities. Residents understood the street as an outdoor room, a negative form of architecture that belonged to everyone and that was open to varied, creative uses. Busy streets like Rua Direita, the city's main commercial space, offered an ever-changing spectacle of sanctioned and unsanctioned utilities.
Source: Johann Moritz Rugendas, "Rue Droite," in *Voyage pittoresque dans le Brésil* (Paris: G. Engelmann, 1835), plate 63. Courtesy of the Acervo da Fundação Biblioteca Nacional, Brazil.

have as much right to stand, sit, chat, negotiate, observe, and argue as they do to move. They stand together in small groups interacting, or alone observing others. They sit on empty carts, on their bundled wares, or, often, directly on the pavement. And they look relaxed, as if they have been there for some time and have no plans to move on. A two-wheeled tilbury, with passengers, presses against their collective body, but it too seems to be seeking interaction rather than transposition. The street folk do not move for oncoming traffic; the traffic will find its way around them. From above, local residents, also unmoving, engage the street from their windows.[13]

[13] Johann Moritz Rugendas, "Rue Droite," in *Voyage pittoresque dans le Brésil* (Paris: G. Engelmann, 1835), plate 63.

This is the street of interest in this chapter: the mundane, the common, the everyday. I resist (not always successfully) the temptation to assume the role of the flaneur, the elite rambler popularized by Baudelaire and Dickens and practiced in Brazil by João do Rio and Aluísio Azevedo, who take to the streets in search of the exotic, the serendipitous, and the lurid. Still, the street of a century ago can be exotic to modern eyes. Modernity simplifies street life, tells us all where it is we should look, subsuming all of our senses to the dominance of our eyes. On the street today, it's "eyes forward, both hands on the wheel." The circus has only three rings; the traditional street, on the other hand, was a stage with too many human dramas to comprehend all at once, all of which overwhelms the modern gaze. It was complex, and it was open to rapid changes – additions and subtractions – in use and meaning. The unsettled and shifting nature of the street's spatial practices impresses, and this chapter's objective is not an exact chronology of evolving street practices but rather a demonstration of its spatial possibilities. When the street was an open commons and not yet dominated by transpositional movement, citizens devised and reinvented hundreds of creative ways to use the street to meet their social, economic, cultural, religious, and other needs, which altogether expressed the street's multifaceted meanings. More to the point, with space, an open urban habitat, residents found a place in which to act out their most basic behaviors: to talk, to buy, to sell, to celebrate, to play, and to simply be with others of their own species.

SYSTEMS AND PERCEPTIONS OF NATURE

The automotive street's dominant flows have been habitually compared to the human circulatory system, which, despite certain limitations, is apt. As with the human bloodstream, where corpuscles flow through a complex system of arteries and capillaries, the streets, avenues, and highways of the city's network serve as the conduits on which bodies and commodities stream from one place to another. As such, these systems are described as serving one function, movement, and when they perform below expectations, or fail, we call them congested or sclerotic. In prioritizing flow, we tend to disregard the street's other functions, many of which still hold, if now attenuated and less visible.

The traditional street, with its multiple utilities, is too complex a reality for this simple analogy. However, if one delves into the bloodstream's more complex functions, the metaphor can again be elucidating. Blood circulates, but it does so in support of the bloodstream's most critical functions, which are access and exchange. First, and quite remarkably, the body's network of arteries and capillaries access essentially every tissue and cell in the body: the bone's marrow, the tooth's pulp, and the hair's follicle. The bloodstream effectively connects every space within the body with every other space, putting all elements in communication. Second, blood, once it has accessed a location, engages its most elegant machinery in the exchange of commodities and information. Blood consists of as many as 4,000 different ingredients that offer energy, nutrition, waste disposal, and antiviral and bacterial security. To the door of every cell, blood delivers glucose fuel, oxygen, both coolant and heat to regulate temperature, minerals and nutrients, protein-building blocks, clotting and healing agents, antibodies, hormones, enzymes, and a host of other elements, many containing vital information. Maybe most impressive is the bloodstream's ability to accomplish all of this within a single conduit. In the same stream that blood carries beneficial sugar, oxygen, and antibodies, it also carries wastes, such as carbon dioxide, toxins, dead tissue, excess water, and salts, all of which it safely exchanges to organs of excretion.

In a sense, the traditional street, although on a large and crude scale, mimicked the bloodstream's access and exchange functions. In a single conduit, a host of activities, utilities, and exchanges took place altogether and simultaneously. It was on the street that the city was provisioned with energy: food, firewood, and lamp oil, many of these peddled door to door, as were hundreds of other necessary items. The substantial peddling classes, referred to as the *ambulantes*, represented a mixed commodity stream in flow seeking exchange. Although there were formal and informal markets also located in the streets, householders did not need to daily enter the street to shop but simply waited for the baker, bookseller, florist, or the milkman, the last with milk cow in tow, to flow past their doors, each peddler sounding his or her characteristic call – a jingle, horn, rattle, bell, or whistle – to signal the potential for a specific exchange. Water was collected at local public fountains, many of them located in the squares and *largos*, and then carried through the streets, mostly on slaves' heads, to households and businesses. Rather than relying on machines, even one as simple as the wheel, movement was effected largely on foot and on hoof: slaves carried their masters slung in hammocks, transported goods upon their heads and shoulders, and engaged pack animals for heavier items. The street was an organic machine without machines. Information flowed in the street in vocalized news and gossip, or it was sold in print form on the street corners by newspaper boys who sang out the headlines.

Likewise, the city's waste found its way to the streets to be excreted beyond the immediate urban bounds. Waste water and human excrement were also dumped onto the streets' surface so that the rain might wash it away, or they were also commonly placed in large barrels such that slaves could carry them away to dump in the bay or a local stream. As in the bloodstream, in the city nearly all things flowed, intermingled, and exchanged in the single conduit of the street. And in some ways the street exceeded the bloodstream: it provided the city's cells with essential light and air, and people, commodities, and wastes flowed not just in a single unidirectional stream but moved in all directions at once. The street formed an exceptional example of a hybrid in which nature's space and culture's activities entangled in ways that blurred the lines we tend to draw between them. The streets also, of course, played a critical social and cultural role that went beyond the ecological and commercial. The street accomplished both its ecological and cultural functions all in the same space, all at the same time.

By contrast, the modern street, while still a hybrid space, is a simplified one where lines are more easily drawn. The modern street zones activities and canalizes functions, simplifying the traditional street's complexity. This began some decades before the car arrived, but the car accelerated the process and, in fact, demanded it. Flow took precedence, which required that many other functions be removed or rechanneled. The bed of the street, typically making up its majority, was progressively converted into an almost exclusive corridor for large, fast moving machines. Curbs separated the street bed from the sidewalks, channeling foot traffic to its own particular corridor. Water, now, rather than originating in fountains and moving in hands, or on heads and backs, was channelized into pipes running beneath the streets and directly into homes. Likewise, sewers and later storm drains were installed to carry away wastes that used to move on the surface. Energy, rather than arriving laden on the backs of slaves as firewood or even in the beds of trucks, increasingly arrived in gas lines that ran beneath, or electrical lines that were suspended over, the street. The power of muscles – thighs, shoulders, lungs, and tongues – was being replaced by actual machines – generators, pumps, motors, and horns and loudspeakers. The automobile did not drive all this change, and there were important benefits to channelizing some of the street's utilities, but by dedicating the street's surface to largely host movement, other utilities suffered in the transformation. In particular, those cultural and social functions provided by the street, that could not be easily and mechanically channelized, were diminished and often displaced.

Rio's pre-automotive residents did not, of course, understand their streets as part of an organic machine. But they also did not see streets as cultural products or monuments. Strikingly, they perceived the street, a space that was unbuilt, unimproved, and held in common, as a remnant of nature itself. The space remained unproduced. In Eduard Hildebrandt's 1844 painting of the space we last described, Rua Direita, the city's busiest commercial street, the street's inhabitants are made up largely of African women like Henriqueta, some walking, some congregating about the doors of the Carmelite church, but the majority are seated right on the street in conversation. Two dogs chase each other about in the foreground, amidst the ruts of cart tracks, but there is not a vehicle to be seen along the street's entire length. If one were to just focus on the ground, the street itself, ignoring the shops, the facing Hotel de l'Empire, and the façades and towers of five baroque churches, one might guess that this, the city's main street, was an unkempt farmyard or country lane. The street, which by 1844 is paved, is still entirely overlain with dirt, has irregular dimensions, and displays no apparent improvements – no curbs, no sidewalks, no planted trees, and no gutters.[14] We notice a striking distinction between the tall, substantial artifices of civilization and the low, rather raw reality of the dirt-covered street from which they emerge.

The traditional street, despite its place at the center of civilization and its intense use by humans, fell fairly firmly into the category of nature in the minds of those who used it. The city's founders built homes, churches, palaces, and offices, but between the walls of their constructions they left strips and chunks of nature, whose main function was not travel or commerce but simple access. Early city builders, including those in Rio, thought of the street's function as primarily a space left as they found it so citizens could maintain direct admission to their homes and monuments. The raw, unimproved, unmarked, and officially unnamed street was a cultural space, but in the minds of its users, it was also a natural resource, not unlike forests or fisheries. This sets the Brazilian street apart from a common perception shared by Lewis Mumford who wrote

---

[14] "Rua Direita, Rio de Janeiro, 1844," in Gilberto Ferrez, *The Brazil of Eduard Hildebrandt* (Rio de Janeiro: Distribuidora Record de Serviços de Imprensa, 1989), 37; there is one ox cart depicted parked off Rua Direita, on the square. Another example from 1832 is Conrad Marten's "A Capela Real & um lado da Grande Praça," in George Ermakoff, *Paisagem do Rio de Janeiro – Aquarelas, desenhos e gravuras dos artistas viajantes, 1790–1890* (Rio de Janeiro: G. Ermakoff Casa Editorial, 2011), 151, which contains no wheeled vehicles.

that "nature, except in a surviving landscape park, is scarcely to be found near the metropolis."[15] In Rio, quite the contrary, the street was nature's residue.

Roberto DaMatta has argued for a pervasive, cosmological dualism that divided the Brazilian's mental universe into the two stark categories of house and street. The house represented honor, fidelity, authority, order, safety, and cleanliness; the street evoked the opposites: dishonor, infidelity, insubordination, danger, and filth. The concepts of house and street pervasively ordered the Brazilian mind.[16] Portuguese expressions further illustrate DaMatta's point: to shout the word "street" at someone was the equivalent of telling them to go to hell; a "thing of the street" (*coisa de rua*) was something dirty, low, and vulgar; and to further contrast the licentiousness of the street with the fidelity of the house, when a couple legitimately married, their civic respectability rose to a new level, for they had become "*casados*," the Portuguese term for "married" which literally means "housed." The house represented civil culture; the street was raw nature, which encapsulated many of its undesirable associations. William Cronon has challenged the common mental separation of nature and culture, of city and countryside, arguing that we can no longer presuppose that "nature is the place that we are not." Nature and culture, if such categories are useful, intermingle in nearly all places, even in large cities.[17] Still, we tend to want to separate them. The Brazilian view, while it saw nature in the city's raw streets, maintained the same false dichotomy. It was just that the lines were drawn at the house's front door rather than along some more distant boundary coterminous with the ancient city wall. Nature was distinctly separate, but it was close at hand, occupied, and used. The traditional street, despite its heavy use, was more "natural" than a carefully plowed field or an orderly planted orchard; it was less manipulated to serve human ends than many farms, forests, rivers, and parks, most of which, despite their obvious, intentional shaping by

[15] Lewis Mumford, *The Culture of Cities* (New York, NY: Harcourt, Brace and Company, 1938), 252.

[16] Roberto DaMatta. *A casa & a rua: Espaço, cidadania, mulher, e morte no Brasil* (São Paulo: Editora Brasiliense, 1985). Others have also identified this divided world: Sandra Lauderdale Graham, *House and Street: The Domestic World of Servants and Masters in Nineteenth-Century Rio de Janeiro* (Austin, TX: University of Texas Press, 1988).

[17] William Cronon, *Nature's Metropolis: Chicago and the Great West* (New York, NY: W. W. Norton & Co., 1991) 16–19. Lise Fernanda Sedrez, "'The Bay of All Beauties': State and Environment in Guanabara Bay, Rio de Janeiro, Brazil, 1875–1975" (PhD diss., Stanford University, 2004), also substantially blurs the urban line between nature and culture.

humans, still largely remain in the category "nature." Street naming
practices demonstrate that street spaces were significant parts of the
city's symbolic world, but giving names to streets, like giving names to
other natural objects, such as lakes and hills, again made them no less
natural in the minds of their namers.

The street's perceived "natural" state can in part be understood by
examining its origin in early urban planning. In laying out Rio, the
founders had a variety of potential influences: Greek, Roman, medieval,
and possibly even indigenous, the last by way of cities discovered elsewhere in the Americas that were often characterized by rectilinear streets
and large public squares. In fact, the Tupi's indigenous villages were
themselves built around a central public space that they referred to as an
ocara (*ocaraçu* if it were large). Some have argued that Rio's urban plan
was capricious, had no forethought, or was meant to imitate Portugal's
medieval cities with contorted narrow streets.[18] Close examination suggests otherwise, and part of this error in observation comes from looking
only to the streets for an answer. Significantly, here as in Spanish
American and European cities, the streets were not the ordering element.
Surveyors did not plot the city by laying out the lines of the streets as is
done today, but by laying out the blocks, or, more specifically, the lots and
their frontages that would form the blocks. We have no founding documents for Rio's plan, but that of Panama City from 1519 expresses well
the approach:

In view of these things necessary for settlements … divide the plots for the houses,
these to be according to the status of the persons, and from the beginning it should
be according to a definite arrangement, for the manner of setting up the houses will
determine the pattern of the town, both in the position of the plaza and the church
and in the pattern of the streets.[19]

What gave the city shape was not its complement of streets but the
arrangement of its blocks. The architect Paul Spreiregen points out that
before the modern era, the street was not "treated as a principal design
element but as the minimal leftover space for circulation."[20] Rio was

---

[18] See Roberta Marx Delson, *New Towns for Colonial Brazil: Spatial and Social Planning in the Eighteenth Century* (Ann Arbor, MI: Department of Geography, Syracuse University, University Microfilms International, 1979), 1–2; and Preston E. James, "Rio de Janeiro and São Paulo," *Geographical Review* 23, no. 2 (Apr. 1933): 283–84.

[19] Cited in Jay Kinsbruner, *The Colonial Spanish-American City* (Austin, TX: University of Texas, 2005), 11.

[20] Paul Spreiregen, *Urban Design: The Architecture of Towns and Cities* (New York, NY: McGraw-Hill, 1965), 3.

a structured mass of irregular cells. The streets were not created. Humans built buildings on demarcated blocks, and the streets simply emerged. To this extent, streets, while not accidental, were not quite yet produced. Streets expressed irregularity and messiness in their composition because they were not composed.[21] João do Rio felt that streets were among the most human of spaces, bodies with souls, and suggested that in much the same way that we create new human beings, in "expectant sighs and fruitful spasms," our streets birthed inadvertently in the human quest for more immediately tangible desires.[22] In Rio, as in New York, Boston, Lima, and Havana, officials did not give streets official names at their emergence between the blocks.[23] Like children, they were nameless when conceived.

In many cases there was almost no plan in the beginning; settlers simply plopped down buildings randomly on open ground. But soon method was imposed. In Rio, the blocks were produced irregularly – in shape and in size – which was reflected in the varied character of the streets. The blocks' only regularity was that each aligned itself pretty well with its neighbors. But one would be hard pressed to find a perfectly square block in colonial Rio, and it would be almost as hard to find one that was a perfect rectangle. In shape, we can characterize the city block only as a four-sided object whose sides were usually straight but often not parallel. Since each block's corners generally aligned themselves with the corners of three other blocks, Rio's streets had continuity and intersections, but they did not have regularity, nor were they rectilinear. Streets broadened, narrowed, and changed direction, all depending on the shape and alignment of the neighboring blocks.[24] What was true of the streets was also true of the squares. Lilian Fessler Vaz's study of Rio's squares notes that not a single one before the nineteenth century was "regular" – that is, had the shape of a square or rectangle. Of the eighteen she examines from the

[21] Mumford, *Culture of Cities*, 56–57, argues similarly that medieval cities started with the construction of buildings that were self-contained "islands" and the streets an urban network made up of footpaths.

[22] João do Rio, *A alma encantadora das ruas* [original edn. 1908] (Rio de Janeiro: Prefeitura da Cidade do Rio de Janeiro, 1995), 4.

[23] Carl Bridenbaugh, *Cities in the Wilderness: The First Century of Urban Life in America 1625–1742*, 2nd edn. (New York, NY: Alfred A. Knopf, 1955), 15, 153–54. New York's streets did not have official names until 1664, Boston still later. Streets in Latin American cities remained officially nameless until the eighteenth century, according to Kinsbruner, *The Colonial Spanish-American City*, 128.

[24] "Planta da Cidade de S. Sebastião do Rio de Janeiro," Impressão Régia, 1812, Museu Histórico Nacional, Rio de Janeiro.

eighteenth century, only three approximated regular geometric shapes. Rio's squares, like her streets, were an odd collection of poorly defined spaces shaped by the blocks and buildings that irregularly surrounded them.[25]

In size, city blocks could range from as many 45,000 square meters with 150 building lots down to a mere 1,200 square meters with as few as three. Yet blocks in Rio substantially dominated the urban landscape. The space dedicated to, or better, left over for, streets was minimal. On average, Rio's central streets were no wider than 5.5 meters, and frequently narrower. Many downtown streets were insufficient for two carts to pass one another without grinding their axle hubs against the sides of the houses. With its narrow streets and busy traffic out of the port, Rio appears to be among the first cities to establish one-way streets, an innovative spatial practice that astonished European visitors. The direction of travel was (and still is) called "the hand" as signs mounted on walls pictured a hand with index finger extended in the direction of travel. The width of the streets was determined, of course, by how far apart blocks and their building alignments were platted, and in Rio we do not know if this was done by rule or custom, although the narrowness of the colonial streets suggests surveyors may have followed the pattern formalized by Spain's Philip II: that in cold climates, streets should be wide to allow the sun to warm its inhabitants, and in hot climates narrow to provide shade. Across the region, colonial streets in tropical Havana, Mérida, and Rio are quite narrow from frontage to frontage, generally less than 6 meters, whereas in highland Mexico City, Quito, and Bogota, streets were 9–12 meters wide.

Blocks provided Rio with whatever order it had, and what determined the alignment of the first blocks was the orientation of the coast. The beach, not the compass, laid out Rio's loose grid. Many of Rio's first streets were technically *boqueirões* – that is, streets that opened onto the port. And as the early port was presumably a naturally curving water-line, Rio's first blocks were built to face the water along a gentle crescent that became Rua Direita. Hence, each block faced the beach sitting at a slightly different angle from its neighbors. This made the transverse streets emerge from Rua Direita at right angles, and hence Rio's east/ west streets fan ever so slightly from the port and are not parallel.

[25] Lilian Fessler Vaz, "Notas sobre as praças do Rio de Janeiro no periódo colonial," in *A praça no cidade Portuguesa*, ed. Manuel C. Teixeira (Lisbon: Livros Horizonte, 2001), 151–53.

The same logic was used in laying out blocks in colonial Niteroi across the bay,[26] as well as more starkly centuries later when laying out the crescent beachfront suburbs of Copacabana. Compared to the city's somewhat orderly blocks, streets were irregular by comparison, appearing as narrow spaces that come at odd intervals and unexpected angles. The sides of blocks are straight and true, but a facing block did not necessarily run parallel to its neighbor, so streets were not always uniform in width, which could vary over their length, sometimes becoming so broad as to form small squares or *largos*. And streets often changed direction slightly from one block to the next as the blocks themselves had slightly different orientations.

Urban maps until the second quarter of the twentieth century attest to this perception of the city as ordered urban blocks built on a raw landscape. Map makers represented the city by illustrating the city's blocks, and sometimes individual buildings, as distinct objects – human constructions on a blank field. The built environment dominates, leaving the streets, squares, and beaches as interstitial remnants of nature's original space. The blocks and buildings made the figures; the streets were artistically and literally the ground. Colonial maps and illustrations of Rio's streets depict the ground, the unbuilt space, as all of one continuous piece, from street to square to beach, with no distinctions.[27] Maps also presented streets at their actual scale relative to the blocks, emphasizing the street's relative spatial insignificance. Yet significantly, streets were always represented as actual spaces, not as abstracted lines representing space.[28] Once the automobile began to dominate streets, maps became complete inversions of their former selves. Now urban maps are called street maps

---

[26] Thomas Ewbank, *Life in Brazil* (New York, NY: Harper & Brothers, Publishers, 1956), 292.

[27] "Navio Lady Stormant na Baia da Guanabara," c. 1816, reproduced in Ermakoff, *Paisagem do Rio: Aquarelas, desenhos, e gravuras dos artistas viajantes, 1790–1890* (Rio de Janeiro: G. Ermakoff Casa Editorial, 2011), front end paper. For another example, see Debret's sketch of Santa Cruz from the 1820s, in *Viagem pitoresca e histórica do Brasil* (São Paulo: Editora da Universidade de São Paulo, 1978), and for Rio itself, see Luis do Santos Vilhena, "Prospecto da Cidade de São Sebastião do Rio de Janeiro," 1775, in Gilberto Ferrez, *O que ensinam os antigos mapas e estampas do Rio de Janeiro* (Rio de Janeiro: Departamento de Imprensa Nacional, 1966), estampa 4.

[28] "Planta da Cidade de S. Sebastião do Rio de Janeiro," Impressão Regia, 1812, Museu Histórico Nacional, Rio de Janeiro; "Nova Planta da Cidade do Rio de Janeiro" (Rio de Janeiro: E. & H. Laemmert, 1867), Division of Maps, Library of Congress, Washington, DC; and João da Rocha Fragoso, "Mappa architectural da cidade do Rio de Janeiro," 1874, Biblioteca National Digital Brazil, http://objdigital.bn.br/acervo_digital/div_carto grafia/cart470826.pdf (accessed Feb. 15, 2013).

because they represent the city as so many abstract lines, not spaces. The built environment is now the ground on which unscaled, colored lines are inscribed to represent the "figure" of the streets.[29]

If manipulation is what begins to unmake nature, then the failure to modify and improve the traditional street extended its status as nature for centuries. Most of Rio's streets persisted as raw, bare ground, unpaved and unimproved until the eighteenth century, and often for another century even downtown. The first improvement to the street was the paving of the *testada*, the street space immediately in front of the house. Sometimes mistaken as a sidewalk, and certainly used that way when the streets were muddy or trafficked by vehicles, the paved *testada*, which was completed at the owner's expense, served more as a front porch and protection against water at the foundations than as a pedestrian corridor. Each *testada* might be paved in different materials, at different widths, and varying grades, but with no curbstones, lying at the level of the street itself. Likewise, as many houses had none, the *testada* was discontinuous.[30] On steep streets, the *testadas* gave the effect of a series of broad, irregular platforms. The rest of the street was generally unpaved and frequently ungraded, making the ground uneven, rough, and poorly drained. At best, a street might be periodically graded, with hand tools, so that water flowed to the center where a narrow ditch was provided. If a street was paved, abutters, those who lived on it (not the city) paid for it. Still, most streets into the early nineteenth century remained wall-to-wall dirt.[31] And while some prominent squares saw pavement in the eighteenth century, none were landscaped, curbed, or honored with statuary until late in the nineteenth century.[32] Even when paved, streets were often filled with dirt. When it rained, some streets became streams and rivers. Soil and water mixed to form deep, muddy thoroughfares that were impassable to all except shod hooves and unshod feet. And in Rio and other coastal cities, such as Paraty even today, the highest tides rose to cover the lowest portions of the public streets with

---

[29] Karen Joyce Roberts, "The Argentine Babel: Space, Politics and Culture in the Growth of Buenos Aires, 1856–1890" (PhD diss., University of Michigan, 1997), 133, observes a similar linear transformation of maps earlier in Buenos Aires due to the railroads.

[30] Relação do Pessoal em Servico, Nov. 26, 1902, AGCRJ 61, 51-4-35, folhas 6–43. See folhas 90 and 138 for charges to residents to pave their frontages.

[31] Nestor Goulart Reis Filho, *Contribuição ao estudo da evolução urbana do Brasil, 1500–1720* (São Paulo: Livraria Pioneira, 1968), 144–45.

[32] Joaquim Maria Machado de Assis, "Singular Ocurrencia," in *Histórias sem data* (Project Gutenberg, released 3 July 2010), 59. See also James R. Curtis, "Praças, Place, and Public Life," *Geographical Review* 90 (2000): 484.

some regularity. As in most commons, there were few incentives for individuals to make improvements to the street. In these circumstances, the urban commons were no more produced than were fish in the sea or timber in the forest.

One might suggest that streets were unnatural in having been significantly reshaped by their very trampling and by the additions of human trash and wastes. But by many reports, even the busiest streets were covered with grass, choked with weeds, and invaded by shrubs and trees. Locals used the term "*mato*," usually translated as "jungle," to describe vegetation in the streets, and in Rio's first suburbs residents complained that it grew a meter high. In the seventeenth century, locals said streets had more vegetation than anything else. Rio's citizens, even those living downtown, were making similar complaints into the early twentieth century.[33] *Tiririca*, a tall, invasive sedge from Africa, was among the most common street plants, well adapted to packed earth and resistant to trampling. In one of the earliest photos of the city, Revert Henrique Klumb framed Castelo Street in 1860 choked in places with an impassable scrub.[34] Pedestrians and drivers of vehicles used streets selectively, avoiding rank vegetation, ruts, high spots, and mud, following the most efficient trajectories available. This strategy resulted in desire lines, urban trails that give the impression that traditional streets were an organic collection of social trails, not single, coherent thoroughfares.[35] Occasionally before religious festivals, the city ordered a crew to uproot weeds, hoe grass, and fill in holes, creating an adequate space for the coming public event. Entrepreneurs pitched new herbicides, such as one branded "Soldier's Water," that they claimed would bring about the final extinction of plants on the public street.[36] However, some street users held the vegetation as beneficial: laundresses, who formed a major sector of the city's employed, laid their expansive washings on the streets' grass and scrubby vegetation to bleach and to dry.[37]

---

[33] *Jornal do Brasil*, April 6, 1928, 10; "Bairros que a prefeitura esqueceu," *Diário de Notícias*, Apr. 10, 1947, section 2, 1.

[34] Reproduced in George Ermakoff, *Rio de Janeiro, 1840–1900: uma crônica fotográfica* (Rio de Janeiro: G. Ermakoff Casa Editorial, 2006), 22.

[35] George Ermakoff, *Juan Gutierrez: Imagens do Rio de Janeiro, 1892–1896* (Rio de Janeiro: Marca da Agua, 2001), 80–81.

[36] *O Diário Oficial*, Nov. 19, 1897, clipping in AGCRJ 58-1-14, folha 157. *O Estado de São Paulo*, Mar. 21, 1915, 5.

[37] Laundry on street vegetation was depicted in Debret's 1822 "Vista geral da cidade do Rio de Janeiro tomada do Convento de São Bento," in Ermakoff, *Paisagem do Rio de Janeiro*, 155, and can be seen in Klumb's photo of Largo da Lapa in 1860.

"Filthy," like "narrow," was a relative term, but it is also one we misunderstand this side of modern hygiene. Foreigners found Rio's streets narrow, but they commented little on their uncleanliness.[38] Locals, on the other hand, rarely mentioned a common street's straitness, but described particular streets as *suja* (dirty) and *imunda* (filthy). However, sources before the turn of the twentieth century strongly counter such local accusations. It is rare to find the smallest evidence of trash, offal, or waste in street depictions, except in active street markets. Some artists might be accused of idealization or pure obfuscation, and of course notable streets got more attention from artists than back alleys, but the available visual record suggests that the traditional street in Rio was cleaner than many streets today. Most of the time, the street was depicted or photographed as nothing short of immaculate. Part of the explanation for the lack of trash and waste is that in pre-industrial societies nearly all materials had economic value. Bent nails, rags, chaffs of paper, even tobacco wrappers were harvested from the street to be recycled or repurposed. Scavengers, Do Rio wrote, "carved out a livelihood clocking hours cleaning the streets."[39] Brazilians also have had a long tradition of street sweeping each morning to remove the previous day's detritus, which was legally required in Rio from the 1820s and which is still common practice in provincial cities. In the 1840s, the city provided daily carters to take away the piles, and in the 1870s, private hauling contracts were established, most famously with a French immigrant Pedro Aleixo Gary; Rio's ubiquitous street cleaner has been known as a *gari* ever since.[40]

What locals and officials complained about was actual dirt and mud, and the other organics that intermixed with them, such as rotting leaves and pulverized manure. Unpaved streets were by definition "dirty," and the main justification for paving was to overlay nature's earthy foundations, to reduce dust and mud in the street. But even once paved, the streets quickly filled with organic and mineral soils: the city's steep surrounding hills were in constant erosion, their components finding their way down to the streets, and the dust and mud from unpaved streets tracked onto the

---

[38] The always critical John Luccock, *Notes on Rio de Janeiro and the Southern Parts of Brazil, 1808–1818* (London: Samuel Leigh, 1820), 132–33, was the exception.

[39] João do Rio, *A alma encantadora das ruas*, 25.

[40] Directoria Geral de Saúde Pública, *Os serviços de saúde pública no Brazil especializmente na ciadade do Rio de Janeiro de 1808 a 1907* (Rio de Janeiro: Imprensa Nacional, 1909), 526. Fernando Agenor de Noronha Santos, *Meios de transporte no Rio de Janeiro: história e legislação*, vol. 2 (Rio de Janeiro: Typografia do Jornal do Commercio, 1934), 42–44.

pavements. In fact, in São Paulo, where the soil was alluvial, residents, after a good rain, panned the contents of the gutters for particles of gold.[41] Elite complaints about dirt were direct attacks on the raw, untamed state of the streets, on their naturalness, not on human trash or garbage. The streets evinced nature because, paved or unpaved, they were ruled by soil.[42] The street's condition as a raw and unimproved space served as an important marker and signal that the street was indeed a common space that belonged to nobody in particular.

There were, of course, rules for street users – humans, animals, and their associated vehicles – which included many prohibitions. The street was and remains the most regulated of human spaces, and one might argue again that a space so heavily imposed upon by official ordinances and informal rules could not have been understood as natural. But regulation is the norm on most commons, be they fisheries, forests, or grazing lands. Because they are common, they demand rules to ensure access to all legitimate parties and to decrease the probabilities of conflict over the resource. This too did not make the street any less natural in the eyes of those who used it, any more than forest regulations did for forests. However, what was being regulated on the street was behavior, not access. And many things were regulated, from legitimate fun to illegal crime. Cabbies and carters had to register their vehicles; streetcar companies and kiosk proprietors had formal concessions; and peddlers and beggars were supposed to be licensed. The street was not to be a free for all. In the months before street festivals and carnival celebrations, clubs, churches, and brotherhoods all petitioned the police chief for the license to parade and dance in the street, and they did so using established bureaucratic forms. In 1906, there were 175 such requests associated with carnival.[43] The chief, it appears, always granted them, but this was a means to give all access to the street while making it clear that the city regulated the space for the common benefit and that all activities fell under specific rules and expectations.

[41] Eduardo Yázigi, *Mundo das calçadas: por uma política democrática de espaços públicos* (São Paulo: Humanitas, USP, Imprensa Oficial, 2000), 62–63.

[42] Machado de Assis himself complained that city officials took no interest in removing mud from the city's paved streets; see Táti, *O mundo de Machado de Assis*, 23, footnote 7. Carl Bridenbaugh, *Cities in the Wilderness: The First Century of Urban Life in America, 1625–1742*, 2nd edn. (New York, NY: Knopf, 1960), 321–22.

[43] Petitions and Licenses, Feb. 1906, Chefe de Polícia, Documentos de Polícia, OI, GIFI 6c170, ANRJ.

Despite police and the city's best efforts, the streets were never orderly. There was too much space, there were too many people, and maybe above all, there were too many rules to make official regulation of the street anything but a vacuous claim. In fact, much of the activity on the street was in direct contradiction to the rules: slaves sang and danced together in the streets, including *capoeira*, a form of martial dance, despite rules against slaves forming groups; peddlers worked without license; drunks and non-drunks became disorderly and abusive toward their neighbors; prostitutes solicited openly; men rode their horses too fast; and wagons went the wrong way on one-way streets. The street also had a distinct reputation for violent personal crimes, including assault, robbery, rape, and murder. Still, the street remained an attractive place, amenable to human presence, and it was safer than the many criminal anecdotes would suggest. Most street crime was petty, and it was the large number of people in the downtown streets in particular that tended to keep it petty. Social policing worked to keep certain illegal activities in check, but the social will also offered collective support for certain, accepted infractions against the rules, even from the police, who worked on the streets, too. Despite its criminal associations, the street, at least by day, offered safeties and protections that the patriarchy of the home, which acted without public censure, would not offer. Most murders, rapes, and slave punishments took place indoors; hence, for many, especially among the servile classes, the street might have been considered safer than houses.

The most vital rule associated with the street was its protection as a common space, a statute so fundamental and recognized that it may never have been written down. Neighbors might complain about an individual's behavior on the street, but they could not challenge their neighbor's presence or right to occupy space there. Luiz Edmundo remembered various street characters from his youth – undesirable sorts who were broadly familiar and ever present in the street.[44] Many held their ground when their space was challenged and declared its common status openly. One Maria da Costa was angry at her friends for not including her in their evening plans. When she spotted them at an intersection, riding together in a coach, she hurled a few stinging invectives at them, and then, to spite their fun, turned up the narrow street ahead of them to walk at the slowest possible pace. The enraged driver shouted insults at Maria, demanding she make way. But Maria calmly turned to the man and asked, "[I]s not the street the king's," a shrewd legal observation to

---

[44] Edmundo, *O Rio de Janeiro do meu tempo*, 87–89.

which the driver could only give quick assent. He and his passengers then held their peace until Maria turned triumphantly down a side street.[45] What Maria had really said, in a politically astute way, was that the street was common, and she had as much right to the space as anyone. The traditional street was contested, in part because it was common, but it was always shared, available to even those who were known to refuse to follow its stated rules. The streets were, hence, both mine and thine, and its perception as nature, raw, unimproved, and unproduced, was a primary indicator of its common status.

AT THE BOUNDARY: WALLS, WINDOWS, AND DOORS

The built and un-built stood in opposition to each other, and since the days of Gilberto Freyre, who also held that house and street were enemies divided, historical work has tended to focus on the undesirable and violent exchanges between them: those who invaded the honorable home – burglars, rapists, army drafters, mosquito abaters, and medical vaccinators – challenging male power and property; and those who attempted to elude the house – domestic servants, and even daughters and wives – flirting through and slipping out of windows to expose themselves to the street's moral and medical hazards. The house was supposed to speak order to the street's chaos, hierarchy to its insubordination. Yet the dualism of the house and the street, although it had very real consequences, was largely a fiction championed by elite men to bolster their insecurities about the limits of their power over either house or street. Despite the cultural separation, physically and practically, the house and street were intimately and unavoidably coupled.[46] It was through the windows and the doors that many of the street's bloodstream exchanges took place, and hence windows and doors figure prominently in the street's function. What was a significant cultural barrier was at the same time a permeable social and ecological boundary.

Houses, shops, and even churches were built on grade, making it possible for bodies to cross the boundary between house and street

---

[45] This altercation, which took place in Porto Alegre, is cited in Roger Kittleson, *The Practice of Politics in Post-Colonial Brazil: Porto Alegre, 1845–95* (Pittsburgh, PA: University of Pittsburgh Press, 2006), 183.

[46] Roberto DaMatta, *A casa & a rua: Espaço, cidadania, mulher, e morte no Brasil* (São Paulo: Editora Brasiliense, 1985). See also Paulo Marins, "Habitacão e vizinhança," in *História da vida privada no Brasil*, vol. 3, *República, da Belle Epoque a era do rádio* (São Paulo: Companhia das Letras, 1998), 138.

FIGURE 1.2 The Barber Surgeon and the interpenetration of the house and street, 1821. The street's most important function was to provide access to the built environment, which included the exchange of goods, services, and information between the house and the street. Walls formed an important, recognized boundary between private and public realms, but an abundance of doors and windows made the boundary porous. Like an ecotone, this ecological transition attracted much of the street's densest uses, and many lived and worked on that critical line. Note the barber's bench, whose legs are specially built to span the gap between the two worlds.
Source: Jean-Baptiste Debret, "Boutique de Barbiers," in *Voyage pittoresque et historique au Brésil*, vol. 2, (Paris: Firmin Didot Frères, 1835), plate 12. Courtesy of the Acervo da Fundação Biblioteca Nacional, Brazil.

without breaking stride or stepping up. Rio's city edifices had neither stoops nor steps. The streets were too narrow to allow them.[47] This put the world of the house and street on the same level, at least on the first floor, and in 1808, of Rio's total 7,500 commercial and residential buildings, 4,800 were single-story, which would remain the pattern for much of the century. An individual on the street stood at eye level with those in the house as they, through windows and doors, exchanged glances, gossip, or goods. The boundary was meaningful, and tenants could prevent much of

[47] Ewbank, *Life in Brazil*, 85.

the street's flow into the house by shutting doors and shutters, making the façade an actual physical barrier. As João Pinheiro Chagas reported, homes and shops were always prepared to slam their doors and shutters tight at the cry of "Close it up!" due to some disorderly behavior: a fist fight, tumult, or an armed youth firing his pistol while denouncing the government.[48] But the reality was that many chose to permit the street to enter the house because such flows were considered positive. Common domestic architecture in colonial and early nineteenth-century Brazil seemed constructed intentionally to interface with the street. Street-facing façades were pierced with an almost overabundance of doors and windows. On many façades, there was as much fenestration as wall. Windows would remain largely unglazed for the entire nineteenth century; the first storefront panes installed on the fashionable shops on Rua do Ouvidor by 1850 were only for show, to be removed each evening for storage.[49] Unglazed windows were shuttered, but most shutters were thrown open during the heat of the day. John Luccock described a one-story apartment he rented, "equal to most in the place" whose sitting room was "enlightened by one window, without glass or lattice, and which, when the shutters were open, completely exposed the room and all that passed in it."[50] Another pointed out how close the house was to the street, writing of a residential room whose "windows ... opened directly upon the pavement, with never an inch of grass-plot or other border of mitigation to isolate the house from street."[51] When shuttered with the typical louvered and pierced jalousies, residents still kept an eye and ear on the street, the source material for much of the neighborhood's gossip. Doors and windows accessed the commons, and more access meant more of the common's benefits: light, air, movement, commerce, and conversation.

Bodies occupied space in the street and in the home, but there was a strong predilection to inhabit the boundary between them. Thinking of it ecologically, the façade formed an ecotone, a uniquely rich habitat formed by the meeting of two others. The exuberance of windows and

[48] João Pinheiro Chagas, *De bond: alguns aspectos da civilização brasileira* (Lisbon: Livraria Moderna, 1897), 181–82.

[49] Ewbank, *Life in Brazil*, 86.

[50] Machado de Assis' *O Alienista* describes the custom of watching what was happening in other's homes as windows tended to be open. See also John Luccock, *Notes on Rio de Janeiro and the Southern Parts of Brazil, 1808–1818* (London: Samuel Leigh, 1820), 187.

[51] Frank D. Y. Carpenter, *Round about Rio* (Chicago: Jansen, McClurg & Co., 1884), 64.

doors played a role in ventilation in a hot tropical city (an insufficient one in the eyes of hygienists), but it also encouraged interpenetration. For many elite women and girls in particular, but also commonly slaves, the favored spot was to sit in a window, shutters wide open, with elbows propped on the sills. Debret made multiple sketches in the 1820s of Rio's women, free and slave, framed by their colonial windows, with arms or chins resting on the sill.[52] Special sill pillows were fitted for the purpose, and the sill itself was called the *peitoril*, the place for one's chest. Young women who leaned into the street were referred to as *moças janeleiras* or window girls.[53] Today, some residents place at their windows *namoradeiras*, life-size mannequins who lean elbows on window sills, gazing at the street below, evoking a time when real bodies found the street a place worthy of spectating. The fact that cloistered women often participated in the street at a distance suggests some separation, but the house was still an outward looking institution and not a convent that focused on an interior courtyard. Despite the street façade's porosity, which side of the line one was on mattered. Prostitutes, for example, who worked "at the window" (that is, soliciting customers from inside the house, even if they leaned out) were legally protected from arrest for vagrancy and were not bound by the rules of curfew. Prostitutes who worked the streets were vulnerable to harassment and arrest. The house lent a certain respectability and security to the most maligned of activities.[54]

Even as suburban homes began to be set back from the street with intervening small gardens, many still clung to the old ways of staying connected to the street. The successful coffee planter and slave dealer Antônio Clemente Pinto, the Baron of Nova Friburgo, built a luxurious manor that would later become the presidential palace just south of downtown on a massive lot that extended from Catete Street all the way to Flamengo Beach. There was some dispute between the baron and the baroness over where to place the house on the lot, but in the end, rather than build in the central gardens or overlooking the bay, the baroness prevailed. The palace's façade was built tight to the alignment of busy Catete Street, which carried traffic south to the new suburbs; the baroness,

[52] Jean-Baptiste Debret, *Caderno de Viagem*, ed. Julio Bandeira (Rio de Janeiro: Sextante, 2006), 60–61.

[53] For *moças janeleiras*, see Rafael Bluteau, *Diccionário da língua Portugueza* (Lisbon: Simão Thaddeo Ferreira, 1789).

[54] Sandra Lauderdale Graham, "Slavery's Impasse: Slave Prostitutes, Small-Time Mistresses, and the Brazilian Law of 1871," *Comparative Studies in Society and History* 33, no. 4 (Oct. 1991): 673.

tired of plantation landscapes, insisted on the ability to enjoy the views and the movement of the street from the windows of her home. Even fifty years later, a writer complained that foreigners had scooped up all the loveliest home sites in the hills and on charming beaches, spaces abandoned by Brazilians because natives "prefer living in the city streets rather than among the natural, supernal splendors."[55]

Like windows, doorways themselves were favored space. While architects have suggested that the placement of a building's main entrance is the "single most important" decision in a building plan,[56] the Portuguese evaded it by multiplying the entrances. Portuguese colonial architecture may have exhibited more doors per frontage than any other national style. It is a veritable architecture of doors. A typical building, just a few meters wide, might have four or more doors at ground level. On commercial streets as well as on the narrowest of alleys, such as Beco da Moura, frontages were essentially wall-to-wall doors, as if every room needed its own access to the street, or, as in many cases, each room needed multiple entrances. In 1820, one Miss Peppin sketched seven narrow buildings along Rua Direita with a total of nineteen doors on their frontages. In a short stroll, a pedestrian would pass hundreds of doors, many of them wide open in the daytime, as they are in Peppin's depiction.[57] And, of course, many upper story colonial windows were in fact full-size doors, giving access to small, projecting balconies, of which there are thirty-three in Peppin's illustration. The doorways' thresholds were not just passed over but lived on. If women ensconced themselves in windows, men preferred to lean against door frames. Gathering at the doors appears common at night as well. Manuel Antônio de Almeida's *Memoirs of a Militia Sergeant* intimates that on moonlit nights, few stayed inside in the early nineteenth century. Residents gathered family and friends at their thresholds on mats set on the street's surface, in this instance on Rua da Vala (today, Uruguaiana), to while away the evening hours with food, drink, conversation, and song. Some, he claimed, slept the night on the street right around their doorways as the coolest option on hot summer

---

[55] *Fon Fon*, Jul. 22, 1916, 38.

[56] Christopher Alexander, et al. *A Pattern Language: Towns, Buildings, Construction* (New York, NY: Oxford University Press, 1977), 541.

[57] A Richard Bate watercolor based on Miss Peppin's sketch is reproduced in Gilberto Ferrez, *O que ensinam os antigos mapas e estampas do Rio de Janeiro* (Rio de Janeiro: Departamento de Imprensa Nacional, 1966), estampa 11.

nights.[58] In an early nineteenth-century depiction of carnival, the usual water fight does not take place in the street, as one typically assumes, but between the houses. Revelers throw wax balls full of water from inside one house, across the narrow street, and into the neighbor's windows and doors, an excellent example of interpenetration permitted by multiple orifices facing across narrow public spaces.[59]

Façades, windows, and doors formed the walls that enclosed the street's room, and their décor adorned and graced the street as much as they did the house. If walls were built to enclose interior rooms, they were decorated for the benefit of those in the street. Significantly, walls enfolded Rio's old streets at a scale that humans found congenial. Architects who criticize the broadness of modern streets have argued that to create street spaces amenable to human experience, the proportion of street width to building height should not exceed six to one, and some hold that the ideal is closer to one to one.[60] On a typical Rio street, 5.5 meters wide, with a mix of buildings of one to three stories, the average ratio was very close to that ideal. At that scale, walls gave the street a sense of airy enclosure without being stifling. In the early twentieth century, incipient skyscrapers, which were much maligned by some local commentators, blew colonial proportions out of scale. Even in cases where streets were widened, the ever-greater heights of new buildings made street spaces feel oppressive and dark.

Possibly more important than the street's shape was the built environment's physical and social arrangement around it, which impacted the street's place in the construction of community. The frontage of a typical building, regardless of height or purpose, was narrow, less than 5 meters except in the homes of the wealthiest.[61] This meant that in a short length of street, one would find numerous households. Narrow façades created a density of settlement that contributed to the street's liveliness, to the

---

[58] Manuel Antônio de Almeida. *Memórias de um sargento de milícias* (MetaLibri, 2005), ver. 1.0, 114–15, at www.ibiblio.org/ml/libri/a/AlmeidaMA_SargentoMilicias_p.pdf (accessed Jun. 10, 2013).

[59] Augustus Earl, *Games during the Carnival at Rio de Janeiro*, watercolor, c. 1822, in Jocelyn Hackforth-Jones, *Augustus Earle: Travel Artist* (London: Scolar Press, 1980), 62.

[60] Andres Duany, Elizabeth Plater-Zyberk, & Jeff Speck, *Suburban Nation: The Rise of Sprawl and the Decline of the American Dream* (New York, NY: North Point Press, 2001), 78.

[61] Louis Léger Vauthier, *Um engenheiro Francês no Brasil*, vol. 2 (Rio de Janeiro: José Olympio, 1960), 819, 823–24, who wrote of Recife, noted that some elite homes were as wide as 8.8 meters, but that was a rare enormity.

large number of bodies on the streets, at the doors, and in the windows. They also contributed to a diversity of activity and class. Early cities were not economically zoned; along any typical street one would find residential housing, retail shops, workshops, churches, convents, government edifices, bars, and, later, cafés and restaurants. Even the royal palace, which was the residence of his imperial majesty after 1808, Marco Morel points out, was nothing like Beijing's insulated Forbidden City but surrounded on all sides by shops, fish and vegetable markets, a slave cemetery, warehouses, and barracks.[62]

Likewise, the house/street arrangements did not express class segregation. The rich and the poor lived intimately side by side and on top of each other, in the city and also in the early suburbs.[63] Aluísio Azevedo set his late-century novel, *The Slum*, in the suburb of Botafogo on a street that contained a restaurant, a bar, a tenement, a working quarry, and a rich merchant's house, all within the space of three façades. That small space contained residents who were slaves, former slaves, immigrants of diverse origins, thriving merchants, student boarders, laundresses, titled nobility, police sergeants, debutantes, prostitutes, and tradespeople. The walls of edifices and tenements might segregate by color and class, but once bodies passed out their doors, they came into immediate contact with next-door neighbors who were different in color, age, wealth, origins, and gender. The street's extreme density and diversity – of both users and utilities – contributed to the production of a lively community, one in which instances of connection, interaction, and exchange were sustained at a fever pitch. Historians tend to focus on the street's contests, divisions, and conflicts, which were no doubt real, but significantly, despite many ongoing tensions, people in the street mostly tolerated each other, accustomed to mingling with individuals and crowds of disparate means, origins, and aims.

COMMUNITY AS STREET UTILITY

If streets remained physically unproduced and largely unimproved to this point, they still served as an important resource – a place, for the

---

[62] Marco Morel, "A política nas ruas: os espaços públicos na cidade imperial do Rio de Janeiro," *Estudos Ibero-Americanos* 24, no. 1 (1989): 62–63. Morel notes the intense intermingling of social classes.

[63] Paulo Marins, "Habitacão e vizinhança," in *História da vida privada no Brasil*, vol. 3, *República, da Belle Epoque a era do rádio* (São Paulo: Companhia das Letras, 1998), 137–38.

production of the city's commerce, sociality, and play. Among their most important products was community, a concept that is a central feature of human settlements, but unlike commerce, transit, or even kinship, is rather difficult to measure and document. Streets also produce communities that are difficult to define and bound. They did not produce communities of interest – that is, Rio's diverse neighborhoods did not form groups who shared an occupation, a political view, a class, race, or hobby. The interests of the street were often contradictory, divided, and factional, containing individuals of diverse concerns, origins, statuses, and languages. Nor did the traditional street necessarily produce much in the way of social capital. As with the members of any ecological community, street users exhibited mutualism, but also competition and predation. Although mutual assistance was not uncommon, residents did not expect members of their street community to collectively stand ready to aid them in their hardships. Hence, the street did not aspire to the production of a utopian community. Streets were merely communities of place, where membership was determined organically by simple geography. Yet the space provided by the street offered residents free membership with community privileges and essential human amenities: a sense of belonging that, however hard to measure, was part of what it meant to live in a city and neighborhood. Today we think of the city as a place of anonymity, but Rio's neighborhoods were places where people were known.[64]

Today, streets make convenient and effective boundaries between individuals and all kinds of administrative units. In the past, streets, because they linked people together, were neither seen nor used as boundaries. For example, the limits between parishes, which later became the bounds for the city's secular, administrative districts, were not marked along streets, which would have placed people living on the same street in different ecclesiastical and civic entities. Rather, such boundaries were drawn down the backs of blocks. The Sacramento Parish, for example, included residents on both sides of Marechal Floriano Peixoto and both sides of Ourives but excluded their immediately rear neighbors who were parts of other parishes. The street was the space of community, and hence it did

---

[64] Robert Colls, "When We Lived in Communities: Working-Class Culture and Its Critics," in *Cities of Ideas: Civil Society and Urban Governance in Britain, 1800–2000*, edited by R. Colls and R. Rodger (Aldershot: Ashgate, 2004), 283–307, offers a clear-eyed definition of what communities of place entail, challenges revisionist writers who have tried to make community little more than a contractual set of relations, and laments community's decline, including the street life, which he concludes is today, at least in England, is "as dead as that of the North American Plains Indian."

not make sense to divide residents and parishioners with the same streets that made their community.[65]

Available space alone, of course, is insufficient to produce even communities of place. People living, working, and moving together, sharing urban space, as in a modern apartment building or a bedroom suburb, can fail to create anything but the thinnest sense of community, and many of our modern living arrangements produce little as well because in part they provide insufficient and ineffective public spaces on which to build it. A community of place requires the sharing of information, largely personal information; to be part of a community, one must know one's neighbors and be known by them. And this was an essential function of the street – a space on which to meet one's neighbors and share information about each other, directly or indirectly. The difference between a stranger and a neighbor is an introduction, or often little more than second-hand gossip. When one learns that an oft-seen face on the street goes by the name Pedro and lives in the tenement behind the bakery, Pedro ceases being a stranger and becomes a small part of one's community, even if you have not physically met or been formally introduced. On the traditional street, one's knowledge of Pedro increases over time: he is married to Maria, who is from Minas and sells homemade sweets; he has three young children, one of whom is sick; he works as a mason; he is honest, neat in appearance, and enjoys a well-pressed suit on weekends; he is introverted but not unfriendly, except if drunk, when he becomes combative toward even his friends. Soon, Pedro knows as much about you as you do about him, and thus includes you in his community. The street was a space where such information about one's neighbors was trafficked and observed, and that information formed the community's essential links. The histories and characters of hundreds of individuals were spoken, recorded, and retransmitted on the street, often over multiple generations, and it was this information that gave the community its foundation and identity. Community was written on the street where character and plot were under constant development and revision. And although neighbors might share a few local events in their memories, they often did not share a common history in the way a nation or an ethnic group might. The community's identity consisted mostly of personal information, hundreds of individuals' narratives, rather than a single cohesive story.

[65] João da Rocha Fragoso, "Mappa architectural da cidade do Rio de Janeiro," 1874, Biblioteca National Digital Brazil, http://objdigital.bn.br/acervo_digital/div_cartografia /cart470826.pdf (accessed Feb. 15, 2013); *Recenseamento do Rio de Janeiro (Districto Federal)* [1906] (Rio de Janeiro: Officina de Estatística, 1907), after 194.

The communication of personal and other information took place in myriad ways, and it was interaction itself that gave the street much of its meaning. The streets, which were relatively quiet and slow-paced, offered a space amenable to talking, and the talk was reportedly incessant. Thomas Ewbank portrayed Rio's mid-century streets as quietly communicative relative to his experience during long residences in London and New York. He described the common mechanism to initiate conversations: a restrained "pshiu" or shooshing with the lips accompanied by a hand signal, palm down, the fingers repeatedly closing, drawing the targeted conversant to the signaler, a practice not entirely dead today. He noted that there was no loud bawling after each other in the street. "In this quiet and ingenious way all classes communicate with passing friends with whom they wish to speak."[66] If the streets were quieter than in other major cities of the time, which is doubtful, they were quiet enough for easy conversation. However, residents did not reportedly speak quietly, did not seem to cherish privacy, nor did they have to be interrogated to extract personal and confidential information. Olavo Bilac argued that Brazilians could not live without the noise of human voices and could not keep their mouths shut, which explained why throughout their history they could not launch a political conspiracy before news of it reached the ears of authorities.[67] Living in close proximity with so many others, observing and sharing the comings, goings, and doings of one's neighbors, formed the core of much of the street's exchange. Gossip, which carries a negative connotation in both English and Portuguese (*fofoca*), served a positive, community-building function. It was of little use or meaning to those outside the community, which in part explains the growing opposition to it in an increasingly anonymous city, but it was essential information for insiders. One needed to know one's neighbors with some intimacy to be able to spark a conversation with ease, to interact with them judiciously, to avoid unnecessary offense, or to keep information from those, such as the jealous husband of an unfaithful wife, who all agreed ought to be the last to know.

The community's social life and social health depended on chatting. Biological life depended on economic exchange that also took place largely on the street, person to person, which intensified the street's role and its opportunities for building community. Street peddlers, as a chief form of commercial exchange, were among the most commonly treated

[66] Ewbank, *Life in Brazil*, 94.
[67] Olavo Bilac, *Crítica e fantasia* (Lisbon: A.M. Texeira, 1904), 337–38.

subjects of city life – exotically by foreigners in the nineteenth century, who found them a colorful and lively topic, particularly slave peddlers, and then nostalgically by Brazilian writers in the early twentieth century, by which time peddling had begun to sharply diminish in the central city.[68] The practice extended back into the colonial period and seems to have peaked at the end of the nineteenth century due to emancipation in 1888 and rising foreign immigration.

Residents depended on street peddlers, the *ambulantes*, for their daily needs, and peddlers contributed substantially to the diverse forms of movement and activity of the street. They called out to potential customers and approached residents intimately, at the windows and doors. The traditional street was a sort of reverse shopping mall, one in which the shoppers stayed at home and the "shopkeepers" came to them in a steady stream with their wares on their heads, in trays, or pushcarts. Some peddlers, consisting of men, women, and even children, came every day at anticipated hours offering bread, milk, newspapers, water, lemonade, juiced sugar cane, dried beans, fresh fruit, ice cream, poultry, rice, cigarettes, pastries, eggs, cigars, matches, candy, and ice. Many clients had subscriptions for the regular scheduled delivery of fresh roasted coffee or firewood. Jorge Americano could remember from his childhood the very hours in which specific commodities arrived at his door each morning, and in the afternoons, his street was full of candies, ice cream, and cool drinks.[69] Other peddlers came intermittently: those who sold pots and pans, brooms, baskets, houseplants, fabric, popular novels and devotional books, flowers, horses, edible roots, goats, hay, furniture, and pets; those who offered such services as knife sharpening, letter writing for the illiterate, chair caning, message delivery, or family portraits; or those who purchased old rags, metal, shoes, or bottles. While some of these offerings could be found in weekly markets and shops, residents liked the low prices and, significantly, that the price included delivery. To carry goods in the street, even your own shopping, was an indicator of low status, so acquiring goods at your door evaded the need to carry your own purchases or to engage a slave or carter to convey them for you. By the early twentieth century, some local merchants with rents to pay complained about the peddler's unfair competition, but housewives often came to the *ambulantes'* defense due to their competitive prices and

---

[68] Debret, *Viagem*, vol. 1 (Editora Itatiaia, 1978), 224–25, 251, 296, 297, 341; Ewbank, *Life in Brazil*, 93, 94; Yázigi, *Mundo das calçadas*, 117–19.
[69] Jorge Americano, *São Paulo naquele tempo*, 111.

convenient service. In other cases peddlers served as salespeople for the local merchants.[70]

For foreigners who reported on these activities, the peddlers were strangers and strange, outsiders who roamed local streets in search of reluctant customers. But locals recognized the peddlers as neighbors or, at the very least, as familiars, many of whom had worked their daily routes for years. The peddlers reciprocated these sentiments. In Portuguese, the term *freguês* today generally refers to any customer, but in the past it referred to one's habitual clientele, those repeat customers a peddler relied on for daily commerce. The term derived from *freguesia*, which was the smallest administrative unit in Portugal, smaller than a parish, and hence is the equivalent of neighborhood. Customers were neighbors in the literal sense, and many peddlers did not work an anonymous street but their own communities. Some, like the breadman or the milkman, might have come to one's door for years, building bonds and familiarity. Sales took place through windows and doors, but some salespeople, such as those who sold fashions, fabric, and furniture, demonstrated their wares inside the home. Peddlers sold merchandise on credit, which required a certain degree of trust as well as repeated, regular visits to collect payments. In the earliest years of photography in the city, peddlers were a popular subject. Most such photographs seen from our distant present appear to be of types – broom vendors, candy peddlers, and knife sharpeners – but to residents, these were recognized people. One such portrait was of Castro Urso in a ragged collar and pristine boater, a widely recognized seller of lottery tickets.[71] In 1933, the artist and cartoonist Anísio Oscar Mota, better known as Fritz, produced a sculpture of a newsboy which was placed on Ouvidor Street. The boy, in ragged clothing and floppy hat, did not represent all news peddlers but specifically José Bento de Carvalho, a notoriously loud and single-minded purveyor of the news, at the age of ten.

One resident's interaction with his bread boy suggests that community building was based on frequent, intimate contact. The narrator wrote of his association with an industrious *padeirinho*, a young boy who delivered bread on the street at 6 AM sharp, regardless of the weather. He was not much for gossip, but his maturity and businesslike responses made him a popular figure as he literally ran with baskets of hot bread produced by

---

[70] Yázigi, *Mundo das calçadas*, 117–19.

[71] George Ermakoff, *Rio de Janeiro, 1840–1900: Uma crónica fotográfica* (Rio de Janeiro: G. Ermakoff Casa Editorial, 2006), 204. The photograph was taken c. 1880.

his father. The boy, who wore long pants like a man, got upset with customers who did not come to the door promptly as it made him late to his next customer, and to those who complained of high prices, he diplomatically noted the rising cost of flour. The narrator reported that daily interaction created in him a deep bond of affection for the boy. Then, suddenly, the boy stopped coming, and the whole neighborhood asked after him. His father, who now took over the duties of delivery, explained in tears how his boy was down with the recent epidemic, and his daily reports noted his son's decline into fever and deliriousness such that he no longer recognized his parents. Evidence of the plague's virulence was in the street as doctors themselves made house calls, peddling medicine and hope. The plague became so severe that the delivery of bread ceased for a time. Then, one morning, the narrator responded to the boy's familiar call once again, to find him hale and hearty. The boy was greeted, to his embarrassment, by hugs from his customers, by which he felt detained in his duties. By the simple process of daily exchange, intimate information was shared, and it was in these kinds of mundane interactions, not exceptional events like carnival or religious processions, that meaningful communities were built on the streets.[72]

Not all the interactivity of commerce took place door to door; it also took place on the streets proper. Customers went to known street corners where barber/surgeons, almost always of African descent, offered services as varied as haircutting, the removal of parasites, bleeding, and tooth pulling, right on the street where all your neighbors observed what ailed you. Many vendors of drinks and treats targeted customers gathering in or passing through crowded squares. Debret noted that it was typical for men of the more leisurely classes to assemble in the palace square every day at 4 PM to enjoy the breeze, watch the shipping, and converse. Female vendors charmed and flattered regular customers, offering drinks of cool water from the fountain with the purchase of a sweet or pastry. And the men, he described, were generous in the exchange because of their long acquaintances with particular women.[73]

The streets were a place for productive work and entrepreneurship. Basket weavers, spinners of thread, stocking knitters, lace makers, and other such "cottage" artisans worked in the street.[74] Boys, of course, made the street a place of play, but many children also found employment

---

[72] "O Padeirinho," *Fon Fon*, Mar. 22, 1919.   [73] Debret, *Viagem*, 202.
[74] John Luccock, *Notes on Rio de Janeiro and the Southern Parts of Brazil, 1808–1818* (London: Samuel Leigh, 1820), 110.

there. The ubiquitous boot blacks so often associated with street work do not seem to make an appearance on Rio's streets until the twentieth century, when less dirt-filled streets made it possible to maintain clean shoes for more than a few minutes, but boys worked delivering goods, running errands, and selling newspapers. Newsboys hawked their wares with one arm raised while the other, with multiple copies of multiple papers tucked in the armpit, carefully guarded the coins in their purses. Boys also comprised the city's many tattoo artists. This was big business with entrepreneurs hiring, training, and supplying the boys with needles and ink. Each tattoo had a set price, and some were still done, as in Africa, by scarification. One Madruga, who himself had Jesus on his chest, pagan charms on his arms, a snake on his leg, and the initials of his love conquests on his bare shoulders, ran a crew of boys who in a single month tattooed 319 customers. João do Rio reported that nearly everyone in the lower classes, regardless of gender or ethnicity, had tattoos. They were popular with Africans, Jews, Maronites, and Muslims, who received the symbols of their religions, as well as more generally with workers, soldiers, sailors, and peddlers. Pimps tattooed their fists with signs of power; prostitutes had moles placed on their faces. Some tattoos protected one symbolically from unseen evils while others served more directly: one sailor had Christ and the cross placed respectively on his chest and back because they would prevent ship captains and port authorities from giving him a whipping as it would appear "they were thrashing upon Christ." Women tattooed the initials of former lovers on the soles of their feet, as an act of spite, and some inked their children's names or initials on their breasts. The Portuguese, who arrived in Brazil with clean skin, soon sought out the tattoo boys whose art was performed publicly on street curbs and fountain steps. Tattoo artists might make as much money as a respectable office clerk.[75]

Rio's informal economy was made up largely of street workers, not to mention all those engaged in transportation and street maintenance. Jaime Benchimol asserts that even though Rio was Brazil's industrial center until the 1920s, the *ambulantes*, as an economic category, were larger than Rio's industrial class.[76] The street was a place of work, and as long as the street remained common, it enriched and diversified the city's economy.

---

[75] João do Rio, *A alma encantadora das ruas*, 29–34.
[76] Jaime Larry Benchimol, *Pereira Passos: um Haussmann tropical: A renovação urbana da cidade do Rio de Janeiro no início do século XX* (Rio de Janeiro: Secretaria Municipal de Cultura, 1992), 280.

For some, like policemen, lamplighters, and slave catchers, the street was merely incidental to their work, but for thousands, the street was essential to gainful employment. Many could not afford to buy or rent private spaces in which to produce or offer their goods and services. The common street made it such that one could be productive. Many peddlers worked for merchants, but some chose the profession because it offered independence. To work anywhere but the street typically meant to work for someone else or at least under someone else's eyes.

Today, streets are full of unintentional, largely meaningless sounds; most of the street's information is conveyed by visual signals and signs. The traditional street was a place in which aural communication dominated. There were remarkably few signs, even of a commercial nature, and one was as likely to know what was going on outside one's door, at the neighbors, or in a shop by the sounds that emanated from their usage. Houses of prostitution were discovered by visiting sailors – not by signs or shapely figures in windows, but by the salacious whispers that passed through eye-level shutters. Bars, with their characteristic soundscapes of chatter, music, and clinking glassware, no more needed signs than did churches.[77] With the rise of manufacturing in the city, there were local complaints about noise[78] and there had long been gripes about the whining of oxcarts with their fixed, un-lubricated axels and of steel tires on stone cobbles, but most of the city's incidental sounds, if cacophonous, were full of meaning. Aluísio Azevedo, who spent many hours in Rio's streets to get material for writing his realist novels, wrote of a morning in the city in which the first sounds to be heard were the yawns, throat clearings, and spitting of those poking their heads out of windows. "The day's first greetings were exchanged from window to window; conversations interrupted the night before began again." As women hung out caged birds, which added birdsong to the mix, conversations became louder, quarrels commenced, and talking escalated into shouting, curses, and guffaws. The breadman's call, followed by the milkman tinkling bell, caused shutters to be thrown open. Azevedo also noted the repetitive chuffing of a steam engine at the local macaroni plant, and by this time electric streetcars were becoming common sights on some city

---

[77] For a wonderful description of noise in England's medieval streets, see Goronwy Tidy Salusbury-Jones, *Street Life in Medieval England*, 2nd edn. (Oxford: Pen in Hand, 1948), ch. "Time and Tune."

[78] Locals complained about sawmills and smithies in particular. For one example, see newspaper clipping, *Jornal do Brasil*, Aug. 2, 1912, GIFI 6c373, ANRJ.

streets, but such unintentional, meaningless sounds were often intermittent and rarely rose to a level to make verbal conversation on the street
difficult.[79] Henry James described Venice, Italy, in 1882 as having no
noise except human noise: "all articulate and vocal and personal ...
Venice is emphatically the city of conversation; people talk all over the
place because these is nothing to interfere with its being caught by the
ear."[80] Rio was not that quiet, but conversational possibilities were
similar.

Music was pervasive. Indeed, Azevedo noted that the first sounds one
perceived in the morning streets of Rio were the faint strains of guitar
strings. João do Rio observed that Rio was in its very essence musical and
that songs and singing were not merely an accompaniment to the city's
urban life; rather, music "presided" over the city. Music could be found at
home, in bars and cafés, and at the theater, but it was also a stock in trade
of the street; and as a form of wave energy that in a dense city moved
farther and penetrated better than light, music crossed all boundaries.
Many noted that one could hear music almost anywhere one went, and
that "it is impossible to pass through [the city] without encountering the
ambulant musicians" who peddled commodities more ethereal but no less
appreciated or saleable than those of the other merchants of the street.[81]

Among the most noted musical sounds were the calls, jingles, and
musical instruments employed by the peddlers. Each product had its
distinct means of getting customer attention; C. S. Stewart observed in
1858 that "each kind of vegetable and fruit seems to have its own song,"
and then each peddler seemed to have her own peculiar turn on the
method.[82] For example, the ubiquitous bread sellers used a small tin
horn to announce the presence of fresh bread in the morning, but each
played a unique melody. By sound, without having to get out of their beds,
residents knew not only that bread was coming up the street, but whose
bread. The seller of fabric and notions vigorously clacked his folding
measuring stick in a particular rhythm. The poulterer played his tune on
the African *mbira*, a finger harp, each model of which had its own distinct

---

[79] Aluísio Azevedo, *The Slum* (New York, NY: Oxford University Press, 2000), 21–23.

[80] Henry James, "Italian Hours," cited in J. J. Norwich, ed., *A Traveler's Companion* (Northampton, MA: Interlink Books, 2002), 227–28, which was originally published in 1882.

[81] João do Rio, *A alma encantadora das ruas*, 66. For a full chronicle of street music, see José Ramos Tinhorão, *Os sons que vêm da rua*, 2nd edn. (São Paulo: Editora 34, 2005).

[82] C. S. Stewart, *Brazil and La Plata: The Personal Record of a Cruise* (New York, NY: A. O. Moore, 1858), 72.

scale. Others clapped their hands, used a variety of rattles and percussion devices, including those they sold, like drums and pots and pans.

Jingles, sung by voice, were yet more distinctive, with tune and lyrics unique. In addition to the native and immigrant Portuguese speakers, Africans, Syrians, Jews, and Italians sang out their wares with distinctive accents on top of original compositions, from simple to elaborate.[83] Most such creations have been lost to history, and much of the evidence for the actual content of these musical sales pitches comes from the nostalgia of writers remembering the traditional streets of their youth or vestiges of them, which in some places survive in diminished forms. Mário Quintana wrote, "[M]y street is full of jingles, as if I was seeing cauliflower, pineapples, persimmons, and melons with my ears."[84] One contributor to the magazine *Fon Fon* in 1910, after first criticizing the peddlers for being the city's general alarm clock each morning, regretted peddling's decline. He reminisced fondly of a childhood of mornings in which he waited, half awake at the window, for the song and the scent of the baker's hot corn cakes.

Bento, Machado de Assis' main character in *Dom Casmurro*, who grew up in Rio, waxes nostalgic for home while studying in São Paulo. He fixates on the memory of an African candy seller who jingled regularly on his street: "Cry, little girl, cry! Cry because you haven't got a Penny," a unique song "so well known in the neighborhood," which Bento remarked was intended to provoke a child's vanity. Bento remembers leaning out his window to make the fond exchange on many afternoons. To make his nostalgia concrete, Bento calls on a professor of music who he asks to transcribe the jingle, which he entitles "The Jingle of the Black Candy Man on Matacavalos Street," into musical notation, and in later years required his young son to play the piece at the piano before he was rewarded with candy.[85] Unfortunately and somewhat uncharacteristically, Machado

---

[83] Edmundo, *Rio de Janeiro do meu tempo*, 52. The musical sales pitch was referred to as a *toada* or, more commonly a *pregão*, which can be literally translated as a strong sermon, *pregar* meaning, "to preach."

[84] Mário Quintana, *A rua dos cataventos* (Porto Alegre: Livraria do Globo, 1940), 26, "Minha rua está cheia de pregões. / Parece que estou vendo com os ouvidos: / 'Couves! Abacaxis! Caquis! Melões!'" Jorge Americano, *São Paulo naquele tempo*, 111.

[85] Machado de Assis, *Dom Casmurro* 2nd edn. (São Paulo: Edicões Melhoramentos, 1968), 59, 246–47. "Chora, menina, chora! Chora porque não tem Vintem." Here is one example that well justifies the use of literature to recover the past. Machado de Assis himself expected that his novels, in one hundred years, might be used to understand his time, how people dressed, what they thought of women, and even trivially, on what arms they wore their watches. See Táti, *O mundo de Machado de Assis*, 11.

de Assis, despite his intentions, did not provide the transcribed notes for his readers, whom he feared would not appreciate them. He noted he saved his publisher the cost of engraving and left us the lyrics without the tune.

Daniel Kidder and James Fletcher, American evangelicals who peddled Bibles in Rio mid-century and hence knew Brazil's streets first-hand, were astounded by the slaves' widespread use of music to cope with their hard work. On one occasion the city had banned worker singing, but the result was a near strike and lots of singing, and the city soon rescinded the order. Kidder and Fletcher observed, "[C]ertain it is that they now avail themselves of their vocal privileges at pleasure, whether in singing and shouting at each other as they run, or in proclaiming to the people the various articles they carry about for sale. The impression made upon the stranger by the mingled sound of their hundred voices falling upon his ear at once is not soon forgotten."[86]

A broadly sonic city conveyed additional sorts of information. Each morning, construction foremen called laborers to work by hammering a known pattern on a plank in the scaffolding. Ewbank did put his publisher to the expense of representing the pattern musically. The signal began with three strong blows followed by an increasingly rapid rapping that extended over some time, and then concluded as it began. Likewise, pavers called their employees to work with a different beating pattern, this time with a hammer on an iron lever. Ewbank noted that these calls could be heard for many blocks, and woe to the laborer who failed to respond promptly.[87] Likewise, visitors generally did not knock on doors to get the attention of residents; they would clap their hands. This might bring dozens of residents to their windows to see if the clapping were for them. Church bells for centuries had been used to signal noon and the nighttime curfew in addition to sounding alarms, calling parishioners to Mass, or celebrating holy days. In Rio, bells conveyed personal information, too. Luiz Edmundo noted that the newspapers dealt in opinions, but that "bells dealt solely in facts." When a child was born, parish bells announced the new addition to the community: nine chimes if it were a boy, seven if a girl. The churches would ring their bells to signal that a woman was passing a difficult and dangerous labor, in the expectation that hearers would

---

[86] Daniel P. Kidder and James C. Fletcher, *Brazil and the Brazilians, Portrayed in Historical and Descriptive Sketches* (Philadelphia, PA: Childs & Peterson, 1857), 30.

[87] Ewbank, *Life in Brazil*, 185–86, 193.

pray for her.[88] And when a person died, bells announced their passing, usually the largest bell if the deceased were male, and a small one if female. Based on who was pregnant or lingering, many knew immediately for whom the bells tolled and left their homes to congratulate the new parents or console the grieving. Bells were distinctive, and based on their tone, direction, and distance, residents also knew in which parish such events occurred.[89]

At the beginning of the twentieth century, Do Rio expressed some worry that recordings might threaten the living music of the streets, but the street still vibrated with spontaneous music, the echoes of slaves who sang rhythmically in their work, informal percussive sessions, sad Portuguese *fados*, and the ever popular love songs, the *modinhas* – all of which combined and recombined to create one of the most expressive and diverse musical cultures. It was on the street that new music was introduced to the city and disseminated to the broader population, who rejected it with inattention or applauded it with their hands, coins, and the movement of their bodies. Laws were passed against certain kinds of music, particularly African drumming, but, as we have seen, often to little avail.

Music brought people together in big events and small. Carnival called out the city's every musical instrument and every passable voice, but it was the smaller, mundane gatherings that pervaded the streets day in and day out, and these were conversations in and of themselves. The street was music's audience, and one writer spoke of his youth in Rio chasing after one *fado* group "from street corner to street corner almost throughout the whole city."[90] Those who developed to a certain level their writing and performing talents on the street began to enter bars and cafés; by the early twentieth century, they made recordings, although Do Rio noted that most of Rio's musical tradition, even after the arrival of the technology, went unrecorded and unpreserved for posterity. He noted a variety of locally famous musicians who worked the streets, individuals that residents knew by name and whose lyrics they knew by heart.[91] And despite the theatrical presentation of some music, much of the street's music was participatory, where one did not so much spectate as join in with voice,

---

[88] Manuel Antônio de Almeida. *Memórias de um sargento de milícias* (MetaLibri, 2005), 89, www.ibiblio.org/ml/libri/a/AlmeidaMA_SargentoMilicias_p.pdf (accessed Jun. 10, 2013).

[89] Luiz Edmundo, *Rio in the Time of the Viceroys*, 73–82.   [90] *Fon Fon*, Jun. 12, 1915.

[91] João do Rio, *A alma encantadora das ruas*, 65–68.

clapping hands, or dance. Foreign artists depicted these informal gatherings of spontaneous song. Music was not some extraordinary appendage but an elemental part of the community and one of the factors that bonded residents together, whether in particular neighborhoods or more broadly in celebrations such as carnival or the feast of the Holy Spirit. Young men serenaded at windows that framed their affections, many with lyrics that had hardly changed in lusty intent or poetic content since medieval times. Much of the city's musical work was produced by the street and for the street.[92]

Citizens, of course, came together in broader communities during Rio's religious and national festivals that littered that annual calendar.[93] The streets and squares were crowded with participants and spectators, and residents hung their best carpets and fabrics from windows to decorate the streets' walls. Residents took to the streets to celebrate the inauguration of new streetcar lines and new monuments, they formed and followed religious processions, and they feted visiting dignitaries and national heroes in great throngs.[94] But again, the more mundane and spontaneous causes for street gathering probably served more successfully to bind neighbors into communities of place. When friends returned from abroad, neighbors welcomed them at the port and then escorted them to the front door of their homes, sharing stories and missed gossip along the way.[95]

Likewise, death was a public event. As burial came soon, often the same day in the hot tropical city, a death was an immediate call for family and friends to gather to carry and accompany the body to the parish church, or in later decades, the cemetery. Mourners followed the bier in ranks, taking turns at carrying the body. John Luccock experienced one such procession accompanying the body of a beautiful young girl on her

---

[92] The entire discussion here was taken from João do Rio's, *A alma encantadora das ruas*, final chapter on poetry, "A Musa das Ruas." See also page 16 and his selection of popular lyrics of the period.

[93] On the nature and purposes of nineteenth-century urban festivals, see Hendrik Kraay, *Days of National Festivity in Rio de Janeiro, Brazil, 1823–1889* (Stanford, CA: Stanford University Press, 2103); Martha Campos Abreu, *O império do divino: festas religiosas e cultura popular no Rio de Janeiro, 1830–1900* (Rio de Janeiro: Nova Fronteira, 1999); and John Charles Chasteen, "The Prehistory of Samba: Carnival Dancing in Rio de Janeiro, 1840–1917," *Journal of Latin American Studies* 28, no. 1 (Feb. 1996): 29–47.

[94] Rosa Maria Barboza de Araújo, *A Vocação do prazer: a cidade e a família no Rio de Janeiro Republicano* (Rio de Janeiro: Rocco, 1993), 332.

[95] *Fon Fon*, Oct. 21, 1908, reported that on the return of former President Rodriques Alves, residents walked from the port all the way to his suburban home in Botafogo.

way to burial. As the body passed through the tight crowd of spectators, one of the pall bearers grabbed Luccock's sleeve and placed his hand on the bier where he became a participant in the occasion, staying at his new assignment to the very door of the church. Debret observed in the 1820s that family and friends walked with their hands resting on the exposed body throughout its journey. Residents along the procession's route observed such processions, removed their hats, and placed candles in their windows. If the deceased had any prominence in politics, letters, or business, crowds that gathered at the deceased's home to join the procession could reach into the tens of thousands, as was reported for the deaths of Machado de Assis, João Pinheiro, Baron of Rio Branco, and Artur Azevedo – events that were widely publicized and photographed in newspapers and magazines. If, in the days of slavery, the deceased were of noble African origins, the procession was preceded by song, dance, and entertainers doing somersaults, and the square in front of the church would be crowded with well-wishers who continued to make noise during the burial. For the poor, for whom no bells rung and no procession formed, death was still a public event. Persons paused respectfully as the body, in a hammock suspended from a pole carried on the shoulders of two unshod slaves, passed. The remains of the poorest, those without friends, family, or membership in a religious brotherhood, were placed on the street, in front of the local parish church or a local shop where passing residents might donate coins to cover the cost of burial. Debret suggested that street collections in the 1820s rarely failed to finance a simple, respectful burial.[96]

The street was quintessentially a place for public displays of affection, often expressed in song and verse. There were cruder forms, of course, and residents complained of men who were too effusive or suggestive in their pledges of love, especially if they went long into the night. But marriage itself often had its origin on the street. And marital status itself was publicly expressed there. Again, Machado de Assis evokes this most intimately in describing a couple who were anxious to complete their honeymoon so they could return to their own neighborhood and walk the streets arm in arm. For the couple, neither the church wedding nor the nuptial bed fully consummated their union, and they invented reasons to go walking together in the streets, to be seen and recognized as

---

[96] Debret, *Viagem*, vol. 2, 187, 205, 257; Luccock, *Notes on Rio de Janeiro*, 57. *Fon Fon, Careta,* and other popular publications reported on major funerals with numerous photographs of their associated street events.

a respectable, married couple.[97] The street was the platform on which marriage was proposed, declared, and finally performed to the community's satisfaction. It officialized and publicized much that counted in the life of the city.

Community was the city dweller's birthright, built in myriad ways, and essential to not only one's identity and sense of belonging, but to happiness and mental health. The street gave space for citizens to be a community, to be fully human, to develop what made urban cultures unique. "In Vain," a short story written in 1919, expressed the popular notions of the street as a place of social danger but also one of social necessity in the Brazilian mind. A poor mother, Senhora Fortunata, refused to let her teenage daughter, "cheery, chubby, and with skin the color of ripe wheat" outside the confines of the house. Whenever she found her curious daughter at the door or sticking her head through the window's shutters, she cursed her, "may the devil take you," and chased her inside: "get back in the house, shameless girl; how often have I told you." Fortunata confided to her neighbor that she had lost two older daughters to bad influences, but she would not lose this one. Yet the little girl, who was by nature gregarious, yearned for contact. She would climb and straddle the wall of her backyard to make small talk with the neighbors. She made it a particular habit to stand on an empty box at the window in order to get the attention of the baker who lived nearby. A group of neighbors gossiped in the street about the woman's rigid cloistering of the girl. A passing peddler offered his opinion that "this is a crime, my friends, this is a crime."[98] In the end, the girl ran off with the baker, and the story illustrates that while some worried about the moral dangers of the street, the consensus was that everyone, even the young and the female, had a right to take part in the community that was the street. To keep someone from the street was its own sentence of social death.

The meanings and uses of the traditional street are too many to fully enumerate. What is important to comprehend is the street's almost limitless possibilities. The street was a public good without peer, one whose common status was accepted and successfully defended, permitting Rio's residents to occupy and use the space to meet many different human needs. It was, at its core, a raw natural resource of near universal consumption. The street belonged to no one; rather, everyone belonged to the street. The space was regulated, but poorly; it was not much improved,

[97] Machado de Assis, *Dom Casmurro*, 231.
[98] Murilla Torres, "Em vão," in *Fon Fon*, Feb. 22, 1919.

decorated by civilization's walls, but full of dirt and vegetation. Its status as a commons was essential to the city's organic function and to the creation of community. João do Rio suggested that the street was a living thing that modified human beings and made them its "perpetual and delirious slaves," as if it were a force of nature itself.[99] Quite the contrary. Humans, with access to the street, made of it exactly what they needed. If it was nature, it had no deterministic power. As a common, the street fostered independence, enhanced a modicum of equality, built community, and, above all, permitted creativity in human urban behavior.

[99] João do Rio, *A alma encantadora das ruas*, 19.

2

The Street's Apotheosis

Avenida Central

I have never seen anything that occupies less space than poverty.
Oswaldo Dias da Costa[1]

In 1903, Francisco Pereira Passos, the aged but vigorous mayor of Rio de Janeiro, tore an audacious linear gash in Rio de Janeiro's colonial fabric by demolishing homes and businesses to create the new Avenida Central – a dream he had had for decades. Now, with near autocratic powers, he acted without the consent of the municipal council, which he suspended, and because Rio was the nation's capital, he had almost unlimited access to federal credit, which he used to purchase, under eminent domain, the private property that was in his way. He cleared a swath some 50 meters wide and nearly 2 kilometers long, running north and south through 400 years of the city's architectural history. While there were precedents for this kind of destructive creation – from Haussmann's Parisian avenues, the creation of which Pereira Passos had witnessed as a young engineer in France, to Buenos Aires' Avenida de Mayo – Avenida Central was unprecedented for the speed of its creation. Within three years, Pereira Passos had demolished more than 1,600 buildings and displaced 20,000 people, thus reducing the population in the downtown parish of Candelaria by 54 percent. The mayor was caricatured as running in the street in tailcoat and top hat, pickax in hand, barking "Hurry! Hurry!" and threatening to skewer any merchant on Uruguayana Street who did not vacate in five days'

---

[1] Oswaldo Dias da Costa, *Canção do beco: Contos* (São Paulo: Editora Rumo, 1939), 137. "Nunca vi coisa que ocupe menos lugar do que a pobresa."

time.[2] In the same three short years, Pereira Passos had paved the Avenue's roadbed with smooth, hygienic asphalt and its broad sidewalks with some of the city's first and now ubiquitous intricate black-and-white mosaics. By late 1906, many of the Avenue's new, ostentatious Beaux-Arts buildings lined the thoroughfare with fully finished façades, while spindly brazilwood saplings, as national symbols, stood evenly spaced among florid, electric streetlights along the Avenue's median and sidewalks. The broad avenue and the handful of existing streets that were concurrently widened allowed daylight to pour into the downtown, and the area and volume of the city's total public space swelled substantially. What began in 1903 as a ragged, cavernous laceration on the city's face was soon transformed into a stunning beauty mark. The city's residents, newspaper reporters, and even critics, some of whom asserted that such willful destruction would be reprehensible even in a ghetto, were astounded to see that in a short period of time a sizable segment of the city went from colonial uniformity to modern showcase, complete with sumptuous retail shops, luxury hotels and clubs, and eventually an opulent opera house, national art gallery, and soaring national library. The mere passage of time could not make a city modern. The passage of space, from old to new, served as the chief marker of the city's progress.

It is difficult to overstate the emotional, civic impact this new street had on Rio's citizens – at least those not displaced by its creation. For the next two decades, Avenida Central would be the most talked about, photographed, and vaunted space in the nation. The Avenue was the object of poems and essays that sang its praises, and it seemed to form the stage for every event in the city. On ordinary days, the Avenue offered a public playground that represented, in its sophisticated consumer goods and grandiose architecture, the city's rising good taste. Shoppers and walkers flowed seamlessly from their old haunts on Rua do Ouvidor, which the Avenue intersected, to the smart, spacious shops on the Avenue. On special days, the Avenue served as the red carpet to every visiting foreign dignitary and the funereal passage of national heroes. Carnivalesque groups and religious celebrants immediately commandeered the new street and made it part of their traditional spaces for dance and worship. The Avenue became the physical and spiritual center of the nation's deepest aspirations for international respect and domestic

---

[2] *O Malho*, Mar. 18, 1905, 27.

FIGURE 2.1 Avenida Central, 1906. Looking north, Avenida Central, lined with rising Beaux-Arts façades, was the most ambitious example of the street's modern production in Rio. Despite its breadth, the avenue was not designed primarily for transportation; it is best understood as an extended public square – a space whose principle aims were aesthetic: to impress the foreigner, delight the elite, and civilize the poor. Later renamed Avenida Rio Branco, it remained for decades the most celebrated and referenced space in the nation.
Source: Marc Ferrez, "Avenida Central, vista para o norte," Nov. 15, 1906, postcard. Courtesy of the Acervo da Fundação Biblioteca Nacional, Brazil.

delight. The street as public space had exceptional power in shaping the citizenry's collective identity and self-opinion.

Historians have paid careful attention to these events, examining the creation of the Avenue and the modernization of Rio from the perspectives of the rich, the poor, the law, art, and architecture, making much of the motives and the immediate consequences. The most significant story for historians has been the official effort to displace the poor from the city's core and the loss of inexpensive housing downtown where tens of thousands of poor residents had lived and worked. By the late 1890s, anyone of consequence, observed João Pinheiro Chagas, had already moved to the southern suburbs, which were deemed beautiful, clean, and gardened spaces, segregated from the working masses.[3] Now it was time to sanitize and beautify the downtown that the elite had abandoned but to which they still had to commute and in which they still worked and shopped. Removing a backward population was the ultimate means to achieving urban hygiene. But despite losing their downtown homes in the process, many of the poor refused to leave, according to Everardo Backheuser who addressed the housing crisis as it was unfolding. They were attached to their local parishes and unable to afford public transportation to their downtown employments, so rather than move to the northern suburbs or to promised workers' housing, many gathered the rubble of their ruined homes and carried it up the nearby hills to build the city's famous slums, the *favelas*. If the Avenue did not give birth to the *favelas*, which sprung up the decade before, it helped populate them.[4]

Hence, the creation of Avenida Central can be seen as an attack on the poor's place in the city, an attempt to remove undesirables by destroying their homes. That is, we have looked at the building of the Avenue from the perspective of the house, the elite world view of civilization that decided what counted as civil behavior and who counted as civil people. It might be said in this context that Pereira Passos' overall intent was to transform the public street, which was associated with dirt, crime, and disorder, so that it would take on the noble qualities of the house. And from the perspective of housing, the poor literally lost ground. My intent here, though, is to look at the change from the perspective of the street and

---

[3] João Pinheiro Chagas, *De bond: alguns aspectos da civilização brasileira* (Lisbon: Livraria Moderna, 1897), 155–56.

[4] Everardo Backheuser, *Habitações populares* (Rio de Janeiro: Imprensa Nacional, 1906), 44, 106–07, 111. Some notable works on the motives, construction, and implications of the Avenue are Jeffrey Needell, *A Tropical Belle Epoque: Elite Culture and Society in Turn-of-the-Century Rio de Janeiro* (New York, NY: Cambridge University Press, 1987); Jeffrey Needell, "Rio de Janeiro and Buenos Aires: Public Space and Public Consciousness in Fin-de-Siècle Latin America," *Comparative Studies in Society and History*, 37, no. 3 (July 1995): 519–40; Jaime Larry Benchimol, *Pereira Passos: um Haussmann tropical: A renovação urbana da cidade do Rio de Janeiro no início do século XX* (Rio de Janeiro: Secretaria Municipal de Cultura, 1992), see particularly 228–29 on sanitation and the lower classes; Verena Andreatta, *Cidades quadradas, paraísos circulares: os planos urbanísticos do Rio de Janeiro no século XIX* (Rio de Janeiro: Mauad X, 2006); Monica Pimenta Velloso, *A cultura das ruas no Rio de Janeiro, 1900–1930: Mediações, linguagens e espaço* (Rio de Janeiro: Edições Casa de Rui Barbosa, 2004). For the formation of the city's first *favelas*, see Maurício de Almeida Abreu, "Reconstruindo uma história esquecida: origem e expansão inicial das favelas do Rio de Janeiro," *Espaço e Debates* 14, no. 37 (1994): 34–46.

street life, which gives the event a more positive spin, for while many poor lost their former homes, they did not relinquish the downtown or its streets, which remained very much within their sphere of action and influence, at least for another decade or two. Unlike modern urban highways, the Avenue did not precisely target the poor and slums, nor did it divide neighborhoods. Housing for the poor had been accurately targeted since the 1890s by city officials with tenement clearances. The engineer's compass, more than contemporary political and social concerns, determined the Avenue's orientation, and the homes of the rich came down as did retail shops, commercial houses, workshops, taverns, and bakeries. Only the churches were spared in the routing. What went up, if you will, was a new public space. Regardless of one's interpretation of this new space, the street conquered the house rather than the other way around, and the public realm took precedence over the private. Pereira Passos created Rio's last great public commons: the street's final hurrah before the revolution of the street through the rapid rise of modern transportation. Larger spaces would be ripped from the city in the future, but only for the introduction of multilane highways that were built strictly for automotive movement. Although housing – the city's constructed blocks and buildings – came down with a noted violence, no streets were harmed in the construction of the Avenue. The streets gained territory, as did the people who used them.

Significantly, it was the elite's desire to make the street in its image that distinguished the Avenue from all of Rio's streets before it. The Avenue was no longer the street as raw, natural space. The Avenue was emphatically produced space, built to meet the needs of particular favored groups and to emphasize particular uses. The Avenue was designed in marked detail, with a specified width, known length, perfect alignment, and a carefully considered orientation. The space, rather than being an organic blank, was zoned in three broad segments, and its appointments, including pavements, curbs, sidewalks, trees, medians, and monuments, were all committed to paper before they were effected on the ground. Also unlike the traditional street, Avenida Central was born with an official, fitting name. Contractors built the street first, and thereafter constructed the buildings to grace and define the public space – a complete inversion of the way streets came about before. Colonial streets were narrow; the Avenue was emphatically wide, a public statement in itself produced for named ends addressed later in this chapter. The building of the Avenue attempted to rationalize and socially stratify public space, to move it from the category of messy nature, which was all things to all people, to ordered civilization with particular priorities and publics in mind.

This street was now an extraordinary place, but the attempt to remove the poor, or at least eliminate certain behaviors associated with the poor, from the public realm was a failure. Hence, the Avenue, while produced space, did not yet become a dominated space. It remained a part of the commons, all citizens retaining equal access. The elite's attempt to make it a lovely pleasure ground was a success, but no particular group, class, or set of behaviors could be realistically excluded, and the Avenue's beauty and spaciousness made it a *logradouro* that might be best characterized as an elongated public square rather than a broader street. The Avenue was a new creation, but its utility expressed a great deal of continuity. For now, walking, talking, singing, peddling, and playing, although sometimes in modified forms, continued and expanded onto the new space. Hence, the Avenue stood as a triumph of public space over mere private or class interests and remained part of the connected public realm where all people and nearly all activities were found, if not always officially welcomed or legal. In this chapter, we will first go back to the period before the Avenue and investigate its designers' intended motives. Then, we will move to the period after its completion, after 1906, to see how the Avenue was received by its public.

SANITATION: ROOM TO BREATHE

The motives for the construction of a broad, downtown avenue are apparent in the sources; plans for it, in various forms, went back at least to 1843, when Henrique de Beaurepaire Rohan suggested that all of Rio's downtown streets be widened into spacious public spaces. While each subsequent plan differed in design – width, location, orientation, and decoration – each was fairly consistent in its motives, which can be condensed under three proclaimed headings: sanitation, circulation, and beautification.[5] All these terms might be placed under the category of civic modernization, but it appears that each originated as a separate line of reasoning that only by the end of the century merged into a single refrain

[5] The four most influential plans were the Relatorio apresentado a ilma. Camara Municipal do Rio de Janeiro por H. de Beaurepaire-Rohan of 1843; the Relatórios da Comissão de Melhoramentos da Cidade do Rio de Janeiro, one each in 1875 and 1876; and the Melhoramentos da Cidade projetados pelo Prefeito do Distrito Federal, Dr. F. Pereira Passos of 1903, all of which have been published in Verena Andreatta, *Cidades quadradas, paraísos circulares*, anexo documental, 3–29.

of modernity and civilization. Yet, it is striking that the street itself was seen as both a primary problem and an obvious solution to the city's most noted medical, economic, and aesthetic ills.

For much of the nineteenth century, sanitation was the primary justification offered for the city's street reforms, an attempt that might be cynically seen as the official appropriation of an empowering medical discourse to support the city's plans for material modernization. Yet, Rio was a lethal place and widely perceived as such. Mortality rates from chronic tuberculosis and epidemic yellow fever and cholera were frighteningly high, and repeated outbreaks over the latter half of the century took tens of thousands of lives. Officials saw disease mortality as a shameful pockmark on the city, and some accused the imperial government of underreporting the actual statistics to make the nation's capital appear safer and healthier than it was. One interested observer in search of better hygiene in 1895 claimed that yellow fever alone had killed some 47,000 in the city during the previous fifty years.[6] Pereira Passos reminded citizens that in the 1880s, many foreign ships, including Britain's Royal Mail, refused to make port in Rio due to fears of contagion. Italy and Germany advised potential emigrants to avoid Rio, and one Italian doctor claimed with exaggeration that annual mortality in Rio reached 40 percent in the 1880s; without Italian immigrants to replace the dead, he wrote, Rio's population would have declined significantly.[7] City officials, of course, blamed much of the problem on the poor, who they referred to as the "dangerous classes," not only because of their resistance to labor, policing, and good order, but because of their presumed threat to the city's goals of sanitation and hygiene. Tenement clearings attempted to root out what were deemed to be centers of the city's infection. From the tenements, officials perceived corruption radiating outward along Rio's narrow streets to infect every class.[8] President Rodrigues Alves, who appointed Pereira Passos as mayor and fully backed his reforms, lost his daughter to yellow fever. And if the ubiquity of elixirs, ointments, pills, tonics, curatives, and purgatives seen in popular advertising of the period is any indication, health was the primary concern of the reading public.

---

[6] José Simão da Costa. "Memorial apresentado ao Illustrado Conselho da Intendencia Municipal sobre o systema de calcamento denominado Pavimento Sanitario Fluminense, inventado por José Simão da Costa," Rio de Janeiro, 1895, 31, AGCRJ.

[7] Donald B. Cooper, "Brazil's Long Fight against Epidemic Disease, 1849–1917, with Special Emphasis on Yellow Fever," *Bulletin of the New York Academy of Medicine* 51 (May 1975): 681–82.

[8] Sidney Chalhoub, *Cidade febril: cortiços e epidemias na corte imperial* (São Paulo: Companhia das Letras, 1996), 21, 29–35, 86.

The Avenue's promoters proposed to produce a street that was not only a sanitary space, but a space that would help sanitize the rest of the city. According to the theories of the day, the cause of disease could not be exactly pinpointed, but it was widely accepted that hygiene and contagion were spatial issues. While disease may have derived, as they saw it, from filth, soil, standing water, rotting animal and vegetable matter, and dust[9] – all of which were street problems that cities were trying to address – it was also believed that the lack of space in the city's narrow streets and in the city's cramped housing constrained the evacuation or prevented the dilution of these foul substances and their emanations. So, even though the municipality's sanitation programs were multipronged – from street cleaning by the *garis*, obligatory vaccinations by Dr. Osvaldo Cruz, and an early sewage system for the downtown that Pedro II contracted with British interests in 1857 – part of the final solution was to open things up so that city spaces could ventilate and drain. Hence, the broad Avenue could be justified in terms of its width and length as a means to help open the city to the purportedly healthy sea breezes. The Avenue was to be like the trunk run in a ventilation system, supplying itself and every connected colonial corridor with calculated volumes of fresh air. The city's many hills were also seen as obstacles to the flow of good air replacing bad, and it may not have been accidental that portions of São Bento and Castelo Hills, which bordered the bay, were targeted for demolition as part of the construction of Avenida Central. At the same time, Senado Hill was removed entirely, further opening the city to supposed healthy winds. Real estate interests certainly applauded the conversion of useless or unprofitable hills into level lots, but sanitation and hygiene were the primary stated motives for leveling the city's obstructive architectures and topographies, a process that would continue well into the twentieth century.

Drainage too was a spatial issue. Proponents of the avenue complained of the impossibility of keeping narrow colonial streets free of groundwater, puddling runoff, and even tidal seawater. Street grades could not be easily changed, and streets were too narrow to install storm drains. That left, at best, open ditches carrying filthy water and, at worst, surface-level standing water and animal dung that was constantly churned by the hooves of animals and the wheels of vehicles. Another reason given for removing the surrounding hills was to prevent their muddy runoff from

---

[9] *Jornal do Comércio*, Rio de Janeiro, May 18, 1892, 1, features an article on the epidemic dangers of dust.

clogging the streets below.[10] The constant call in such plans for the planting of trees in the streets and plazas had less to do with beauty and shade than with the expectation that tree roots would work to remove much of the soil's noxious dampness. Before mid-century, Rio's streets and squares were almost entirely bereft of trees. The large public spaces of Santa Anna, Praça 15, and Praça da República were all entirely shadeless, without a single tree to grace their contours. Scrubbier street vegetation existed, but it was unplanned and largely unwanted. Only in the 1850s and later would trees be added to the city's squares, and later still to the first new avenues, such as those along the Mangue Canal in the 1870s and the Beira Mar at the turn of the century.[11]

Even street pavements were taken into consideration by the hygienists, who claimed that cobbles, largely of stone but some of wood, also contributed to the city's insalubrious reality. The dirt-filled spaces between the cobbles made much of the road "unpaved," as it were, and this multitude of gaps and crevices harbored the street's deepest filth and organic matter, not to mention even deeper exhalations of the soil, "stuff that oppresses us, suffocates us, and poisons us." In these narrow but wild interstices between the paving stones, impervious to even vigorous sweeping, corruption accumulated and vegetation invaded. For most, the solution was asphalt, which in its seamless smoothness should not harbor such infections and was easy to clean by broom or jets of water.[12]

By decree, Pereira Passos attempted to eliminate some of what he considered the most egregious, unsanitary, natural functions of the street. Stray dogs were ruthlessly killed; the peddling of fresh milk, direct from the cow, and of viscera was banned; spitting and urinating in the street were outlawed; beggars and the sellers of lottery tickets were cast off; and children were prohibited from flying kites into new electrical wires.[13] In addition to directly regulating street activities, there was the utopian hope among elite planners that the construction of the new Avenue – not a natural, raw, dirty street but a hygienic and elegant space – would by itself change the behavior and even the dress of the city's poor residents. A clean, modern space would promote a refined and urbane public

---

[10] Benchimol, *Pereira Passos*, 122.

[11] For a variety of contracts and petitions regarding tree planting and cutting from the late 1870s, see AGCRJ 138, 39-3-29, folhas 1, 2, 4, 7, 10–13, and 17.

[12] José Simão da Costa. "Memorial apresentado ao Illustrado Conselho da Intendência Municipal sobre o systema de calcamento denominado Pavimento Sanitário Fluminense, inventado por José Simão da Costa," Rio de Janeiro, 1895, 13–14, AGCRJ.

[13] Benchimol, *Pereira Passos*, 277–81.

culture. One asphalt contractor argued that more than the lecturing of the hygienists, and even more than the threat of the next epidemic, the beauty of smooth pavement – "polished asphalt," as another put it – would induce the residents themselves to be clean in their habits and civilized in their manners.[14] At the very least, some elite hoped that the Avenue would be so exotically immaculate that the poor and unwashed would simply stay away rather than come and feel out of their element.

CIRCULATION: INTRODUCING THE WHEEL

The movement of air for health was a top concern, but a second major stated objective of building the avenue was to facilitate the movement of bodies and commodities – and the vehicles that carried them. An avenue, it was argued, should be built to serve as a broad thoroughfare that, in the case of Avenida Central, would connect new port facilities on the city's north with the central business district and the expanding suburbs to the south.[15] As Rio grew over the course of the nineteenth century, its narrow, colonial streets, which had often been congested, began to experience jams, particularly on the streets nearest the old port. Pedestrians remained the largest users, but the cause of the slowed circulation was not simply growth but a revolution in spatial use that we glaringly neglected in the previous chapter: the introduction of wheels. This is not to say that the city had no wheeled vehicles before the 1840s; there were a few and in many cases they were limited to the rare royal carriage, a smattering of horse-drawn tilburies, and primitive oxcarts. Kidder and Fletcher claimed that they did not see a single wheeled vehicle in the city of Salvador, Brazil's former capital, in 1840, and Rio's colonial transportation developed on a similar model as Salvador's. Most people and most goods got around on foot. The majority of residents, of course, walked on their own feet, but some, especially upper-class women, were carried by their slaves in litters, and some wealthier men relied on the hooves of horses and mules. Rio's first cabbies were slaves who carried their fares in hammocks slung on poles. The large majority of goods in the city rode on the backs and heads of slaves. Debret explained this practice as the near universal means to

---

[14] José Simão da Costa. "Memorial apresentado ao Illustrado Conselho da Intendência Municipal sobre o systema de calcamento denominado Pavimento Sanitário Fluminense, inventado por José Simão da Costa," Rio de Janeiro, 1895, 22, AGCRJ. *Kosmos*, Oct. 1906.

[15] "Embelezamento da Cidade," *Correio da Manhã*, Apr. 17, 1903, a report by the Club de Engenharia.

move goods due to the complicity of slave owners, many of whom derived their income from their slaves providing the service of carrying goods in the streets for a fee.[16] In some ways, this was a natural solution to the reality of very narrow streets where large wheeled vehicles did not fit. Pedestrians, and humans as beasts of burden, could better negotiate the streets' confines and the crowded bodies of fellow citizens than could carts and wagons that suffered from a comparatively substantial disadvantage in maneuverability. Wheeled vehicles could not sidestep or turn their shoulders – essential skills in the crowded street.

But wheels in number did finally come. Among the first were those that belonged to the generally modest carriages of foreigners, particularly French and British merchants who arrived in Rio after foreign trade opened in 1808. Non-Portuguese immigrants were the first to move from the tight downtown streets out along Rio's bay beaches and foothills, starting an incipient suburbanization. But such vehicles remained few in number. By the 1840s, the first mass transit vehicles, closed coaches known in Rio as *gôndolas* (omnibuses elsewhere) that might carry ten passengers, began to ply their trade between the city and the neighborhoods of Gloria, Flamengo, and Botafogo, although many commuted by steamer on the bay. In 1857, Fletcher and Kidder reported that "every evening presents an animated spectacle of crowded steamers, full omnibuses, and galloping horses and mules" conveying the foreign merchants and their bookkeepers to their suburban homes.[17] Additionally, as the city's commerce grew, particularly in coffee exports and manufactured imports, the general movement of goods in handcarts and small wagons incrementally added more wheeled traffic.

Then, in the late 1860s, mule-drawn trams entirely transformed the city's transportation. Popularly known as *bondes* (because British bonds were the instruments used to finance their construction), the open trams, often drawn by a single mule, carried fifteen to thirty passengers on forward-facing benches. Running on rails installed directly on the street's surface, *bondes* were efficient and proved to be a complete disruption of former systems. *Gôndolas* required four of more mules to drag their small passenger loads over the street's rough and rutted cobbles, making for

---

[16] Gilberto Freyre, *The Mansions and the Shanties* (New York, NY: Knopf, 1963), 310–13; Debret, *Viagem*, 317–18.

[17] Daniel P. Kidder and James C. Fletcher, *Brazil and the Brazilians, Portrayed in Historical and Descriptive Sketches* (Philadelphia, PA: Childs & Peterson, 1857), 27; Robert Elwes, *A Sketcher's Tour Round the World* (London: Hurst and Blacket, Publishers, 1854), 18–19. For more detail, see Needell, *Tropical Belle Époque*, 151–53.

FIGURE 2.2 The *bonde*, c. 1901. The *bonde* (the mule-drawn tram) revolutionized the city's transportation from about 1870, creating the first substantial suburbs. However, the large majority of riders, who appreciated the service's cheapness and frequency, lived and worked downtown. Because *bondes* displaced many cabs, coaches, and carriages, including those of the royal family, and because they moved no faster than pedestrians, this first expression of public transit in fact had a calming effect on the street. The open cars, which continued under electrification, often mixed classes and always kept passengers in intimate contact with the street.
Source: "Bonde de bitola estreita da Companhia Carris Urbanos," c. 1901, Arquivo Brício de Abreu, Biblioteca Nacional, Rio de Janeiro. Courtesy of the Acervo da Fundação Biblioteca Nacional, Brazil.

a jarring commute. Their comparative inefficiency more than their discomfort forced *gôndolas* from competition.[18] An 1868 illustration depicted a pitiful *gôndola* coachman and his mules hanged by their necks from their reins in a tree, which meant to express the violent rapidity with which the service vanished from the street.[19] Cabs and carriages declined in number as well because they were not as comfortable or as

---

[18] Clay McShane, *Down the Asphalt Path: The Automobile and the American City* (New York, NY: Columbia University Press, 1994), 14, notes that a horse or mule could pull 30 percent faster and twice the load on rails than with wheels on pavement. New York's mayor called the horse tram "the greatest invention in the history of man."

[19] Published originally in *Vida Fluminense* 42 (Oct. 17, 1868), 504 and reprinted in Maurício de Almeida Abreu, *Evolução urbana do Rio de Janeiro* (Rio de Janeiro: IPLANRIO, J. Zahar Editor, 1987), 45.

cheap as *bondes*. The smooth-running *bondes* were a brilliant, financial success, and by the mid-1880s, tram lines owned by four private companies, had concessions to run on most of the city's central streets. Each line originated on a public square and provided convenient transit within the downtown and out to the suburbs. Already in 1870, the trams served 6 million annual riders. By 1885, they served 41 million in a city of about 400,000 people. Most of the unique riders took short, downtown hops, not long rides to and from the suburbs, so the trams were as much about efficient downtown movement as they were meeting the needs of the growing suburbs. Only the downtown trams had cars that were labeled *descalços* (shoeless), which at half price were reserved for the poor, most of whom now wore shoes; these cars also permitted baggage.[20] There were special *bonde* cars for carrying the mail, and there were more elegant versions that a family could rent for baptisms, weddings, and funerals. Members of the royal family used reserved *bondes* when traveling from the palace to attend Mass or the theater, suggesting that *bondes* had attractions superior to their baroque coaches. Mule-drawn trams dominated Rio's public transportation for twenty-five years and then were replaced starting in the early 1890s by electric versions.

The mule *bondes* moved a lot of people, but they did not move rapidly. Their typical top speed was about 5 miles per hour, and they stopped a lot, so the pace of the street did not change much and in fact slowed with the demise of the *gôndolas* and the decline of private cabs and carriages. The tram's appeal was not speed but the savings in effort and perspiration at a reasonable price, especially on long or hilly routes. They plodded along compared to the *gôndola* coaches that had raced across "gutters as if there were none, and rush[ed] through narrow streets as if Negro water carriers had no existence. It is curious to behold the heavy-laden slaves clearing the street and dodging into open shop doors as an omnibus appears in sight."[21] It was reported that in New York City, the horse trams' slower movement reduced pedestrian deaths to one-sixth of the

---

[20] Hastings Charles Dent, *A Year in Brazil with Notes on the Abolition of Slavery, the Finances of the Empire, Religion, Meteorology, Natural History, etc.* (London: Kegan Paul, Trench & Co., 1886), 22, 235–36. Fernando Agenor de Noronha Santos, *Meios de transportes no Rio de Janeiro*, vol. 1 (Rio de Janeiro: Typografia do Jornal do Comércio, 1934), 329. The rapid expansion of the trams lines is evident in João da Rocha Fragoso, "Mappa architectural da cidade do Rio de Janeiro," 1874, Biblioteca National Digital Brazil, http://objdigital.bn.br/acervo_digital/div_cartografia/cart470826.pdf (accessed Feb. 15, 2013); and "Plan of the City of Rio de Janeiro" produced for the *Handbook of Rio de Janeiro* (Rio de Janeiro: Rio News, 1887), foldout map.

[21] Kidder & Fletcher, *Brazil and the Brazilians*, 38.

former, faster omnibuses.[22] In Rio, in their constant search for passengers, the *bondes* crawled through intersections looking up and down the cross streets for potential fares. Machado de Assis observed that if a driver on Rua do Catete saw a fare wave him down from two blocks away on a side street, as far away as Flamengo Beach, the driver would stop the tram, take a pinch of snuff, and jump down to engage in conversation with locals on the corner until he could load the passenger. Then the tram would proceed on its slow way and repeat the operation at each new intersection.[23] In early photographs, with their longer exposures, a pedestrian in motion would blur their own image, particularly that of their legs and arms, but passengers on the poky *bondes* are always in sharp focus.

The trams became a significant spatial presence on the streets of the city, and one might argue, as has Clay McShane for North American cities, that as they electrified and pick up some speed in the 1890s, the trolleys began to transform citizens' views of the streets as exclusive corridors for transportation as opposed to social, commercial, and recreational gathering spaces.[24] In Brazil, however, this seems to have been a much slower process. While the trams, with their rails implanted in the street, must have given the street a sense of linearity, the use of the street did not seem to change yet as a result. Pedestrians and *bondes* mixed with few conflicts. The rails certainly occupied space, as did the trams, but the trams came and went, slowly, and space occupied by the rails themselves, although private property, remained public and people walked on them, gathered over them, and conversed over them, as they had before on the same street space. The rails are noted in one city map from 1886, identified in colored lines, but in early photographs, especially from low angles, the rails are largely invisible, embedded into the pavement. In some ways, the trams made the streets safer and less chaotic. Compared to a carriage, omnibus, cab, or a man on horseback, which came by at random times, at rapid speeds, and along unpredictable paths, the trams were not only slow, they were orderly. And no matter how frequently they might pass, they always ran on the same track and pedestrians knew what parts of the street were safe and which were not when the tram came up the street. There were accidents associated with the *bondes*, especially the electrics, but the large majority involved passenger falls as they climbed on and off.

[22] McShane, *Down the Asphalt Path*, 8.
[23] Tati, *Mundo de Machado de Assis*, 47, footnote 2.
[24] McShane, *Down the Asphalt Path*, 29.

Early trams were relatively quiet, and some referred to them as *leiteiros* (milkmen) because with their small bells they sounded like the milkman on the street peddling with his cow, a familiar sound. Electric trams, on the other hand, increased street noise.

While the trams were technically private property, street users perceived them as public spaces, mobile extensions of the street itself. The polity and sociality of the street entered the trams, and one often saw the same drivers and same riders daily, part of the community. When one passenger entered, all saluted, and when another left, all tipped their hats; conversations were started, and tobacco was kindly offered to one's seating partner. And as open cars, the trams remained connected to the street, so one could hail a friend or make comment to a pretty girl. As trams came up the street, children placed objects on the tracks for effect, including nails, rocks, glass shards, and even the occasional bullet.[25] When the trams stopped, children climbed on them as if they were playground equipment. During carnival and other celebrations, locals decorated their trams, which often had their neighborhood's name printed prominently on the rollsign or tram scroll, and "hijacked" their usual route to parade while singing and dancing on the running boards, a practice that continued until the middle of the next century. Social classes continued to mix on the trams, and commerce and crime, just as on the street, kept up a lively business. The city too saw the tram as an entity not unlike the street that they could and did regulate, both its hygiene and what counted as proper behavior. Like the street, the tram was to be swept, spitting was not allowed, and one might see it as one more space the elite tried to sanitize and bring up to their own acceptable standards.[26] But it became increasingly seen as a space dirty and diseased, much like the traditional street, and so while the Avenue's designers aspired to more modern circulation, they concluded that the popular tram would have no place or role on its broad, civilized surface.

---

[25] Marco A. C. Sávio, *A cidade e as máquinas: Bonde e automóveis nos primórdios da metrópole paulista,1900–1930* (São Paulo: Annablume, 2010), 109–10.

[26] Anton Rosenthal, "Dangerous Streets: Trolleys, Labor Conflict and the Reorganization of Public Space in Montevideo," in *Cities of Hope*, edited by James Baer and Ronn Pineo (Boulder, CO: Westview Press, 1998), 37; Fletcher and Kidder, *Brazil and the Brazilians*, 42; *Reglamento higiénico para ferrocarriles, tranvias, coches urbanos, diligências y carros funebres* (San Salvador, Brazil: Imprenta Nacional, 1901).

BEAUTIFICATION: A SECOND THOUGHT

Of the three motives I have identified, the avenue boosters had the least to say about the street's beautification and how to accomplish it. Plans repeated themselves in the details of sanitation and circulation. Beauty got the occasional nod, but not much print. For many, it seemed, form would follow function, and solving the problems of circulation and sanitation would indirectly bring about the street's transformation into a modern, civilized space, the assumed equivalent of beauty. Reformers were assured that if the city's colonial architecture – which many judged to be not only unhygienic but also squat, dull, and monotonous – were removed from the avenues, whatever replaced those structures would be a significant improvement. Even in the 1903 plan, there was initially no proposal to vet the design and stylistic influences on the buildings that would go up along the Avenue. It was assumed that if you gave buyers the opportunity to build on new broad plots in a high-rent district, they could not fail to build something pleasing, even though previous experience on Avenida do Mangue, where brand new structures were built in the dated colonial style, suggested otherwise.[27]

City officials did indeed concern themselves with beauty. Congress explicitly stated in 1882 that city councils had control over streets, ditches, alignments, and paving, and in planning decisions should prohibit anything "that might come in conflict with the beautification of the city."[28] Beauty was subjective, however, and little was said of what constituted its primal essence or its specific, Brazilian cultural expression. The visage of modernity, on the other hand, was concrete and widely agreed upon. To achieve modernity, Rio simply needed to imitate European models, particularly those of France, but also England. Replication would be the automation of beauty. This was accomplished architecturally on the Avenue with the construction of the Municipal Theater, which was a downscaled copy of Paris' Palais Garnier, and the design of the national art museum, which was a good likeness, though again on smaller scale, of the Louvre. Beauty was the declared essence of the City Beautiful Movement, a North American development that also sought to mimic Europe's monumental cities. It was best expressed in Chicago's 1893

---

[27] Reproduced in Verena Andreatta, *Cidades quadradas, paraísos circulares: os planos urbanísticos do Rio de Janeiro no século XIX* (Rio de Janeiro: Mauad X, 2006), anexo documental, 3–29.

[28] *Annaes do Parlamento Brazileiro, Camara dos Srs. Deputados, Sessão de 1882*, vol. 5 (Rio de Janeiro: Typographia Nacional, 1882), 257.

World's Fair, whose grand but temporary architecture did serve as a model. This too was imitated in some measure on the Avenue's southern end. In fact, the Palácio Monroe, which was originally built as the Brazilian pavilion for the 1904 St. Louis World's Fair, was dismantled in pieces, shipped to Rio, and rebuilt at the Avenue's southern tip. And Chicago was imitated most fully in Rio's own National Exposition of 1908, held in Urca; the architecture there was also temporary.

But imitation in some spaces had begun well before. Jeffery Needell notes that the crown, which represented an agricultural elite who showed weak urban interests, had largely neglected the city and its reforms over the whole of the nineteenth century – "Rio rotted in its colonial shell" – but this criticism is specifically applied to the city's architecture.[29] City officials significantly imitated European street forms from about 1850, and went well beyond the important changes in infrastructure that came with the mule trams and electric streetcars. Before mid-century, nearly all of Rio's streets retained their colonial contours, nature not much disturbed. They were often paved in cobbles in poor repair, but usually still full of dirt, and characteristically pitched to the center where a shallow "∨" or an excavated ditch ineffectively carried away rainwater and refuse. There were no trees, and gaslamps, which were few, hung from the walls of buildings, particularly at corners. However, by the 1890s, many of the downtown streets had been given more consistent paving, high granite curbs, raised sidewalks, a reverse grade that pitched the street to the curbs instead of to a center ditch, and gutters, many attached to storm drains. To that were added, all in the finest European style, shade trees, almost an excess of decorative streetlight posts anchored at the curb line, and eventually asphalt pavements. Likewise, the public squares began to be treated like parks and public gardens rather than pastures and dumping grounds. These were changes that for the most part had become prevalent in northern Europe itself only since the middle of the eighteenth century.[30] This was all done apparently with little fanfare, as such changes and beautifications were drawing less attention than the oft-repeated concerns about sanitation and movement, but the accumulating changes of the street's appearance, the beginnings of its production, set a precedent for Avenida Central, where it was all done of a piece, on the grandest scale.

[29] Needell, *Tropical Belle Epoque*, 26, 32. Needell does note the changes that came to some public squares in the period.
[30] Michael Southworth and Eran Ben-Joseph, *Streets and the Shaping of Towns and Cities* (Washington, DC: Island Press, 2003), 18.

SANITATION'S LIMITS

The motives of Pereira Passos and his collaborators are easily summarized, and the evidence of their produced work, which we will examine now, is fairly concrete. What the streets and the Avenue in particular meant to the people who received it, however, must be divined largely by what they said of, and more importantly, what they did in, the street. Most users had almost no other voice than what they did with their feet. Because the Avenue was produced as a public space, its elite designers could not accurately predict how people would use the street, what utilities receivers would emphasize. If the designers focused most of their attention on producing sanitation and circulation, the receivers rarely mentioned those benefits. The new Avenue was celebrated for its beauty and enjoyed for its broad utility; it was a grand space where citizens could go for a walk, make a shopping jaunt, spectate a parade, or simply socialize – all activities associated with the traditional street but now celebrated and sanctified by the most splendid space in which to engage in them. Rio's nickname, "The Marvelous City," which was popularized by a samba tune of the same name in the 1930s, was reportedly coined by the poet and dramaturg Henrique Coelho Neto in 1908. In fact, the name had come into use some time before – not in the sense of Rio's natural beauty, as is now assumed, but in the context of Rio's urban improvements, in particular, Avenida Central.[31] Ten years after its completion, the editors of the magazine *Fon Fon* compared the Avenue to the great thoroughfares of New York, Buenos Aires, Chicago, Berlin, and Rome, which they said epitomized each city. The Avenue for Brazil had become the "center of all human sensations, of all the greatest national happenings, the center of things elegant, of all our happy gestures, felicities, miseries, and revolts, and in the life of great cities, such things dominate our souls – whether

---

[31] Daryle Williams, Amy Chazkel, and Paulo Knauss, eds. *The Rio de Janeiro Reader: History, Culture, Politics* (Durham, NC: Duke University Press, 2016), 8, footnote 1, identify the first usage of *Cidade Maravilhosa* in reference to the city in a poem published in *O Paiz*, Feb. 16, 1904, 2, although in this case it is used in irony, the verses lamenting, not praising, a heartless city that was shooting all the stray dogs. The first nonsarcastic use that I can find is in the same newspaper, *O Paiz*, May 4, 1904, 1, which praises the work of Pereira Passos and Rodriguez Alves who "transformed, beautified, and sanitized this marvelous city," although still in lower case. It appears that the first usage of "*Cidade Maravilhosa*," uppercase, was in connection to the November 1908 exposition held at Rio's Praia Vermelha, with its ostentatious but temporary pavilions. See *O Paiz*, Nov. 17, 1908, 1.

momentary or eternal."[32] From the eyes and under the feet of the receivers and users, the street's civic beauty and cultural utility pushed the practical concerns of sanitation and circulation well off center stage.

And rightly so, for the claims of improved sanitation and circulation promised by the Avenue's creators were overblown. The city may have looked cleaner and more salubrious in some precincts, but if the incidence and morbidity of disease had at all declined (and even that was debatable),[33] it was due to focused campaigns of forced vaccination and mosquito abatement and not to better ventilation and more consistent sweeping. Whatever sanitary benefits the Avenue may have brought were mostly cosmetic and limited to small parcels downtown. Most of the city's streets remained narrow, colonial, and full of dirt. One observation noted that the unsanitary housing situation overall did not improve with the Avenue; it simply moved elsewhere and not far away at that.[34] Despite the Avenue's new breadth and smooth flooring, many still described it as infiltrated with mud and dirt. The Avenue flooded during heavy rains, just like any other street. Dust, whose insalubriousness was feared more than that of mud, became increasingly a concern as rapid electric tram and the new automotive traffic raised it into the air. In summer, dust was the "tired and repeated complaint of the street"; newspapers professed shock that this was occurring right on the Avenue. Regarding mud on the Avenue, one wag observed that at least the new muck was "civilized" like that of the streets of Paris and London, because it was blackened by petroleum oozing from the asphalt.[35]

Pereira Passos did seem to have a permanent impact on the number of animals, particularly pigs and cattle, roaming the downtown streets as pasture. Farm animals were banned from downtown streets, and dogs were exterminated such that their reported numbers declined significantly. Families in the city were permitted to own dogs, but they had to be licensed and controlled. If the press sometimes praised the decline of beasts that barked all night and threatened citizens' legs, among many classes, the capture and killing of stray dogs was extremely unpopular, and residents worked to save them, harboring canines in their homes and

[32] *Fon Fon,* Mar. 20, 1915.
[33] Teresa Meade, *"Civilizing" Rio: Reform and Resistance in a Brazilian City* (University Park, PA: Pennsylvania State University Press, 1997), 126.
[34] Backheuser, *Habitações populares,* 3, 111.
[35] *Fon Fon,* Jul. 13, 1913; *Fon Fon,* Dec. 20, 1913; *A Noite,* Jul. 4, 1921, 4. See the collection of contract bids for signage, Oct. 30, 1896, AGCRJ 175, 32-4-20, folhas 35-36.

courtyards and working to thwart the dog catcher. In the 1904 carnival, one group of revelers created a float imitating the dog catcher's paddy wagon. Inside the bars, energetic actors wearing dog masks protested the municipal act that "deprived the canine race the right to live and enjoy the full freedom of the capital's streets." This may suggest an understanding of the street as a place not only for humans to enjoy, but for other creatures as well. The protesting revelers passed out flyers with the lyrics of a song criticizing the dog catcher's "pretty prison" as the genial mayor's most "captivating invention." The dog catcher and his murderous squad patrolled the streets, making a hell of a noise as they yelled "Circle it; grab it; capture it." Then, the poem makes allusion to the sound of multiple guns discharging. The poem concluded that indeed, for the murder of innocent canines, there was no other city in the world like Rio: "Marvelous City, indeed; God Save Rio de Janeiro."[36] In fact, this satirical sense of "Cidade Maravilhosa," employed in carnival during Pereira Passos' reforms, may have been the beginning of its popularization rather than its use by the city's boosters thereafter. The mayor would later brag that he had caught and killed thousands of the city's dogs, whose numbers and freedom had made Rio repugnant, "like many Eastern cities," but later press reports noted that the next mayor was not as keen on the effort, and the number of dogs began to rise to former levels.[37]

One of the incontrovertible reforms – related to the sanitizing or attempted removal of certain residential classes – that the Avenue introduced to the city was a modicum of zoning. First, the Avenue itself was organized in three separate sections. On the south, very much influenced by the City Beautiful Movement, the Avenue was graced almost exclusively with monumental buildings: an opera house, a national library, a national gallery, an obelisk, the federal courthouse, and two palaces inhabited by the federal house and senate, respectively. Here also were constructed the city's newest theaters that along with the opera house gave the southern portion of the Avenue the name Cinelândia, the cinema district. The central segment of the Avenue was reserved for posh shops, hotels, private clubs, and professional offices, including the city's major newspapers. On the upper length near the new port, the Avenue became the city's financial district, lined with merchant houses, transportation providers, and banks, including the national bank.[38] Second, the entire Avenue was zoned as nonresidential, apparently not yet by law but by

[36] *O Paiz*, Feb. 16, 1904, 2.
[37] Benchimol, *Pereira Passos*, 277. *Fon Fon*, Mar. 14, 1908.   [38] *Kosmos*, Oct. 1910.

intent. The result was possibly the only street in the city without a single resident, other than some well-known, long-term residents at the Hotel Avenida. This had never been seen before in the downtown city, where previously all uses and buildings of all types had been mixed at random. It was not gentrification but rather commercialization and professionalization. And it changed the nature of the street substantially. Community, particularly business communities, could still be built on a street with no residents, but an exclusively commercial street was a new creature that would not have the domestic atmosphere of other streets, and community would be transient and limited. Peddlers of bread, milk, fruits, and fashions, without resident customers, had no reason to amble up the avenue proper; local gossip, child's play, and serenades did not make much sense on the Avenue. As a home for nobody, everyone in the city could be possessive about the Avenue, and it became the street for everyone, a place primarily for civic play and display. Like many modern downtown streets without residents, it was lively when it was lively but it could otherwise be lifeless, especially weekends.

CONFLICTS OVER CIRCULATION

The Avenue's promoters argued that the new space would increase the city's capacity to move goods and people and would lower the cost of haulage. In reality, the Avenue did little to help the city's transportation for the first few years; in fact it was an impediment to public transit. Although the automobile eventually would stake out the Avenue – a long, unobstructed space with smooth pavement – as its preferred environment, the Avenue was not built for the car. In 1905, there were only four automobiles in the entire city, and nobody at the time could have predicted the revolutions the car would bring.[39] There were, however, during the same year nearly 5,000 other wheeled vehicles, consisting largely of carts and wagons that moved goods to and from the old port. There were also eighty-four bicycles. City authorities considered granting concessions to autobus companies to run on the Avenue even before it was finished, but other than a short-lived experiment by the Auto-Avenida Bus Company to run people from the downtown to the 1908 Exposition, buses would not run consistently on the Avenue, or anywhere in the

---

[39] [Census of Vehicles Registered in Rio de Janeiro, 1905], AGCRJ, cod. 375, 58-1-22, folha 140.

city, until the late 1920s. In 1922, there were only seven licensed buses in the entire city.[40]

In the way of goods and workers, despite intentions to reorient the city on a more north and south axis, much of the city's traffic continued to move east and west, from the old port to the commercial district. Ferries continued to arrive at the old port locations. Hence, the Avenue offered ease of movement in the wrong directions for most movers. Trams, increasingly electrified, were the real people movers, but the city essentially banned them from the Avenue as eyesores whose tracks would mar the pristine, smooth asphalt. Tram companies were never allowed to establish rail lines along the Avenue itself, thus limiting the Avenue's contribution to moving people. The Avenue in a sense created an inconvenient transportation break for the majority moving east and west.[41] There was resistance to letting the trams even cross the Avenue. From the 1880s, trams from the port had run on nine streets, essentially every street that reached the old port except two, Rua do Ouvidor and Rua São José, crossing the area that was now the Avenue. The pressure to rebuild these lines was great, but it took some time. The line crossing at Rua da Assembléia was rebuilt in July of 1908, but local businesses complained about the noise, referring to the electric tram as the "yellow peril" whose "criminal drivers" would disturb the peace and beauty of the Avenue.[42] While no tram lines were permitted to run on the Avenue itself, a number of lines eventually crossed it, remaking the city's east-to-west connections. Still, some complained that the electric trams brought no real benefits in speed but the inconveniences of noise, dust, and discomfort. Mário Pederneiras, a poet who wrote an irregular column on street happenings, noted that little was gained by moving from animal to electric traction. The former mule-drawn trams were more comfortable, cleaner, quieter, and did not jolt one's bowels. The small gain in time – a 40-minute trip now took 35 minutes – was insufficient to compensate for being uncomfortable, or particularly "for the loss of the freedom to have a discussion or even to exchange simple

[40] G. Frankel & Cia to Lauro Muller, Ministro da Industria, Dec. 10, 1904, Comissão Construtora da Avenida Central, Viação e Obras Públicas, 4/70–4, ANRJ; Noronha Santos, *Meios de transporte*, vol. 2, table: "Resume de estatistica de veiculos terrestres . . . 1922"; *Fon Fon*, Jul. 11, 1908.

[41] Samuel Malamud, *Recordando a Praça Onze* (Rio de Janeiro: Livraria Kosmos Editora, 1988), 34.

[42] "Na calçada," *Fon Fon*, Jul. 11, 1908.

phrases," with one's fellow riders. The electric *bonde* had become "the school of enforced silence" and "of deafness."[43]

Neither wheels nor traffic, both of which had been around for some time, initiated the vehicular dominance of Rio's central streets; it was the arrival of velocity. In possibly the earliest case, it was the arrival of the more rapid electric tram that threatened the city's ubiquitous handcart workers, another critical transit reality in the city's downtown, where sturdy men moved goods of all kinds through busy, narrow streets.[44] The old horse trams and handcarts got along fine for forty years. They moved about the same speed and literally used the same spaces. The speed of the electric trams, however, made obstacles of the handcarts.

Sometime after their installation in the late 1860s, the horse tram rails, especially downtown, were utilized by carters. Cartage before this period was done largely on slaves' shoulders or in oxcarts. The new rails, which were private, were treated as common, forming an opportunity. Handcart builders designed carts specifically so that the vehicle's axle had the same gauge as the narrow-gauge trams, which permitted the handcart workers to pull their loaded carts right on the rails. This greatly eased the labor. Carters no longer had to drag their loads over rough cobbles and potholes. On smooth rails, carters doubled their loads to 600 kilograms, and as the rails expanded, handcarts increased. By the turn of the century, street photography frequently and inadvertently recorded carters pulling their sizable loads on the tracks, which confirms the practice's commonplace-ness. The handcart pullers, who were referred to as "asses without tails," a title many wore with pride, provided ship-to-shop and shop-to-door service faster than could carts or wagons. Augusto Malta photographed a dozen such carts lined up at the bottom of the hill in Gamboa, a working-class neighborhood. Each was neatly parked with one wheel on the curb, its registration number painted on its side, and a well-worn rope coiled neatly around the handles. Each represented a family's livelihood.[45]

---

[43] "Diário das Ruas," *Fon Fon*, Nov. 29, 1913; Pederneiras' identity as the author of the column "Diário das Ruas" was revealed in his obituary in *Fon Fon* in February of 1915.

[44] For New York's handcart removal under LaGuardia, see Daniel Bluestone, "The Pushcart Evil," in *The Landscape of Modernity: Essays on New York City, 1900–1940*, edited by David Ward and Olivier Zunz (New York, NY: Russell Sage Foundation, 1992), 287–312.

[45] See George Ermakoff, *Augusto Malta e o Rio de Janeiro, 1903–1936* (Rio de Janeiro: G. Ermakoff Casa Editorial, 2009), 71. A Marc Ferrez photo of Praça XV in 1870 shows that many handcarts were still not yet built for the tram rails: Ermakoff, *Rio de Janeiro, 1840–1890*, 159. But they seem to be universally so-built by the early 1890s; see

The battle began in late 1902. The Companhia de Carris Urbanos, which owned most of the narrow-gauge tram lines in the downtown, prohibited the handcarters, who had "fraudulently engineered" their carts to fit the company's rails, from carrying goods on their infrastructure. The legal issue came down to whether or not the space directly above the rails was available for common use or if its use was exclusive to the tram company. Carris Urbanos hired lawyers to provide opinions on the matter, and not surprisingly, they all spoke in favor of the tram company. While the company did not own the space through which their rails passed, it had been given by contract the exclusive right to move people and goods on the rails. People and vehicles could pass over the rails, use the space above them, but nobody was to profit from the tram company's direct investments and maintenance.[46] The tram owners claimed that heavily loaded handcarts damaged the paving around the rails, which the company had to maintain. But this, while possibly true, could have been no worse than the damage done by thousands of the heavier vehicles – wagons and carriages – that also drove on and over the lines. Significant legislation had been passed in the latter half of the nineteenth century regarding the number and width of wheels that wagons had to employ, based on their weight, as these were the main culprits in destroying pavements. But the new difference in velocity defined the conflict.

The city sided with Carris Urbanos, banned the handcarts from using the rails in December 1902, and began enforcing the law in early January. On January 8, handcart workers, who made up a sizable contingent of the street's occupied laborers, went on strike and rioted in the street. The brawny strikers, each capable of dragging a half a ton single-handedly through the street, intimidated both scabs and police. At first, they overturned the cart of any colleague they caught not running his cart on the tram rails near Praça 15. Then, once a general strike had been successfully organized, they refused to move any goods at all, shutting down much of the city's internal commerce. Strikers now overturned the cart of any scab, on or off the rails, who dared to ignore the strike. President Rodrigues Alves, aware of the carters' grievances and the potential for violence, instructed the city police to use extreme caution. One newspaper reported that things were black in certain parts of the city: merchants "closed shops" as handcart workers "opened heads." There

George Ermakoff, *Juan Gutierrez: Images of Rio de Janeiro 1892–1896* (Rio de Janeiro: Capivara, 2001), 55.
[46] *Correio da Manhã*, Dec. 15, 1902.

were so many strikers and altercations that unfounded rumors spread that the strike was nothing less than an attempt to overthrow the republic and restore the monarchy. Handcart workers accused Mayor Pereira Passos of taking bread from the mouths of their children. Then, as the strike escalated to block the movement of all traffic, including the trams, carters chanted boisterously that "either we pass over the rails or the Mayor passes over our cadavers." The street was their forum, and they did not cede their ground. They asserted to the mayor, "[W]e are not asses – with or without tails." Police whistles, commanding the protesters to move aside, had no effect, so the police desisted, awaiting further orders.[47]

Carris Urbanos maintained an ongoing newspaper campaign against the handcarts. The company mocked the carters for their weakness relative to electric motors, suggesting that they, mere humans, were too puny to move their loads expeditiously and should hence step aside. They also played the modernization card by damning handcarts as an outmoded form of transportation, a disgraceful display that ought to be eradicated on modern avenues like so many other obsolete and unfashionable street behaviors. Handcarts were placed in the same dated category as slaves carrying ladies in sedan chairs. Downtown businesses, however, which suffered because of the lack of haulage, came to support the carters' cause. Facing business pressure, violent protest, and commerce coming to a halt, Pereira Passos backed down and permitted the carters to use the rails. The carters kept a showing on the streets for a few more days for good measure, more in celebration than anything else, but then went back to work on the rails.[48] Others in the city also celebrated. The Theatro Lucinda posted announcements on their marquee of a lecture on the question of handcarts on Carris Urbano's iron rails, of a play entitled "Leiteiros sem Leite" ("Milkmen without Milk"), a reference to the tram company's failure, and of a new song, "Esta Bom. Deixe" ("Things Are Good; Leave Them Be"), which was a refrain against a variety of changes being imposed on the city by the mayor.[49] The handcarters' victory was as unusual as it was lasting. While many former, unmodern users of the street were banned and regulated, the handcarters' service was so essential to the city's downtown streets that they remained a fixture.

---

[47] *Correio da Manhã*, Jan. 8, 1903; *O Paiz*, Jan. 8, 1903.

[48] *O Paiz*, Feb. 27, 1903; *O Piaz*, Apr. 22, 1904; *O Pharol*, Juiz de Fora, Jan. 9, 1903.

[49] *Correio da Manhã*, Feb. 27, 1903. "Leiteiros sem Leite" could also refer to new laws against selling fresh milk in the street, but trams were also known as *leiteiros*.

Even in 1937, there were still 4,496 handcarts licensed in the city.[50] They were finally banned in the 1950s when motorists succeeded in their arguments that handcarts as well as streetcars were backward vestiges, too slow for the city streets. Just the same, till the end, motorists liked to place their driver's side wheels on the streetcar rails to smooth their ride on potholed streets.

Among the broader motives that led to the building of the Avenue was the desire to give the public good precedent over private interests. This was nothing new, and throughout the colonial period and empire officials argued in favor of the common good and frequently legislated in that vein. So, in some sense, the early Republic was a continuation of a paternalistic culture among city officials. Even if the tram companies were in their legal rights to obstruct common carters in the use of the rails, the city eventually sided with the latter, although admittedly only after threats of violence and disorder. But other acts suggest this was not outside their overall interest. The building of the Avenue itself was a triumph of public space over private property. One might argue that it was really built to benefit private real estate interests, but much of the Avenue was lined with public buildings, and, as we will see, many of the private ones were of little real utility because of their shallow lots. The public space the Avenue created was more important to both its builders and receivers than the private edifices that lined it.

The means with which the city dealt with the growing traffic problem also suggests a strong interest in protecting the commons for the common good. With the rise of the trams and the growing number of wheeled vehicles of all kinds, especially in the city's commercial areas, congestion on the narrow downtown streets had become a real if intermittent issue by the 1880s. To the city's credit, officials recognized that most of the city's traffic was pedestrian, and spatial street reforms reflected that. The most common solution to traffic before the Avenue was simply to increase the number of streets that were demarcated as one-way, but in a number of cases such as Rua da Alfandega, Rua do Carmo, and other busy colonial streets, traffic was considered so difficult that the city banned wheeled vehicles on them entirely between 9 AM and 10 PM, just as they had decades before on Ouvidor. Local businesses complained and even appealed to the constitution's guarantee of free commerce, but to no avail. Handcarts, which were granted exception, certainly benefitted

---

[50] *Anuário estatístico do Distrito Federal, 1938* (Rio de Janeiro: Serviço Gráphico do IBGE), 130.

because of they did not have to compete with horse-drawn vehicles. Residents of these streets also probably found these blockages beneficial to making pedestrian movement easier and in keeping the street in a state that allowed activities other than mere movement. City officials were increasingly interested in movement, but pedestrians were given some spatial priority over vehicles, even on the new, broad street designs. In the 1875 proposal for an avenue, the designers recommended a width of 40 meters, 22 (the majority) of which would be dedicated to sidewalks.[51] On Avenida Central itself, which was 33 meters wide from frontage to frontage, 17 meters, just more than half, were dedicated to pedestrians as well. And in São Paulo in 1910, some streets were widened by demolishing buildings, but the curbs were left in place, meaning all the gains went to pedestrians, a sharp contrast to New York City in the same period, which was adding automotive lanes to its avenues, such as Fifth Avenue, entirely at the expense of pedestrian sidewalk space.[52] In Rio, some observed that pedestrian traffic increased its speed and fluidity, and residents experienced fewer bumps and foot treadings as a result of the expanding sidewalks.[53]

These changes did indicate the beginnings of a zonation of street use: the roadbed for vehicles and sidewalks for pedestrians. But few pedestrians obeyed these changing expectations, and for decades to come citizens would walk on the street, although not without increasing risk. The expansion of pedestrian spaces introduced Rio to the "footing," a borrowing from the English. The broad sidewalks on fashionable avenues invited strolling for the sake of strolling, the procession gone informal. This had long been common on Sundays and holidays in the Spanish American square, and it had some precedents in Brazil, but it was reported as something of a new phenomenon in Rio, probably because now it had greater appeal to the upper classes. The "footing" became a bit of a rage within a couple years of the Avenue's completion, as well as along Beira Mar Avenue; they were places to see and be seen.[54] The street's utility as leisure recreation pleased the elite, and society magazines published

[51] Decreto 29, Dec. 24, 1894, AGCRJ, 58-1-14, folha 52; "Veiculos," 1881–1890, AGCRJ, 373, 58-1-3, folhas 55, 277, 287, 301, 304; Primeiro Relatório da Comissão de Melhoramentos da Cidade do Rio de Janeiro, 1875, in Verena Andreatta, *Cidades quadradas*, anexos, 13.

[52] *O Estado de São Paulo*, Dec. 10, 1910, 4; McShane, *Down the Asphalt Path*, 217.

[53] *Fon Fon*, Mar. 3, 1910.

[54] Rosa Maria Barboza de Araujo. *A vocação do prazer: A cidade e a família no Rio de Janeiro Republicano* (Rio de Janeiro: Rocco, 1993), 326–28.

photographs and lists of prominent strollers on the Avenue each week, with comments on their fashionable dress, lovely daughters, and sizeable shopping bags.[55]

Public space also took precedence over private interests, namely the hundreds of private kiosks in Rio's streets and squares that had initially sold papers and magazines, but which increasingly offered helpings of coffee, rum, cheese, fried fish, and lottery tickets – whatever the public was buying. This was a relatively recent private street invasion with its origins in the 1870s. Kiosks served the needs of the working classes who gathered around them at all hours of the day. They were not owned by independent shopkeepers but by a single large corporation, the Companhia dos Quiosques. The kiosks, whose tin and wood bodies were usually in an exotic, orientalist style, collectively occupied a not insignificant portion of public space, especially in the downtown. Vendors strategically placed their stalls permanently on the squares, sidewalks, and streets – often half on the sidewalk and half on the street bed propped up with loose cobbles – to serve customers at the street's busiest points. In 1911, Pereira Passos denied their license, indemnified the company at a price significantly below its stated value, and removed the kiosks, sometimes with violence and fire. Thus one more private impediment on the street was removed for the benefit of the broader public and their collective movement, as Pereira Passos saw it.[56]

Hence, whether tram companies or kiosk vendors, the public interest in the street overrode private claims. The press joked that when Pereira Passos vacationed in Egypt in 1907, he had suggested to the Egyptians that they not only place the Nile conveniently in a culvert, but that they turn the Sphinx and the deserts into public *logradouros* with Sunday bands, and that they dismantle the pyramids, employing the stones to pave new streets. Pereira Passos would be remembered by his contemporaries, for good and ill, for converting private edifices into public spaces and placing private street uses subordinate to those public.[57]

[55] *Fon Fon*, from its inception, had a weekly column entitled "Na Calçada" documenting the fashionable *Who's Who* on the Avenue.

[56] Benchimol, *Pereira Passos*, 282. Augusto Malta, a supporter of Pereira Passos' reforms, photographed a score of kiosks in 1911; he also recorded the burning of kiosk #124 in 1906 that dared to post a banner attacking the mayor; see Ermakoff, *Augusto Malta e o Rio de Janeiro, 1903–1936*, 25, 98–107.

[57] *Fon Fon*, Apr. 27, 1907.

EMBRACING THE AVENUE'S BEAUTY

Over time, and particularly in hindsight as citizens responded to the new Avenue, beauty, more than hygiene or circulation, became the focus of civic attention. Even for Pereira Passos, a practical engineer who had spent most of his life in railroads and hydrology, moving passengers, goods, and sewage, the new Avenue was not just a colonial-dectomy, an amputation of the hills, or a draining of the city's infectious abscesses. Above all, it was to be cosmetic surgery that would create of the new public space an expression of Brazil's cultural refinement. If function was the talk before construction, form got nearly all the attention thereafter, and most of the project's critics changed their tunes as the Avenue emerged fully formed. In a eulogy to Pereira Passos at his death in 1913, Mario Pederneiras praised the ex-mayor for being the best friend of the Brazilian street. "Of all his vast and active glories and competencies, this, the transformation of the street in Rio de Janeiro, is that which most consecrates his dear memory and illustrious name." And not only did he decorate, tree, pave, and line the street with magnificent buildings, he also lived the street, the Avenue being his preferred place to be and where he took his frequent walks. Pederneiras claimed the mayor had a bohemian and free spirit, "and the life of the street seduced and enchanted him."[58]

Beauty stood front and center almost from the opening of the Avenue's line of sight. In July 1903, one newspaper ran a front-page spread listing the streets that Rio's most noted poets, men who were supposed to know beauty, identified as the most lovely in the city. Pederneiras chose São Clemente in Botafogo; Guimarães Passos elected Senador Vergueiro; Coelho Neto nominated his own street, Rua Rozo. A few, including Euclides da Cunha, chose Avenida Central, even though at the time it was little more than a sunlit pile of rubble. In June 1903, *O Malho* published a cover depicting the yet unfinished avenue as a beautiful, bare-shouldered blond woman equably contemplating her admirers who have caught her regarding herself in a mirror. The mirror's reflection shows a straight, graceful avenue lined with tall buildings and lovely trees.[59] Once completed in 1906, admirers of the Avenue's beauty tripped over each other with ever more formidably supernal adjectives: glorious, delightsome, transforming, stirring, stately, modern, and, above all, civilizing. The choice of words betrays that this was beauty in the service of

[58] *Fon Fon*, Mar. 15, 1913.
[59] *Gazeta de Notícias*, Jul. 5, 1903; *O Malho*, Jun. 13, 1903, cover.

something greater, the evidence of Rio's cultural and material arrival. Jeffrey Needell writes that the Avenue was an "annunciation, ... a monument to Brazil's progress."[60] The Avenue, a tiny fraction of national territory, symbolized, all by itself, Brazil's arrival as a civilized nation. At the Avenue's tenth anniversary, the space was still working its magic on locals and foreigners alike. Rio's writers spoke of the city's transformation with a glee undiminished, and for years thereafter, foreign travelers and journalists snapped the Avenue's photograph to publish Rio's modernization in books and papers abroad.[61]

Like many symbols, the Avenue's beauty and enlightened appearance were only a thin veneer. This is not to discount its importance or its power. Culturally, appearances mattered. On the Avenue, the asphalt, the mosaic sidewalks, the window glass and dressing, and even the frontages were skin thin, literally often no more than a few centimeters in thickness, but they served their purpose well, and that was to give grace to the very real space and volume that the Avenue created. These façades too were widely celebrated and published, first by Rio's pioneer photographer, Marc Ferrez. His album, *Avenida Central*, published in Rio and Paris, presented more than a hundred images of the Avenue's new façades that, much like colonial buildings, tied themselves to the street with myriad doors and an abundance of windows, many of which had small or false balconies.[62] Windows of the upper floors had their shutters thrown wide open, and on parade and festival days, they filled with spectators.

The Avenue's architecture, in a modern Beaux-Arts style that nearly all agreed was lovely, was itself spatially shallow. It would be fair to call it a facial or façadal architecture. The new wide frontages of the buildings were not mere façades, for they did in fact front actual buildings, but the buildings were often only a few meters deep. The city could not afford to purchase more than a narrow lot or two beyond the Avenue's new trajectory, which left them building plots of little depth. Unfortunately, in part because their shallow depth made them of little utility, few of the Avenue's original buildings survive. Many were shallower than the sidewalks that fronted them. This too was a modern contrast: the city's

[60] Needell, *Tropical Belle Époque*, 33.
[61] *Fon Fon*, Jan. 1, 1916; Alured Gray Bell, *The Beautiful Rio de Janeiro* (London: William Heinemann, 1915); William Gibbs McAdoo, "Rio de Janeiro, 1916," Photographic Album, Library of Congress Prints and Photographs Division; Hugh Gibson, *Rio* (New York, NY: Doubleday, Doran and Co. Inc., 1937).
[62] Marc Ferrez, *Avenida Central: 8 de Março 1903–15 de Novembro 1906* (Paris: Erhard, n.d.).

colonial buildings had been very narrow and very deep; the Avenue's constructions were wide, some extending the whole block, but startlingly shallow.

But they were deep enough to serve their main purpose, which was not to house offices, shelter residents, or even display and sell European consumer goods: their main purpose was to gracefully enclose the new Avenue. The Avenue's creation was about the street, the appearance and utility of a public space. Few of the Avenue's buildings had strong individual identities but ran together as a large curtain. They were to be appreciated as the walls of the Avenue, not as individual monuments. The façades were all built on a strict alignment, all vetted by committee, all different yet coherent in style, and all of a height that maintained roughly the same street proportion of width to height as colonial streets, but on an enlarged scale. They delimited and decorated the Avenue's primary function, which again was neither sanitation nor circulation. Nor was it merely shameless ostentation. Pereira Passos himself believed that the Avenue's space would serve as the "simple 'habitat' of a civilized people," using the Latin term "habitat" to express his understanding that the street was a place to inhabit, a chamber for civilized populations.[63] And when residents thought of the street, they still thought about it in human scale rather than monumental or circulatory terms: one publication showed no interest in how many new buildings there were, in how many offices were available for rent, in how hygienic the asphalt was, nor in how many vehicles could flow over its course per minute; it declared with pride that the new Avenue, 59,400 new square meters of public space, could enfold 237,600 street users, assuming four persons per square meter. The street was still primarily seen as a space for people – people on foot.[64]

GLORIOUS HETEROPIA

An essential hope of the Avenue's designers was that if they built it, the street's age-old problems would vacate the premises. However, despite the hope that the poor would depart and leave the Avenue as an exclusive elite pleasure ground, or would self-reform in their newly civilized environment, the unwashed, the noisy, the criminal, the handcarter, and the prostitute did not go away. They behaved on the new Avenue as they

---

[63] Cited in Luiz Edmundo, *O Rio de Janeiro do meu tempo* (Rio de Janeiro: Imprensa Nacional, 1938), 27.
[64] *Fon Fon*, Aug. 27, 1910.

had in the old streets. The so-called *Bota Abaixo,* the "knocking down," as locals referred to it, did not banish its refugees to the city's outskirts. If affordable housing was decimated in the valley, it began to flourish on the peaks.[65] And all those citizens who went to the hills and the northern suburbs at night to sleep, descended upon the city by day to work, shop, and recreate. The elite could not spatially dominate the street, and their hoped for civic utopia remained a heterotopia, a space that refused to order itself according to the expectations of authorities.[66] One newspaper prophesied at the Avenue's commencement that such dreams of exclusionary modernity would end in the same elitist's nightmares. It reported old Mayor Pereira Passos, nodding off in his official chair, dreaming of a city that shown golden in its sanitary cleanliness, its broad, graceful Avenue, more beautiful than that of Buenos Aires. But while admiring his Avenue, he spies coming in his direction hundreds of trundling handcarts pulled by athletic men who unceremoniously run him down on the pavement. He is startled awake, feeling the pain of an elbow that had been badly positioned on the armchair. He dozes again, this time to envision thousands of cows in the street and men crying "Milk, Milk," only to awaken to hear the cry of a real milkman just outside City Hall, despite recent legislation prohibiting his existence.[67] You could, with some success, ban kiosks and cows, but the street still belonged to the people – people of all sorts.

Still, some saw what they wanted on the Avenue. Pederneiras claimed by 1912 that "the typical rube, a genuine street feature, disappeared with the Avenues and with Civilization," replaced by politicians, poets, and beautiful women. He even named "Mamae" and "29," two of the Ouvidor's best-known eccentrics described by Luis Edmundo, as among the disappeared. They and their related company of buskers, beggars, and hawkers had all been "cut off by civilization or cast out to the unknown corners of the dark suburbs."[68] But those with less romantic eyes still saw much of the same old company in the streets, new and old. Beggars, many of them children, were ubiquitous, as the continuous calls for their removal or institutionalization made evident. In 1911, a photographer

---

[65] Maurício de Almeida Abreu, "Reconstruindo uma história esquecida: origem e expansão inicial das favelas do Rio de Janeiro," *Espaço & Debates* 37 (1994): 34–46.

[66] Tim Edensor, "The Culture of the Indian Street," in *Images of the Street: Planning, Identity and Control in Public Space,* edited by N. Fyfe (New York, NY: Routledge, 1998), 218–20, describes many contemporary Indian streets as heteropias despite colonialism's attempts to reduce them to single uses.

[67] *O Paiz,* Jan. 11, 1903.   [68] *Fon Fon,* Sep. 21, 1912.

for the magazine *Careta* captured a poor man in suit coat and sandals extending a simple cap with his good arm to two well-dressed ladies in extravagant hats. His right sleeve is rolled up to expose an amputated limb. In the women, there is a familiar reticence mingled with the demands of expressions of public charity: one woman, conversing with the man, opens her closely held purse while her friend looks on with obvious concern. All three of them stand in the street, not on the sidewalk, and the positions of their feet – his squared to his benefactors and the women's turned tentatively, the weight shifted to one foot, ready to move on – speak to the nature of such cross-class exchanges.[69] The street was the only place where such interactions were inevitable, even on the Avenue, and Lima Barreto noted that by 1915, the city's social center, which embraced elegant dames as well as persistent peddlers and "those without hope," had unmistakably moved from Ouvidor to the Avenue.[70]

If the elegant Avenue could not exclude the undesirables, cast them out as Pederneiras claimed it might, many among the elite still hoped that its beauties, polity, and urbanity could refine the people's dress, speech, and behavior. Just as promoters of the City Beautiful Movement argued, the right urban environment would shape and determine the proper deportment and civil discourse among the city's inhabitants and users. Pederneiras joined fellow writer Luiz Gonzaga for a stroll along the entire Avenue in 1907. Taking their refreshment at a "modernizing" café table on the sidewalk, they noted how bright and cheerful the citizens had become because of the Avenue. Before, in the old streets, "we were lethargic, bad humored, indecisive in stride, our faces jaundiced and callused with annoyance." Today was a brighter day, citizens walked with a smile and a spring in their step, because civilization had been "published" on the Avenue. Gonzaga noted that Rio's women in particular were now more beautiful than ever as a result of the Avenue. This new perception, he insisted, should not be attributed to his advancing age. The new, form-fitting French fashions certainly did not hurt their cause either, but what feminine beauty really needed was lots of sunlight, lots of space, and a smooth surface over which to pass. On the dark, crowded, uneven colonial streets, women could not be fully appreciated, nor could they walk with their common grace, Gonzaga believed. It is probably little

---

[69] *Careta*, Sep. 9, 1911. See *Fon Fon*, Feb. 15, 1913, as one example of many complaints of beggars.

[70] Afonso Henriques de Lima Barreto, *Toda Cronica*, vol. 1, edited by R. Beatriz and R. Valenca (Rio de Janeiro: Agir Editora, 2004), 212.

wonder that men of previous periods, such as Machado de Assis, seemed to have been connoisseurs of women's arms, because in the old crowded streets, they were all one could see of the female body, in brief glimpses. But on the new Avenue, Gonzaga argued, smooth pavements gave woman a stately, queenly gait, and the new buildings "framed" her entire body and all its curves.[71]

But these, however real, were superficial changes compared to the kind of modernization and civilization that men such as Pederneiras and Gonzaga hoped for. Pederneiras contradicted his own civilizing claims about the modern, produced street by observing in 1913 that citizens still shouted too loudly, still went about in their shirtsleeves, still walked barefoot, still spoke with cigars clenched in their teeth, and still bumped into others and stepped on toes without asking pardon. Rio's citizens, he lamented, remained vulgar despite their palatial surroundings. European immigrants arrived on Rio's Europeanized avenues properly attired in suit jackets and shined shoes, but as soon as they saw the locals running around the street shirt-sleeved and unshod, the immigrants went native.[72] But even the forward-looking Pederneiras could be ambivalent about the rapid changes he saw. On another stroll along the Avenue, his companion asked if there was among the stately buildings and now honking automobiles anything at all evident of the old, unlovely realities before the reforms. Both agreed there was not – until they spotted an old Bahian woman peddling peanuts in her striking, white traditional dress near the Palácio Monroe. Pederneiras exulted that yes, there she was, "opposing the clamor of a dominating Civilization with the simple geniality of her primitive trade." The same woman was depicted on the cover of *O Malho* with the ambivalent label "a dying type."[73] The street would remain a casual, comfortable place for the lower classes, and such behavior persisted, working against the city's oft-repeated maxim: "Rio Civilizes Itself."

The first murder on the Avenue, in early 1906, proved a genuine shock to those who had hopes the Avenue might civilize its users. Murders and attempted murders in Rio, a large percentage perpetrated with handguns, were reported at least weekly in the newspapers, so the shooting on the Avenue had nothing remarkable about it other than its taking place on the

---

[71] *Kosmos*, Nov. 1907. Evidence of Machado de Assis' fond appreciation of the female arm can be found in a number of his works, but particularly in his short story "Uns braços."

[72] *Fon Fon*, "Diario das Ruas," Nov. 22, 1911; see also Araújo, *A vocação do prazer*, 333.

[73] *Kosmos*, "Tradições," Oct. 1906; *O Malho*, Oct. 1, 1904, cover.

Avenue. Accidents and crimes, including murder (except titillating crimes of passion), were generally placed in the newspapers' middle pages, but this felony went on the front pages, and the weekly magazines highlighted it as well. Two working men who lived respectively on the steep streets Ladeira da Conceição and Ladeira de João Homem, both located in the Conceição *favela* at the north end of the Avenue, exchanged eight shots as one chased the other down the Avenue toward Largo da Carioca. The pursuer, José Joaquim de Souza, a carpenter, aged twenty-three, hit his victim, Manuel Hermida, in the neck, severing the carotid artery. Hermida, after dutifully giving his name and address to authorities, expired, his blood staining the Avenue's brand new sidewalk tiles. The *Revista da Semana* illustrated the altercation in an image that expressed astonishment that a brutal crime could happen on a civilized Avenue. A well-dressed woman walks passively up the street, her shopping in her arm, her eyes looking demurely to the ground, the Avenue's lovely façades as backdrop, while directly behind her, unnoticed and certainly unsuspected, two men, guns drawn, fire at one another as if it were the Wild West. The barbarous event was called the Avenue's baptism by blood, a traitorous entrance into the New Year, one that betrayed the highest expectations for the city's civilized birth. The Avenue, given voice, spoke: "Only in this am I like other streets." But it was a conceit. Other than in its superficial beauties and its lack of residents, this street and its activities were very much like other streets in the city. Appearances, despite all hopes, did not change behavior, and the poor, as the elite press saw it, continued to run amuck on the public domain and endanger the city's civilized citizens.[74]

The modern street's conceits, and those of its builders, were in danger. The more the elite patted each other on the back for their creations, fashions, and supposed modernity, the more they expressed a hostile arrogance against the poor. The rich wanted respect, but what their pride perceived in the poor was envy. Envy might have its own rewards, but it carried liabilities. Listen to a conversation between two successful men of the city:

My friend, everything in this world causes envy, a furious envy, which manifests itself in looks and gestures, which seek occasion to explode, provoke, and insult.

It's true. They envy you an article of clothing, the position that you've conquered, the obvious happiness you possess, the advantages that you've earned.

---

[74] *Jornal do Brasil*, Feb. 5, 1906; *Revista da Semana*, Feb. 11, 1906.

Then begins the cursing! Outrages arise! And thus forms and commences the formidable campaign against the envied individual.

Today, one fears walking on this Avenue. There are those who look on us with an injurious displeasure. There are those whose demeanor towards us is a provocation. There are those who turn their backs to us in fury. There are even those who with intent shove and bump into us with their bodies.

Yes, there are times when I desire to walk in the city equipped as an explorer of the African continent, with a loaded blunderbuss at the ready.[75]

Although there is exaggeration here, the poorly veiled racism is real, and the fear of the working man is palpable. There had been a long tradition of defiance by subordinates to their superiors in Brazil, from the plantation to the barracks, a reality that reportedly worsened as the new republic, established in 1889, promised greater equality.[76] The new streets, even if clean, beautiful, and modern, still embraced the lowest classes, and hence still held threats of impudence and even violence against the self-styled civil classes. If inadvertent collisions could not be avoided on the colonial lanes, now that there was sufficient space, such bumps appeared to carry malicious intent. Legislation could only go so far to remove the poor in their various categories, and even if successful, they just came back to the street in different guises. The rich could exclude the poor from their clubs, operas, and art galleries, and suburbanization had begun to segregate rich and poor residences. But the street, as commons, remained contested.

Just as men could better appreciate the beauty of women on the broad Avenue, the poor could not fail to see the obvious pretensions of their betters walking on spaces that, while beautiful, also suggested they were being left behind spatially. Maybe the most common complaint about the Avenue was that its benefits and beauties had not reached other streets.[77] Street improvements would not come to hillside *favelas* or commuter neighborhoods, many of which were repeatedly characterized as having no pavement, many potholes, open sewers, and none of the many police who made the Avenue their beat. In the mid-1920s, a radical workers' magazine, *A Classe Operaria*, employed spatial arguments to raise worker

[75] *Fon Fon*, Sep. 9, 1916.

[76] João Pinheiro Chagas, *De bond: alguns aspectos da civilização brasileira* (Lisbon: Livraria Moderna, 1897), 180. He identified coachman, streetcar operators, and even waiters as among the most impudent of Rio's citizens.

[77] Residents' complaints about the condition of streets were rampant in newspapers and seem to increase with the completion of the Avenue. The *Jornal do Brasil* was among those that printed reader complaints. Browse September and October of 1909 for many examples. See also *Fon Fon*, Jun. 4, 1910, for an argument for better distribution of the city's street improvement funds since taxes were paid everywhere.

consciousness, particularly of municipal street workers. The editors asked: How is that you work at poor pay to maintain our downtown streets, where the rich can travel easily in cars, but you commute hours in perspiration just to get to and from your homes on muddy, dusty *ladeiras*? How is it that our *garis*, who pick up bourgeois trash day after day, themselves live on streets piled high with filth and permeated with stench? And how is it that those of you who work for the city's emergency services, the Assistência Médica, who provide first aid in fast vehicles to the rich in their palaces and mansions, watch your own children teeter at death's brink because you live on steep, poorly maintained streets where ambulances cannot or dare not go?[78] The poor did not just lose housing with the city's remodeling. They lost out on the quantifiable benefits of modernity. These included aesthetic but valuable superficialities, such as well-appointed façades, decorative pavements, and street cleaning, but they also included the more concrete benefits of potable water, sewers, police, and ambulance service.

But they still had the street. Shy working girls walked the fashionable avenues and streets in pairs after their day shifts. Before catching the crowded streetcars to their distant or hillside homes on dirty, unlit streets, they ended each weekday strolling arm in arm under the cast-iron streetlamps and between the beautiful storefronts. This too was an exercise in envy, though without the threatening behavior. The girls moved slowly, pausing now and then to huddle before shop windows. Wearing modest skirts and thin, printed blouses, always meticulously laundered, the same items of clothing they had worn the day before, they whispered in awe at the displays – hats, dresses, handbags, silk fans, inevitably presented against velvet backdrops – that they could not afford. "Just look at that, Jesuina." "Ah, girl! How beautiful!" "It must be expensive, don't you think?" For the most part, they were ignored other than by the occasional lovelorn clerk. One of the girls dared ask the price of a strange carpet. "Beautiful, aren't they," the shopkeeper replied. "It took 40 ostriches just to make the smallest one. Would you like to buy it," he teased. The girls laugh in their humiliation: "No, sorry, no. Just asking out of curiosity."[79]

Contrary to what João do Rio claimed in this chapter's epigraph, the street did not equalize its users. The street, because it was common, was a space where the social gulfs between rich and poor, black and white, men and women, and natives and immigrants, were on constant display.

[78] *A Classe Operária*, Rio de Janeiro, May 1, 1925.
[79] João do Rio, *A alma encantadora das ruas*, 101–05.

While working girls might find the courage to address natty shopkeepers, the men who served as the gatekeepers to luxury, the women did not venture to enter the elite shops. They did not belong. Had they tried to step across the threshold from public to some private spaces – the chic retail shops, the private clubs, the fancy restaurants, the national library, or the opera house – they might have been physically obstructed or forcefully removed. But significantly, the exclusive world that Pereira Passos and his colleagues had tried to create of the city's downtown streets still only began at the thresholds, as it always had. As fancy as Ouvidor and the Avenida were, they remained, as all streets, public commons. These poor girls knew they were not considered full citizens in their own city. They lived on the margins, not quite *gente*, a term used to describe those who were deemed full members in polite and political society. But they still belonged on the street, and the commons gave all a place to literally rub shoulders with those who were different, whether they liked it or not. The Avenue, for a period, served its primary purpose: a place to be and a place for all. The American Harry Franck, who visited Rio a decade after the Avenue's inauguration, noted that "the direct and hurrying northerner comes to realize that the Avenida is not designed to be merely a passageway from somewhere to somewhere else. It *is* somewhere itself."[80]

The elite had not yet found the means to exclude or separate themselves from undesirables on the public commons. However, they had now produced spaces – linear, broad, and smooth – on which a new technology was about to enhance their social separation by transforming a place to be into a place between. At the Avenue's completion in 1906, nobody could have foreseen the car's stunning rise.[81] But as the automobiles arrived, their first fields of operation were these broad, unobstructed spaces that had been created primarily to beautify rather than move the city. Soon, to be in the Avenue was to be in the way. The avenues were the first to experience the automobile's transformations but also formed the scenes of debates about the changing meanings of working, talking, dancing, and even walking on the commons.

[80] Harry A. Franck, *Working North from Patagonia* (New York, NY: The Century Co., 1921), 176.
[81] *The Rio News*, Sep. 8, 1890, opined that the proposed Beira Mar Avenue would have been great for improving the quality and number of carriages in the city, which would come out in hundreds instead of handfuls, in refining the breeding of horses, in making excellent space for strolling, the so-called footing, and in improving bicycling. But they would not predict the car's predilection for the space.

3

Putting the Car in Carnival

Avenida Rio Branco

And suddenly, it's the age of the automobile. The snorting, transformative monster erupted amidst the rubble of the old city and, like magic, like nature, the harshest teacher, transformed everything.

João do Rio[1]

POLICE OFFICER: "You two cannot be there. You are blocking the traffic."
WOMAN: "Where, then, can we be?"

O Pirralho[2]

Brazil's first automobile, a Peugeot Type 3, was imported from France in the luggage of a future national hero. Acclaimed for his pioneering contributions to the birth of human flight, Alberto Santos Dumont was the first person to engineer powered flight, in a motored dirigible, and the second to build and fly a craft heavier than air, an accomplishment achieved in late 1906, publicly, before crowds, independent of the Wright brothers' contemporary, secretive work. In fact, the modern airplane's standard configuration follows Santos Dumont's designs rather than those of Wilbur and Orville Wright. His Damselfly was the first mass-produced aircraft, and by freely giving away the plans and licensing rights, he hoped the plane would be a technology that could potentially benefit all people.

In the early twentieth century, automobiles and airplanes – the two inventions that best expressed a modernizing world – were frequently

---

[1] João do Rio, *Vida vertiginosa* (Rio de Janeiro: Garnier, 1911), 1.
[2] *O Pirralho*, Sep. 1917 (first bi-monthly issue), 8.

spoken of in the same breath. And their motions were often compared. Gutzon Borglum witnessed an early flight piloted by Orville Wright, who, he wrote to a friend, "handled his [wings] like a chauffeur, and rode the air as deliberately as if he were passing over a solid macadam road."[3] Here were two personal machines that conquered space and time, not for the masses and the commodities of mass production, as had the train, but for the individual. From all other identities, what set apart the pilot and chauffeur, the model individualists of a new age, was the peculiar personal power to pack ever more meters into the second, kilometers into an hour, in the direction of one's choosing. As did the Wright brothers, Santos Dumont made patented contributions to the internal combustion engine, which was the horsepower behind both technologies. But if the engine's potency gave greater acclaim to Santos Dumont the pilot, Santos Dumont the chauffeur, by his less feted introduction of the car, had the greater impact on a nation's modernization, urban forms, and vital statistics.

The 1892 Peugeot that Santos Dumont and his brother Henrique drove around the passable streets of São Paulo was little more than a four-wheeled bicycle steered with a tiller and powered by a 3.5 horsepower engine. It could "race" at 11 miles per hour, which was frightfully fast at the time, and of course drew a great deal of attention. As a teenage driving pioneer in France, which was his grandfather's homeland, Santos Dumont had been forbidden by the Parisian police to stop his car in the public street because it attracted such a crowd as to obstruct all other traffic.[4] So one can imagine that he drew crowds in São Paulo as well, but the reactions of street folk were not always in the categories of excitement and exhilaration. The automobile's infernal banging, its relentless panting of noxious smoke, and its apparent demonic possession, a contraption that moved with no apparent mover, caused some early observers to cry "devil," "demon," and "monster," associating the automobile with hell's minions.

We do not know with certainty when the first automobile arrived on Rio's streets, but among them was a French steam-powered Serpollet, which the abolitionist journalist José do Patrocínio imported in 1893. He enjoyed giving friends rides, but many refused the invite out of fear: "Sorry, but I have a family to support." Olavo Bilac, a fellow poet and

---

[3] Private letter from Gutzon Borglum, Sep. 10, 1908, cited in Tom D. Crouch, *Wings: A History of Aviation from Kites to the Space Age* (New York, NY: W. W. Norton & Co., 2003), 6.

[4] Alberto Santos Dumont, *My Airships: The Story of My Life* (London: Grant Richards, 1904), 28–29.

newspaperman, was not one to forego a new experience, despite the peril. After terrorizing a few pedestrians on the city's narrow streets, Bilac himself took the wheel and turned toward the hills of Tijuca. But the velocity exceeded his ability, and the vehicle crashed into a ditch. Both men were thrown clear, getting off unscathed, but the car was a total wreck and had to be removed with "oxen and heavy chains." Patrocínio quipped that as he had failed to have the car formally christened, the beast died without sacraments and had hence gone straight back to the hell from which it had come.[5] Patrocínio remained as strident a promoter of mechanical modernity as he had been a tenacious opponent of slavery. He praised the machine, as he did abolition, for its power to make Brazil civilized. He died suddenly in 1905 giving a public address extolling Santos Dumont's contributions to the modernizing world.

From these small but auspicious beginnings, the automobile would become a substantial spatial presence on Rio de Janeiro's streets. In a relative sense, the growth of the car in Rio de Janeiro was rather slow, when compared to the United States in particular, but also compared to Buenos Aires and even São Paulo. New York City had 31,000 vehicles in 1910 and 213,000 in 1920. In the US generally, there would be 8 million cars by 1920, and by 1926, one per household.[6] There were twelve passenger cars in Rio in 1905. By 1915, there were just 1,996. Actual growth rates ran a remarkable average of 53 percent per year to 1926, but still, by that date, there were fewer than 10,000 passenger cars in the Federal District, about one vehicle for every 150 inhabitants, if you include trucks.[7] But relative numbers belie the reality on the ground. Cars did not spread themselves over the breadth of Federal District; they were concentrated on a few of Rio's downtown streets. Significantly, more than half of the passenger cars in the District up to 1924 were taxicabs, a proportional presence downtown that declined only after 1927 when

[5] Coelho Neto, "Discurso de recepção," Oct. 31, 1905, Rio de Janeiro, Academia Brasileira de Letras, www.academia.org.br/academicos/mario-de-alencar/discurso-de-recepcao (accessed Nov. 15, 2015). This incident has been considered apocryphal, but Coelho Neto's account was pronounced at the 1905 election of Mário de Alencar to the Academia Brasileira de Letras to replace Patrocínio. Coelho Neto's speech formed an extended eulogy to Patrocínio's life and contributions, which, according to Coelho Neto, included introducing the car to Rio de Janeiro. João do Rio also referred to the incident in his *Vida vertiginosa* (Rio de Janeiro: Garnier 1911), 3–4.

[6] Clay McShane, *Down the Asphalt Path: The Automobile and the American City* (New York, NY: Columbia University Press, 1994), 105.

[7] Fernando Agenor de Noronha Santos, *Meios de transporte no Rio de Janeiro*, vol. 2 (Rio de Janeiro: Typografia do Jornal do Comércio, 1934), 107.

buses were introduced in any numbers.[8] The first automobiles in Brazil were chiefly urban phenomena. The *New York Times* reported optimistically in 1911 that Rio had 200 miles of paved streets to house the travel of American-made cars, but it lamented that the nation's highways were so poor that most cars could run no more than a few miles beyond the city limits.[9] The cars that arrived, mostly from Europe before World War I, and predominantly from the US thereafter, had the city as their only reasonable destination. Hence, a relatively small number of cars came to inhabit a notable spatial volume of the city's streets. A cartoon in two frames published in an automotive magazine in 1926 illustrated the change as well as any other evidence. In the first frame, dated 1900, there is one car, a primitive model not unlike that the one driven by Patrocínio, being chased down the street by a crowd of outraged pedestrians. In the second frame entitled "Today," hundreds of cars chase a single pedestrian running for his life.[10] This, of course, was an exaggeration. Pedestrians would outnumber automobiles on the city streets for much of the century and resisted the automobile's presence, reportedly refusing to run or even walk to make way for the car. But the car had become ubiquitous in the city center, effectively consuming more space than pedestrians, and the battle lines in what would be a long territorial conflict had been definitively drawn.

In 1912, Avenida Central, the space of interest in the previous chapter, was renamed Avenida Rio Branco, after the nation's most celebrated diplomat, the Baron of Rio Branco, who after remarkable service in securing Brazil's broad national borders, died in February that same year. The rechristening was timely because by the early teens the Avenue was already a new space, with new uses and meanings. The changes were not immediate. Unlike in the United States, where car growth was astounding and the streets were converted to motorways in a single generation, in Brazil, the process was slower. Yet, however slowly, the street became a space not just produced but dominated, and its benefits would be increasingly channeled to an elite class in ever-faster vehicles.

Generally, we associate modernism with change, but it is arguable that the city street saw more change and evolution over the course of the

---

[8] Howard H. Tewksbury, *The Automotive Market in Brazil* (Washington, DC: US Dept. of Commerce, 1930), 57–58.

[9] "Car Market in Brazil," *New York Times*, Feb. 7 1915; "Boom in the Auto Industry," New York Times, Oct. 29, 1911.

[10] *Automobilismo: a revista pratica do automovel*, Jul. 1926, 21.

nineteenth century, even in transportation, than it would in the twentieth. In the nineteenth-century commons, individuals were free to invent new uses for the street – commercial, recreational, religious, and communal – which tended to increase the diversity of its utilities, the pace of change, and the intensity of negotiation by which users competed for the resource. The dances changed, the songs changed, the commodities changed, the crimes changed, the festivals changed, even the names of the streets changed. With the arrival of the automobile, the street's diversity declined and negotiations became lopsided. The street would still see change, but it was largely change by elimination and simplification to serve the single utility of automotive movement. Thomas Hughes has suggested that modernity's urban technologies – primarily new technical systems such as subways, elevators, and skyscrapers – transformed the city from a simple, two-dimensional space to one of three dimensions, and it is true that such systems allowed the city to take on a stunning vertical aspect.[11] However, on streets where automobiles would dominate, quite the opposite occurred: in both perception and utility, the car simplified public spaces, reducing them from three-dimensional volumes to the two-dimensional line. And once automobility fully emplaced itself, Rio's streets would largely express continuity.

AUTOMOTIVE ATTRACTIONS: SPEED, STATUS, AND SPACE

In addition to the usual automotive attractions, such as the practical benefits of the car's economy, its mobility, and its powerful associations with independence, freedom, and modernity,[12] sources suggest there were three particular charms that drove the adoption of the automobile in Rio: play, display, and spatial power. For a nation that had only recently emancipated its slaves and had guaranteed "freedom of movement" to all its citizens with the 1891 Constitution,[13] it is surprising how rarely freedom appears in sources related to the car. The car's appeal and

---

[11] Thomas P. Hughes, *Human-Built World: How to Think about Technology and Culture* (Chicago, IL: University of Chicago Press, 2004), 50.

[12] For motives for car adoption elsewhere, see James J. Flink, *America Adopts the Automobile, 1895–1910* (Cambridge, MA: MIT Press, 1970), ch. 3; Matthew Paterson, *Understanding Global Environmental Politics* (London: Macmillan, 2000), 101–05; and David Blanke, *Hell on Wheels: The Promise and Peril of America's Car Culture, 1900–1940* (Lawrence, KS: University of Kansas Press, 2007), especially ch. 3.

[13] *Constituição da República dos Estados Unidos do Brasil*, section 2, article 72, paragraph 22, Feb. 24, 1891, Palácio do Planalto, Presidência do Senado, www.planalto.gov.br /ccivil_03/Constituicao/Constituicao91.htm (accessed Jul. 1, 2015).

multiplication were driven less by a yearning for individual freedom, which the elite had long enjoyed, but rather as a novel means to express their social superiority, something to be flaunted to its best effect on city streets.[14]

This is not to discount that rapid movement had its attractions. For some, the car's capacity for speed was exhilarating fun. Among the first buyers were young thrill seekers such as Santos Dumont, the sons of wealthy fathers, who found on the city's new, broad avenues an un-policed playground for velocity. As the car's horsepower and numbers increased, spontaneous racing broke out, followed by official and rather dangerous competitive events that the city organized on downtown streets.[15] The earliest cars were not so much about getting anywhere because there was nowhere to go beyond the avenues. Motorists drove up the new avenues and then come right back down, over and over, as fast as conditions allowed. The Detroit journalist Karl Miller observed that "the Brazilian never hurries unless he is in an automobile and then he goes as fast as the gas will burn."[16] Miller insinuated that Brazilians were overcoming their tropical lethargy through the power of the machine, but the auto's appeal was more about visceral stimulation than utilitarian work. Cars and speed, Adelmar Tavares observed in 1926, were "a mania, a seduction we cannot resist, like gambling, cocaine, sex, and alcohol."[17] One promoter argued, without intended irony, that fast rides in powerful cars were the answer to the city's perennially high suicide rates. "Before you do something rash, take a ride in a car, if you can afford it, ... refresh your brain cells, and perhaps you will be converted back to good sense and reason."[18] Still, velocity was the seduction of a certain set of male motorists. As elsewhere, already by the 1920s, motorists began to prioritize reliability, mileage, and comfort over speed.[19]

---

[14] Blanke, *Hell on Wheels*, 72.

[15] In 1935, the city considered banning racing on city streets. "Prohibe as corridas de automóveis ou outros vehículos, em aposta de velocidade; com paracer contrário da Comissão de Justiça," Projecto n. 53-A, Câmara dos Deputados. Rio de Janeiro, 1935, IHGB.

[16] Karl W. Miller, "Sunny Rio: Beautiful, Bizarre, Unique," in *South America: Continent of Opportunities* (Detroit, MI: Evening News Association, 1925), 26, 28.

[17] Adelmar Tavares, "O automóvel perante a justiça criminal," *Vida Policial*, Jul. 25, 1926, 6.

[18] Gregório Garcia Seabra Junior, *Accidentes de automoveis: Delictos profissionaes dos automobilistas: doctrina, jurisprudencia, legislação* (Rio de Janeiro: Leite Ribeiro & Maurillo, 1918), 80; *Auto Federal*, Feb. 15, 1917, 7.

[19] Gijs Mom, *Atlantic Automobilism: Emergence and Persistence of the Car, 1895–1940* (New York, NY: Berghahn Books, 2015), 376, 382.

The automobile's second significant attraction to Brazilians was its growing association with high social status. The car, at first, was questionably fashionable, but by the 1910s, it was eminently so. That cars were prized as markers of social status is an observation so obvious it needs no belaboring, but in Brazil it takes on a special significance because unlike in the US where there was soon one car per family, the car in Brazil would remain an exclusive status symbol for the entire century. In the United States, per capita income permitted the widespread adoption of the car, and after a period of concern radically expressed by Woodrow Wilson who feared that the "possession of a motor car is such an ostentatious display of wealth that it will stimulate socialism," Americans could characterize the car's success as the appending of a technological democracy to an existing political democracy. All American drivers were not economic equals, but broad car ownership made of them civic equals.[20] What displayed one's status was the model and age of the car one drove; velocity itself belonged to everyone, even those who drove dilapidated Chevrolets. Brazilian authorities desired the car's technological symbolism and political benefits for Brazilians, too, but low per-capita income and stark income inequality made repeating the success of the car's rapid conquest of North America an impossibility. So the car in Brazil acquired strong and often rather negative status associations that endured. Roberto DaMatta suggests that over time the main social distinction on Brazil's streets was no longer how one dressed or the color of one's skin but who had a car and who did not.[21]

Thus, the arrival of the car invented two oppositional categories: chauffeur and pedestrian. Technologies create vocabularies. Before the arrival of the automobile, people in the street had been referred to as people, citizens, souls, and most commonly as residents. None of these terms had strong class connotations. One term that was found in general use in the late nineteenth century was that of "transient" (*transeunte*); its use appears to have been created by the arrival of the streetcars. Earlier in the century "transient" was the equivalent of "foreigner," but over time it came to refer to persons on foot in the street, to distinguish them from riders of public transit who were newly

---

[20] Blanke, *Hell on Wheels*, 76–78, argues that while the car could never entirely express economic equality, it did come to express a civic equality, that all might drive and that hence all had rights to the road as a public amenity. Blanke cites Wilson, 77.

[21] Roberto DaMatta's *Fé em Deus e pé na tábua: ou como e por que o trânsito enlouquece no Brasil* (Rio de Janeiro: Rocco, 2010), 45.

referred to as "passengers," the landward transfer of a maritime term. The term "chauffeur," which referred to all automobile drivers, was a French loanword employed in Brazil after about 1903, although by 1930 the English-inspired *"motorista"* became the more common term for non-professional drivers.

"*Pedestre,*" on the other hand, was not a borrowed word but the rebirth and redefinition of an old term. Up to about 1880, the *pedestre* was a low-ranking policeman associated with such undesirable tasks as managing the street's drunks and, most characteristically, with the capturing of runaway slaves. Often black, the *pedestres*, were unpopular street characters. With the demise of slavery, the office disappeared, and the term fell into disuse. As an adjective, *pedestre* continued to describe anything on foot, but as a noun, *pedestre* disappeared from the language for two decades. In about 1899, *pedestre* was resurrected to name any person on foot in the street, and it became more common by 1910 with the increasing number of cars. By 1920, *pedestre* was the preferred legal term for people in the street who were not in vehicles. Although the car created the upper-class category of driver, it created many more pedestrians.[22]

There was enmity between these new classes from the beginning. The chauffeur saw the pedestrian as a detestable object, something to impress, terrorize, and ultimately remove. To the chauffeur, speed abstracted all who moved more slowly than he, and velocity became a new mark of social differentiation. In Monteiro Lobato's *Clash of the Races*, Ayrton, the main character, who had recently acquired a car, described his former pedestrian status in deprecating terms.

Pedestre, the caste into which I was born and lived until the age of 26, was a poor and unhappy station, one that forced me to spoil good shoe leather, sweat profusely in heat, suffer sodden in rain, and engage in prodigious acrobatics to avoid being crushed by the superior, heedless, man, the *rodante*, who did not walk but whose swifter status was to glide effortlessly. How often I stood on the sidewalk to spectate my brother pedestrians reduced to mere insects, scattering

---

[22] Textual analysis was accomplished using the Biblioteca Nacional do Rio de Janeiro's "Hemeroteca Digital Brasileira," a massive database of scanned newspaper and magazine sources that are word-searchable and return quantitative results, at http://memoria.bn.br /hdb/periodico.aspx (accessed Oct. 15, 2013). *Pedestre* was also a term used in the 1830s that also fell into disuse for "postman." For *pedestre*'s first modern nominative usage, see *O Paiz*, Jan. 1, 1899. Thomas Holloway, *Policing Rio de Janeiro: Repression and Resistance in a 19th-Century City* (Stanford, CA: Stanford University Press, 1993), 110, addresses the role and unpopularity of the *pedestres* as slave catchers.

to make way for an arrogant, metallic Cadillac – the snort of its Klaxon horn seemed to say to me: "Make way, scum."[23]

His greatest pride in life was his rise to the status of chauffeur. Now he too looked on all pedestrians, his former caste, with the vitriolic hatred one held toward the pariah. With the purchase of his first car,

> everything ran for the better, in the best of all possible worlds, and I exceeded myself in a fury to "Fordicate" at every opportunity just to make the pedestrian's jaw drop ... I paid various tickets, killed half a dozen dogs, and ran down a pitiful deaf man who had not responded to my honking demand to "Move It!" To me, the pedestrian became an odious creature, an obstacle to my right to speed and the straight line. I thought I would petition the government, suggesting a law that would ban all these mobile stumbling blocks from transiting the asphalted streets. In the end, I had acquired the mentality of the chauffeur, coming to despise the pedestrians as vile things less worthy of life.[24]

When Ayrton inevitably crashes his car, more than the pain of his broken limbs, more than death itself, he fears returning to the "miserable caste of the pedestrian."[25]

Pedestrians, on the other hand – mild and good-hearted by nature as one described them – could be inflamed all of a sudden when a car threatened their person, inspiring in them desires to destroy the machine or more commonly throw stones at the driver. "We all hate Popes, Berliets, Renaults, and Fiats," and those who drive them, "whose desire is to be better than others, to place themselves above what is common," and who, due to velocity, "have a natural indifference to the poor devil who moves retrograde on foot."[26] The social distance between the chauffeur and the pedestrian was described as being as far apart as life and death.

For men, the car played a particularly valued role marketing masculine status. Four wheels and an engine enhanced a man's suitability as a mate, or at least increased the range of his options, and sources in Brazil are shot through with the theme of men who utilized the car to flirt, woo, and pick up women – and cheat on wives. Men took mistresses for late-night rides and shopping excursions during working hours. Others ran up debts in car rental fees to keep up appearances. One man stole a government vehicle in a crime of opportunity; rather than sell or dismantle it for

---

[23] José Bento Monteiro Lobato, *O choque das raças: ou,o Presidente negro; romance americano do anno de 2228* (Rio de Janeiro: Companhia Editoria Nacional, 1926), 15.
[24] Monteiro Lobato, *O choque das raças*, 132–34.
[25] Monteiro Lobato, *O choque das raças*, 134.   [26] "Delenda," *Fon Fon*, Jun. 7, 1913.

parts, he rushed straight to the red light district, where he picked up three prostitutes who he raced up and down Avenida do Mangue until the car was recognized.[27]

Intensifying the new class divisions that the automobile introduced were the large number of official cars in the nation's capital. As power attached itself to the car, the powerful sought the association, even if their government salary could not afford it. The first official car appears to have belonged to the commission in charge of building Avenida Central in 1905. The mayor got one the same year. By 1907, a number of elected officials and political appointees had government-issued cars, including President Afonso Pena, who purchased a luxury model named the "Presidential." US President Taft would not have his White House issued Pierce Arrow, the office's first car, until 1909. Brazil's official cars carried special plates demanding special privileges, including right of way at intersections and reserved parking.[28] In 1913, some legislators tried to limit the total number of official cars to fewer than twenty, with strict restrictions on their non-official use,[29] but soon, cabinet members, congressional presidents, generals, and the heads of nearly every agency had both a vehicle and a professional driver provided at state expense. And the privilege kept trickling down; Lima Barreto joked in 1921 that the benefit was now enjoyed by secretaries, messengers, and servants. By 1926, there were 1,052 official cars – roughly 10 percent of all passenger cars on Rio's streets. Congressman Pessoa de Queroz pointed out that the cost of buying, maintaining, and driving Rio's official cars required a budget that exceeded the entire annual expenditures of the states of Sergipe, Maranhão, and Santa Catarina; "Rivers of Money" (the headline, "*Rios de Dinheiro*," a play on the capital's name) could no longer be justified.[30]

It was the misuse of official cars, more than the poor use of government funds, that angered the population. Outside of official functions, ministers, military officers, and chiefs of police engaged their state cars and government-paid chauffeurs in shopping trips for their wives, beach outings for their families, and weekend joyrides with their friends. No longer

[27] See, as examples, just from 1915: *Fon Fon*, Mar. 6, 1915, 29, Dec. 11, 1915, 52, May 29, 1915, 30, Nov. 27, 1915, 27.

[28] *Gazeta de Notícias*, Nov. 20, 1905; *The Brazilian Review* Nov. 7, 1905, 966; *O Paiz*, Apr. 19, 1907, 1.

[29] *Retrospecto Commércial do Jornal do Commércio* (Rio de Janeiro: Typografia de Rodrigues & Co., 1914), 50.

[30] *A Rua*, Oct. 8, 1926, 1; Lima Barreto, "Automóveis Officiaes," *Careta*, Feb. 26, 1921.

would the children of officials condescend to get to school in "a vulgar streetcar or on foot, accompanied by the maid." Officials were unflatteringly caricatured taking Sunday drives, their family and friends piled high in the seats behind uniformed drivers.[31] The public display of the misuse of government property had become so common that in 1915 the editors of one magazine published an open letter to President Wenceslau Braz, in which he was sincerely thanked for renting, at his own expense, a car in which to enjoy carnival, insinuating that while a small gesture, it spoke to his character relative to the rest of the government's shameless thieves parading up and down the Avenue in cars meant for public service.[32] Lima Barreto called the rise of the official car "bureaucratic democratization" and made the rather insightful leap that it was possible the government invested substantial funds in the purchase of numerous official cars as the best means to give the nation's capital the appearance of modernity, for every capital ought to appear "sumptuous, rich, and in constant motion." Despite many complaints and legislation, the official car remained a stock character of elite consumption and public outrage for decades.[33]

The official car invigorated the perception that automobile usage was consumption by the rich at everyone else's expense. Even cars legitimately owned by private individuals were accused of elitism, abuse of position, and suspected corruption. And rich car owners certainly got their tax breaks: nearly all imported goods to Brazil were taxed at rates of 50 percent or greater, which included carriages, wagons, and even handcart and wagon wheels. Automobiles entered the country at a mere 7 percent, and tires at 10 percent.[34] The acerbic pseudonymous writer, Jotaenne, sat one night in the Passeio Público, now separated from the bay by the Beira Mar Avenue, the city's most amenable new speedway and the primary connector between the old downtown and Rio's growing upmarket suburbs. As the luxury cars left the city's clubs and theaters for home that night, he observed the partiers in their "posh Popes, noiseless Renaults, and gleaming Humbers," murmured the name of each well-dressed and perfumed owner, and identified their route to economic success: "this one got rich by selling goods on contract to the state; that one earned a fortune granting corrupt concessions; this other ran a large law firm defending the current administration; and that one backed our dissolute government with

---

[31] *Revista da Semana*, Nov. 17, 1907.   [32] *Fon Fon*, Mar. 27, 1915.

[33] Lima Barreto, "Automoveis Officiaes," *Careta*, Feb. 26, 1921.

[34] *Retrospecto Commércial do Jornal do Commércio* (Rio de Janeiro: Typografia de Rodrigues & Co., 1911), 162–63.

editorials in his newspapers." While watching this stream of "gallant men" and "shapely women" in "lustrous automobiles," he remembered the miserable poverty in the city's streets, the unemployment, and the debts that were sinking the nation.[35]

Lastly, social distancing, a less familiar factor, seems to have played a significant role in the Brazilian elite's broad adoption of the car. This appeal went beyond sociologist Georg Simmel's social distancing theory that argued that city residents, to avoid overstimulation in the maddening crowd, adopted a detached or blasé attitude to maintain social distance.[36] The car offered a material, physical distance from other people, especially other classes. The car brought the protection and decorum of the house to the street. Because it is architecture, with foundation, walls, windows, and roof, the car offered its owner a remarkable capacity for spatial control. Like carriages before it, the car segregated the upper classes into privileged spaces. The carriage, as a vehicle reserved for the most privileged, had remained few in number in Rio, and many private carriages sat idle in stables, reserved for weekends and special occasions. In 1908, there were 210 private carriages in the city; by 1920 that number declined to almost zero. Automobiles would already substantially outnumber carriages by 1911 and were heavily utilized by comparison.[37] The appeal was similar: the carriage and the car placed their passengers above the common press of the street. One critic, who had never ridden in a car because he joked he had no friend in the government, looked with admitted envy on those in official cars, the beautiful girls and adorable children of the elite who had long been associated with the house, "filling the enviable commodiousness" of the automobile.[38] A 1916 cover of *Fon Fon* magazine depicted a brand new hardtop automobile parked on Beira Mar Avenue overlooking the bay, its passengers – two men, two women, and one girl – were all dressed to the nines. The hardtop, with closeable windows, would come to dominate the car market by the late 1920s due to its cocoonlike compartment. The passengers in the illustration sit and converse under the vehicle's bright interior lights, as if at a private party, the driver leaning on the steering wheel as if it were the armrest of a lounge chair. With glazed and curtained windows, well-appointed furniture that faced passengers to

[35] Jotaenne, "Na Beira-Mar," *Fon Fon*, May 20, 1916.

[36] Georg Simmel, "The Metropolis and Mental Life," in *The Sociology of Georg Simmel*, trans. Kurt H. Wolff (Glencoe, IL: Free Press 1950), 408–24.

[37] Noronha Santos, *Meios de transporte*, vol. 2, table "Vehiculos Terrestres, 1906–1916," after 177.

[38] *Fon Fon*, Apr. 2, 1910, "enchendo a commodidade invejável."

each other rather than to the windshield, and eventually lockable doors, the enclosed car, in a sense, introduced to the street the trimmings and trappings associated with the house. In fact, the interior of the car took on a variety of roles associated with the intimate house. In a space exclusively held for family, friends, and servants (chauffeurs and mechanics), owners dined in their cars at the horse track, partied in them at carnival, and played card games in them at the beach. When a private car or cab progressed along the avenues slowly, its curtains drawn and its driver winking, oncoming chauffeurs recognized the car had also taken on the function of the bedroom.[39] And significantly, the luxury cars, the Popes, Cadillacs, Humbers, and others, which made up a majority of private cars in the first decades of the twentieth century, could be as large as nineteenth-century carriages, with widths and wheelbases exceeding those of many modern SUVs. These, indeed, were rooms, not merely transportation.

Privately run streetcars, the only viable option for most before the car, formed a new kind of public space, but they retained the old dangers. One automotive magazine argued that even the most democratically minded individual – he who claimed that to rub shoulders with the popular classes on one's daily commute made one a man of the people – sought the privacy and spaciousness of an automobile, if he had the money to purchase one.[40] Ladies were considered most at risk in the presence of uncouth men who cozied up to a captive audience on public transit. These included the *bolinas,* a nautical term gone slang which referred to men who made premeditated physical contact with females on loaded streetcars or congested streets. At first, *bolinar* referred to the perpetrator using his knees to caress the backsides of women sitting on the bench in front of him. The term broadened to include those who sought to sit close beside a girl, pressing leg against leg, at first distractedly, an apparent inadvertence. One eager contestant got well along into his deviancy before realizing the skirt on the shapely leg that he had chosen to snuggle was in fact the robe of a priest. There were also the *tira-camisas* who undressed women with their eyes and the *encaradores* who stared at women provocatively. Laws were passed, police made arrests, and women frequently fought back, beating lechers with umbrellas and handbags, but it was a difficult outrage to avoid.[41]

---

[39] *Fon Fon*, May 17, 1913.   [40] *Auto Sport*, Nov. 15, 1912, 382.
[41] Luiz Edmundo, *O Rio de Janeiro do meu tempo* (Rio de Janeiro: Imprensa Nacional, 1938), 79–80; Raul Pederneiras, *Geringonça carioca, verbetes para um diccionário da*

On the streets, the elite formerly had to share the public commons, including public transportation, on equal footing with their inferiors, all at the risk of rude encounters, begging, theft, spitting, peddling, spiteful envy, and even exposure to vile diseases strongly associated with the unwashed and immigrant classes. The car represented safety, a defensible redoubt from which to fight – or in which to take flight – from indigents and criminals who the better classes had long maligned but could not easily avoid. As we saw in the previous chapter, the wealthy saw themselves as envied by the average man in the street; their swank clothing, which identified their class, put them at risk of not only dislike but perceived physical threats, bumps, and shoves. The car, which as a status symbol also inspired envy and hostility, was the perfect, safe platform from which to be envied. The driver, rather than the destitute poor, became untouchable. With the car's enclosing protection, envy could be enjoyed rather than feared, and drivers could be haughty and inconsiderate with impunity.

The car was embraced as a prophylactic against uncouth street behavior. Even epidemic disease was to be avoided, kept at a distance, by the use of the car's controlled spatial bounds and speed. Streetcars, as had streets, became increasingly associated with dirt and potential infection, with civic campaigns to sanitize them. But this was of no concern for those in cars. Hiram Bingham, who visited Rio briefly in 1908, wrote confidently that despite the fact that the city was suffering from smallpox and a number of other communicable diseases, "if you are content to spend your time in the fashionable end of town or speeding along the fine new thoroughfares in a fast motor car ... think no more of Rio's bad record as an unhealthy port"; the mere possession of a fast car quarantined the city's infected masses to the pedestrian street and the streetcar.[42] Hence, Rio's elite abandoned their passenger and pedestrian status for the socially safer and more spacious life of the motorist.

PRIVATE OBJECTS ON THE PUBLIC COMMONS

From the perspective of the newly created pedestrian class, there were many early complaints about the car, its attendant noise, danger, and

gíria, Rio: Jornal do Brasil, 1922), see "bolina." These thoughts offer historical evidence to DaMatta's *Fé em Deus e pé na tábua*, 18, that comments on the search for social separation.

[42] Hiram Bingham, *Across South America* (Boston, MA: Houghton Mifflin, 1911), 18.

dust, and its impact on the use and habitability of the street. One described a lovely afternoon in the city in 1908, a mother and child, dressed in their best on a treed avenue, enjoying a walk, the bay, the mountains, and the fresh air that were integral parts of what made the city a pleasant place. Yet, charging into the midst of their enjoyment "came the vertiginous hideousness of a rented car at full velocity, kicking up a fouling dust." The child's formerly bright eyes blink in painful blindness, her lace dress covered in a yellow pall, while her mother attempts to wipe the dust from her formerly rosy cheeks. The observer concluded that those who matter tell us that "a capital of any renown must have cars. But it would be an unpardonable gaffe to give any dispensation to this unsightly depravity, braying and fouling everything, a machine that the *snob* has taken from the highways and rural paths into the sanctity of our immaculate avenues, our modern streets."[43] It was the modern automobile threatening the very values associated with the modern street. The comments reflect the hygienist's point of view, concern about an unaesthetic, uncivil contraption that raced up and down the very same space, the hallowed Avenue, on which the streetcar itself had been effectively blocked. They also identified the car as a class issue, employing the English term "snob" to finger the haughty who had dared bring the car to the public street in Rio. Those who were well traveled had already seen the future and worried about the consequences for Brazil's cities. Manuel de Oliveira Lima, who served as one of Brazil's most active diplomats, would not go so far as to say that Paris was decadent in late 1906, but its decline as a great city was obvious to him, having lost its cardinal elegance due in part to the "raw ambience imposed by the introduction of the numerous automobiles – cars, buses, and trucks – all circulating with a license that nothing can effectively restrict."[44]

Despite such complaints, there was a sense of the car's inevitability and the futility of any resistance to its presence. Peter Norton argues that in the United States, motorists and cars were seen as intruders who "had to fight to win a rightful place" on city streets, a fight that was successful but which was fraught well into the 1920s.[45] By contrast, in Brazil there were few so bold to suggest that the car be barred or banned from the city street

---

[43] "Impressões," *Fon Fon*, Jun. 20, 1908.

[44] Manuel de Oliveira Lima, "Coisas Extrangeiros: A França e o Sr. Clemenceau," *O Estado de São Paulo*, Dec. 27, 1906.

[45] Peter Norton, *Fighting Traffic: The Dawn of the Motor Age in the American City* (Cambridge, MA: MIT Press, 2008), 7.

altogether. There was certainly anger against the car. The reality was that there was no precedent to stop the automobile. As a common, the street had embraced a wide variety of vehicles in the past, from luxurious carriage to utilitarian handcart. In the US, there were in fact legal challenges to the car's presence on the city street and over the street's legal definition as either a thoroughfare or as a public space. But already by the end of the first decade, the automobile's boosters were arguing that the American courts' only role with the car was to shape its adoption and use on the street, not judge its right to pass there. The car was to have a right equal to that of pedestrians, despite its tendency to injure and kill them.[46] Similarly, Jennifer Bonham finds that in Australia, pedestrians complained about cars and tenaciously resisted changes to their own behavior in the street, but gave little direct resistance to its presence.[47] Despite conflicts and collisions, Rio's citizens did not challenge the car's place but demanded that the car and its drivers be effectively regulated. The solution to the problem of the car would focus on neither its numbers nor even its speed but in segregating the street's uses, which resulted in giving the car the greater share of the street. This happened more quickly in the United States than in Brazil, but it seemed an inevitable solution once the car's place on the street had been acknowledged.[48]

The first public spaces whose meanings and utilities began to change were the new avenues. Many photos celebrating Avenida Central in 1906 and 1907 depict a street largely devoid of vehicles, barring the rare cab. Bodies tend toward the sidewalks, the majority on the shady side of the street, to window shop and stroll, but individuals also occupy the street indiscriminately, often as many bodies mid-street as on the sidewalk, still walking in all directions, not necessarily parallel with the street, with notably confident steps. Individuals interact, pedestrians loiter, and the street is inhabited by all classes, genders, and races, and ages. Children are boldly conspicuous. The space has all the feel of an extended public square, almost a public fair, even on non-holidays, a space broadly open to creative invention. In less than a decade, the aspect of the Avenue, now Rio Branco, was transformed. The street had not changed physically. Photos show that the curbs, trees, and lampposts are in the same place.

---

[46] Xenophon P. Huddy, *The Law of Automobiles*, 2nd edn. (Albany, NY: Matthew Bender & Company, 1909), 41–45, 96. The first edition was published in 1906.
[47] Jennifer Bonham, "Transport: Disciplining the Body that Travels," in S. Boem, et al., *Against Automobility* (Oxford: Blackwell, 2006), 63.
[48] Norton, *Fighting Traffic*, 65–72.

The real change was in what occupied the space, for the now ubiquitous automobile, at most times of the day, collectively occupied substantially more street space than all the pedestrians combined. Cabs and luxury cars park in congested lines along the central median and curbs, sometimes double parked, while moving vehicles, their tops down, shoot the narrow lane remaining between parked vehicles. Bodies still venture into and stand about the middle of the street, handcarts and men with loads on their backs mix with the cars, and youth converse amidst the traffic, but there is a wariness that was not present before, and with every step, every pedestrian seems tentative, ready to alter direction or position based on changing conditions monitored by eyes that now dart nervously about the street rather than gaze upon it. Some festival days and parades make exceptions, with bodies dominant, crowding and slowing the cars. But invariably, everyday spaces and routine activities were being increasingly interposed by the machine.[49]

Motorists enclosed in the protection and power of the machine, demanded ever-greater spaces among those claiming rights to the street. Within a decade of its arrival, the car would kill and injure daily. The driving class, in addition to exacting regular deaths on their pedestrian counterparts, made explicit claims to the street and its space with what were essentially poorly veiled threats, as in a 1924 poem entitled "Get Out of the Way"

> Noble son of Adam, made of clay.
> On the street, keep your pretty little head;
> Out here, do not let it suffer a collision
> With an automobile of massive iron.
> Pay attention to the horn, the snort of the machine . . .
> And when you move in the street, watch out
> If something comes smelling of gasoline.[50]

By the early 1930s, one writer described automobiles as swarming ants "occupying every free space" and marveled how the pedestrian's primitive instincts prevented accidents from being worse than they were.[51] For motorists, the car merited space by its very power to consume it, and those who ignored that power did so at their peril. Nicolau Sevcenko

---

[49] "Na calçada," *Fon Fon*, Aug. 8, 1908. See also Massimo Moraglio, "Knights of Death: Introducing Bicycles and Motor Vehicles to Turin, 1890–1907," *Technology and Culture* 56, no. 2 (Apr. 2015), which makes a similar argument regarding the perception of diminishing street utilities as a result of the arrival of the bike and the car.

[50] "Sae da frente," *Voz do Chauffeur*, Oct. 13, 1924.

[51] "Andar nas ruas," *Diário Carioca*, Aug. 31, 1932, 1.

FIGURE 3.1 The machine displaces, c. 1919. Private and official automobiles, for the most part chauffeured, became the dominant users of many downtown streets by 1920, occupying a growing share of the public commons. Avenida Rio Branco would not long be used as an elongated public square. Despite a noted resistance and sporadic anger from nonmotorists, the car diminished and displaced many traditional street uses with its spatial, sonic, and deadly presence.
Source: Augusto Malta, "Avenida Rio Branco," c. 1919. Courtesy of the Acervo da Fundação Biblioteca Nacional, Brazil.

remarks that the automobile in Brazil inherited the legacy of slavery that "associated positions of power with the exercise of brutality."[52] Central to the car's success at occupying the street was the fact that the chauffeur class backed their claims to the street with violence and its ever-present threat.

Pedestrians answered with anger and sometimes their own violence, but resistance was reactive rather than organized. When a car hit a pedestrian, other pedestrians occasionally attacked and even threw rocks at the driver at fault. But pedestrians had little power to punish guilty drivers, and even less to prevent subsequent accidents. At most, they complained, and the press attempted to highlight the intolerability of the car's dangers. Already in 1909, in a series of cartoons, Raul Pederneiras portrayed the automotive

---

[52] Nicolau Sevcenko, *Orfeu extático na metrópole: São Paulo, sociedade e cultura nos frementes anos 20* (São Paulo: Companha das Letras, 1992), 74.

absurdities that pedestrians were forced to face. One frame depicts a pedestrian's body lying in the street, cut up into neat little chunks by the wheels of a passing car. In another, he sketches a mixed race family, the Pardavascos, crossing the Largo do São Francisco with handguns drawn. Every member of the family is armed but they still enter the street with a great deal of trepidation on their faces and in their body language. Only the infant, in the nanny's arms, carries his weapon with any boldness.[53] Yet public opposition to the car rarely advanced beyond complaints and caricature.

RULES FOR WALKING

Avenida Rio Branco was exceptional in that it lacked residents, but on nearly all other public spaces, the automobile posed a challenge to the role the street had played in the building of communities of place, which is a central concern. But before we speculate on the impact of automobiles on community, which is not well documented, let us first examine the particular bodily and spatial changes the car brought to the street.

The automobile's increasing velocities and numbers, and, hence, growing demand for public space, had the effect first of compressing other street activities. One such compression was movement for the majority who still got around on foot. Many pedestrians continued to brave ever-faster and more congested lanes of automotive traffic, but the car condensed most pedestrians to the sidewalks, resulting in pedestrian congestion.[54] For a decade or so, cars had a field day in the streets, experiencing little to no congestion of their own. But these fast-moving cars slowed everyone else. The pace of walking slowed. Crossing the street was not only dangerous; it was time-consuming. One pedestrian in 1912 captured the new reality for all those of his class succinctly: "With all these chauffeurs, there is no way to circulate any longer."[55] In more heavily wheeled cities in the US and Europe, this reality had appeared before the car due to the larger number of wheeled vehicles, but the car greatly intensified that reality. In 1912, the city installed new traffic cops at the busiest intersections because without them, pedestrians, women and

---

[53] "Scenas Pavorosas," *Jornal do Brasil*, Sep. 26, 1909, 10. Anton Rosenthal, "Dangerous Streets: Trolleys, Labor Conflict and the Reorganization of Public Space in Montevideo," in *Cities of Hope*, edited by James Baer and Ronn Pineo (Boulder, CO: Westview Press, 1998), 40, cites one actual case in Montevideo in which a father escorted his children across a busy avenue with a well-aimed handgun.

[54] "Si Cette Histoire," *Fon Fon*, May 17, 1913.   [55] *Fon Fon*, Apr. 13, 1912.

children in particular, had found it nigh impossible to cross the street at busy times of the day. Yet still, many complained that the police were more focused on keeping the cars moving than assisting pedestrians – an observation repeated over the next few decades.[56] In a cartoon from 1925 with the caption "Now things move better here," a sharply dressed traffic cop, in the act of pointing his baton to give a car passage, inadvertently strikes a pedestrian in the face, knocking him to the ground.[57] Already by 1913, the automotive revolution was complete enough that a two-day taxi strike in April seemed to set Rio back a decade in time:

> [W]e returned to a day when we walked un-terrorized through our streets without the constant preoccupation of fleeing the rapid fury of the automobile ... Our nerves relaxed in a period of repose, and our attention rested from its relentless worry as we crossed streets without danger, without hurry, at the pace we used to walk, in our former attitude of tranquility.[58]

The presence of cars also channeled pedestrians into ever-more gridded patterns of movement; that is, they had to follow the linear direction of the street, moving along the sidewalks. Previously, walkers had complained when excavations or piles of construction equipment forced them to "break the line" they were walking, thus lengthening their walk and slowing their progress.[59] With more cars, pedestrians lost the freedom to walk the street's most efficient angles. Human motion in the city became increasingly restrained to the rigid matrix of the grid. This was resisted for decades, but it would eventually rule the city. And pedestrians lost even the freedom to pause because the dominion of motion, with new rules, was imposed on pedestrian space. The problem seemed even more acute in São Paulo, where the busy avenues had narrower sidewalks than those in Rio. Merchants there began to complain in 1914 that pedestrian crowds could no longer pause to appreciate the wares of the downtown shop windows. "With the liberty conceded to vehicles, the downtown's commerce has suffered ... The feverish, chaotic transit that moves along our sidewalks does not permit anyone to pause ... because behind them comes the strong, impetuous wave that carries everyone forward in the stampede ... We need to sacrifice the interests of a small minority to

---

[56] *Revista de Automóveis*, Mar./Apr. 1912, 272; *A Rua*, Dec. 28, 1922.

[57] Reproduced in Marco Antônio Cornacioni Sávio, *A modernidade sobre rodas: tecnologia automotiva, cultura e sociedade* (São Paulo: EDUC, 2002), 91.

[58] "Diário das Ruas," *Fon Fon*, Apr. 4, 1913.   [59] *Jornal do Brasil*, Oct. 10, 1909, 9.

the higher interests of what is almost the totality of the population."[60] Commerce suffered in the press for constant movement.

Sidewalk congestion had become so pronounced by the mid-1910s that Rio's police, in addition to legally forcing the pedestrian to the sidewalk, also attempted to regulate sidewalk behavior. As noted, officials legislated against many of the street's former utilities: stray dogs, some peddlers, and all kiosk operators were banished by 1912. With increasing sidewalk congestion, complaints emerged for the first time about newsboys who were described as blocking pedestrian flow.[61] Others grumbled about light posts, trees, police call boxes, and trash bins, which had been seen as the modern means to beautifying and civilizing the street but which now were merely more impediments to pedestrian movement. In 1910, a cartoonist predicted that in 1920 the sidewalks would be even more heavily stocked with civilizing devices such as spittoons, drinking fountains, mailboxes, park benches, and restaurant tables. The space, the artist intimated, would have to be simplified in its uses rather than complicated with more aesthetic obstacles. In the press, loiterers were singled out as useless, shiftless obstacles to their fellow citizens who actually had somewhere to go.[62]

During the 1908 visit to Rio by the US Navy's Great White Fleet of sixteen battleships, a street altercation came to blows between locals and American sailors on the Largo do Paço. The press almost universally condemned the drunken sailors, but *O Malho*, which was suitably impressed by the American's show of power and modernity, placed the blame squarely on Rio's uncouth underclass who had taunted the sharply dressed sailors as if they were "animals in a zoo." "What would you do," it asked, "if you found yourself surrounded by a bunch of filthy carters, deckhands, rubes, blacks, and idle brats?" Despite the city's modern street reforms, the poor and the vulgar remained as before. The solution, looking again to France as a model, was first suggested in *O Malho*: keep the riffraff moving. Rio, they argued, ought to adopt the Parisian policy of the *circulez*, which demanded that all pedestrians on the sidewalks remain in

---

[60] "Coisas de Cidade: O Trânsito," *O Estado de São Paulo*, Sep. 25, 1914, 4. In São Paulo, the blame was placed in part on the transitioning of some downtown streets to two-way thoroughfares for cars; the article called for the return of one-way streets in order to solve this problem.

[61] Afonso Henriques de Lima Barreto, "As Esquinas," in *Toda Cronica*, vol. 1, edited by R. Beatriz and R. Valenca (Rio de Janeiro: AGIR Editora, 2004), 144, first published in *Correio da Noite*, Jan. 9, 1915.

[62] *Fon Fon*, Aug. 20, 1910; *Fon Fon*, Mar. 5, 1910.

perpetual, ordered motion. The term *circulez* was a direct adoption of the French command "Circulate!" that was pronounced by policeman on the streets of Paris. For the next decade, elements of Rio's press would continue to demand that this pattern of civilized movement be imposed on Rio's streets. Pedestrians who were always moving were people who did not cause trouble, and had the policy been in place in 1908, the vulgar classes could have not have harassed the American visitors but would have "left our guests in peace."[63]

São Paulo implemented the *circulez* in August 1910, which prohibited people from "parking" themselves or forming groups on the sidewalk for any reason on the busiest downtown streets, except if waiting for a streetcar. Drivers now had a greater legal right to stop and chat with other drivers, which was not uncommon, than did pedestrians with each other on the sidewalk.[64] In Rio, there was a continued press to implement the *circulez,* with constant comparative references to successes in São Paulo, Paris, and New York. Elsewhere, the main stated purpose of the *circulez* was to smooth pedestrian movement, but in Rio, demands for its implementation continued to be couched in arguments for eliminating undesirable street behaviors.[65] Peddlers, buskers, musicians, men gawking at women, children at play, and even acquaintances engaged in friendly conversation were construed as provincial conduct, uncivil discourse, or as indulgences that could no longer be entertained on the increasingly crowded sidewalks. One argued that the city's citizens must be liberated from the infernal shouting, jingling, and noise making of the peddling classes, a call that in itself was nothing new. But now, the demand for movement became a tool to eliminate the peddling classes. "How many camp out in the same space every day ... making us crazy. In front of our very office it is like martyrdom. There is a well-known seller of pomades for the removal of callouses that needs to be told to keep it moving. In such cases, circulation is the solution."[66] The removal of beggars, which had long been a goal of city officials, was now newly justified to improve pedestrian movement.[67] A visitor from São Paulo noted surprise that in Rio musicians still played music on the sidewalks and street corners, a problem his hometown had eliminated by demanding that they keep moving. Mário Pederneiras particularly targeted the men who gathered

[63] *O Malho*, Jan. 18, 1908.   [64] *O Estado de São Paulo*, Aug. 8, 1910.
[65] *A Gazeta de Notícias*, Dec. 26, 1910, 3; *Fon Fon*, Jul. 25, 1914.
[66] *A Gazeta de Notícias*, Nov. 18, 1911, 2.
[67] Clipping from *Jornal do Comércio*, Nov. 21, 1912, GIFI 6c374, ANRJ.

on busy sidewalks to admire women as they arrived in streetcars from the suburbs. Those who stood drooling before the female, as if she were some rare creature, were themselves nothing new to the city's streets, although he characterized them as more vulgar than their fathers. But these boors who admitted they were there to "examine legs" now bunged up the pedestrian stream. "Our police could sanitize these spaces infected by the epidemic of leering gawkers. Just ban the gathering of persons on the sidewalk and impose constant movement on the foot traffic."[68] Some even believed that the *circulez* would finally eliminate prostitution by forcing both the street girls and their customers to keep moving, thus preventing the contacts that led to vice. "Love sold by the hour" was to be sent "walking," and soon "Rio de Janeiro will finally be sanitized ... nearly purified, worthy to be counted among the most commendable and decent of cities."[69]

Rio's chief of police made what appears to be the first serious attempt to impose and enforce the *circulez* in Rio in April 1914, for which the press congratulated him. Policemen were instructed to ticket and fine chauffeurs who engaged in infractions against vehicle regulations, but the first strictures of the law devoted their attention toward the pedestrian. Citizens were prohibited from walking at all in the street, maintaining their ordered presence on the sidewalk. On the sidewalks, officers were to require them to keep to the right as they walked, forming two opposite streams that were not constantly coming up against each other. Above all, the police were not to permit pedestrians the freedom to stop or even pause, the command being given appropriately and politely in French: "*Circulez, messieurs!*" ("Keep it moving, gentlemen!"). Pedestrians should not form groups, even peaceably, play games, or converse whether in front of homes, shops, theaters, churches, or any public spaces. Stopping to talk was now a crime. And a variety of traditional street "movements" themselves were to be banned: street games, of both adults and children, that "perturbed the public peace and free movement of vehicles and pedestrians," were absolutely impermissible, including soccer, *peteca* (a form of shuttlecock with indigenous origins), top spinning, diabolo, and *malha* (throwing steel disks at pins).[70]

---

[68] "Diário das Ruas," *Fon Fon*, Sep. 19, 1914.

[69] "Pequenas Notas," *Fon Fon*, Aug. 09, 1913.

[70] Clipping from *A Folha da Noite*, Apr. 18, 1914, GIFI 6c520, ANRJ. The federal police interpreted decree 6440 of Mar. 30, 1907, as giving them the power to control all street activities. There is evidence that some aspects of the *circulez* were attempted in Rio in 1913, as well.

FIGURE 3.2 "Keep moving, gentlemen," 1913. From the mid-1910s, city officials attempted to mandate movement on the street, even for pedestrians. Loitering, a quintessential street behavior, became illegal, and police ordered pedestrians to move in the automotive fashion – that is, by keeping to the right. While reportedly successful in Paris and São Paulo, Rio's pedestrians largely sidestepped official efforts to regiment their public movement on the sidewalks, and they often tempted fate in the street.
Source: K. Lixto (Calixto Cordeiro, 1877–1957), "Circulez, messieurs," *Fon Fon* Aug. 23, 1913. Courtesy of the Acervo da Fundação Biblioteca Nacional, Brazil.

Despite occasional fines and rare arrests – loiterers and conversationalists often refused to surrender their static behaviors – pedestrians continued to walk when and in the direction they pleased, and both adults and children played games where they could.[71] The police themselves understood the futility of what was being asked of them and failed to consistently enforce the new, civilizing rules. Among the major resisters were elite men who often responded to the police with either a simple "You cannot do this," or the more status charged "Do you know who you are talking to?" In a cartoon from 1913, a policeman stands authoritatively erect, pointing his baton at two gentlemen conversing on the street: "Look, chief, it is prohibited to walk standing still." One of the infractors

[71] "Um guarda civil inconveniente," *Gazeta de Notícias*, Aug. 16, 1915, 4.

seems ready to move on, but the other stands his ground, his hands in his pockets, sneering at the policeman through his monocle.[72] The press continued to demand the rules be enforced, to which the police responded intermittently. In a major police offensive in 1919, photographed by the press, uniformed officers ordered citizens on Avenida Rio Branco to keep moving. When instructed to keep to the right-hand side of the sidewalk, residents look at police with bewilderment and annoyance, and the operation appears not unlike an attempt to herd cats. For most Cariocas, this was order and progress taken too far. The operation, ironically, attracted spectators, who broke the more fundamental rule against loitering. One humorist noted vulgarly that that day the only persons who "kept to the hand" (*ficou na mão*), a phrase that intimated masturbation, were the police.[73] In São Paulo, a few individuals challenged the *circulez* on constitutional and legal grounds, a development followed in Rio. They sought writs of habeas corpus, pointing to the loss of both their constitutional right to free movement and assembly, and argued that the *circulez* coerced them in their movements, as if they were imprisoned without cause. Stasis, they insisted, was as much a part of their right to freedom as movement, and the coercion to constantly move was an abuse of power. But the court ruled against them, concluding that the street had essentially become a space that only permitted movement, and the majority's need to move trumped the minority's desire to use the street as they always had, to associate, assemble, and communicate with their neighbors. Stopping and gathering infringed on the majority's right to move with dispatch. The chief justice concluded that because the petitioners were not being constrained, because they could move, their constitutional rights remained intact.[74] Although Rio's police would back off and always found it difficult to enforce, the insistence on movement had largely triumphed in the law by 1920, and as the downtown's streets became increasingly occupied by cars, it became more difficult to use the downtown's streets for purposes other than movement, at least during its busiest hours when citizens most wanted or needed to be there.

The car's arrival and proliferation presented the elite with a critical tool for gaining spatial control of the street, something they had been

---

[72] *Fon Fon*, Aug. 23, 1913; "Diário das Ruas," *Fon Fon*, Feb. 29, 1913. See also, *Fon Fon*, Aug. 16, 1913.

[73] "O Circulez no Rio," *Fon Fon*, Mar. 22, 1919, and a cartoon on the next page of the same issue.

[74] *O Estado de São Paulo*, Dec. 13, 1910, 6; *O Estado de São Paulo*, Dec. 16, 1910, 7; *O Estado de São Paulo*, Mar. 4, 1911, 5.

attempting with laws, regulations, and policing for decades. With emancipation in 1888, a growing urban migration, and substantial foreign immigration, the issue, Sydney Chalhoub notes, had become increasingly debated by an elite who saw the streets consistently occupied by former slaves, loafers, beggars, and thieves. They were equally upset by the growing number of individuals who made an independent and noisy living with the street as their workplace. As neither indolence nor independence were to be tolerated, the question was how to put them all to work, ideally, formal work in structured workplaces under someone's direct control.[75] But new rules and new police – old strategies that intensified from the 1890s – were ineffective. Maria Odila Silva Dias asserts that the city had struggled the entire century to regulate streets, banning peddling, dancing, drumming, playing, prostituting, and keeping animals, but all without significant success.[76] Only with the automobile's occupation of the street were many unwelcome behaviors associated with the lower classes finally cast off by progressively taking away the spaces on which those behaviors were acted out. To challenge the car directly for the space required for these activities involved considerable physical risk. Likewise, the city now justified restrictive street usage laws by speaking in favor of the machine's right to rapid circulation. But if automotive preference now justified regulatory street laws, it was the machines, rather than the police, that did much of the enforcing.

Rio's citizens continued to resist, but even pedestrians began to be persuaded by movement's demands. Ten years after the initial effort to

---

[75] Sidney Chalhoub, *Trabalho, lar, e botequim: o cotidiano dos trabalhadores no Rio de Janeiro da belle époque* (São Paulo: Editora Brasiliense, 1986), 27–29, 44–49.

[76] Maria Odila Leite da Silva Dias, *Quotidiano e poder em São Paulo no século XIX – Ana Gertrudes de Jesus* (São Paulo: Brasiliense, 1984), 48–51, 57–58. See also Eduardo Yázigi, *Mundo das calçadas: por uma política democrática de espaços públicos* (São Paulo: Humanitas, USP, Imprensa Oficial, 2000), 75; and Reina Ehrenfeucht and Anastasia Loukaitou-Sideris. *Sidewalks, Conflict and Negotiation over Public Space* (Cambridge, MA: MIT Press, 2009), 116–19. Peter Baldwin, *Domesticating the Street: The Reform of Public Space in Hartford, 1850–1930* (Columbus, OH: Ohio State University Press, 1999), 177–80, 185–89, 194–95, also delineates the decline of the peddling classes in Hartford, Connecticut, giving more weight to restrictive laws which were often justified by the automobile, and he notes the contemporary transformation of the street's space and the city's commerce by the growing number of cars. Andrew Brown-May, *Melbourne Street Life: The Itinerary of Our Days* (Kew, Australia: Australian Scholarly Publishing /Arcadia and Museum Victoria, 1998), 152–72, 202–03, describes a similar process in Melbourne, Australia, where for much of the nineteenth century, city officials had tried to regulate street uses and increasingly prioritized circulation over other activities, but it was not until after 1920, that such laws actually removed the undesirables.

enforce the *circulez*, pedestrians in a hurry now complained about those who used the sidewalks for window shopping, listening to music, or commerce. The street remained a place to gather and talk and engage with one's neighbors, a space where stasis tenaciously competed with movement for priority of place, but there was less space and less tolerance for stasis. Those who attempted to enjoy their right not to move were scorned as "loafers," "flirts," "loiterers," "drivellers," and "flaneurs" who impeded "the free locomotion of those who give themselves to the more productive activities of life in the urban center."[77] For those who refused to move or remove themselves, the automobile's introduction of increased crowding, danger, and noise made many of the streets' traditional activities not only hazardous but disagreeably impractical.

MACHINES DISPLACING COMMUNITY

In addition to its spatial conquest, the automobile overwhelmed the city's sonic landscape, jamming communication of various kinds and diminishing the street's role as a space to build community and engage in commerce. The car produced considerable noise with its whirring tire treads, aerodynamic inefficiency, primitive powertrain, and squealing brakes, each sufficient alone to interrupt conversation; but the sounds that came to dominate the city were those of its engine and horn. The technical, English term, "internal combustion engine," is something of a euphemism. A candle in a church counts as internal combustion. Portuguese refers to the auto's engine more accurately as the "motor by explosion." In fact, driver's licenses into the early 1920s in Rio specified that what they authorized was the operation of "automobiles by explosion."[78] The car engine's rapid, serial ignition of fuel and oxygen creates deafening bangs, whose volume reaches well beyond the threshold of human pain, as loud as gunfire, but sustained like a machine gun. Before the muffler, which came into common use after the turn of the century, the automotive engine was a frightening terror to humans and animals. Without the muffler, it is quite likely the car would have been banned outright for making street spaces virtually unbearable. Yet, even with the early mufflers, cars were loud contrivances. By 1910, it would be common to be within earshot of scores of engines, each of four, six, and eight cylinders, all firing in quick, timed succession in variable pitches.

[77] "Por que não se restabelecem a mão e contra mão," *Jornal do Brazil*, Oct. 10 1928, 10.
[78] "Carteira de habilidade, 5470," Mar. 23, 1923, DL 1470.014, IHGB.

A typical street experienced a half a million such explosions per minute. The collective effect was to overpower most other sounds, even in streets that were only modestly trafficked. Mufflers improved, especially with Hiram Percy Maxim's early-century silencers, co-developed to both quiet automotive engines and firearms, but as the number of cars grew, the net effect was an ever-noisier city. Some argued that the best motorists, as examples of modernity, demanded silence as a form of luxury, and hence cars would someday soon be entirely quiet.[79] But the reality was that many drivers seemed to enjoy their automobile's potent sound, another source of its dominating power and a means to clear essential space before them, and they worked to keep it loud.

As already noted, the street before the car was not a quiet place, and many complained of hooves on pavements and steel tires on cobbles, of clanging streetcars, church bells, arguments among neighbors, and the shouting of the peddlers. But the car brought a significant change in noise's quality and level. The car's noise was constant, and people complained they could not get away from it. Even at a distance, or in the suburbs, the car's noise found them.[80] Like space, a soundscape is imminently renewable, as one sound comes and goes, another can follow. Unlike two bodies, two sounds can share the same space; but the louder sound will tend to displace the quieter one from the perception of the ear. The car's noise was the constant hum of the machine; it never stopped competing with and overpowering other sounds. Automobility became the soundtrack to urban modernity. Even while parked, chauffeurs tended to leave their engines idling loudly because of the danger involved in hand-starting early vehicles. In 1913, Cadillac began advertising its automatic starter in Brazil; it suggested that the primary benefit of an automatic starter was not an easy start but the increased willingness of drivers to turn off their cars while waiting curbside, which reduced noise and saved gasoline.

The car's mechanical noise, unlike most of the street sounds before it, had no meaning. Bells, shouts, conversations, music, and even silence conveyed intelligence of various sorts to the city's residents. The car's collective noise communicated largely nothing, except traffic volume and driver frustration. Oswald de Andrade, a modernist who enjoyed touring in a green Cadillac, observed in 1922 that the music of the street suffered

---

[79] *Horseless Age*, Sep. 15, 1909, 288; *Horseless Age*, Dec. 15, 1909, 686.
[80] *Fon Fon*, Jun. 11, 1910. In this story, a man heads up a river to find peace, but even there he can't get away from the car's sonic reach.

an abrupt transition with the arrival of the car. Before, song and conversation did not have to compete with horns, crashes, screeches, and clangs, but now such intrusions were constant, "breaking on our former Brazilian calm and rapping on the very desks of our work and meditation."[81] In 1930, with the invention of the decibel as a measure of sound's relative volume, Rogers Galt published an influential chart that illustrated the automobile's sonic intrusion in the city. Galt described 30 decibels as the sound of a quiet street without any traffic. By comparison, the average home today, with its appliances, heating, and cooling, runs about 40, which is perceived as twice as loud as 30. Galt measured the sound of conversation, when the speakers were 3 feet apart, at 65 decibels. By comparison, an automobile averaged 66 decibels at 50 feet. Auto-congested streets in New York and Chicago rated 75, which nearly drowned out all but those who shouted to be heard. In 1911, Mayor Carter Harrison of Chicago, responding to local complaints of peddlers calling out their wares, observed that he personally would rather have ten peddlers in front of his house than a single car.[82]

Thus, the street, which had been alternately a quiet or a noisy place, became one of constant rumbling punctuated by deafening ruptures. Pederneiras noted that smooth asphalt was an improvement over uneven cobbles, but the quieting of tires had been replaced by siren horns and exhaust pipes emanating endless "series of short bursts that afflict their banging on us," like nothing they had known before. He and others noted that while the older sounds of church bells and voices diminished, the sounds of modernity, which went so far as to shake the homes of the residents, were taking away sleep, creating crabby faces, and possibly even increasing the numbers entering the city's asylums. For Pederneiras, the new movement of the streets had its appeal; it was the clamor that had become "insupportable." In the past, people had complained of noise, but horns, exhaust pipes, police whistles, and the attending roars of the car, he noted, "afflicted and stupefied" in ways the old streets never could. This is why, he asserted, Rio's citizens walk about "irritable with surly countenances." He lamented that there appeared to be no measures that might

---

[81] Cited in Paulo César de Azevedo, et al. *Século do automóvel no Brasil* (São Caetano do Sul: Brasinca, 1989), 36.

[82] Galt's work is cited and commented on by Karin Bijsterveld, *Mechanical Sound: Technology, Culture, and Public Problems of Noise in the Twentieth Century* (Cambridge, MA: MIT Press, 2008), 110–11. Derek Vaillant, "Peddling Noise: Contesting the Civic Soundscape of Chicago, 1890–1913," *Journal of the Illinois State Historical Society* 96, no. 3 (Autumn 2003): 272.

repress such torments. A cartoon of the period depicted an anguished resident kneeling in bed, fists clenched, failing to find sleep due to the din of "auto-honking" which entered his bedchamber from every direction.[83] Was it any wonder, Amadeu Amaral observed, that the rich in large cities move from the center to the suburbs where they may hope to find some peace, at least at night?[84]

Horns were not entirely new either. A few carts, carriages, and especially bicycles had bulb horns installed before the arrival of the car, but they were of limited power and volume. The car, which produced electricity and exhaust gases that it tapped for noise, adopted horns that were not only substantially louder but effortless to operate. The Sireno electric horn, which arrived in Rio about 1910, advertised its easy push-button operation. It produced a sound with a signal strength of one mile, which was projected in all directions even though a pedestrian to the front may have been the only intended target.[85] The city banned the use of train whistles on automobiles, but it was feared that if horns were prohibited, morgues would triple, one quipped.[86] Others remarked that those who used their horns most often in the 1920s, low-class young men, did so not with the safety of others in mind but seemingly at random, to get the attention of a girl on the sidewalk, to show anger at congestion, or even to express themselves musically, "as if they were in a jazz band."[87] Honking, which even at its most earnest communicated little more than "get the hell out of the way," had become the new street music, effectively drowning out former styles.

Louder still were the large number of cars equipped with exhaust bypass valves. The mechanism, which was controlled by a pedal on the floor, claimed increased engine power as its stated function. By bypassing the muffler, which created negative back pressure, one could get a few more horsepower out of the engine, and hence it was used to climb hills, pass streetcars, and accelerate at signals. The practice was ear piercing, exposing people on the street to the completely unmuffled explosions of

---

[83] *Fon Fon*, Mar. 9, 1912.
[84] "O ruido nas grandes cidades," *Correio da Manhã*, Sep. 4, 1909. Pederneiras also identified streets in Rio where he doubted it was possible to sleep; "Diário das Ruas," *Fon Fon*, Dec. 7, 1912.
[85] *Country Life in America*, vol. 16, May–Oct. 1909, 249.
[86] *Fon Fon*, Mar. 19, 1910; Adelmar Tavares, "O automóvel perantes a justiça criminal," *Vida Policial*, Jul. 25, 1925, 6.
[87] *O Cruzeiro*, Nov. 10, 1928, 5; *Automobilismo: A revista prática do automóvel*, Jul. 1926, 16; *Annuário de Automobilismo*, 1929, 112.

the engine, usually at full acceleration. But more than for speed, drivers found that by tripping the bypass, due to its louder, more aggressive force, they got more responsive behavior out of pedestrians. And it could be effectively modulated, like the growling of a fierce animal, by playing with the accelerator pedal. It was so loud that it overpowered car horns, which police worried made the street less safe as pedestrians could not hear a car's typical warning. The device and practice was outlawed, first in 1911 and then again in 1913, as it had been elsewhere, but it remained an ordinary reality on Rio's streets well into the 1930s. Throughout the period, complaints and calls for enforcement were incessant. Foreigners were stunned. Auto clubs and automotive magazines spoke out against it, appealing to reason and decency, but to little apparent avail. One described streets so noisy that those few, poor peddlers who remained "sought to overpower the continuous noise" of the traffic and preferred to seek out their customers in the hours before sunrise when their voices had fewer mechanical competitors. During the car's first noisy decades, the only time citizens found relief was when it rained, as cars, being largely open, stayed in their garages. The rains, one noted, returned the city's calm: temporarily, dialogue returned to replace dissonance.[88]

The automobile's spatial impositions and sonic cacophonies combined to confound the street's role as a place on which to build and maintain community. Community is an ecology that requires a viable habitat. Surprisingly, even while many noted the street's essential changes, social scientists paid little attention to the car's transformation of urban community.[89] In fact, it was not until the late 1960s that Donald Appleyard made the first direct study of automotive traffic's impact on community. He examined three parallel, neighboring streets – Octavia, Gough, and Franklin – in a strictly residential area of central San Francisco that each exhibited different rates of traffic. All three streets had attractive housing in Victorian and modern styles. The study first established traffic volumes and street noise levels. Octavia Street had the lightest traffic at 2,000 vehicles per day, 200 per hour at traffic peak with

---

[88] Brazilian's referred to the bypass valve as *"escapa livre."* For examples of car noise being constantly addressed to little avail, see *O Paiz*, Nov. 23, 1911; *Auto Sport*, Nov. 15, 1912, 318–20; *A Noite*, Jan. 9, 1913; *Revista de Automóveis*, Mar. 1913, 524; *Fon Fon*, Apr. 8, 1916; Seabra Junior, *Accidentes de autómoveis*, 175; *Jornal do Brasil*, Dec. 9, 1928, 8; *Annuário de Automobilismo*, 1929, 117.

[89] See José Francisco Bernardino Freitas, "Townscape and Local Culture: The Use of Streets in Low-Income Residential Areas in Vitória, Brazil" (Diss., University of London, 1995), for an excellent survey of Appleyard and the few studies that followed.

an average speed below 20 mph. Gough Street fell in the middle with just over 8,000 cars passing per day, peaking at 550 per hour at an average speed of about 25 mph. And Franklin, which had been converted to a one-way street, carried some 16,000 cars per day, peaking at 1,900 per hour with an average speed of 35–40 mph. Unlike six-lane Van Ness Avenue to their immediate east, none of these streets was a major arterial; rather, they were typical residential streets. Sonically, noise levels on busy Franklin Street exceeded 65 decibels 45 percent of the day, a level that was off the charts in the Traffic Noise Index of 1968. On the least trafficked, Octavia, noise exceeded 65 decibels only 5 percent of the time.

Appleyard surveyed the residents, adults and children, regarding their perceptions of community on their streets. Appleyard found that traffic volume was the primary indicator of a variety of perceptions. On lightly trafficked Octavia, the average length of residence was 16.3 years, and families with children predominated. On heavily trafficked Franklin, residents only stayed on average eight years, and residents consisted largely of single adults. In general, residents on Octavia, with light traffic, had a better knowledge of their street's architecture and features, and a stronger sense of ownership of the space or belonging to it. They described their street as friendly, clean, and safe, and they noted on provided maps the various places that residents gathered, neighbors talked, and children played, which often extended beyond the sidewalk into the street. Residents living on Franklin, by contrast, disliked the street they lived on and rarely spent any time outside of their homes. Maybe most telling, residents of Octavia claimed three close friends on their immediate block and 6.3 acquaintances on average. On Franklin, residents claimed fewer than one friend and only 3.1 acquaintances.[90]

Appleyard concluded that when traffic increased on residential streets, the inhabitants were forced to "adapt, withdraw, or migrate," and a 1972 follow-up study of those who did move confirmed that traffic was a major reason for leaving the central city.[91] The automobile hounded people from the city as much as it carried them on new highways to the suburbs. More recent studies confirm Appleyard's findings. In 2006, surveys in six New York City neighborhoods, which noted that traffic studies still focus almost exclusively on economic and public health issues rather than community concerns, found similarly strong correlations between

[90] Donald Appleyard, et al. *Livable Streets* (Berkeley, CA: University of California Press, 1980), 15–28.
[91] Appleyard, *Livable Streets*, 26.

traffic volumes on particular streets and the quality of life and sense of
community perceived by the residents living on them. Those who lived on
the busiest streets held more negative perceptions of their neighborhood;
were more frequently interrupted in their conversations, meals, and sleep;
and spent less time playing with their children, walking in their neighborhoods, or even shopping. Residents on busy streets also had fewer neighbors they called friends. In Highbridge, a Bronx neighborhood just north
of Yankee Stadium, a community that is largely Hispanic, residents on the
two busier categories of streets, with 2,000 to 5,000 or more cars per day,
claimed to have an average of seven to nine friends on their street.
However, for those on the least busy streets, with fewer than 1,000 cars
per day (half the volume of quiet Octavia in San Francisco fifty years ago)
residents claimed twenty-eight local friends.[92] Of course, it is difficult to
project such studies back chronologically and culturally to early twentieth-century Rio de Janeiro, and a number of other factors have played
a role in damaging the fabric of urban communities such that today fewer
of us know even the names of our immediate neighbors. But the weakest
part of these studies, for our purposes, is that there were almost no
available controls, not a single residential street that had survived the
century without the invasion of cars. Even those living on relatively
quiet Octavia complained of car noise and "hotrodders," who took
advantage of the street's light traffic to attain speeds that endangered
children and adults. Likewise, we can never know how many friends
and acquaintances Rio's citizens had on their streets before the arrival of
the car's transformation, but based on anecdotal evidence the three friends
and six total acquaintances claimed by San Francisco residents even on the
most lightly trafficked streets seem depressingly low. As late as
1913, Mário Pederneiras insisted that Rio was more like a village than
the industrial cities of Europe. The street, he wrote, "popularized everyone," such that everybody on a street knew almost everybody else, at least
by sight.[93]

Some specific changes in the period were strongly noted. By the 1920s,
some lamented and some cheered the obvious decline of the peddling
classes, an occupation that would never disappear entirely but

---

[92] Transportation Alternatives, "Traffic's Human Toll: A Study of the Impacts of Vehicular
Traffic on New York City Residents," New York, NY, Oct. 2006, Transalt.org, www
.transalt.org/files/newsroom/reports/trafficshumantoll_executivesummary.pdf (accessed
Nov. 11, 2013).
[93] "Diário das Ruas," *Fon Fon*, Nov. 1, 1913.

substantially deteriorated. Some peddlers, in response, set up shop on squares or in the growing number of official, municipal markets. Customers now had to come to the peddlers. The result was that more people had to leave their homes to get the daily items they needed, which in fact added to the street's congestion. Peddling had been an extremely efficient means to distribute goods to the city's population. *Vida Policial*, which reported on police interests and activities in the city, was among those who cheered the peddlers' decline: "We do not miss them a bit."[94] Others, such as the caracaturist Raul Pederneiras, lamented their decline, a loss to the city's life and essential color, as he saw it. In a 1924 montage, he illustrated with evident nostalgia "Some Figures of Yesterday," that by inclusion evidenced their disappearance: purveyors of fresh sugar cane juice, vendors who scooped ice cream from carts made to look like little ships, shoe shine boys, musicians and entertainers, clowns and water carters, kiosk keeps, match sellers, and drovers of turkeys and geese.[95] As early as 1914, the *Gazeta de Notícias* published an idealized photo of a fishmonger and claimed that he and the vegetable peddler were the only *ambulantes* left in the city, who themselves were described as not long for the world.[96]

Likewise, there seems to have been a rapid decline in traditional street festivities in this period, which during the nineteenth century were cele- brated on an almost weekly basis. In the eighteenth century, Portuguese officials complained that there were too many street festivals, which only promoted "prayer and idleness." Festivals were seen by a secularizing elite as a tax on the nation's industry that consumed a third of society's labor value. Even to the 1920s, with the exception of some traditional Sunday festivals, officials were still trying to reduce the religious calendar to a half dozen sanctioned holidays.[97] Most festivals consisted of religious proces- sions down main streets: without direct permission from the city and the use of police force to block automotive traffic, such events became difficult

---

[94] *Vida Policial*, Apr. 11, 1925, 26.
[95] Raul Pederneiras, *Scenas da vida carioca: caricaturas de Raul* (Rio de Janeiro: Jornal do Brasil, 1924).
[96] *Gazeta de Notícias*, Mar. 10, 1914, 2. The same process is still observable. Angela Jain and Massimo Moraglio note that in India in recent decades, traffic "is displacing the established" low-income work opportunities long offered by the street; see "Struggling for the Use of Urban Streets: Preliminary (Historical) Comparison between European and Indian Cities," *International Journal of the Commons* 8, no. 2 (Aug. 2014): 524.
[97] Emílio Carlos Rodriguez Lopez, *Festas públicas, memória e representação: um estudo sobre manifestações políticas na Corte do Rio de Janeiro, 1808–1822* (São Paulo: Humanitas FFLCH/USP, 2004), 105, 109.

to organize. The city now used the need for traffic movement as an excuse to deny permits. The festivals that did survive were those, such as the famous celebration at Penha in the suburbs, which rather than being a street celebration had its own, large carless space on which the festival found continuity. Lima Barreto noted the declining number and declining interest in festivals, blaming it in part on religious leaders now having little sway with republican legislators, some of whom were "heretics," in his opinion. The citizens and maybe the city itself, as it enlarged, he claimed, seemed to be fragmenting along the lines of religion, politics, and immigrants.[98] But the loss of public spaces, of the streets themselves, for spontaneous or planned merriment contributed to the decline.

Many aspects of the traditional street persisted in the face of the car in the century's first decades. Because there was nowhere else to go, children still played there, with consequences. A significant percentage of children hit by cars were hit on their own street, within sight of their front door. Some insisted that children keep themselves to parks and gardens, but there were few such spaces in Rio. Playgrounds for children appeared in the United States in part as a response to the automobile, and Rio got its first in 1910, but it was only one in a large city.[99] In poor neighborhoods, which were still not affected much by cars, toys and children still dominated. A character in a 1915 Lima Barreto novel described the "tranquility of his poor street," without streetcars, without transit, populated every afternoon by the toys of the children of the neighborhood. Children could be found playing in the streets during the day and well into the night. In 1916, crowds of boys were observed playing army – with pine swords, red sashes, and newspaper tricorns – on a busy street just off the Avenue.[100] One success of the period was resistance to Mayor Rivadavia Correa's 1915 proposal to remove the iron gates that surrounded the city's public garden, the Passeio Público. He had wanted to let cars enter and traverse the space, to turn its garden paths into automotive carriageways, but protests secured the garden against cars, although this was a greater benefit to courting adults than children at play.[101] As with peddlers, musicians, and partiers, there had been

---

[98] Lima Barreto, "Festas Nacionais," in *Toda crônica*, vol. 2, 82. Originally published in *Careta*, Nov. 29, 1919.
[99] Norton, *Fighting Traffic*, 83–85; H. C. Tucker, "Rio de Janeiro's First Playground," *The Playground* 5, no. 11 (Feb. 1912): 382–85.
[100] *Fon Fon*, Jun. 21, 1913; *Fon Fon*, Jul. 22, 1916; *Fon Fon*, Jul. 8, 1916. Lima Barreto, *Numa e a ninfa* (Rio de Janeiro : Gráfica Editora Brasileira, 1950), 59.
[101] *Fon Fon*, Jan. 15, 1915, 38; *Fon Fon*, Jan. 22, 1915, 36.

FIGURE 3.3 Largo do Castelo, 1921. Hilltop spaces such as the Largo do Castelo, with streets too narrow or steep for cars to ascend, remained havens for former street uses, such as child's play. Augusto Malta thoroughly photographed Castelo Hill's streets in the year before the hill's scheduled demise in 1922, documenting some of the last of the downtown's car-free streets. As was typical of many colonial streets, only the *testadas*, the housing's immediate frontages, were paved. Source: Augusto Malta, "Largo do Castelo," Dec. 28, 1921. Courtesy of the Acervo da Fundação Biblioteca Nacional, Brazil.

attempts to get kids off the street before the car, but the car's danger put teeth in the legislation. Mothers were shamed in the mid-1920s in an effort to put the onus on them to keep their children off the street, but it was fear of the car's ever-more evident lethality, more than shame or legislation, that diminished child's play on the urban commons in a substantial way.[102]

---

[102] Baldwin, *Domesticating the Street*, 155, 172–75; *Voz do Chauffeur*, Oct. 6, 1924, ran a cartoon showing a car about to run down two small children playing with toys in the street; the cartoon maligned "unnatural mothers" who let their kids wander at random in the streets.

Adults, on the other hand, defied the car longer. When chauffeur associations complained of soccer being played in the street, it was not children but adult, working-class men who were the targets of their ire. Illustrations unflatteringly depicted unshod Afro-Brazilians in shorts and hairy-limbed immigrants in feathered hats chasing balls around the streets, lit cigarettes between their lips, disrespectful of the civilized traffic.[103] Others complained that men playing ball were insufficiently dressed for the polite demands of the modern street. Police publications unfairly and inaccurately associated them with criminal behavior, asserting that many soccer playing thieves "infested the city on all sides," whose real intent was not clean fun but burglary. Players, it was claimed, strategically kicked the ball into courtyards and vacant lots, and then "jumped the wall in search of the ball and whatever else they might pick up." The police also presented street soccer players as menaces who liked to bump into girls, cut off ladies, and even target the occasional shopper with a well-aimed kick. One reported an old man hit square in the back who, upon crying out, dropped his groceries, which included a live chicken, causing an uproar among the players who gave full chase to the loose fowl. Such behavior was described as laughably and shamefully disagreeable, and the police pledged on numerous occasions their commitment to eliminate such unbecoming street conduct. By the mid-1920s, players technically needed a license to play the game on the street, a rule that was universally flouted.[104]

Also, in some respects, car culture, rather than effecting new utilities of the street, imitated the street's traditional and pedestrian uses. Into the late 1920s, drivers complained of fellow drivers who cruised the city's streets casually, at the pace of a stroll, as if they were out for a Sunday walk with the family or on the hunt for a pretty girl. Many new car owners stopped their vehicles mid-busy street so they could blithely converse at length with friends, apparently oblivious to the honking cars piling up behind them. One automotive magazine lamented that too many drivers had not caught the vision that all the other drivers and their passengers had the inherent right "to arrive at their destination rapidly." For the established driving class, those who claimed to understand the true and singular meaning of the street, hurry was the street's essential utility, an efficient

---

[103] *Voz do Chauffeur*, Sep. 15, 1924; *Careta*, Apr. 10, 1937, 19.

[104] *Vida Policial*, Mar. 14, 1925; *Vida Policial*, Oct. 31, 1925, 21. *Jornal do Comércio*, Jul. 26, 1935, noted that street soccer was a problem of working-class areas, and accidents were frequent.

thoroughfare, and their frequent complaint was that novice drivers, as they saw them, still acted as if they were pedestrians behind the wheel.[105]

THE CAR IN CARNIVAL

Many of the street's traditional activities persisted, but they also changed form due to the presence and bulk of the car. Carnival, Rio biggest annual event and the quintessential street festivity, itself experienced a substantial evolution due to the arrival and multiplication of the car. Over the course of the nineteenth century, street carnival had been the almost exclusive domain of the poor. None were excluded, and a few brave and exuberant elite, such as Joao do Rio, as individuals, and the Fenianos, Democráticos and Tenentes do Diabo, as clubs, descended to the streets in costumes to dance, celebrate, and spectate the popular bands, the dancing troupes, and the African drum corps. But most of the better classes watched street carnival safely from the windows and balconies of their homes, if they watched it at all, refusing to condescend to street level, fearing the street's clamor and vulgarity. One newspaper depicted street carnival in 1913 as a negation of the city's desire for modernity, a mockery of a capacity to engage consistently in productive labor, and as a plebian indifference toward attempts to sanitize and even lift the poor from their downtrodden state. Street carnival was seen as immoral: "an infernal shouting by the celebrants, the youth of both sexes wrestling bodily in the open street with neither modesty nor shame, and engaging in the most scandalous contacts without regard to race, color, or education." There had been attempts throughout the nineteenth century to outlaw and regulate various aspects of street carnival play, also with very little success. In 1913, celebrants in the street sang in verse of their intent to have fun and make noise, despite the police presence that had been deployed to censor some of their rowdy behavior.[106]

Due to such associations and incriminations, carnival celebrations for the elite consisted chiefly of private parties at home and larger, elaborate events in private clubs. The clubs partied and danced in costume, but in a much more subdued, interiorized manner, as evidenced by flash photos in the vanity pages of newspapers and magazines, although the conduct at some private clubs was depicted as rather bawdy, where nudity and salacious behavior were not out of bounds.[107] Outside, writes Sandra

---

[105] "Deveres do bom automobilista," *Annuário de Automobilismo*, 1929, 110–11.
[106] "Idéas de Carnaval," *O Paiz*, Feb. 3, 1913, 1 and following.
[107] *O Malho*, Feb. 13, 1904, cover.

Lauderdale Graham, "the poor declared the street to be *their* territory, publically and triumphantly," converting "familiar streets into festive and glittering places ... The street remained the street, only more so – exaggeratedly, excessively so." Remarkably, while the press provided heavy coverage of the staid indoor carnival, it largely ignored the poor's flamboyant street festivities. Carnival, despite its collective and almost universal celebration, a celebration that some have claimed brought all Cariocas together, in fact attested to the social gulf between the honorable house and the disreputable street.[108]

Some had hoped that the completion of the Avenue would in itself have tamed street carnival with its more civilized ambience, or that at the very least the celebrants, who had packed themselves onto narrow Rua do Ouvidor in the past, would spread themselves out, making both real and social space for the better classes to enjoy a more civilized street carnival. But part of the attraction of carnival was to gather in dense crowds. Streetcars and trains from all directions brought the city's poor to their final downtown stops from which they converged in pedestrian masses on Ouvidor Street, Praça Onze, and Avenida Rio Branco. Despite Rio Branco's new spaciousness and length, one complained that still, rather than spreading out, celebrants concentrated themselves in a dense pack along just one short segment of the Avenue, leaving much of it as empty as "Siberia."[109]

The one place the elite did celebrate outdoor carnival consistently was in the so-called Battle of Flowers. For those who could afford a carriage, horses, and a liveried driver, families had long paraded weekly along Botafogo beach in an activity called the *corso* to enjoy the grand views and to be grandly viewed by their neighbors. During carnival, the *corso* moved to downtown and families decked their carriages in carefully arranged flowers, from the wheels to the horses – a single event in which judges picked a winner from families typically riding sedately and politely together, dressed in white suits and dresses. As noted earlier, there were few carriages in Rio, and while the press recorded the event each year, it took little time, little space, and had limited appeal compared to carnival's other activities. The event was held not on the street but in the broad Santa Anna Square, by this time a landscaped park with groomed carriageways.

[108] Graham, *House and Street*, 68–70; Marco A. C. Sávio, *A cidade e as máquinas: bondes e automóveis nos promórdios do metrópole pualista, 1900–1930* (São Paulo: Annablume, 2010), 261.

[109] "Carnaval na Rua," *Fon Fon*, Feb. 5, 1910.

It was in the context of the *corso*'s respectably florid battle that the automobile, also covered in exuberant flowers, made its first appearance in carnival celebrations, in line right behind the carriages in the park. After about 1910, the automobile had largely displaced the carriages, and by the mid-teens, it broke free of respectable Santa Anna park to take a place in the midst of the traditional street carnival. There, in a rather quick coup, private and rented automobiles moved brashly through the poor's pedestrian marching, drumming, and dancing, on the main downtown thoroughfares. John Chasteen, who examines carnival dancing into this period, asserts that "the processions of family cars overflowing with stylish occupants became, rather understandably, the center of attention in the early years of motoring in Brazil, and they necessarily reduced the street dancers' freedom of movement."[110] With some exceptions, such as Praça Onze, the car occupied many of the traditional places associated with the poor's downtown street carnival celebrations, and the *corso* went from being a small, horse-drawn affair that offered a few hours of colorful flowers to being the dominant activity, exhibiting not flowers but a lot of noise and exhaust that would now span two of the three days of the official carnival calendar and the entire length of Avenida Rio Branco.

The press now, in print and photos, thoroughly covered the new automotive street carnival. The photographs evidence that through the 1920s pedestrians on the Avenue had largely become spectators of the car that had taken the spotlight. Carnival street activities shifted from poor folks playing and dancing in the streets to rich folks playing and not dancing in their cars. From afternoon into the evening with their headlights beaming, those who could afford to own or rent a car during the holiday cruised up and down, literally filling the Avenue end to end and bumper to bumper, four cars abreast in two directions. With the spatial power of the car, motorists not only captured the public space but finally felt safe and secure in it, riding high in their automobiles with the pedestrian classes forced to spectate from the sidewalks. Of the city's few thousand cars, it appeared that nearly all of them converged on the Avenue, and demand was so high for rented vehicles that per hour rates climbed to seven times their normal level. The cost became so prohibitive for some middle-class residents that they demanded price controls for the days of carnival, to which the city responded with strict caps.[111] Car dealerships used the occasion to pitch

[110] John Charles Chasteen, "The Prehistory of Samba: Carnival Dancing in Rio de Janeiro, 1840–1917," *Journal of Latin American Studies* 28, no. 1 (Feb. 1996): 43.

[111] *Vida Policial*, Feb. 26, 1927; here one also finds reference to the fact that the *corso* ran two of the three days of carnival. See *O Estado de São Paulo* for similar developments in

FIGURE 3.4 The car in carnival, 1915. Automobiles became the center of street carnival on Avenida Rio Branco. The elite, now protected in their machines, descended from their private clubs to introduce noise and mechanical display to spaces that had formerly been occupied by the dancing, singing, and parading of the lower classes. Automotive carnival persisted on Rio Branco, the city's main public space, until World War II.
Source: Augusto Malta, "Carnaval, Rio de Janeiro," 1915. Courtesy of G. Ermakoff Casa Editorial Ltda and Arquivo Images2You.

their wares to those desirous to have their own car for the occasion, one offering prices "so low" that they headlined their ad with the claim that "anyone who doesn't own an automobile must not want one." The price of a car seemed to be the cost of entry to the modern carnival street celebration.[112]

Open cars, tops down, filled to standing-room capacity with family and friends, became carnival's private, mobile, exclusive party. And the larger the car, the bigger the party. Vehicles meant to carry six passengers were loaded with a dozen.[113] Carnival's pedestrians continued to dress as they always had, as kings and dukes, priests and peasants, slaves and prostitutes, to mock the standing social order. But the rich in their cars wore the standard, fashionable fantasies, which they had sported in the private

São Paulo, Feb. 9, 1915, 4; the price of car rental there rose by a factor of seven during carnival.
[112] *Revista da Semana*, Jan. 22, 1921.   [113] *Fon Fon*, Jan. 15, 1915, 28.

clubs and masked balls, that consisted of non-threatening and matching costumes of sailors, damsels, pirates, clowns, nurses, Mexican cowboys, American Apaches, brides, flappers, and platinum blond showgirls, to name a few, with plenty of males cross-dressing in the same themes.[114]

The street carnival *arrivistes* proclaimed the automotive *corso* as the refining of carnival itself, and their participation was a modernizing example to the pedestrian carnival, now sidelined. The magazine *A Cigarra* asserted that the "civilized carnival is the *corso* in open automobiles ... Everything else is barbaric, primitive, and low class."[115] The view from the sidewalk was not universally one of admiration. The elite partied in their cars as if the lower classes were not there, interacting with shouts and tossing handfuls of confetti and colorful streamers to cars in the next lane. The poor were meant to be passive observers of their betters under the new regime. But the observers still posed social and even potentially physical threats, so much so that in São Paulo, where automotive carnival was on the same trajectory as in Rio, a 1920 law prohibited pedestrian onlookers from insulting anyone in a passing car during carnival.[116] Not all of the traditional elite were keen on the new carnival. One described the automotive *corso* on Rio Branco as an absurd carrousel whose cars were filled with wearisome celebrants, whose tedium was evident as they reclined and yawned through the motions imposed on them by the machine. Augusto Malta abundantly photographed the automotive carnival, a fan of both Mayor Pereira Passos and his new Avenue, but in addition to the standard poses of smiling and waving passengers, he also captured festivants with faces soured by the aggravation of being stuck in the celebration's stop-and go traffic.[117]

Before the car, street carnival exhibited a great deal of group activity, individuals organized into troupes and bands that sang, danced, paraded, and roamed the streets together as coherent assemblages. The organizing principle might be a community of place, such as a poor neighborhood or

---

[114] For a variety of photos of automotive carnival from the mid-teens, some at night, see the issues of *Fon Fon*, Feb. 6, 1915, and Feb. 27, 1915. See also *Fon Fon*, Jan. 8, 1915, 36, for a more descriptive piece about the respectability and equality claims of the *corso* in this early period.

[115] *A Cigarra*, São Paulo, Feb. 15, 1922; cited in Sávio, *A cidade e as máquinas*, 263.

[116] Sávio, *A cidade e as máquinas*, 264.

[117] *Fon Fon*, Jan. 29, 1916, 40. For one example of unhappy automotive carnival celebrants, see Augusto Malta, "Carnival, Rio de Janeiro, Brazil," 1916, G. Ermakoff Casa Editorial Image Archive, www.images2you.com.br/v1/info.php?f=250&dat=1505748562970 (accessed Jan. 14, 2017).

a single street, membership in a club, religious brotherhood, or professional association, or it might be a shared musical interest, such as being part of a marching band or African drum company. The groups went by a variety of labels: *cordões, préstitos, ranchos, congos, congadas, coretos, blocos*, and by the late 1920s, the *escolas de samba* or samba schools, but they all shared a group identity. Carnival groups gave themselves outrageous and often portentous names with political overtones. The Democratics favored the Republic; the Fenians named themselves after the revolutionary Irish opposition to Britain, and the Devil's Leftenants gave the impression of favoring mayhem. Also, there were the Sons of New World Thunder, the Poppies from Japan, the Undaunteds from Hell, We Play so We Do Not Cry, the Chills, Spice in the Frying Pan, the Conquerors of the Dark-skinned Girls, and What's Left over Is Ours. But above all, these groups were about singing and dancing together, as communities, having their own songs and lyrics written for the occasion of carnival, these also often carrying political overtones or claims to the commons. Some groups totaled hundreds of participants, and João do Rio described their collective and competitive music and percussion on Ouvidor's pre-car celebrations as "a street convulsing itself as if it were about to split down the middle and explode in its exuberance and clamor."[118]

Through the 1930s, group dancing and singing continued on narrow streets such as Ouvidor and at Praça Onze, but they did seem to diminish during a period when carnival's focus moved to the automobilized Avenue.[119] Automobiles had the effect of atomizing the celebratory groups. Initially, wealthier clubs organized themselves into the automotive *corsos*, but on the increasingly congested Avenue, they found it difficult to stay together, and soon it was every car for itself. The group and community aspects of the celebration were frustrated by the cars' inability to form groups. Carnival brought people together, but the car separated them on arrival. This made the elite feel safer in the celebration, but it changed the carnival's communal and interactive function. Cars

---

[118] João do Rio, *A alma encantadora das ruas* (Rio de Janeiro: Prefeitura da Cidade do Rio de Janeiro, 1995), 89–97. See also *Jornal do Brasil*, Feb. 27, 1920, 11. In Portuguese, the names are Filhos do Relâmpago do Mundo Novo, Papoula do Japão, Destimidos do Inferno, Brincamos para não Chorar, Arrepiados, Tempero na Panela, Triunfos das Morenas, O que Sobrar é Nosso, the last, reported in *A Manhã*, Jan. 1, 1928, 8.

[119] For a description of various expressions of carnival in the mid-1930s, including private parties, street dancing in Botafogo and Praça Onze, and automotive carnival on Rio Branco, see Hugh Gibson, *Rio* (New York, NY: Doubleday, 1937), 136–45.

made carnival, which had been a gathering and mixing, a linear and segregated event, one in which movement through space was more important than sharing it.

The car's sonic presence also had the effect of diminishing the former preponderance of music and verse. Not even drums could effectively compete. Intentional noises, music, and song were replaced by voices trying to shout above the sound of engines constantly revving to engage their clutch plates in the stop-and-go traffic. Gleeful honking and throwing confetti became the *corso*'s stock interactions. The car moved the body, but not the way music did, and one could not dance with much satisfaction – nor in unison – to the rhythms of the internal combustion engine. And now the scents that dominated carnival were not human perspiration and cheap alcohol but those which derived from incompletely burned gasoline. *Revista da Semana*, which often depicted the elite domestic carnival's seamier side, declared in 1923 that old, Carioca street carnival, which they asserted had been the "apotheosis of prostitution," exhibiting "public delirium" and "raucous lasciviousness, is now positively dead."[120]

Automotive carnival became so popular by the 1920s that substantial regulations had to be put in place to avoid traffic jams and keep the revelers moving. *Cordões* and *préstitos*, with their traditional singing, dancing, and marching on foot on the Avenue, were now relegated to the third and last day of carnival, the first two being dedicated solely to wheeled carnival. There was not room for both at the same time. All regular car traffic was banned on the Avenue for the duration of the *corsos*; to enter, one's car had to be full of costumed bodies, the evidence of one's festive intentions. The Avenue's side streets were closed to prevent congestion, and one could enter the exclusive wheeled party only at the extreme ends of the Avenue. From 1917, parking was banned on the Avenue and drivers were required to maintain a maximum (not a minimum) of two meters between cars, which tried to force cars into a rigid moving chain, not unlike linked rail cars. Neither stopping nor passing were permitted. Those who drove through the festivities were forced, by the very nature of the car's presence, to conform to rigid regulations, especially compared to the pedestrian carnival of yesteryear, whose intent was to throw off the street's usual rules and strictures. Car carnival regulations consumed multiple columns in the newspapers. Only curfew went out the window during the automotive carnival; the papers

---

[120] *Revista da Semana*, Feb. 17, 1923, 28.

reported that "the automobiles, in considerable numbers, persisted on our beautiful artery until daybreak." The nature of carnival dangers changed, too. Pedestrian accident rates rose during carnival. During the 1914 carnival, thirty-eight people were hit, and eighteen children were killed by cars.[121] The catastrophe only seemed to grow. During the three days of carnival in 1934, the Assistência Médica, the city's emergency medical service, reported that 199 people had been hit by cars, the worst year that anyone could remember.[122]

Marco Sávio notes that the automotive *corso* in São Paulo ceased in the early 1930s because the streets had become too congested, shutting down the city's regular traffic, and too egalitarian for elite car owners who no longer found the event sufficiently exclusive. He also blames the somber mood of the global Depression.[123] Others have argued more simply that car models of the 1930s had closed cabs rather than open tops, causing the *corso* to lose its communal appeal entirely. In Rio, however, the automotive celebration of carnival seems only to expand through the same decade. More cars showed up downtown, and the overflow spilled down Beira Mar Avenue, all the way out to Copacabana's Atlantic Avenue, and even to some suburban communities. Downtown congestion may have fomented the phenomenon's spread and decentralization, but it remained an event of the central city as well. In Rio, the car in carnival seemed inextricable. Only World War II, which made it nearly impossible to purchase gasoline, finally shut down the *corsos* in 1943, to much lamentation in the press. Photos show a carnival whose streets are entirely devoid of moving vehicles and whose pedestrian participants walk about subdued in slim numbers – numbers that had been decimated by the car's reign. Celebrants could not even find confetti, and the annual battle of paper projectiles had to be fought "without arms." They called it the Year without Carnival. *Revista da Semana*, a weekly that had long given the automotive *corso* heavy photographic coverage, considered a future reader fifty years out looking back with incredulity at their photos of Carnaval 1943, but they insisted the images were indeed taken during the festival's peak hours when the streets should have been nothing less than a tornado of activity. The elite, without their cars, took their

[121] *O Estado de São Paulo*, Feb. 13, 1915, 10; *Auto Federal*, Feb. 15, 1917. 21; *Vida Polícial*, Feb. 26, 1927. Sávio, *A cidade e as máquinas*, 263–65; *Fon Fon*, Feb. 18, 1909; *Jornal do Brasil*, Jan. 8, 1928, 22. "Os Mata-Crianças: uma Hecatombe em Seis Dias," *Fon Fon*, Mar. 7, 1914; *A Imprensa*, Feb. 26, 1914, 6.
[122] *Jornal do Brasil*, Feb. 16, 1934, 5.   [123] Sávio, *A cidade e as máquinas*, 268.

celebrations back indoors. Through the war years, with the car sidelined by empty gas tanks, the common people returned to fill the streets again to capacity with costumed bodies, sing songs, and share dances, although sadly the most exuberant carnival celebrations of Praça Onze ended the same year due to the car's more mundane spatial needs, which we will examine in Chapter 6.[124] The car made a brief comeback in Rio's 1969 carnival – a number of shops repaired 1930s convertibles and war-vintage Jeeps for rent to cruise Copacabana and Leblon, the southern beach neighborhoods. The director of transit approved of the event as an historical reenactment but correctly predicted it would "be a hell of a mess for traffic in the South Zone," and it was not approved in any subsequent year.[125] The rising spatial demands of the automobile first displaced elements of the traditional pedestrian carnival, and then its intense need for public spaces at all times ruined the automotive carnival itself.

Due to Rio's rapid change in the early twentieth century, in no small part due to the automobile, a number of authors and artists wrote and illustrated rather nostalgic works that looked to their childhood as an idyllic yesteryear. They evoked a quieter but active street of singing peddlers, chiming bells, child's play, and community, lamenting what was lost by describing it in sentimental detail. They did so generally without attacking modernity or the car, in part, because they assented to the changes. But they pined for something lost. As one example, Jorge Americano reminisced in his retirement about how different the Brazilian city had been at the turn of the century during his childhood. One distinct memory was of a man who had been widely known in his neighborhood simply as O Brodo; the name, from the Italian, might be translated as "The Broth." O Brodo always sang as he walked in the streets, a newspaper under his arm, his powerful baritone bouncing off the walls. He was not a peddler but a common working man who was admired for a purposeful, authoritative stride that matched his booming voice. He took large steps, his arms swinging purposefully from his straight-set shoulders, and he never moved off his preferred line. Americano claimed that everything parted from O Brodo's path, even horse-drawn carriages: the power of his personage projected the message "Get out of the way because here comes a force of nature." While he had never seen O Brodo encounter a car, Americano asserted, "I know with certainty that in such a contest, O Brodo would have crushed the

---

[124] *Revista da Semana*, Mar. 13, 1943, 24–26.   [125] *Veja*, Feb. 19, 1969, 42.

automobile." Here was possibly the most nostalgic comment in a book
conceived in nostalgia: the pining for a day when human bodies and voices
ruled the street.[126] The reality of the automobilized street was unfortunately quite different. While there may still have been personages as
potent as O Brodo, all violent confrontations between cars and human
bodies ended badly for the bodies. As in industrialized warfare, where fast
bullets and powerful shells were insensible to bravery and war whoops,
street machines showed little consideration for even the most potent
pedestrians, and their noise diminished the vocal power of the most
thunderous and shrill. The car populated and dominated the city's public
spaces, converting streets into roads, and violence was an essential part of
the transformation. Pedestrians in the headlights were mere obstacles.
Pedestrians in the newspapers were mostly statistics.

---

[126] Jorge Americano, *São Paulo naquele tempo (1895–1915)* (São Paulo: Saraiva, 1957),
182–83. O Brodo walked the streets of São Paulo, not Rio. For a similar nostalgic
account of Rio first published in 1938, see Luiz Edmundo, *O Rio de Janeiro do meu
tempo* (Rio de Janeiro: Conquista, 1957).

4

Death by Blunt Instrument

Largo da Misericórdia

I almost threw myself under the wheels of an automobile running with its headlights off. But I made out that it was a Ford and wanted none of that – a death too ordinary.

Mário Graciotti[1]

The cadaver is of a young child, black in color, whose body is in good physical condition, now rigid, with slightly swollen contusions on his back. The anterior portion of his cranium is compressed with multiple fractures ... The cause of death sufficiently explained, the examiner concludes the exam responding to the first question, "Was there death?": Yes. And to the second, "By what means did death occur?": A blunt instrument.

Coroner's Report[2]

Largo da Misericórdia, a small, irregular plaza on the downtown's southeast peninsula, took its name, which translates as Mercy, from Rio's venerable charitable hospital, the Santa Casa da Misericórdia, which it faced. Founded in the sixteenth century by the Brotherhood of Our Lady, Mother of God, Virgin Mary of Mercy, the Santa Casa, as it was popularly known, was one of Rio's most prominent institutions, led by a long succession of illustrious benefactors. The lay brothers who administered the hospital's charitable work took vows to care for the community's poorest: to cure the sick, bury the dead, console the sorrowful, and,

---

[1] Mário Graciotti, O automóvel de luxo (São Paulo: Casa Editora António Tisi, 1926), 47.
[2] Coroner's Report, "O caso de Oswaldo Garcia, filho de Joanna Garcia, de cor preta, com quatro annos de idade, residente à rua Conselheiro, 914," Jun. 8, 1935, Inqueritos sobre atropelamentos, BR AN Rio CS.o.IQP 7232, 1935, folha 8, verso, ANRJ.

most commendably, "suffer our neighbor's shortcomings."[3] The Santa Casa established its first hospital in Lisbon in 1498. With crown support, by 1600 it had spread its branches to nearly every settlement in the Portuguese empire, from Nagasaki and Macau to Mombasa and Bahia. Rio's Santa Casa, founded in 1582 at the base of Castelo Hill, was rebuilt on a grand scale in 1852 at its original location. The largest edifice in the city, it sprawled along the shore, fronted by the street known as Santa Luzia Beach. The hospital purposefully faced the presumed healthy breezes coming from the mouth of the bay, and for all who came to Rio by ship, which was pretty much everyone until the mid-twentieth century, the Santa Casa's broad façade dominated one's first view of the city's historic center.

The Largo da Misericórdia was among the city's first *logradouros,* and the steep, curving Ladeira da Misericórdia, a narrow street that began in the Largo and climbed to the top of Castelo Hill, is credited as the city's first official street and the first to be paved, in 1617. A remnant of the colonial Ladeira remains, rising abruptly, still clothed in cobbles, but terminating like an unfinished freeway onramp. Misericórdia Street departed the Largo and then, within a few blocks, became Direita, the city's main commercial street. The Largo was once the space where medical students in training relaxed between their rounds and took refreshments from street peddlers, including the succession of Sabinas, market women, who themselves often offered charity to the penniless student body and the hospitals' many patients. Moreover, the Largo, as the hospital's informal lobby, witnessed the perpetual arrival of the city's sick and injured poor who, without means, had no alternative destination for critical medical attention. Likewise, because the crown had granted the hospital a monopoly on funeral services that remained in effect until 1890, the Largo also received many of the city's dead, including those who died in the hospital's care.[4] Before the late nineteenth century, when the hospital purchased two suburban properties for modern cemeteries, many of the dead were buried right on the hospital grounds. Even with the monopoly's end, private mortuary services still congregated around the Largo as the most profitable location for their line of business.

---

[3] A. J. R. Russell-Wood, *Fidalgos and Philanthropists: The Santa Casa da Misericórdia of Bahia, 1550–1755* (Berkeley, CA: University of California Press, 1968), xi, 19–20, 40. It was also referred to as the Misericórdia.

[4] Donald B. Cooper, "Brazil's Long Fight against Epidemic Disease, 1849–1917, with Special Emphasis on Yellow Fever," *Bulletin of the New York Academy of Medicine* 51, no. 5 (May 1975): 687.

The Largo as public space, in a sense, served as the city's antechamber that marked the boundary between health and sickness, life and death.

In the latter half of the nineteenth century, death was a growth industry. After 1850, epidemics lashed the city's residents with an unrelenting fury. Yellow fever returned in devastating cycles after an absence of almost two centuries. It was particularly virulent among the sailors who took up housing on Misericórdia and Dom Manuel Streets situated behind the hospital. African slaves, who generally survived the epidemics, were blamed for bringing to Brazil the black vomit, as yellow fever was known. Brazilians imported more slaves in the 1840s than in any previous decade – 34,000 per year[5] – and the perceived link between Africa and yellow fever played a role in the crown's decision to finally end the slave trade in 1850 after the first outbreak infected a third of the city's population and may have killed more than 10,000. Yellow fever afflicted even the royal family, sickening the emperor and his wife and killing their son, Pedro Afonso, who had not yet turned two. Recent European immigrants, who made up most of the yellow fever victims, were deemed, in their crowded conditions, to exacerbate outbreaks of smallpox and cholera, as well as contribute to the chronic presence of tuberculosis. Emigrant nations, such as Italy and Germany, warned off their citizens from migrating to Brazil, in particular to ports from Rio de Janeiro north; one German doctor who was working for the royal family in Rio warned all who considered coming: "Foreigners, prepare to die."[6]

After the turn of the century, the capital made measurable progress against its virulent microbes through projects of sanitation, mandatory vaccinations, mosquito eradication, and targeted quarantines, programs in which the Santa Casa Hospital played a role. Yellow fever in particular declined rapidly due to the work of Dr. Oswaldo Cruz. By 1908, his measures had chased the scourge from Rio forever, even though yellow fever would continue to plague smaller cities and rural areas for decades. Other infectious diseases declined as well, although tuberculosis persisted. Some microbial conquests were possibly due to rapid social change rather than to sanitation projects: Ian Read explains that tetanus, which had long

---

[5] Herbert S. Klein, *African Slavery in Latin America and the Caribbean* (New York, NY: Oxford University Press, 1986), 151.

[6] Sidney Chalhoub, "The Politics of Disease Control: Yellow Fever and Race in Nineteenth-Century Rio de Janeiro," *Journal of Latin American Studies* 25, no. 3 (Oct. 1993), 441–42. Sidney Chalhoub, *Cidade febril: Cortiços e epidemias na Corte imperial* (São Paulo: Companhia das Letras, 1996), 61, 74–77. Cooper, "Brazil's Long Fight against Epidemic Disease," 672–92.

inflicted excruciating deaths on infants and adults, declined in the city in part due to the demise of slavery – the former slaves began to wear shoes in the streets as symbols of their new status, thus reducing an opportunity for tetanus infection.[7] To many, a new age of health and hygiene was dawning, expressed not just in the construction of modern avenues but the documentable disappearance of age-old plagues. To the most hopeful, it seemed as if the days of the Santa Casa itself were numbered.

BACILLUS AUTOMOBILIS

As Rio's officials celebrated their evident if incipient liberation from the capital's persistent epidemics, the Largo da Misericórdia began to count a growing body of new casualties, both injured and dead. These victims were not infected by tropical microbes nor covered in pustules; rather, they arrived at the Santa Casa with excoriations, fractures, and contusions. In a matter of a couple of decades, the hosts of yellow fever, cholera, and tetanus, who had occupied many of the Santa Casa's beds, were being replaced in part by the bodies of those who had been bludgeoned and trodden by the automobile.[8] Unlike in deaths by microbes, coroners performed autopsies on the automotive and pedestrian dead to establish guilt in what were at first considered crimes of recklessness and negligence. When a patient died due to an infection or poisoning, the cause could have been one of scores of microbes or toxins whose identification could be a matter of great medical skill. For the victims of automotive accidents, the forensics were a simple diagnosis of obvious trauma, and the cause of death was most commonly identified as "a blunt instrument."

In 1908, the same year that yellow fever died in Rio, the first Model T Ford showed up in the city's downtown Ford dealership. Within a few years, it became the city's most common model. Initially, before the Model T's arrival, the number of cars were very few, most of them large, European luxury models, but the deadly potential and reality of the automobile was already apparent and widely remarked. In 1907, the popular illustrator Raul Pederneiras depicted on the front page of the *Jornal do Brasil* a gig pulled by an emaciated horse over the caption "In light of all the disasters of electricity, the knaveries of steam, and the

---

[7] Edmundo, *O Rio de Janeiro do meu tempo*, 29. For the decline of tetanus see Ian Read, "A Triumphant Decline? Tetanus among Slaves and Freeborn in Brazil," *História, Ciências, Saúde* 19 (supp., Dec. 2012): 107–32.

[8] See Blanke, *Hell on Wheels*, table 4.1.

atrocities of gasoline, how the horse has risen in our esteem." Seven years later, on the same front page, he depicted a murderer menacing the streets of Rio with a revolver in one hand, a knife in the other, and a miniature automobile under his arm to the caption "Stop! There are no children left."⁹ By 1921, the car had been labeled *Bacillus automobilis* and identified as a public health emergency. While life insurance corporations celebrated mortality's decline in nearly all disease categories in the United States in 1921, the 15 percent rise in automobile deaths that year evidenced a new epidemic, one whose potential for growth, by the car's rapid multiplication, created alarm. One insuring agency estimated that 10,000 people had died in car accidents globally in 1921, a poorly informed guess as the same year the US census counted 13,253 auto-related fatalities.¹⁰ In Brazil, too, the automobile's boosters had to admit the epidemic nature of automotive injuries and deaths. They still argued that because humans were ultimately in control of their machines, this epidemic too, by rational regulation, could be fixed, and with greater ease than defeating microbes. In fact, some argued that because the car "kills and decimates ... like a pestilence," the solution was to "sanitize the driving classes," using language against the working-class chauffeurs similar to that used in the previous century against slaves and the urban poor in their infectious tenements.¹¹ The solution did not require the elimination of *Bacillus automobilis* but of its most virulent drivers.

After two decades of attempts to make the car safe, Renato Almeida and others subscribed to a more fatalistic prognosis. In a 1932 book entitled *Velocity*, he embraced the ideology of the Italian futurists who had argued for a technological horizon in which machines and noise would be held up as the evidence and substance of modernity and progress. Almeida noted that while Brazil's hygienists had successfully combated deadly germs, he observed that "cars are killing more than any of those old outbreaks." Little, he asserted, could or even should be done about it. There was ambivalence about what to do with this new killer,

⁹ *Jornal do Brasil*, Jan. 7, 1907, 1; *Jornal do Brasil*, Jul. 8, 1914, 1.
¹⁰ Robert Lynn Cox, "National Health in the Life Insurance Mirror," in *Proceedings of the Fifteenth Annual Meeting of the Association of Life Insurance Presidents*, New York City, Dec. 8 and 9, 1921, Life Insurance Association of America, 72–75. US Census Bureau, "Transportation Indicators for Motor Vehicles and Airlines," Statistical Abstract of the United States, n. HS-41 (2003), n. HS-41, 77, www2.census.gov/library/publications/2004/compendia/statab/123ed/hist/hs-41.pdf (accessed Sep. 28, 2015).
¹¹ *Vida Policial*, Jul. 25, 1925, 2, 3, 5.

a creature of our own creation, one that was considered the very embodiment of national progress. For Almeida, the thought of eradicating the triumphal machine, or even limiting the speed that made it attractive and useful, was not to be countenanced, so he argued that Brazil, like the rest of the modern world, would have to embrace the automobile for the sake of progress, and simply accept the blood price: "Civilization," he shrugged, "demands a heavy tribute."[12]

Streets before the car, of course, were not places safe from dangerous and deadly collisions between vehicles and bodies. Streetcars, especially once electrified after 1890, intensified the street's vehicular hazards, becoming the most common cause of street accidents. Residents sometimes reacted violently to streetcar incidents, and streetcar companies were among the most hated institutions in the city, not only for increasing their fares but for presumed negligence and an apparent lack of concern for human life. Collisions with pedestrians, especially when they involved children, might incite citizens to tear up rails and damage company property.[13] Because all injuries were assumed to have a moral cause, before the car, the city almost universally took the side of victims, nonwheeled street users, in drawing up regulations and punishing infractors. Pedestrians made up the majority of street users, both elite and poor, and had a friend in the law.

The arrival of the automobile transformed the scale of vehicular accidents by introducing not only higher velocities but also higher vehicular volumes. The opportunity and intensity of spatial violence changed.[14] Cars quickly outnumbered all other kinds of vehicles moving in the streets, creating more opportunities for accidents, and even the earliest cars moved at speeds that trebled those of the electric streetcars. In addition to going faster, cars ran on unpredictable trajectories. With streetcars, if one stayed clear of the rails, one was generally safe. Moreover, many streets segments had no streetcar lines, so the car introduced the danger of large moving vehicles to streets that had rarely had them. With cars, no passable street, and no place on the street was entirely secure, not even sidewalks, as many accident reports demonstrated. Already by 1910, cars were hitting and injuring people in the street at

---

[12] Renato Almeida, *Velocidade* (Rio de Janeiro: Schmidt, 1932), 115.

[13] *Jornal do Comércio*, Jul. 16, 1890, 1; *O Estado de São Paulo*, Oct. 26, 1892.

[14] Sávio, *A modernidade sobre rodas*, 163, notes that in São Paulo, too, collisions with vehicles were fairly common, but that with the "arrival of the automobile, this dispute over the streets' space became far more intense and more violent."

FIGURE 4.1 "A perilous crossing," 1909. As the number and speed of automobiles increased, pedestrians, who remained the street's primary users, found simple movement becoming difficult, slow, and increasingly dangerous. Newspapers consistently reported the city's daily pedestrian accidents, from the minor to the deadly, for half a century. Here, the artist Raul suggests confronting the threat of violence with the threat of violence, to reestablish a balance of power.
Source: Raul (Raul Pederneiras), "Travessa arrojada," Sept. 29, 1909, *Jornal do Brasil*. Courtesy of the Centro de Pesquisa e Documentação de História Contemporânea do Brasil and the *Jornal do Brasil*.

rates that were closing in on those of streetcars and horse-drawn vehicles, even though cars were still rather few in number by comparison.[15]

The decline of infectious disease was accompanied by the fall of gravity as the main cause of accidental death. With the notable exceptions of firearms, before the automobile only gravity had the force to accelerate bodies and objects to speeds that threatened the integrity of flesh and bone. The newspapers' nineteenth-century "Disasters" columns were dominated by stories of workers falling from ladders and scaffolding,

---

[15] *Jornal do Brasil*, Sep. and Oct. 1909. During these months, wagons, carts, trains, and streetcars figure prominently, but the car by itself begins to match them all for total accidents.

FIGURE 4.2 A new vehicular violence, 1907. As an automotive victim flies through the air, he cries out: "If I don't fall beneath the wheels, I'm saved." But the illustrator spells out the nature of modern transportation in the caption – that now it was no longer gravity, being crushed under wheels, that posed the major threat, but velocity, the violence of the actual collision, that injured and killed. Compared to the prior vehicular threat, which was not insignificant, residents perceived the car as having introduced violence to the human body on an appalling scale.
Source: "Si não caio em baixo, 'stô sarvo!'" *Fon Fon*, Apr. 20, 1907.

residents falling down wells or out of windows, or of bricks, hammers, flowerpots, and entire walls falling onto the heads of people below. Sinking vessels and drownings, which always ranked high among causes of accidental death, were also in a sense clinched by gravity. Because transit was relatively slow, the majority of transit accidents consisted not of collisions, although these were not uncommon, but of individuals being thrown from horses, coachmen tumbling from their perches, and, most commonly, streetcar passengers falling hard to the street while either boarding and disembarking. Particularly after the arrival of the electric streetcar, which braked and accelerated faster than the horse trams, falls associated with transit were the common fare of the daily injured.[16] The police blamed these injuries on careless streetcar operators who refused to come to full stops at streetcar stations. Even those who did stop, they claimed, did so too briefly for passengers, especially children and the elderly, to get on and off safely.[17] Most of these unfortunates fell clear of the vehicles in which they were riding, experiencing mild abrasions, sprains, and an occasional broken bone. Less commonly, pedestrians fell beneath horses and vehicles, and then the power of gravity crushed them under hooves or wheels, which was occasionally fatal.

Gravity, as a force, remained more powerful than the internal combustion engine. Cars could not accelerate their own mass with anything close to gravity's motive power. But they did not have to. Even today the average passenger car has only half the force of gravity for its weight. In the early twentieth century, with just a few horsepower, the car's power was less than a tenth of gravity's. Ford's Model T only had twenty horsepower for most of its long period of manufacture. However, early internal combustion engines had acceleration sufficient that they could, on the speedways which the streets had become, accumulate more than enough speed to put the body at risk to life and limb. Even at moderate speeds, cars created conditions in which decelerations – collisions with other vehicles, pedestrians, trees, poles, and walls – achieved massive forces involving many times the force of gravity that were often not survivable.

Brazilians used the term *atropelar* to describe being run over by a vehicle, an ancient term that literally meant to be trodden or trampled by the hooves of pack animals (*tropas*). Street users understood quite correctly that being trampled by a mule or run over by a vehicle, not being hit, was the primary physical danger of the vehicular street before the car. As a result, some streetcars sported cowcatchers or low bumpers to push a fallen pedestrian off the tracks, to prevent the victim from being crushed.[18] When the car arrived on the scene, transit's dangers substantively changed due to the car's increased velocity, and the meaning of

---

[16] Noronha Santos, *Meios de transportes*, vol. 1, 329.
[17] *Vida Policial*, Dec. 19, 1925, 34.
[18] Rosenthal, "Dangerous Streets," 38, reports on the cowcatcher or *salvavida's* use in Montevideo. It was a rarer feature in Rio, but low bumpers are common.

atropelar changed with it. With the car, the danger now lay in being hit by
the vehicle at high speed, whose initial impact was likely to throw a body
clear of the wheels. *Atropelar* came to describe any automobile pedestrian
accident and would primarily carry the connotation of being hit violently,
not necessarily being run over. Even in the earliest years, car impacts were
often of such violence that they propelled bodies a good distance and
removed pedestrians from their shoes, which might remain poised in the
exact spaces the victim stood. Such violent phenomena, if occasionally
seen with trains, had been largely unknown on city streets. A cartoon from
as early as 1907 illustrated the new automotive risks starkly. A man,
a provincial bumpkin by his accented comments, flies threw the air after
being hit by a car, his contorted expression evincing pain and bewildered
astonishment. With hope he cries out: "If I don't fall beneath the wheels,
I am saved." But the illustrator's caption disabused the victim and the
reader of any such optimism. "Now, things are otherwise, in our new age,
and with automobiles! In the past, the coachmen would secure the horses
by the reins, and everything would be fine; today, all has changed: honk-
honk in your ears, gasoline's smoke in your eyes, a bludgeoning from
above, and the wheels may follow." [19]

Hence, velocity and volume, not horsepower and mass, were the car's
lethal additions to the street. With its increasing numbers and accumula-
tive velocities, the car's size, ungainly maneuverability, and dangerous
shape made it a technology with outsized spatial implications. For private
transportation, automobiles were remarkably large, as long and as wide as
the early streetcars. Cars cut a large swath of street space before them, the
largest private object on the street. On Rio's narrowest streets, a passing
car consumed most of the street's width, leaving little refuge.

In part due to its size, the car was not as easily maneuvered and
controlled as its boosters claimed. Proponents touted the new vehicle's
safety compared to capricious equines and ponderous streetcars. Unlike
the horse, which was skittish, had a mind of its own, and was prone to
bolting unpredictably, the car, they claimed, responded immediately,
without thought, fear, or resistance to every command of the human at
its controls. Unlike the streetcar, with its many tons of steel and strap-
hanging passengers trundling on rails, which could neither stop quickly
nor swerve around imprudent pedestrians, the car could brake with
rapidity and take evasive action. One American enthusiast claimed that
the car's "ability immediately to stop, its quick response to guidance, its

[19] *Fon Fon*, Apr. 20, 1907.

unconfined sphere of action, would seem to make the automobile one of the least dangerous of conveyances."[20]

But claims of the car's inherent safeties were exaggerated, and its "unconfined sphere of action" was limited by both its controls and the small spaces most streets offered its motions. Although many were impressed with the car's ability to stop relative to horse-drawn vehicles, its speed negated any such gains. Even for chauffeurs paying attention, with quick reflexes and good will toward men, early brakes did not have the power to effectively slow or stop a car moving at even moderate speed. Until the early 1920s, cars typically had only rear brakes, and most of these consisted of a fabric band that wrapped around the rear axle or around rear brake drums, both operated by human muscle – a hand brake or foot pedal – with a little mechanical advantage.[21] Rear brakes alone were extremely ineffective because a car, once it begins to brake, throws its weight forward onto the front tires, causing the rear tires to potentially lock and skid, whether or not they were brittle and bald, which they often were. The addition of drums and linings at the wheels, hydraulic actuators, and of brakes on the front wheels took three decades to become common. Henry Ford, who liked to keep things simple and cheap, considered front-wheel brakes to be unnecessary, even on the Model A, and some Ford vehicles did not have front brakes until 1938. Overland Automobiles claimed in a 1928 advertisement in the *Jornal do Brasil* that its Whippet was the first light passenger car to have brakes on all four wheels. The ad pictured the Whippet stopping abruptly, just short of a child playing in the street.[22] The inability to brake well meant that when pedestrians were in front of speeding cars, they really had to get out of the way because a driver could not significantly slow his vehicle unless he had a lot of space and sufficient warning. His most common safety recourse was to apply the horn rather than the brakes and hope the more maneuverable pedestrian had time to get out of the way. Drivers accused of negligence in accidents frequently pointed to skidding tires to show a good faith effort at trying to avoid hitting a pedestrian.

Early tests demonstrated just how bad early brakes were. Trials completed in 1909 by the Automotive Club of New York, which had every reason to get the best results, were appalling. The fabric band brake, they

---

[20] Huddy, *Laws of Automobiles*, 28.
[21] See Gijs Mom, *The Evolution of Automotive Technology: A Handbook* (Warrendale, PA: SAE International, 2014), 151–53.
[22] *Jornal do Brasil*, Mar. 11, 1928, 17.

claimed, was far more effective than the brakes on horse carts, yet a car traveling at 15 mph required 34 feet to come to a stop. At 25 mph, it required 90 feet; and at a mere 30 mph the early car required all of 136 feet to come to a complete stop. If conditions were wet, those distances, one noted, would have to be greatly increased, and none of them included the driver's reaction time that in today's tests accounts for half the stopping distance at 20 mph.[23] Soon, cars sped along at more than 40 or 50 mph. Over the decades, stopping distances have improved, but the gains again were ephemeral as cars became faster. A modern car still requires 110 feet to make a complete stop from 30 mph, if one includes the reaction time. An early car at the same speed, including reaction time, would have required more than 200 feet. As a car's speed doubled, the distance it required to stop quadrupled.[24]

The automobile's steering was likewise overrated. Due to the lack of any kind of hydraulic or electrical assistance, turning the wheel required some physical strength, and because tires were narrow and convex, they made little contact with the road and responded poorly to a driver's steering adjustments, especially if abrupt, at high speeds, or in wet conditions. And because cars only steered at the front wheels, even when a driver steered the front end safely around a pedestrian, the rear fender or wheel often hit them anyway, a fairly common occurrence. The early car was largely a poorly controlled projectile, and its backers eventually concluded that because the car was neither safe nor entirely controllable, the onus of behavior change would have to fall most heavily on pedestrians.

Lastly, it was the very shape of the car – a blunt instrument fashioned to meet the needs of mechanical function and aesthetic form – that posed substantial dangers to pedestrians. A horse would veer or rear if it perceived that a collision were eminent, but probably more importantly, horseflesh, barring its hooves, served as an effective bumper for the vehicles it pulled behind it, often sparing pedestrians a collision or trampling. Streetcars, in addition to sporting bumpers, presented broad and rounded front ends that tended to distribute their impact over much of the body. The early automobile's body was often wider than early electric streetcars and formed a panoply of sharp and blunt objects crafted smartly of steel, brass, and glass. Even at moderate speeds, steel chassis, projecting

[23] *Horseless Age* 24 (Dec. 22, 1909): 738.

[24] See Tilton E. Shelburne and Jack H. Dillard, "An Appraisal of Skid Prevention," in *Proceedings of the 9th Pan American Highway Congress* (Washington, DC: 1963), 656.

leaf springs, headlights, narrow wheels, and sharp fenders all posed serious threats to a pedestrian's lower extremities. The car's grilled radiator, radiator cap, hood, and plate glass windshield threatened the more vital organs.[25]

COUNTING THE QUICK AND THE DEAD

Examining the conflict of oil and blood on the street is critical to understanding the car's spatial conquest. Pedestrians did not cede the street's space without defiance, and for years, many, including children, continued to maintain their presence, to retain the roles they had long played in the traditional street, in leisure, commerce, and celebration. However, with the increasing number of vehicles, it was a fool's game to challenge the car's spatial dominance. While there is no need to go to any great length in harrowing up the grotesque horrors that the automobile produced on the city's streets, we must do a little. The frequency and the brutality of automotive accidents, particularly of the auto-pedestrian variety that made up the preponderance of deaths and injuries, help explain the rapid diminishment of the street's traditional roles. The car did not just occupy space previously used by bodies; it displaced them with force and regularity. The lethal results were widely witnessed by those who used the streets and written up for all to read in the daily newspapers.

Although observers repeatedly described the automobile's virulence in graphic anecdotes, statistics on automotive accidents in Rio, even unreliable ones, are hard to come by. The dearth of good data remains the reality through most of the century. Despite the fact that the automobile was a public health emergency of epidemic proportions, officially, the car's virulence was ignored and sometimes outright denied; hence its statistics went uncounted or unreported.[26] In this, Rio and Brazil were not atypical. One American scholar observed in 1963 that different US agencies offered radically different estimates of the casualties, varying by millions of incidents, and lamented that "we do not know how big the problem is we are trying to resolve, only that it is tremendous."[27] In Rio, no single agency took on – or appears to have even been given – the responsibility of

[25] *Auto Federal*, Aug./Sep. 1917, 24. Seabra Junior, *Accidentes de automoveis*, 258.
[26] Seabra Junior, *Accidentes de automoveis*, 307; and Fructuoso Moniz Barreto de Aragão, *Delictos do automovel e outros carros (sentenças)* (Rio de Janeiro: n.p., 1924), 10.
[27] David M. Baldwin, "Needed Improvements in Traffic Accident Reports," in *Proceedings of the 9th Pan American Highway Congress*, May 6–18, 1963, vol. 1 (Washington, DC, 1963), 393.

documenting and reporting automotive accidents. The police kept some statistics but failed to maintain or report their findings, and they were often found to be unwilling to share what they knew. The crime magazine *Archivo Vermelho* (*The Red Archive*), which covered the city's most audacious crimes from 1918, seemed to have some access to police information, including investigation photographs. But they observed that the police were unwilling to share information about some forms of crime because the numbers reflected badly on the police forces themselves. "The results are not divulged because the highest police authorities guard the number and extent of such crimes with the maximum secrecy ... for they give the impression that there is no policing in Rio de Janeiro."[28]

With the statistics the police would give them, the magazine decided to publish, beginning in late January 1921, weekly tables that enumerated vehicular accidents and deaths along with suicides, murders, fires, falls, explosions, and drownings. All this was to be aggregated quarterly. However, reporting never made it through its first quarter since the police apparently retracted their cooperation. The tables ceased to appear after eleven short weeks. City officials elsewhere showed a pattern of obfuscation on such matters, and automotive statistics – like those surrounding epidemics, whose presence and severity were frequently manipulated or withheld out of fear of the consequences for immigration, commerce, and tourism – were often not made available for public consumption.[29] In the 1950s, Álvaro Altieri specifically accused São Paulo's police of hiding the scale of automotive deaths from the general public by refusing to open their archives to the press.[30] The eleven weekly tables that *Archivo Vermelho* was able to publish indeed make it apparent that the automobile was a major element of accidents and death by the early 1920s, and a significant fraction of the police force's daily concerns. Using data supplied by thirty-three police districts, *Archivo Vermelho* reported 324 vehicular accidents: 58 involving minors and 40 resulting in death. The numbers include tram accidents, but the tables indicate that 71 percent of all vehicular accidents involved automobiles. In the same period, according to the same records, there were only 23 suicides and 19 murders

---

[28] *Archivo Vermelho*, Feb. 2, 1921, 5.

[29] Sonia Shah, *Pandemic: Tracking Contagions, from Cholera to Ebola and Beyond* (New York, NY: Farrar, Straus and Giroux, 2016), 106–09.

[30] Seabra Junior, Accidentes de automóveis, *307*; Aragão, Delictos do automóvel e outros carros, *10*; *Álvaro Altieri*, Variações sobre o trânsito paulistano (São Paulo: Amigos da Cidade, 1953), 111–12.

in Rio, suggesting that vehicles were already as deadly as other age-old forms of violence.[31]

Archivo Vermelho's brief window into automotive accidents also shows that police records were incomplete. The magazine admitted as much, explaining that "great are the number of cases of aggression, accidents, suicides, and robberies that are not brought to the attention of the police and do not figure in their statistics." They pointed out that the chief of police did not communicate and in fact had a poor relationship with the medical services that cared for most automotive victims, and hence knew nothing of many of the city's accidents.[32] Most automotive accidents that involved injuries never came to the attention of the police, a reality that is borne out by newspaper reporting. During the first full week of 1921, *Archivo Vermelho*, relying on police records, reported twelve automobile accidents, two of which resulted in death. Nine of those accidents, including both deaths, were not reported in any of Rio's four major papers the same week, showing that the police did not share with the newspapers. However, that same week the newspapers themselves reported thirty-one automotive accidents with injuries that the police did not have on record. To the mid-1920s, newspapers not infrequently concluded accident reports with the accusatory phrase "the police remain ignorant of this incident."

One might expect that the police had at least a loose handle on the number of automotive dead, but various sources suggest otherwise. *Voz do Chauffeur*, the publication of the chauffeur's union, tried to "honestly" report the number automotive dead in 1924, counting some seventy-four victims (fifty-one men, five women, and eighteen minors) through September who had passed through the police morgue. But it noted that those who died at the scene rarely entered the morgue or became part of its statistics because relatives were permitted to remove the bodies to the family home directly, which it estimated would increase the number of deaths by 30 percent (but it offered no basis for the magnitude of the addition).[33] Some subset of mortal accidents did enter the courts with substantial reports and detailed autopsies, but it is impossible to know what fraction went through this process. The National Archive in Rio has 1,563 such police inquiries spanning the years 1891 to 1938; they provide a great deal of information about the nature and circumstances

[31] See the "Boletim seminal" tables published weekly in *Archivo Vermelho* beginning on Feb. 2, 1921.
[32] *Archivo Vermelho*, Feb. 2, 1921, 5.   [33] *Voz do Chauffeur*, Nov. 24, 1924, 2.

surrounding automotive deaths, but they are not much help in quantifying the problem.[34] And while death records for the city are available in every administrative district and decade that concerns us, they only state the immediate cause of death (asphyxia), not the proximate – sometimes referred to as the legal – cause (strangulation).[35]

Rio's many newspapers offer us a source on automotive accidents that are flawed and incomplete but that have the advantage of being remarkably consistent. For half a century, some of the city's longer-running papers reported on the streets' daily collisions. Searching Rio's papers, particularly by the mid-1910s, a researcher might feel that he or she was suffering from confirmation bias – that is, finding exactly what he or she was looking for all over the place.[36] Already by 1914, newspapers commonly reported more than twenty accidents per week; by 1921, they totaled 30, and by 1928, newspapers reported an average of 45 automotive incidents every week. These numbers were by no means exhaustive because the newspapers missed a great deal of the carnage and rarely reported on accidents beyond the downtown streets. But the newspaper reporting establishes a minimum to the disaster at the city center.

Rio's papers seem rather exceptional in the magnitude and consistency of counting automotive accidents in the national capital. Newspapers in Brazil's provincial capitals make no such effort, nor do the major papers in the United States, even though automotive accidents there were also

---

[34] See the scattered Inquéritos Policiais dealing with *atropelamentos* that can be most easily found and aggregated in the Aquivo Nacional do Rio de Janeiro's digital catalog "Sistema de Informações de Arquivo Nacional." We do not know how complete these records are.

[35] For examples: Antonio Monteiro de Faria, aged sixty-four, was killed by a car on Avenida Salvador de Sá on April 2, 1914 (*Correio da Manhã*, Apr. 3, 1914); and Luiza Sonia Cosme Pinto, aged thirty-four, was killed on Avenida Beira Mar while riding in her husband's car on July 6, 1935 (*Jornal do Brasil*, Jul. 7, 1935). But their death records only state that they respectively died of "traumatic rupture of the liver" and "radiated transversal fracture of the base of the cranium," not that they were the result of automobile accidents. Death record for Antonio Monteiro de Faria, Brazil, Rio de Janeiro, Civil Registration, 1829–1912, 3rd Circunscrição, Óbitos, Aug. 1913–Jun. 1914, n. 115, at Family Search, https://familysearch.org/ark:/61903/3:1:S3HY-66YQ-2T2?i=148&wc=9GBQ-2NL%3A113334201%2C122849201%2C117545901%3Fcc%3D1582573&cc=1582573 (accessed Jun. 8, 2016); and for Luiza Sonia Cosme Pinto, Family Search, Brazil, Rio de Janeiro, Civil Registration, 1829–1912, 6th Circunscrição, Óbitos, Jun.–Oct 1935, 75, https://familysearch.org/ark:/61903/3:1:S3HT-68T6-R6?i=79&wc=9GR1-MNP%3A113334201%2C135195401%2C143811901%3Fcc%3D1582573&cc=1582573 (accessed Jun. 8, 2016).

[36] Many of the statistical claims that follow are based on a 10 percent time sample (five random weeks per year) taken every seven years from 1907 to 1935. They include more than 700 accident reports taken from Rio's largest newspapers, most consistently the *Jornal do Brasil*, *Correio da Manhã*, *A Noite*, and *O Paiz*.

notoriously common. For example, during the first week of January 1921, Rio's newspapers reported thirty-three automotive accidents – six per day – with forty-two injured just in the city's downtown. By comparison, during the same week the *New York Times* published only three accidents with five dead, and the *Chicago Tribune* reported seven accidents with as many deaths. The same pattern held in 1935: during the first week of July, the *Jornal do Brasil* reported forty-five accidents compared to the *New York Times'* three and the *Tribune*'s six. From the early teens, American newspapers, in part due to the scale of the problem, focused their attentions on the spectacular; they reported only sensational incidents that involved multiple cars and multiple deaths, and they even reported on dramatic automotive tragedies occurring in other parts of the nation.[37] In contrast, the newspapers in Rio and São Paulo focused on the local, day-to-day accidents where the majority of collisions were between cars and pedestrians, and they included the most mundane, least sensational examples.

There are a number of cultural and moral reasons for the newspapers' consistent, almost obsessive attention to automotive accidents in Rio. In the early decades, the papers certainly took up the cause of the lowly pedestrian, and accident reports frequently spewed a venomous rage toward privileged drivers who not only daily hit unprotected pedestrians but also often sped away, leaving the victims for dead. But what made the actual reporting possible was a significant development in the city's public medical services. In response to the increasing number of auto accidents, Mayor Aguiar de Souza established the city's first first-aid post, known as the Assistência Médica, in late 1907. The service's central post downtown became the primary destination for accident victims of all kinds. Accident reports in the newspapers before this date, whether for cars or other street disasters, were fewer in number, much as they were in other city's newspapers of the time. Before 1908, accident victims in Rio for the most part were treated in local pharmacies and then sent home. Wealthier individuals were treated by private doctors who were scattered throughout the city, and the most serious cases ended up in various hospitals and morgues. Nobody, including the police, could keep track of so many random and distributed cases. The central Assistência Médica, then, became in essence a clearinghouse of information about the city's accidents. Because

---

[37] American newspapers, because they limited themselves to larger tragedies, had more dead and injured per accident than Rio's papers. However, they were as keen in reporting non-automotive types of crime.

medical care there was prompt and free, as was the ambulance ride, accident victims concentrated at the new post. This made it possible for the newspapers to send their reporters to the central post to gather information on the daily automotive toll. Between 1914 and 1935, 93 percent of all automotive accidents reported in Rio's papers derived from information that originated in the various Assistências established throughout the city. The medical posts did not report their statistics; reporters regularly visited their patients and collected the data themselves.

However, while the newspapers in Rio now found it relatively easier to report automotive accidents, their reports were skewed to particular kinds of accidents. They missed minor incidents: those with lesser injuries that continued to be treated in local pharmacies, and especially those with no injuries. Over the eleven weeks of *Archivo Vermelho*'s statistical reporting, there were 192 auto-pedestrian accidents in police records identified as being without treatable injuries.[38] These were ostensibly victims making direct complaints to the police, and the newspapers reported none of them. Likewise, the newspapers often missed the most serious accidents where victims died at the scene and never passed through the Assistência, or when the injuries were serious enough that the victims were taken directly to the city's various hospitals. They also often missed the deaths of those who survived treatment in the Assistências but then succumbed later once interned in a hospital. Of those victims treated in the Assistências, 18 percent, all with serious injuries, were transferred to local hospitals, and only rarely did the papers follow up on those cases. The newspapers also substantially missed the tragedies in the suburbs. In the first couple decades, nearly all the accident reports came directly from the Assistência's central post downtown. By 1928, the Meier post, which was located just to the west of the central city, accounted for less than 10 percent of reports, but the papers seemed to make no effort to gather information from posts, all established by 1922, in Copacabana, Gávea, Engenho Dentro, Paquetá, or beyond. And lastly, it is apparent that the papers were inconsistent in utilizing even the Assistência's sources. Many automotive accidents were reported in only one paper; all the other papers, not to mention the police, failed to record or report the cases. In 1914, in comparing the accident reports in three major papers, 45 percent of all accidents reports were unique to just one paper. In 1935, examining four papers, 58 percent of the cases were entirely unique. The same was true of deaths, although the papers did somewhat

[38] "Boletim seminal," *Archive Vermelho*, Jan.–Apr., 1921.

better: 25 percent of all automotive deaths went unreported in all but one of the city's papers.

Despite these flaws and omissions, the newspapers provide us a floor on the size of the calamity. Between 1914 and 1935, I estimate that the newspapers reported about 5,000 dead and 41,000 injured in automotive accidents. Again, these are only the minimums we can document of automotive disasters. Newspapers did not report on the southern suburbs, where most of the city's daily car trips originated; there are almost no accident reports from Laranjeiras, Botafogo, Copacabana, Jardim Botanico, Ipanema, Leblon, or Gávea. Likewise, newspapers did not report accidents in the burgeoning northern suburbs beyond Engenho Velho and Sao Christóvão. Certainly, accidents were more common downtown where automobiles and pedestrians mixed most intensely, but cars were in every district by the 1920s, and average speeds and speed limits tended to be higher outside the downtown. The newspapers, then, offer a limited downtown view of the car's mortal impact.

They do offer a view of who was being brutalized. Victims represented nearly every neighborhood and suburb across the city, but the large majority lived downtown. The dead and injured, then, were not typically strangers but neighbors, and it is surprising how many are casualties on their home streets. However, the most serious car accidents happened disproportionately on the city's broad avenues where cars achieved the highest speeds and pedestrians had to cross numerous lanes. The downtown corridor that ran along avenues Mangue, Senador Euzebio, Visconde de Itaúna, Marechal Floriano, Rio Branco, and Beira Mar figures prominently. Throw in the avenues Mem de Sá, Frei Caneca, Salvador de Sá, Haddock Lobo, and São Christovão, and the squares Tiradentes, República, and Onze, and you encompass the larger majority of the locations of newspaper-reported accidents. All of these, excepting Rio Branco, were streets with many residences. Striking for their almost complete absence in recorded accidents are the downtown's narrow, colonial streets, spaces that cars also occupied, but in smaller numbers and at far lower velocities, forming something of a pedestrian refuge where traditional street uses might better endure.

Above all, it was the unprotected pedestrian who took the brunt of the violence. Cars, of course, collided with trees, walls, posts, houses, streetcars, and other cars, all of which were reported, and the results could be deadly and might "profoundly disturb public sentiment," especially when they involved the better classes or the famous.[39] But such accidents paled numerically in comparison with the more mundane, pedestrian reality. Drivers and their passengers found protection in the car's considerable body. Pedestrians were vulnerable. Pedestrians posed almost no direct threat to drivers. In fact, drivers and passengers injured in auto-pedestrian accidents were usually the result of the driver taking extraordinary means to avoid the pedestrian and crashing into something more substantial.

In newspapers through the mid-1930s, pedestrians make up just over 80 percent of the car's victims (87 percent in 1928). That is higher than in São Paulo, New York, and Philadelphia where pedestrians made up about two-thirds of automotive casualties.[40] Restricting the sample to deaths in Rio in 1935, 79 percent of the dead were pedestrians. In São Paulo in 1936, among 1,003 automotive accidents over nine months, pedestrians accounted for fifty-two deaths (85 percent) while drivers and passengers made up only nine deaths. As early as 1910, in a cartoon published in Brazil's first automotive magazine, a man visits his insurance company's doctor who declares him in good health, until he learns he has no car. "As a pedestrian, you are uninsurable ... buy a car if you want to live a long life": an urban prescription for longevity. A few years later, *Fon Fon* observed that poor pedestrians killed while walking the public commons experienced the greater comfort and safety of the car only in the hearse that carried them to the cemetery.[41] One police publication suggested, in all seriousness, that the city incentivize the reduction of auto-pedestrian accidents by offering public prizes to all drivers who did not hit a pedestrian during the course of a calendar year.[42] The blind, the deaf, and the drunk, for whom the slower street of the past had been an integral part of their spatial domain, also suffered a disproportionate share of casualties. And some of the pedestrian dead, without driver's licenses, were anonymous, lying on the coroner's slab unidentified until a family member came looking for them, first with hope in the Santa Casa, or then with dread in the morgue. A few were never identified, disappearing from

---

[39] For an early case that shocked even beyond Rio, see *O Século*, Jun. 22, 1909, 2; *O Estado de São Paulo*, Jun. 23, 1909.

[40] Costa Netto, *Relatório* (São Paulo: Directoria do Serviço de Trânsito, 1936), 142; for US statistics, see Norton, *Fighting Traffic*, 21, 25.

[41] *Revista de Automóveis*, Oct. 1911, 66; "Automoveis, automoveis, automoveis," *Fon Fon*, Jan. 15, 1916, 28.

[42] *Vida Policial*, Jul. 25, 1925, 8.

a family, neighborhood, or social circle without notification or explanation, to be buried unnamed in a pauper's plot.[43]

The car discriminated by gender and age as well. Men made up the largest proportion of the victims, accounting for 89 percent of the car's injured and dead from 1914 to 1935. Men made up the majority of casualties in part because they made up the larger share of drivers and of street workers. Yet still, the most common occupation of pedestrian victims in São Paulo in 1936 was female domestic servant, followed by student.[44] During the month of July 1930, a single Rio newspaper reported fifty-nine auto-pedestrian accidents. Of those, forty-three were identified as male, and only three as female. And among children, thirteen boys were involved compared to only two girls. Of the five total reported dead, all of them were male. The majority of street workers were male, and hence police, street cleaners, peddlers, postman, handcart men, cabbies, and streetcar employees suffered higher rates of accidents.[45] This high incidence of male casualties might suggest that the street, which many had described as becoming increasingly feminized in the late nineteenth century, showing an ever greater number of women participants on the glorified and sanitized avenues, was again becoming masculinized by the dangerous presence of the automobile. Men effectively occupied more street space than women as cars were almost universally driven by men until the 1930s in Brazil, and far outnumbered women drivers for decades to come. The first female drivers in Rio made their debuts in the mid-1920s, and the first documented accident with a female driver was by an American, Adele Stein Elysson, attached to the US embassy, who hit and injured a motorcycle officer in 1924.[46]

At least to 1935, children made up the largest subset of the automobile's victims. Those between the age of ten and nineteen formed the largest decadal bracket, accounting for 26 percent of all automotive victims. If you add those under the age of ten to the teenage bracket, minors accounted for almost 40 percent of all the car's deaths and injuries. Adults in their twenties made up 24 percent; those in their thirties, 12 percent. And the aged did not escape either, those over fifty accounting for 14 percent of victims. If there were an average victim, he

---

[43] Typical cases here were gleaned from all accident reports in *Jornal do Comércio* during July 1935.

[44] Costa Netto, *Relatório* (São Paulo: Directoria do Serviço de Trânsito, 1936), 149.

[45] Statistics were gleaned from all auto accidents reported in *Jornal do Comércio* during the month of July 1930.

[46] *Voz do Chauffeur*, Nov. 10, 1924, 8.

was a teenage male who worked or played in the street, a boy like the
street peddler Florivante Christovão, aged fifteen, who was hit on Frei
Caneca on April 6, 1920, by Leonel Augusto Santos driving car number
1,356. He, like most who suffered "grave injuries," was transferred from
the Assistência to the Santa Casa for long-term treatment.[47] Or little
Mario Bianco, aged nine, a poor child from the *favela* on Conceição Hill
who sold newspapers: he was run over by the rear wheel of a bus on Rio
Branco on January 30, 1929. The *Jornal do Brasil* published a photo of
Mario's wake, his alarmingly small body lying beneath his mother's
hands. Sensing an occupational connection with this "humble servant"
of the press, the newspaper paid his funeral expenses. The same day, the
Jornal reported sixteen other auto-pedestrian accidents, two of which
involved young children, both of whom died.[48] It is possible children's
deaths and injuries were better documented in the newspapers out of
deep public sympathy or outrage, but for children and their parents, the
streets had been and were expected to remain a place for children to be,
to move, and to play. For some time, citizens believed that cars and
children could share the street (as children and streetcars and horse carts
had shared the street before), if only motorists drove responsibly and
cautiously. Accidents would be expected, of course, but they would be
minor and occur only occasionally. But the car changed children's relationships with the street, their former playground. Children were being
run down with a horrible frequency, many times each day by the 1920s.
More than half of the children were hit within a block or two of their
own residence. A number were hit in the act of running out their own
front door into the street.[49]

Because of their short stature, children's heads and vulnerable
organs often suffered the primary, direct blows from the cars' body,
and children more often seemed to go under the wheels, which might
also explain their higher death rates. But accidents occurred mostly
due to the child's lack of judgment and experience with such fast
moving objects, something new to adults as well in the first years.
Before 1920 in Rio, an oddly common source of auto-pedestrian
accidents was the pastime on stormy days of standing along Beira
Mar Avenue to watch waves crash into the sea wall. As the spray
ascended, the participants in this game, adults and children, would

[47] *Jornal do Brasil*, Apr. 7, 1920, 8.
[48] *Jornal do Brasil*, Jan. 30, 1929, 11; *Jornal do Brasil*, Jan. 31, 1929, 11.
[49] *Diário de Notícias*, Apr. 10, 1947, 2.

dart into the Avenue, avoiding the spray but also running into the path of passing cars.[50]

Rio's experience with childhood automotive disasters was not exceptional. Children were vulnerable everywhere that cars went. In São Paulo in 1936, pedestrian accidents among children under the age of eighteen numbered 241 compared to 240 among adults aged nineteen to forty. Teachers in São Paulo were told to educate their students about the dangers of the car because children, it was reported, made up 75 percent of all auto deaths.[51] In 1928 Philadelphia, 75 percent of automotive accidents involved pedestrians, and half of those killed or injured were children under the age of sixteen. Across the entire United States in 1925, some 7,000 children had died on American streets and highways, one-third of the national toll. And in Mexico City in the late 1930s, cars were the cause of 77 percent of all deaths among children aged five to fourteen.[52] Just during Rio's 1914 carnival, the papers reported that eighteen children had been killed by the automobile, which was labeled the "Mata Criança" (Child Killer). The holiday was described as "A Hecatomb in Six Days" with all the outrage the press could muster to demand the arrest, prosecution, and severe punishment of the heartless drivers who universally fled the scene.[53] At such incidents, anger flared, but court testimonies frequently implied that death and injury were occurring even when the motorist was driving conscientiously, under the speed limit, and when the car was in good repair.

The newspapers, coroner reports, and police periodicals published many thousands of the street's tragedies, but the facts tend to be curt, dry, and cold. Initially, automobile accidents were front-page news, but they quickly found their way to secondary pages, enumerated in brief along with all the other streetcar incidents, falls, drownings, occupational disasters, and petty crimes. Unlike murders, daring robberies, and crimes of passion, whose reports could run on for many columns and sometimes over a number of days, automotive accidents had neither motives nor

[50] *Auto Federal*, May 1, 1917, 22. See Sávio, *A modernidade sobre rodas*, 163–64, who briefly examines child victims in São Paulo, many in the act of play.

[51] Costa Netto, *Relatório* (São Paulo: Directoria do Serviço de Trânsito, 1936), 148, after 150.

[52] Norton, *Fighting Traffic*, 21; V. Cortés Sotelo, *Consejos y ejemplos relativos al tránsito en la República mexicana* (Mexico City: Tipografia Morales, 1938), 14.

[53] *Vida policial*, Oct. 24, 1925, 33; "Os Mata-Crianças: uma Hecatombe em Seis Dias," *Fon Fon*, Mar. 7, 1914; "Farrapos," *Fon Fon*, Apr. 10, 1920. During the three days surrounding this year's carnival, there were thirty-eight people hit by cars compared to only three by trams and one by wagon; see *A Imprensa*, Feb. 26, 1914, 6.

plotters, no conspiracies, neither anger nor jealousy, no cruelty, no narrative, and commonly no denouement in justice. As a result, auto accidents
were neither remarkable nor fascinating in and of themselves. Automotive
deaths were tragic but senseless, so reports were short and formulaic.
Repeated reports – only the victims' names, the locations of the accidents,
and the perpetrators' license plates changed – provided neither closure nor
comprehension.[54] Already by 1914, newspapers had begun to report
auto-pedestrian accidents with a brief rubric, evidence that the new terrors
caused by chauffeur had already become mundane. For three decades,
a number of newspapers headlined their automotive accident reports with
"Sempre os Automóveis" ("As Always, It Is Automobiles"), which
demonstrated the anger and awareness that cars were doing a great deal
of harm, as well as intimated that such reports were always the same old
story. In some cases, the headline was merely "Sempre Eles" ("It's Always
Them"), since everyone already knew to what the papers were referring.[55]

The press was schizophrenic about the automobile. On the one hand,
editors could not deny the weight of the ink describing the blood on the
streets, and they often lamented and condemned the new reality. On the
other, car makers, tire manufacturers, and oil companies were increasingly important as advertisers. One might in fact explain the explosion of
new publications in Rio in the early twentieth century by the expansion of
automotive advertising revenue, including the growing number of cars for
sale in classifieds. From the beginning, large, illustrated automotive ads
occupied print space, and this presence only increased over the decades, in
some papers to entire sections dedicated to things automotive. Brief
accounts of accidents could not well compete for space and visibility
with the half- and full-page ads promoting not only the car but frequently
its touted safety features, including brakes, horn, and acceleration. It is
arguable that newspapers, with this obvious conflict of interest, down-
played the car's depredations. In early 1914, the *New York Times* promoted itself as the biggest advertiser of automobiles in the city: over the
course of 1913, automotive advertising amounted to the equivalent of
491,764 lines of text (more than 200 pages), a major source of the *Times'*
revenue that the paper sought to expand.[56] As Clay McShane has found

---

[54] *Vida Policial*, Apr. 18, 1925, 22.
[55] Newspapers used this heading with some consistency through the thirties, including the
Jornal do Comércio, Jornal do Brasil, O Imparcial, O Paiz, and others.
[56] *New York Times*, Jan. 8, 1914, 11. Norton, *Fighting Traffic*, 210, observes that at least
some were suspicious that the auto industry, which provided so much advertising revenue, was influencing what was being reported in New York's newspapers in 1924.

was the case in the US,[57] the press in Brazil was initially sympathetic to the pedestrian in cases of accidents. Reporters attacked the car with "clamorous ingratitude," as one of Rio's boosters put it.[58] But over a decade or two, the press moved to the driver's side of the debate. Editors and reporters, as they joined the motoring class, also began to view their city from behind the wheel. Rio's newspaper coverage of accidents remained widespread, but reports became more terse and less visible.

The press also treated the realities of pedestrian accidents with a certain apathy, fatalism, and commonly with humor. No small percentage of cartoons in magazines and papers took the automotive accidents as their subject: cars crashing into restaurants with their bumpers bellying up to diners' tables, silly stories of families out for a drive that usually ended in some accident in which the madam loses her hat, and illustrations of official vehicles racing up avenues, crushing pedestrians, tossing peddler bodies, or forcing shoppers to jump through windows to escape. Some cartoons were often darker. In a typical cartoon, entitled "Poor Chauffeurs," the driver looks down on a pedestrian cut to pieces by his car and says, "I must have bad luck; this is the seventh time this has happened to me"; and his passenger adds "the bad luck is mine; this is only the tenth car I've ridden in, and this has happened every time." During a period when it was difficult to get newsprint, an official in charge of rationing the resource asks the journalist, "Why do you need so much paper?" to which the journalist replies, "Dammit! How else am I going to cover all the city's automobile accidents."[59] The morbid humor of the automobile certainly kept the issue of mechanical street violence in the public mind and served to criticize and condemn the new street's new reality. But by making light of it, such humor also had the effect of trivializing the very real statistics of deaths and injuries. To laugh at tragedy, even in a generalized way, is to diminish its horror. Laughter was not an expression of approval or assent; quite the contrary. But it was in some sense an expression of acquiescence. Within decades, most of society would come to consent in and officially facilitate the intolerable: tens of thousands of national deaths each year just to get around.

[57] McShane, *Down the Asphalt Path*, 129, 184, also argues that while much newspaper copy about cars was negative, the overall space dedicated to cars was positive.
[58] Seabra Junior, *Accidentes de automoveis*, 1.
[59] Paulo César de Azevedo, et al. *O século do automóvel no Brasil; The Century of the Automobile in Brazil* (São Caetano do Sul: Brasinca, 1989), 15; Herman Lima, *História da caricatura no Brasil* (Rio de Janeiro: J. Olympio Editora, 1963), 454–56; *Fon Fon*, Jan. 15, 1915, 14. *Fon Fon*, Jan. 22, 1915, 12.

The press and its readers grew weary of and waxed apathetic to the carnage that surrounded them. A cartoon from 1921 illustrated a man tumbling down the street behind a speeding car with the caption: "Our frequent automobile disasters, no matter the number of victims, already no longer cause among us the minimum of upset."[60] In one case, automotive death was welcomed. In a poem published on the front page of *Jornal das Moças,* a magazine for young women from the 1930s, the poet described a poor little boy, legs bowed from walking too early, filthy mouthed from too much exposure to the street, forced from the age of six to sell peanuts in the streets by his mother. He often cried in his plight, his heavy basket rubbing his shoulder raw, and he looked with longing on those children who had the privilege of riding bikes or playing ball in the streets. When the author learned that the familiar boy had been killed in his employment by a passing car, the poet felt a "painful happiness, a sadness mixed with contentment" for there was still something with the power to liberate the downtrodden, and that automotive death, "good and compassionate, adopted those children that life abandoned to harsh destinies."[61] Still, much of the reporting identified the car as a cause for genuine mourning. Another poet humanely exulted in the chauffeur's strike of 1915: for one glorious day, "cars will not race about the city with their usual velocity, and our nerves will run with more serenity. And if our legs grow weary in walking, we will not tire of crying less during this holiday from the city's usual disasters."[62]

Automotive victims were usually hit one at a time in solitary and random events, but even when they went unreported in newspapers, news traveled rapidly along the traditional street's usual channels, and many individuals were direct witnesses of the car's violence. The sheer number of witnesses that might be rounded up in any particular case is surprising. On December 30, 1921, two young boys, aged seven and four, attempted to cross busy Avenue Senador Euzébio, which made intersection with their own street, Marques de Pombal, at Praça Onze, one of the city's most trafficked spaces and ostensibly where they had been playing. The boys, Romeu Santoro and Romeu Chappeta, friends who shared the same Christian name, were on their way home. The elder took the younger by the arm and ventured out into the evening street. Within a few steps, they found themselves in the headlights of Victorino

[60] *A Noite,* Oct. 10, 1921, 1.
[61] Corynthia Vianna Cavalcanti, "Pela vida," *Jornal das Moças,* Mar. 10, 1938, 1.
[62] Antomil, "Féria de Desastres," *Fon Fon,* Jan. 29, 1915, 37.

Lopes Ribeiro, a professional chauffeur driving a car with license number 589. Both the driver and children realized the danger at about the same time. Victorino honked. The boys leapt back at the same moment Victorino applied the brakes and swerved hard to the right. While successfully missing the boys with his front end, the car's rear left fender caught them both, throwing them violently to the ground. Victorino, rather than fleeing, went to the boys' aid. Pedestrians rushed into the street, blocked traffic, and then, as was common, verbally threatened and physically apprehended the driver. The police arrived, arrested Victorino, and summoned medical attention, but the ambulance only served to transport the boys to the morgue.

Numerous witnesses gave official testimony to the incident: a civil guardsman who was walking his beat on the square; a military police lieutenant who was riding in a passing streetcar; a fireman, also in a streetcar; and a resident who had been sitting on the sidewalk at his own front door. All made sworn statements, and all agreed that the children, arm in arm, stepped abruptly out into the street, that the driver attempted to avoid them, and, most importantly, that the driver was going at a moderate speed. Above all, the fact that the driver stopped to give assistance gave him the benefit of the doubt. Victorino, a Portuguese immigrant, married, aged forty-two, was jailed, but was bailed later the same night by the Chauffeur's Beneficent Union. Neighbors, strangers, the police, the courts, ambulance personnel, morgue staff, newspaper reporters, and a professional organization all became thoroughly involved in the case. The ensuing investigation found Victorino innocent, he was released, and his bail bond was returned to the union. Reports, as usual, told nothing of the boys, their families, or the pain of their loss. But the case demonstrates that automotive accidents and deaths could be both intimate and broad public knowledge. Praca Onze was one of the busiest spaces in the city, a place of gathering but also one in which numerous streetcars and buses consistently passed. It is likely that thousands of Rio's citizens were directly aware of the two Romeus' deadly accident or its consequences, and there were many incidents every day on Rio's streets by this period. Just weeks before, seven-year-old Álvaro, a resident on the Morro da Viúva, had been killed on Praia de Botafogo Street while running an errand for his mother. Trams and cars slowed, and necks craned to witness his little, soiled body laid out on the sidewalk. As his mother wept against a nearby wall, passing car tires picked up the pooling blood, leaving their several "signatures" on the pavement, in the words of one reporter. Blood literally ran in the streets, and everyone, excepting

possibly children of Álvaro's age, was conspicuously aware of the car's
depredations.[63]

Much as before with wagons, streetcars, and coaches, the legal consequences of vehicular accidents focused not on machines nor their owners,
but on their operators. Liability attached itself almost exclusively to working-class men: coachmen, motormen, cabbies, and chauffeurs. When the car
first appeared, a few fingered the new machine as the cause of so many
disasters and called for its "excommunication" from the streets. But this
was the position of a small minority, and the automotive press defended
"this most excellent, civilizing vehicle," and labeled such attacks as "vulgar,
contradictory, unfounded, and mawkish drivel."[64] Continuity prevailed,
and the laws of automobile accidents focused on operators who were
accused of recklessness, speeding, inattention, belligerence, and even lack
of chivalry. In fact, what seemed to anger the public most were drivers who
did not have the human decency to stop and offer assistance to those they
hit, negligently or otherwise.[65] To them, the automobile was a moral issue,
a crisis of human virtue, more than a technological one. Sometimes these
accusations and sentiments were expressed popularly, as when General
Bernardino Bormann, in his official Ministry of War vehicle, hit and badly
injured a boy on Anna Nery Street. Bormann's chauffeur, by instinct, fled,
but the general turned him back to the scene. As pedestrians took up rocks
to stone the car, General Bormann stood in his car and adeptly appeased the
crowd by promising to pay the boy's medical expenses. The appeal worked,
due to the general's authority, but also because he had not been the driver of
the car. The general, and the elite more broadly, learned the benefits of
continuing to divert attention away from themselves and their cars and
place blame squarely on their drivers.[66] Massimo Moraglio has found the
same strategy among Italian car owners who argued that "safety problems

---

[63] Inqueritos sobre Atropelamentos, Dec. 30, 1921, BR AN Rio 6z.o.IQP 5894, ANRJ.
Álvaro's case was reported in *A Noite*, Dec. 9, 1921, 4, and also in *O Paiz* the next day,
which named him Bernardo, son of Álvaro Barbosa. See also *Diário de Notícias*, Apr. 10,
1947, section 2, 2.

[64] "Os desastres de automóveis e os detractores do vehículo civilizador," *Automobilismo:
a revista pratica do automovel*, Apr. 1928, 20; *Jornal do Brasil*, Apr. 15, 1920, 8.

[65] *Vida Policial*, Dec. 12, 1925, 31; *Vida Policial*, Nov. 28, 1925, 32.

[66] *O Estado de São Paulo*, Jan. 11, 1910, 2.

were a consequence of the numerous incompetent, dangerous drivers and not from the introduction of new technological instruments."[67]

This dodge, it turned out, was easy to perform before the 1920s as few car owners drove their own cars. As with the private carriage, the large majority of cars were driven by employees, professional chauffeurs, as were taxis. Driving was not yet a universal behavior but a profession, a category of men made up of either immigrants (in Rio, mostly Italians) who had picked up their driving skills in Europe, or of working-class Brazilians who learned the trade on Rio's streets. Despite the job's apparent modernity and the drivers' reputation for brazenness, the occupation was still in essence servile. A number of Rio's chauffeurs were of African descent, as photographs of the uniformed employees of the city's garages attest. And they were often very young. One family portrait from about 1920 was posed in the back of rented car driven by a uniformed black chauffeur who cannot be more than fifteen years old.[68] *Fon Fon*, which intentionally associated itself with the modern, brash aura of the car, initially took the black chauffeur as its mascot, illustrating him in early editions and on covers literally driving roughshod over the backs of the white elite on Avenida Central.[69] The message was that the new magazine would shake things up, speak its mind, and pull no punches aimed at sacred cows. But it illustrated the increasingly negative stereotypes associated with chauffeurs as not only brash and uncouth but a danger to the more genteel population, most of whom still relied on their legs to get around most of the time. *Fon Fon* would soon change the color of its chauffeur mascot, who now made his appearance as a natty British mechanic in tweed cap doling out a somewhat more reputable sauciness. Still, car owners were essentially accusing their own drivers, men in their employ, of the same rudeness on the street as their ill-bred pedestrian brothers. Some suggested that driving was a means of rising in the world, yet, regardless of any social mobility, chauffeurs were among the most maligned classes, described as barbarous deviants and assassins of children. One editorialist in *O Paiz* promoted vigilante justice: the only solutions to the problem of the chauffeur were "the club, the rock, and the revolver."[70] Car

---

[67] Massimo Moraglio, "Knights of Death: Introducing Bicycles and Motor Vehicles to Turin, 1890–1907," *Technology and Culture* 56, no. 2 (Apr. 2015), 375.

[68] Photo by A. Mathias, in George Ermakoff, *Rio de Janeiro, 1900–1930: Uma cronica fotográfica* (Rio de Janeiro: G. Ermakoff Casa Editorial, 2003), 121. *Fon Fon*, May 13, 1911, photo of the chauffeurs of the Garage Nacional.

[69] *Fon Fon*, Apr. 20, 1907, cover, and Apr. 13, 1907.

[70] "Os Mata-Crianças," *Fon Fon*, Mar. 7, 1914. *Auto Federal*, Feb. 15, 1917, 6; "Deveres do Bom Automovilista," *Annuário de Automobilismo*, 1929, 112.

owners, dealers, and manufacturers leveraged this vehement hatred of the car's actual drivers to parry anger and criticism away from their automobiles and to resist legislation that attempted to limit the car's speed and scope of movement. Automobiles were criticized for their "snobbish" associations, many using the English word to describe them, but car owners turned the criticism back to their lower-class drivers with notable success.

Hence, if there was a strident, defensive car lobby, the chauffeurs made a better show than did the more respectable Automobile Club of Brazil, which was made up exclusively of elite car owners. Seeking sympathy, the chauffeurs portrayed themselves as a class wearied by the difficult nature of their work, oppressed and made scapegoats by their employers, and maltreated by the population generally.[71] The Centro de Chauffeurs was formed in 1910 on Lavradio Street in response to the frequent attacks on drivers in the press and the occasional assaults on their persons in the street. They created their own publications in which they defended themselves as hard-working, honest men striving to support their families. They reported how honest their drivers were, always making an effort to return items, from jewels to umbrellas, left in their cars by fares. Their most emphatic, repeated claim was that they were not criminals. If the elite effectively blamed chauffeurs for the problems of their own cars, initially the chauffeurs also made scapegoats of the few, they claimed, of their own number who refused to drive by the rules, or more typically, the growing number of "amateurs" who drove their own cars without training or skill. Chauffeur societies created their own ten commandments, which included being alert, polite, clean, and obedient to speed limits, and avoiding alcohol. They tried to professionalize the occupation by creating rules and by adopting a standard uniform. Accused drunk drivers were kicked out of their associations, as was an inebriated member who killed a little girl in 1917. They even promoted professional drivers' licenses as they felt the regular license was too easy to get.[72] But they also resisted direct regulations on the use of the car itself.[73]

Many of the chauffeurs' most deplored behaviors were in reality legacies from a fully developed pre-automotive traffic culture; these included

---

[71] *Auto Federal*, Feb. 15, 1917, 11–12.

[72] For the chauffeurs' self-defense and recommendations to solve the dangers associated with automobility, see the publications *Auto Federal*, which began publication on Feb. 2, 1917, and *Voz do Chauffeur*, which began Sep. 15, 1924. See specifically *Auto Federal*, Mar. 15, 1917, 21.

[73] Marco A. C. Sávio, *A cidade e as máquinas: bondes e automóveis nos promórdios do metrópole pualista, 1900–1930* (São Paulo: Annablume, 2010), 217–18.

the unwillingness to brake for pedestrians and the predisposition to flee accidents. The failure to brake was an inheritance from the electric street-car motormen. The streetcars' ability to brake was even more limited than that of the early car; its mass and steel-on-steel traction could make stopping a block-long affair. Hence, streetcar drivers rarely braked or slowed for pedestrians in the street. The expectation was that pedestrians would move off the tracks, and the driver's responsibility was to ring his bell in warning. Chauffeurs behaved just like streetcar drivers. They did not brake for people in the street – they honked at them. Like the streetcar, the car placed the onus for safety on the pedestrian, even if the law stated otherwise. Like trolley dodgers everywhere, pedestrians were expected to elude the car. Drivers did not want to hit pedestrians, but missing them by a few inches, even at high velocities, was entirely acceptable. Unlike the streetcar, the automobile's maneuverability not only made its behavior unpredictable but also gave drivers the sense that their right was the entire right of way.

When accidents did happen, the large majority of drivers fled the scene, which was the common practice for decades.[74] In 1920, car number 2,433 hit José Lourenço de Souza, a thirteen-year-old identified as a worker, on Visconde do Rio Branco. As José picked himself up off the pavement, another vehicle, number 1,353, hit him as well, leaving him badly injured. Both drivers, rather than stop and offer assistance, increased their already excessive velocity and escaped capture despite being chased by mounted soldiers who happened to be at the scene.[75] Yet flight, too, was an inheritance from the pre-automotive era. When horse cabbies, wagon drivers, and streetcar employees were involved in an accident, they had also run from the scene, although most commonly they jumped from their vehicles and fled on foot. In one case in 1906, a cart driver and his assistant had to whip their mules to get their cart over the streetcar tracks, but in doing so, the driver was thrown onto the trolley line where he was hit by a streetcar, which killed him. Not only did the streetcar driver, who was not at obvious fault, flee the scene on foot, so did the victim's assistant, who was also not at fault.[76] Coachmen, streetcar operators, and chauffeurs had various reasons for flight beyond the simple evasion of the legal consequences of their actions. Drivers fled knowing that even if caught

[74] *Diretrizes*, Dec. 1938, 14–15.
[75] *Jornal do Brasil*, Mar. 28, 1920, 6; see also, as another typical example, Inqueritos sobre Atropleamentos, Jan. 7, 1911, ANRJ BR AN Rio CS.o.IQP 881, 1911, 135.
[76] *Jornal do Brasil*, Jan. 16, 1906.

later, the consequences would be less significant. If caught *in flagrante*, they almost always went to jail. But more significantly for many, flight was not an expression of callousness but an act of fear, a means of avoiding any reactionary violence from victims and bystanders who were incensed enough at automotive accidents to occasionally mob, beat, and stone those who ran down pedestrians, especially if the victim was a child. When a bus driver hit and killed a child of four in the suburbs, the driver stopped briefly, but due to the "exaltation of the residents" and specific threats from the child's godfather, he jumped back into his vehicle and took his leave.[77] In a case in 1928, the motorist Joaquim Ferreira Andressi, while backing up, lightly hit a streetcar employee, the kind of common occurrence not likely to make the papers. But in this case the victim responded by drawing his knife and stabbing the driver in the abdomen while he sat in his car; Andressi died two days later.[78] There was also the possibility of police brutality, of which there were occasional complaints. The motorist who hit Alberto, aged eight, in early 1928, tried to flee the scene but was stopped by police who beat him publicly at the scene. The press complained about this incident as well as another on the same day, and deplored it as a problem with a long history.[79] Motorist flight was almost an institutionalized act, and even if their cars were damaged beyond function, chauffeurs still jumped from their vehicles and took to their heels. When a motorist did stop to help his victim, that was indeed news, and these rare cases were generally praised in the press, regardless of fault. Even ambulance drivers fled their own depredations: in 1909 an ambulance driver, rather than stopping to assist the man he had just run down, fled, leaving the victim to wait for a new ambulance that had to be called. And in a 1914 case, an ambulance driver hit a pedestrian, dutifully transported him to the Assistência, parked the ambulance, and then fled on foot.[80]

By the late 1910s there seems to have been a growing sense of the segregation of the street into two zones: the bed of the street, as it was called, for automobiles, and the sidewalk for pedestrians. Some pedestrians were practical and took to the street only with great caution. But

---

[77] Inqueritos sobre Atropleamentos, Jun. 7, 1935, ANRJ BR AN Rio CS.o.IQP 7232.

[78] *Jornal do Brasil*, Dec. 8, 1928, 11, and Dec. 11, 1928, 9.

[79] *Correio da Manhã*, Jan. 6, 1928, 2 and 3.

[80] *Jornal do Brasil*, Oct. 6, 1909, 12; *Correio da Manhã*, Apr. 5, 1914. *Diretrizes*, Dec. 1938, 14–15, notes that flight remained the default response for drivers in accidents and continued to blame it on what it considered laws that were too harsh, laws that had been written even before the car appeared on the streets.

many others boldly, if imprudently, resisted their segregation, insisting that the street – all of it – belonged to everyone, and no individual's right exceeded another's, regardless of social status or mechanical enhancement. Pedestrians demonstrated by their behavior that they had as much right to stand, stop, and talk in the streets as cars had to drive upon them. "Driving on Rio's streets," wrote the pseudonymous Otto Prazeres in 1917, "inspires fury." When a driver came upon pedestrians in the street, some took umbrage at the offending horn, refused to move out of the way, or did so with spiteful slowness, forcing the car to swerve or brake, "firm in the national philosophy that 'the street belongs to everyone.'"[81] And when the pedestrian did get out of the way, he or she often did so just barely, like a matador in the bullring.

In Rio, the street remained important as a place to be, to spend time. Hence, many of those on the street not in cars were not in the strict sense pedestrians but locals passing time on their home streets. The poorest continued to rent apartments so small and stuffy – "like a sepulcher" – that they spent much of their days, evenings, and nights in the freshness and liveliness of the streets. Mário Pederneiras observed that Rio's citizens remained very much home bodies who refused to "let go of the old habit of hanging about their homes and doors" at all hours. Rio's beaches, parks, and gardens, he argued, remained empty by comparison because "we prefer the unfortunate custom of parking ourselves outside our front doors."[82] Drivers complained that pedestrians walked in the busy downtown streets as if they were "taking a stroll through the wilderness." Men walked in the street reading the newspaper, and poor women carried loads on their heads whose overflowing goods obscured their vision of oncoming cars.[83] By the late 1910s, drivers became so bold as to blame pedestrians for some accidents and demand that laws be passed against pedestrians who refused to yield the street or show proper caution to the car.

Drivers, represented by their chauffeur organizations, realized by this time that they could no longer deny the car's deadly role, and that now, by admitting and even emphasizing the toll, the new, terrible reality could actually work in their favor. Seabra Junior noted that of the 3,028 found guilty in auto-pedestrian accidents between 1910 and 1916, two-thirds

---

[81] Otto Prazeres, "Os desastres de automóveis," *A Noite*, Jun. 26, 1917, 1.

[82] Lima Barreto, "Uma anedota," *Careta*, Oct. 16, 1920; *Fon Fon*, "Diário das ruas," Aug. 30, 1913; Herman Lima, *História da caricatura no Brazil*, 435.

[83] Seabra Junior, *Accidentes de automóveis*, vii, 303–05, 309.

were automobilists; the rest were drivers of streetcars and wagons. Not a single pedestrian was accused, showing the initial, insurmountable bias against the operators of vehicles.[84] Chauffeur and automotive magazines, such as *Auto Sport*, liked to march out the even more appalling statistics coming out of the United States. In 1915, they reported, the US saw 5,000 deaths by car; ten years later, it was 25,000, fifty-five dead per day, not including the roughly half million people injured. They suggested that per capita deaths in Rio were yet higher. The point of such dire stats was that auto-related death was the price of modernity, and the solution was not just to enforce existing penalties for bad driving but to create new penalties for incautious walking. Because many families in Rio and São Paulo lost loved ones each year to automobile accidents, these losses should serve to modify human behavior, mostly that of pedestrians, not place additional restrictions on the car.[85] The chauffeur, who was modern, embraced and fully understood the new reality; pedestrians were in denial. *Auto Federal* argued that pedestrians were slow, inattentive, and preternaturally backward: "It is a proven fact of psycho-social studies that our people are not educated sufficiently to be able to adapt easily to great developments of modern evolution." The chauffeurs that *Auto Federal* represented complained that Brazilians could handle progress about as well as "Guaytacazes, Botocudos, and Troglodytes," lumping pedestrians with cavemen and the most loathed of Brazil's indigenous cultures. *Auto Federal* argued that pedestrians, like indigenous people, refused to comprehend either the benefits or the consequences of another new technology and were dying off as a result.[86] In addition to American death statistics, *Auto Federal* published photographs of American streets, such as Fifth Avenue in New York, where pedestrians, reportedly, had learned their place: "As you see, pedestrians do not walk in the center of the street, as they do in Rio de Janeiro; they stick to the sidewalks."[87]

Above all, the chauffeur's union argued in favor of the accidentalness of modern life. "We are not assassins,"[88] they repeated. The union argued that chauffeurs spent their long days trying their best to avoid hitting humans. Murder, they said, required motive, and we do not wish to harm anyone. Hence, auto-pedestrian deaths and injuries, they insisted, were neither homicidal nor negligent. They were accidental, and *Auto Federal*

---

[84] Seabra Junior, *Accidentes de automóveis*, 307. *Auto Federal*, Aug./Sep. 1917, 24.
[85] *Auto Sport*, Jun. 26, 1926, 39; *Auto Federal*, Feb. 15, 1917, 26.
[86] *Auto Federal*, Aug./Sep. 1917, 24.   [87] *Auto Federal*, May 1, 1917, 15.
[88] *Auto Federal*, Feb. 15, 1917, no pagination.

stressed that "accidents are accidents." The driver's lobby claimed that it sympathized with the anger of one Mr. Evaristo José Rodriguez, a father whose daughter had recently died in the street in front of her home, and could even forgive him for protesting that the driver, who the union represented, had been let out of jail. "His pain makes it such that he cannot think rationally, cannot put thoughts together, and says crazy things."[89] But they would not forgive journalists who exaggerated, lied, imputed motives, and referred to drivers as murderers. In 1913, they requested that the *Jornal do Brasil* stop using "The Champions of Death" as the headline for their daily traffic accidents reports, to which the paper complied, although only for a short period. Another rash of deadly accidents brought the headline back. The chauffeurs associated themselves with the oppressed classes, accusing the papers of only attacking drivers as an occupational class when they inadvertently ran down an individual of some importance or one of his children. "At least," they insisted, "attack those drivers who hit poor people as well."[90]

Eventually, class itself finally helped the chauffeur to rise in the estimation of the law. By the 1920s, more elite car owners had begun to drive their own cars. They could no longer blame the car's hazards on unruly and reckless employees. Rather than become the new bad guys, they joined the chauffeurs in their campaign to implicate pedestrians in their own deaths and injuries. Pedestrians, they argued, could no longer see the street as belonging to them, a place of multiple uses, a space in which to commerce, converse, or recreate. The street was now a place for rapid movement, and pedestrians should show proper deference to speed. As children, the aged, and the disabled seemed unable to adapt, motorists specifically attacked their presence on the street. They cast blame on parents, particularly on "denatured," callous mothers. Children, the chauffeurs demanded, should essentially now be "incarcerated in their own homes," by their parents instead of being allowed to "go to hell on the streets" which can no longer be their "field of diversion."[91] *Auto Federal* went so far as to suggest that in every case that a child was hit by a car or streetcar, the mother be whipped in the public square for negligence. As for the aged and disabled, the driver's lobby decried "this exhibition of the lame and the weary, who drag themselves about the

[89] *Auto Federal*, Feb. 15, 1917, no pagination.
[90] *Auto Federal*, Feb. 15, 1917, 6 and other, unnumbered pages. *Jornal do Brasil*, Apr. 5, 1914, 21.
[91] *Auto Federal*, Mar. 15, 1917, 12–13.

streets," like mendicant beggars. They too should remain indefinitely safe
at home.[92] By the late 1920s, in increasing cases, pedestrians, including
the parents of children, were judged as the negligent parties in accidents,
a significant change from previous decades.[93] This substantially changed
the legal liabilities of driving a car on Rio's busy, pedestrian-congested
streets, and drivers could expect some favor in accidents in which pedestrians acted rashly.

In later decades, the whole issue of blame or who was at fault seemed
beside the point. Death at a new scale became the tolerated reality. Well
into the 1920s, newspapers did their best to identify drivers involved in
accidents. By the 1930s, accident reports seemed to give up on naming the
perpetrators at all, and reports, while enumerating the dead and injured,
did so with a growing sense of fatalism. Eventually, many papers ceased to
report on car accidents at all. *O Paiz*, which had been among the most
dutiful recorders of traffic incidents, desisted in the mid-1920s. Many
others dropped their "Disasters" columns in the 1930s. The *Jornal do
Brasil* continued to publish auto-pedestrian accidents until the late 1950s,
but then it too stopped. When automotive accidents became systemic,
accountability through coverage seemed a fruitless pursuit.

The automobile began to figure in a variety of popular forms of entertainment – burlesque theater, folk poetry, street song, and even film –
where it often served as a vehicle of humor or an object of derision. But it
rarely made a central appearance in Brazil's more serious literature.
The poet Carlos Drummond de Andrade noted in the 1950s that he
could think of no single Brazilian novel where the car figured prominently
"despite its role as our friend, servant, accomplice, and executioner."
As a central symbol of modern culture, this seems surprising, but as we
will see later, many of Brazil's literary elite were ambivalent about the car
if not outright opposed to its vulgarities.[94] We have to look to São Paulo
for the single collection of stark exceptions to this literary omission:
António de Alcântara Machado, in his short stories, made the automobile
a central if mundane part of the poor and immigrant worlds he narrated in
the late 1920s. He wrote of unchaperoned nighttime rides and elite men
seducing working girls with flashy cars. His stories express the lack of

---

[92] *Auto Federal*, Feb. 15, 1917, 18; Seabra Junior, *Accidentes de automóveis*, 263; *Auto
Federal*, Mar. 15, 1917, 12–13, 16; *Fon Fon*, Mar. 14, 1908.

[93] *Jornal do Brasil*, Dec. 2, 1928, 5.

[94] Carlos Drummond de Andrade, "O automóvel na literatura," *Revista de Automóveis*,
Jan. 1955, 1; Seabra Junior, *Accidentes de automóveis*, 1, introduction by Evaristo de
Moraes.

human control over the machine, the car's lopsided benefits to the rich and costs to the poor, of the unpremeditated nature of street death, and of the urbanite's growing fatalism about fatalities.

In "The Wheeled Monster," Alcântara Machado describes the aftermath and funeral of an Italian girl who was run down by a rich young man in a speeding car, depicting, where few others tried, the familial costs and community reactions to the car's depredations. Sadly, only in literature do we begin to see the car's full consequences. The girl's broken body lies at home, in the parlor in a pink casket. Friends, neighbors, and strangers all come to pay their respects – most of them doing so from the street, leaning in on the window sill, observing the body and offering condolences. Children, hands held uncomfortably tightly by their mothers, jump up to get a view of the body. Alcântara Machado describes the girl's mother, who weeps, prays, and struggles to keep the flies off her daughter face, as oblivious to the commotion around her. The women of the house busy themselves in funeral preparations; the men talk angrily, wondering if *Fanfulla*, the local Italian language paper, will cover the accident at all and help bring justice to the perpetrator. One man counters that rich boys like that will no more be held accountable for their crimes than are the corporations of their fathers. The girl's father swears, spits on the floor, gulps a glass of cheap liquor, and then swears and spits again, to which another responds, "yes, this is just the way things are, the way things are." In the funeral procession, little girls in their Sunday best carry the casket in rotation, followed by women carrying palm leaves and dahlias. Boys in the cortege argue about who the best soccer player is, and the young pall bearers accuse one girl, who forces her way to the casket's side on the busiest street, of posing. But the community pays attention. Men on the street, in buses and streetcars, remove their hats; women cross themselves; policeman accommodate the procession by clearing the way; and the traffic stops respectfully to let the funeral party pass every intersection. In the end, one local paper publishes the girl's photo, but it is only a sad, uncomplaining obituary, not the hoped-for condemnation and call for justice. The story ends with the father having departed to speak with a lawyer. While the story portrays the survival and strength of the community – the street still a common where friends and neighbors gather in good times and in mourning – it also evokes the now routine character of automotive accidents, the futility of grief and anger, and the powerlessness to make one's family safe.[95] And if the newspapers and coroners publicly

---

[95] António de Alcâtara Machado, *Novelas Paulistanas*, vol. 1 (Rio de Janeiro: José Olympio, 1961), 96. The story "O Monstro de Rodas" was originally published in 1927.

recorded and documented the actual accidents, the pain, sorrow, and loss associated with them remained private matters that went largely unremarked.

Deaths by illness usually gave warning; murders had motives; suicides might have notes; and epidemics at least offered commiseration in the crowd of casualties. Automotive deaths, on the other hand, which were random and singular, were by more than one definition senseless and painfully inexplicable. Sudden death proscribed opportunities to say goodbye, prepare oneself emotionally, or make amends with the dying. But this did not prevent surviving family members from trying. Some attempted to reach out to their dead by visiting the nation's most famous medium. Chico Xavier, beginning in the 1930s, penned hundreds of books about the afterlife, the details of which were communicated to him, he claimed, by the spirits of the dead, a ghostwriter for ghosts, if you will. Families came from Brazil's coastal cities, even from as far away as Spain and Italy, to consult with him personally at his spiritualist center in the remote, interior city of Uberaba. Xavier offered the despondent consolation, producing unique written missives in the voices of the dead, or, when the victim was very young, in the caring words of deceased grandparents. The message was one of comfort, that things were well on the other side, that Mother should no longer grieve nor worry, and that all were pardoned of their faults and offenses against the recently and untimely deceased. That the automobile had become a central player in the drama of accidental death is evidenced by a study of Xavier's psychographic letters from beyond the grave. More than 40 percent of all his supplicants came to hear from loved ones who had died in automobile accidents.[96]

DISCOUNTING THE DISASTER

The imprecise and incomplete nature of Rio's automotive accident statistics gave officials the power of plausible deniability. Edgar Estrela, who would serve for some twenty years, off and on, as Getúlio Vargas' appointed transit director in the capital, exercised the largest share of his administrative energy in resolving traffic congestion, which he considered the city's primary automotive difficulty. The dictatorship emphasized efficiency over safety. He was of the opinion that automotive accidents

---

[96] Ademir Xavier, "First Study on the Statistics of Chico Xavier's Automatic Writing Messages," Sep. 1, 2012, Spiritist Knowledge, http://spiritistknowledge.blogspot.com/2012/09/first-study-on-statistics-of-chico.html (accessed Nov. 1, 2013).

were not a serious issue. In the capital, Estrela asserted, "accidents are few in number, and the majority of auto-pedestrian accidents are due to the faults of the very victims," a comment that demonstrated that the pedestrian as culpable party had become an official position by the early 1930s. When asked what he thought of Cariocas as drivers, he again insisted that "given how much traffic we have, the coefficient of accidents is minimal ... I attribute this to the skills of our drivers." The reporter agreed enthusiastically with Estrela's expert opinion of the city's expert drivers, despite the fact that on the very same page his newspaper reported five auto-pedestrian accidents that included multiple broken limbs, a skull fracture, and one death. The same day, another paper reported four additional auto-pedestrian accidents, including an additional death. The papers described some of the pedestrian victims of that day as imprudent, and the police did not apprehend or apparently even cite a single driver, which represented a complete and rapid inversion of the legal reality that reigned a little more than a decade before.[97] Streetcar drivers remained (and bus drivers became) scapegoats for street accidents, as had been appropriate to their class, but when it came to the automobile's depredations, pedestrians were increasingly implicated; they were rubes and perpetrators deserving of their own injuries. Popular opinion on the street, of course, still held the motorist at fault. Pedestrians noted how many lampposts were destroyed by motorists and their wayward cars – lampposts innocent of negligent behavior and which remained obediently planted on the sidewalks. One local wit declared: "Give me the lamppost concession, and you can have the treasury."[98] But the official position is the one that mattered at the police station and in the courts. Hence, by the 1930s, auto accidents and their attending deaths and injuries were officially not a priority. Public concern for the injured, while it never disappeared, was increasingly replaced by complaints about traffic congestion, about too many buses and streetcars, and above all about the lack of parking. The world of the street, by those in power, was increasingly viewed through the frame of the windshield, and no transit director was fired or resigned based on his traffic safety record.

Into the 1940s, with Estrela again at the wheel of the transit office, the stats continued to pile up and officials continued to deny them, discount them, or make excuses. Traffic accidents and deaths declined substantially

[97] "Um dos grandes problemas da cidade: o congestionamento da Avenida e os onibus," *Correio da Manhã*, Jun. 22, 1933, 8. See also *Jornal do Brasil*, Jun. 22, 1933, 11.
[98] *Life*, Nov. 14, 1949.

during the war years, much as did automotive carnival, due to the rationing and high price of gas, which was almost unattainable. But after the
war, the carnage ensued, and the press, which no longer functioned under
the eyes of a dictatorship bent on controlling information, noticed.
In 1946, *Revista da Semana* published a rare article for the period illustrated with photos of accidents and of the injured. They reported the
rapid rise in accidents and claimed that in the last decade, even with the
war, more than 30,000 people had been run down by cars in the city, all to
too little notice. They reported that a single, downtown hospital, the Cruz
Vermelha, treated 260 persons per month, half of them victims of car
accidents, and of the 100 x-rays they took each day, 60 percent were for
the same class of victims. Forty percent of automobile victims, they
reported, had injuries with permanent consequences, "a souvenir for
many years from a moment of carelessness." Pedestrians as victims were
here also characterized as incautious, but the magazine claimed that
80 percent of all pedestrian accidents were the fault of the driver. Estrela
parried the criticism explaining that the cause of the problem was too little
space for too many cars. He would continue calling for more highways,
tunnels, and lanes that he argued would be the best means to solving the
problem of the automobile. *Revista da Semana*, while it was unwilling to
blame Estrela himself, astutely pointed out that congestion was in fact
a form of traffic calming, and that the most serious accidents tended to
happen on the broader, modernized streets where cars could achieve the
highest speeds. Some had assumed that the rise in pedestrian deaths at
night was due to darkness and the inability of drivers to see their victims,
but the magazine suggested that as congestion declined at night, drivers
drove faster, and collisions were more lethal.[99]

At the half-century mark, Rio's traffic engineer, Pedro Coutinho,
claimed to have broken the official silence on the scale of the city's
automotive disaster. He asserted that while the world's great cities –
New York, Paris, Rome, London, Detroit – had automotive casualties
that ranged from 22 to 91 deaths per 100,000 automobiles, Rio, by his
count, killed 461, ten times the number in New York City per car. With far
fewer cars, Rio's motorists were also killing more people per population at
15.2 per 100,000 persons, more than double that of New York at 7.1.
Still, it was hard to know if his figures were correct. Infractions, he
reported, were uselessly undercounted as only those without power or
friends received traffic tickets or penalties that stuck. In one significant

---

[99] "30,000 Atropelados em Dez Anos!" *Revista da Semana*, Nov. 23, 1946, 6–11.

improvement over the early century, he estimated that drivers fled the scene of accidents in only 57 percent of incidents.[100] Certainly, the large number of pedestrians relative to cars explains part of the carnage, but many simply stated that Rio's drivers were the most reckless they had ever seen. One American observer opined, as had another in the 1920s, that Brazilians were the most cordial people in the world, unless they were behind the wheel, a comment to which a Brazilian reporter reacted: "[I]f that is true of all Brazilians, what would be said of Cariocas." In 1973, a local study of the "epidemiology" of the automobile in Brazil, reported that cars killed more people than all diseases combined except tuberculosis. It also claimed that Brazil's death rate per car was higher than in any other country that reported statistics. And it was still the pedestrian who received the largest share of the car's violent cost. Some 60 percent of all car accidents did not involve a pedestrian, and yet pedestrians accounted for 70 percent of all auto-related deaths.[101] Rio's citizens, based on their own anecdotal evidence, not infrequently acclaimed their capital as the "champion of death." An automotive expert in the 1950s observed that Brazil's local authorities, mayors in particular, ignored the problem and gave the impression that they did not read the newspaper, did not walk the streets, and did not betray any cognizance that people were dying daily in the streets.[102] In maybe the most shocking account of the problem, São Paulo's *Jornal da Tarde* made a full-press attempt at adding up all of their city's automotive accidents and their consequences over two full days in 1969. Reporters canvassed the city's police reports and its entire hospital network during forty-eight hours and counted forty-nine auto-related deaths. Extrapolated over a full year, the city would have seen 8,943 deaths, but the official statistics for the city in 1969 only came to 649 deaths. The most astonishing finding from the *Jornal*'s report was that of all the people currently admitted in the city's hospitals, 30 percent were convalescing from traffic accidents.[103]

---

[100] Pedro Coutinho, "Rio, Cidade Infeliz, Também no Tráfego," *Diário de Notícias*, Dec. 30, 1952; Coutinho, not surprisingly considering his profession, blamed the death toll primarily on a lack of engineering, including lighting, paving, signs, and signals – issues addressed in the next chapter.

[101] Guilherme Montenegro Abath, *Epidemiologia dos acidentes de trânsito ocorridos no Recife; no período de 1961-1971* (Recife: G. M. Abath, 1973), 15, 165; *Quatro Rodas*, Nov. 1961, 25.

[102] *Revista de Automóveis*, May 1956, 32; see also Altieri, *Variacões sobre o trânsito paulistano*, 112.

[103] Eduardo Fares Borges, *Segurança de trânsito* (São Paulo: Sangirard, 1973), 40. For the continuing scarcity of automotive accident statistics in more recent decades, see

The lack of sound, official statistics betrayed an ongoing lack of interest in the car as a public health emergency. Yet, even inaccurate and imprecise data outlined the general story. Year after year, automobility killed and maimed many thousands in the capital, the large majority of them pedestrians. Even today, World Health Organization officials assert that in developing nations, those most at risk of death and injury from any cause are those two-thirds of citizens who do not own a car.[104] In Brazil, pedestrians had fought and lost a costly battle for their city's public spaces. Chauffeurs and passengers also suffered statistically, and all were at some risk of ending up in the Santa Casa, but the best prophylactic against *Bacillus automobilis* was the purchase of one's own automotive body. Over the century, blame for the car's epidemic mortalities fell on chauffeurs through the 1920s, and on pedestrians in the 1930s. Thereafter, as we will examine, where an act of God was insufficient explanation, blame was placed impersonally on systems and institutions: insufficient laws, the lack of enforcement, or on the street itself, which was deemed deficiently engineered for the needs of modern movement. Whatever the cause, solutions seemed out of reach. Even when cars were well maintained, had a brake at each of their four wheels, and power to assist their steering, when drivers were not criminal, insane, or negligent, when pedestrians were not foolish, and streets were signaled, enlarged, and refashioned, still, fatalities increased. In the fight against epidemic diseases, whose causes were unseen and whose waves of mortality came unpredictably, officials found the means to conquer invisible microbes in city after city. In the case of the automobile, whose lethality was no mystery and which killed consistently and predictably, already by the second quarter of the century, officials preferred to deny the full lethality of its presence or to repeatedly promise that a cure was at hand.

Segurança de Tráfego, Estatísticas e Pesquisas, 1985 (São Paulo: Departamento de Estradas de Rodagem do Estado de São Paulo, Secretaria dos Transportes), 9; Marta Lenise do Pardo, "Caminhos perigosos: uma aproximação ao problema da violência e saude a luz das ocorrencias de transito" (PhD diss., Universidade Federal de Santa Catarina, 1997). Pedro Corrêa *20 anos de lições de tránsito no Brasil* (Curitiba: Volvo, 2009), 81, 85, found that in 2005, the National Department of Transit reported 26,409 auto-related deaths; the federal Mortality Information Service counted 35,753; and the nation's insurance companies paid 63,776 auto-related death claims. He lamented that one needed only establish a 1 percent sample in order to get an accurate number.

[104] Mike Davis, *Planet of Slums* (New York, NY: Verso, 2006), 132; Eduard A. Vasconcelos, *Circular é preciso, viver não é preciso: a história do trânsito na cidade de São Paulo* (São Paulo: Annablume, FAPESP, 1999), 207.

5

Law and the Promises of Safety

Rua da Assembléia

Here lies the anonymous pedestrian
beneath a useless crossing signal . . .
The asphalt's bloodstains
Borne away on the tread of speeding tires.

Sérgio Sersank[1]

Can the Carioca one day dream of living in a city that respects the integrity of the human body . . . without the worry that he will be tossed ludicrous distances like used matchsticks, pinned against sign posts, and crushed under rubber tires that are as unmerciful as their owners and drivers? . . . [The city has become] a veritable jungle in which the strongest dominate because the law guarantees their impunity.

Anonymous[2]

Residents knew today's Rua da Assembléia (Assembly Street) by many names, usually more than one at a time. Running west from the port, as busy as it was narrow, locals once knew it as Manoel Brito Street, after the owner of a popular, colonial bakery. For a time, the street's west end was referred to as the Path to San Francisco as it led to a prominent cross erected to Saint Francis on the Santo Antonio monastery. A portion of the street was also called Padre Bento Cardoso after a notorious priest who resided there in the latter half of the seventeenth century, before he was

---

[1] Sérgio Sersank. "Tragédia Urbana," in *Estado de espírito* (Curitiba: Editora Íthala, 2013), 176–78; "jaz o anônimo pedestre/ sob um semáforo inútil . . ./a mancha de sangue do asfalto/ passa depressa aos velozes pneus . . . ."
[2] "A Cidade dos Loucos," *Folha Carioca*, Nov. 17, 1952, clipping in Serviço de Comunicação, Ministério de Justiça, SECOM, 27,799, BR.AN.RIO, VV.O.JTA, CMJ.3,334, ANRJ.

extradited and later tried for crypto-Judaism by the Inquisition in Lisbon (where he died in prison).[3]

However, the street's more recent, enduring names evoked its recognized functions as a space where laws were made and penalties were imposed. The street's most common appellation during the eighteenth century was Jail Street (Rua da Cadeia) because the municipal building at the street's east end housed the city's notorious Old Prison. It was here that everyone from common street criminals to the now revered conspirators for independence were held over for trial and detained for punishment. In fact, Tiradentes, the nation's most prominent revolutionary, was paraded up the length of Jail Street to his execution near Rocio Square, which is now named for him. Bailiffs of the royal courts sallied forth from their offices housed on and around Jail Street to exercise arrest warrants and serve summons to defendants. Any who saw the colonial bailiff, dressed in black cape, hat, and buckled shoes, approaching with official paperwork in hand, did so with dread, knowing they might be caught up in a lawsuit that could drag on for years.[4] Although "Jail Street" remained a popular moniker, after independence the street was given the more dignified, official name of Assembly Street to honor the colonial municipal building's new role as the nation's parliamentary assembly. Fittingly, the name endured in the twentieth century as Tiradentes Palace, which replaced the old municipal building and jail, hosted the National Congress from 1926 and then housed the State Legislative Assembly after 1960, when the capital moved to Brasília. Even today, a few law firms still congregate along Assembly Street's margins, as does one of the city's law schools. From this space, municipal, national, and state representatives shaped local and federal law, including street rules and automotive regulations, and the city's Transit Service, whose task it was to enforce these traffic laws and which processed hundreds of thousands of moving violations each year, situated itself in a dilapidated townhouse on Tiradentes Square.

With the arrival of the car, hectic Assembly Street, filled with assemblymen between sessions, was considered one of the most dangerous locations for pedestrians, a space where already in 1911 "automobiles,

---

[3] "Processo do Padre Bento Cardoso," Arquivo Nacional da Torre do Tombo, Direcção-Geral de Arquivos, Lisbon, Portugal, http://digitarq.dgarq.gov.pt/viewer?i d=2306332 (accessed Mar. 4, 2014).

[4] Manuel Antônio de Almeida. *Memórias de um sargento de milícias* (MetaLibri, 2005), ver. 1.0, 1, http://www.ibiblio.org/ml/libri/a/AlmeidaMA_SargentoMilicias_p.pdf (accessed Jun. 10, 2013).

pedestrians, bikes, and streetcars are all competing for the same space."[5] Pedestrians on Assembly at the corner of Avenida Rio Branco in particular were described as needing a lesson in acrobatics to survive, and citizens demanded Rio's police be sent to London or New York to learn how to regulate these new, competing demands for the street. Possibly due to the direct concern of legislators who walked this dangerous public space, they installed the city's first primitive traffic signal at Assembly Street and Rio Branco in 1917. A policeman standing on an exposed box in the middle of the intersection operated the handmade, hand-painted contraption, but this early experiment in signalization was short-lived and not tried again until the next decade.[6] Over time, a great deal of hope was placed on legislators and law enforcement to solve the problem of the automobile's depredations, but as with the city's first traffic signal, few such efforts showed much in the way of measurable improvement.

By the car's second decade, Rio's legal scholars had identified what they saw as the car's essential problem: killing without intent. However, they did not know quite what to call it, testing such terms as manslaughter, lethal negligence, *force majeur*, involuntary omission, act of God, and vehicular homicide. As the incidents increased, Fructuoso Moniz Barreto de Aragão, one of Brazil's first investigators of automotive law, noted that modern peoples had found new ways to kill, and "to kill without wanting to."[7] The ubiquity of handguns had been identified as a serious contributor to death rates in Rio in the early twentieth century. And yet the automobile, whose design was for moving people rather than killing them, was soon taking more lives each month than guns, a reality that seemed as absurd as it was undeniable. The street had always been something of a perilous space where violent crimes and traffic accidents were in a sense accepted risks. But with the arrival and multiplication of the car, the scale changed, and behaviors that before had been merely annoyances, such as drunkenness, incompetence, anger, competitiveness, and exuberance, even without malicious intent, now, when expressed in the person of the driver, all too frequently ended in someone's death or injury. Even Chico Navalhada, a notorious local chauffeur whose aggressive driving resulted in ten deaths over a period of a few years, a man condemned by

---

[5] *Revista de Automóveis*, Oct. 1911, 14.

[6] *Auto Federal*, Mar. 15, 1917, 14. Assembly Street had its name officially changed to República de Peru in 1921, but reverted to Assembly in 1937; see *Nomenclatura dos logradouros públicos da Cidade do Rio de Janeiro* (Rio de Janeiro: Departamento de Geografia e Estatística, 1944), 54, 374.

[7] Aragão, *Delictos do automovel e outros carros*, 5.

his own class, never intended to harm his victims nor certainly himself. A nickname earned by his lethal driving, *navalhada*, refers to the thrust of a razor by an assailant, another common weapon in Rio's day-to-day violence; but fittingly, in the context of automotive accidents, most razor cuts, in the mundane act of shaving, are unpremeditated and commonly self-inflicted.[8]

Initially, those who could afford a car, who took pleasure in its speed, found satisfaction in its associated status, and enjoyed a sense of security in its body, resisted attempts to regulate its movements. But as the death toll mounted and became indisputable, drivers changed their tune in part out of a desire for self-preservation. However, rather than admit any universal automotive guilt, they turned on each other, pointing fingers at professional drivers, young drivers, immigrant drivers, inexperienced drivers, and psychologically unstable drivers. They also, of course, blamed incautious pedestrians. But in a defensive strategy that was not entirely disingenuous, drivers, by accepting the need for some regulation, held out the promise of safety to an urban society that was reeling before the car's new dominance. While the promise was ultimately empty, continued reassurances of a safer future worked to thwart criticisms of the car as well as demands for even stronger regulations. Jeremy Packer makes the persuasive point that the idea of safety is not in opposition to automobility but an essential element to the car's social acceptance. Faith in the future effectiveness of automotive safety measures can enable us to discount and live with the car's present hazards.[9] In Brazil, early in the century, there were few automotive laws and fewer safety measures, and one could not deny the carnage. When death in the streets became undeniably pervasive, demand for change was sincere, but it was the promise more than the practice of safety that worked to refute a future of ever more accidents and deaths.

The hope for safety was real, not merely an attempt at deception. *Automobilismo*, a magazine that spoke for automotive interests in Rio, argued in 1926 that just as the laws that regulated trains had reduced the death toll related to train travel to very small numbers, automotive regulation could do the same for cars. They reported that in 1925,

---

[8] *Auto Federal*, May 1, 1917, 17.

[9] Jeremy Packer, *Mobility without Mayhem: Safety, Cars, and Citizenship* (Durham, NC: Duke University Press, 2008), 13.

automobiles in the United States killed 23,300 and injured some 600,000. By contrast, England, a nation of many trains, saw only one death due to rail travel that same year. *Automobilismo* insisted that it was only a matter of time for the same order and safety to be achieved with automobiles, which were merely "passing through a period of anarchy." Earnestly, they argued that cars, like trains, should be able eventually to run at 150 kilometers per hour in complete safety once automotive law and engineering had been as well studied and established as it had been for railroads. They placed a lot of hope in American technocrats, referred to in the mid-1920s as "Hoover's men," to solve, through legislation and engineering, the car's "slaughter and mutilation."[10]

Not everyone officially involved was convinced. *Vida Policial*, a publication that represented the police who had struggled to enforce traffic laws in Rio, countered the culture of safety in 1925, insisting that most auto-related deaths were inevitable, and all the legislation, adopted from any nation one chose, would make little difference. They claimed the city's police did their level best to impose order and enforce existing automotive laws, "but accidents keep happening," and they refused to blame any one person or party. This, they claimed, was the result of the newly "intense life of the city." And worse, they asserted, nobody had the ability to present a viable solution to the problem: not the police, not the automotive lobby, and emphatically not those with the most direct experience, "those who have been run down and killed." The author apologized for publishing an article that while speaking truth offered no solution and hence served no social or moral purpose.[11] Others similarly threw up their hands in fatalism. In 1928, one journalist in São Paulo lamented: "Yesterday, our motorists had a field day. They ran down and they killed, as demands the profession they worship ... But what's the point of banging away at these same keys. There is no remedy, and our motorists have not but to continue depopulating our city for always and forever."[12]

The more pessimistic diagnoses turned out to be correct. Despite new laws, new police forces, proliferating signals and signs, and recurring safety campaigns, automotive deaths and injuries increased. Many sang along with the technocrats, praising the powers of legislation, arguing that "civilization is the victory of rational systems," and that

---

[10] *Automobilismo: A revista prática do automóvel*, Dec. 1926, 29–30.
[11] *Vida Policial*, Apr. 18, 1925, 22. This article's author signed off as Abel Prazer.
[12] *Estado de São Paulo*, Mar. 10, 1928, cited in Sávio, *A modernidade sobre rodas*, 175.

FIGURE 5.1 Police and the promise of safety, 1913. Due to the growing number of automotive accidents, a succession of new police forces was brought to bear on Rio's traffic. The vehicle inspector, wielding a baton in his black, wool uniform, became the most visible figure of authority in Rio's downtown streets. Officials promised order and safety through legislation and enforcement, which mollified some angry citizens, but many were doubtful. In the face of chaos, some police interests threw up their hands; and to the evident violence, some automotive boosters shrugged their shoulders.
Source: K. Lixto (Calixto Cordeiro, 1877–1957), *Fon Fon*, Feb. 8, 1913, cover. Courtesy of the Acervo da Fundação Biblioteca Nacional, Brazil.

FIGURE 5.2 Police and the perception of danger, 1920. As streets became places of visible carnage, the newspapers labeled drivers "child killers" and "the champions of death." The scale of the disaster was beyond the resources of the police, to either regulate congestion or prosecute malefactors. Here, the vehicle inspector commands: "More slowly; not all at once; I cannot enforce the law under these conditions."
Source: J. Carlos (José Carlos de Brito e Cunha, 1884–1950), "A Revanche," *Careta*, Jan. 17, 1920, cover. Courtesy of the Acervo da Fundação Biblioteca Nacional, Brazil.

above all, they would soon make streets as safe as houses.[13] These repeated promises of a coming age of safe streets ultimately safeguarded the car's emergent legitimacy. Detractors found it difficult to attack an entity, as murderous as it was, whose safe and responsible use was relentlessly proclaimed by those in power to be just around the corner.

LAW'S ACCUMULATING SOLUTIONS

One of the first substantive responses to the car's damages was not preventative but curative. In 1905, Mayor Pereira Passos proposed an ambulance and first-aid service for the city. Cesídio da Gama e Silva, who published *Urgent Medical Aid in Rio de Janeiro* the same year, observed that the city had succumbed "to a series of extraordinary accidents in its diverse systems of transportation, the crimes and disasters that are now the theater of all bustling cities."[14] An ambulance service would in a sense fight velocity with velocity, using the same technology that harmed the public to transport its victims to urgent medical care. Pereira Passos' successor, Francisco Marcelino de Sousa Aguiar, firmly established the service because he was particularly concerned about car accidents. In a cartoon from 1910, Mayor Sousa Aguiar berates a uniformed chauffeur whose head is depicted as an early model automobile: "This cannot continue. You are ruining all my efforts. I work in earnest to increase the city's population while you strive to eliminate it."[15] He elsewhere claimed that many accident victims "lay abandoned in the street, at times for hours, suffering without medical attention." His solution was a rapid ambulance service connected not to hospitals, which were largely private, poorly distributed about the city, and typically not set up for emergency medical care, but to free, public, emergency medical stations, which were known as *Postos de Assistência Pública*. Sousa Aguiar established the first such post on Camerino Street on November 1, 1907. Within the first five months of operation, the post had treated 652 street accident victims, compared to 165 individuals who suffered accidents at home or work. Sousa Aguiar added more ambulances

---

[13] Francisco de Oliveira e Silva, *Das indenizações por acidentes nas ruas e nas estradas: automóvel, bonde, estrada de ferro e energia eléctrica* (São Paulo: Saraiva e Cia., 1940), 14.

[14] Cited in Paulo Ernani Gadelha Vieira, "Assistência médica no Rio de Janeiro (1920–1937): Reformas institucionais e transformacões da prática médica," vol. 2 (Master's thesis, Universidade do Estado de Rio de Janeiro, 1982), 235.

[15] *Fon Fon*, Jan. 22, 1910, 15.

to the service, each one celebrated with a ceremonial christening. The mayor claimed that the city's residents, "with ever increasing liveliness and delight, cheered the rapid passage in the street of the ambulance in its incessant charitable journeyings." The ambulances, large vehicles whose stark, white paint contrasted with all the city's other cars, which were black, made a visible impression. By 1912, there were 110 medical and ambulance staff associated with the posts.[16]

Rio's public medical posts appear to be an original innovation. Cities had had ambulance service before, but they carried patients to private hospitals not set up for emergency treatments and not in the business of providing free medical services. Rio's medical posts were honored with a prize in Rome at the 1912 International Exposition of Social Hygiene, of which the city of Rio took great pride. There were few imitators outside of a few Brazilian cities. In Rio, hospitals, doctors, and even pharmacies, the last which had treated most minor injuries in the city, complained at each post's introduction as accidents of all kinds formed a significant part of their business. But younger doctors supported the posts that allowed them to practice surgery on a variety of traumas, paid for by public funds. The initial post on Camerino Street, which proved too small, moved in 1910 to a three-story facility on Praça da República and came to be known, as other posts were established in distant neighborhoods, as the Central Post. Most of the nine smaller downtown posts seemed to consolidate there.[17] Many of the posts were jammed into old and inappropriate buildings. Meier's post was described as a single-room hovel, and medicine and bandages were often in short supply. One doctor associated with the service posted only half-jokingly the following disclosure at the entrance: "Accidents that require medical attention can only occur during regular business hours to people who do not require sterile conditions and who do not require urgent medicines."[18]

Ambulances, like most cars at the time, broke down frequently. The posts needed numerous ambulances just to ensure some were mobile, and in some reported cases, two vehicles were sent on calls so that if one broke down, the second could serve as a backup. By 1932, the Central

---

[16] Mensagem do Prefeito do Districto Federal Lida na Sessão do Conselho Municipal de 2 de Abril de 1908, vol. 1 (Rio de Janeiro: Oficinas graphicas do Paiz, 1908), 9.

[17] *Assistência pública e privada no Rio de Janeiro: história e estatística* (Rio de Janeiro: Typográphia do Annuário do Brasil, 1922), 652–54, 725. *Almanak-Henault*, 1909, 533 lists eighteen posts, ten of which were downtown. The Posto Central grew into the Hospital Municipal Sousa Aguiar, which name it took in 1955 at the same location.

[18] Gadelha Vieira, "Assistencia médica no Rio de Janeiro," vol. 2, 227.

Post had twenty-five ambulances, ten passenger cars, and one funeral car. Ambulances, which averaged very high speeds, were notorious for causing accidents, picking up their own victims as they went. *Fon Fon* insinuated that ambulance operators were the among the city's worst drivers and published photos of their depredations, including one in 1914 in which a rushing ambulance destroyed the Minister of the Interior's official car.[19] Significantly, however, the service evoked the culture of safety. They demonstrated, with their visibility and popularity, that the city was doing something significant in the face of the car's carnage. Ambulance work consisted of picking up the injured and the dead after the fact, because to leave the automobile's victims, dead or injured, lying in the street for any period of time was the worst advertisement against the claims of safety. Sympathetic locals had responded to the neglected dead by encircling the victim's body with lit candles, as they did in 1914 for an unidentified black male whose remains lay unrecovered for hours, right in front of the Catete National Palace.[20] Ambulance staff were the cleaners of crime scenes as much as they were medical specialists.

To prevent the car's depredations in the first place, officials and citizens demanded legislation, but before appropriate laws could be enacted, the causes of automotive death and injury had to be identified and agreed upon, which was no easy task. Drivers, pedestrians, legislators, automakers, and the police had different opinions about the causes of accidents and pointed fingers at different parties and different factors. The debate over the car's unpremeditated deaths produced scores of competing and abetting causes. Many pointed to human error and frailties, including recklessness, inattention, negligence, incompetence, ignorance, imprudence, crankiness, fatigue, sleepiness, and drunkenness. Others focused on the automobile's mechanisms or poor maintenance: engines too potent to control, inadequate steering, deficient suspension systems, bald or burst tires, dirty windshields, inoperable headlights, and failed brakes. In the 1950s, police actually reported "brakes made in Brazil" as the cause in some accidents. There were multiple and sometimes contradictory environmental and urban planning conditions faulted for accidents: both excessive speed and insufficient speed, streets too narrow

---

[19] Noronha Santos, *Meios de transportes no Rio de Janeiro*, vol. 2, 58–59; Gadelha Vieira, "Assistencia médica no Rio de Janeiro," vol. 2, 228, 232–33; *Fon Fon*, Feb. 18, 1909; *Fon Fon*, Jun. 27, 1914. Even to the mid-1960s, ambulances were identified as causing a great deal of accidents with their rushing to and from accidents; see *Quatro Rodas*, Dec. 1966, 59.

[20] *Jornal do Brasil*, Jan. 8, 1914.

and streets too wide, bright sunlight and dark nights, as well as rain (wet cobbles, muddy asphalt, slippery streetcar rails), fog, failed traffic signals, poorly engineered curves, steep streets, potholed streets, congestion, a lack of streetlights, illegible or non-existent signage, and even too many signs. By the 1920s, psychological disturbances became popular explanations: mania, depression, commonly referred to as melancholy, as well as dizzy spells, fainting, and blackouts resulting from the sheer stress of driving a car. Fashion was not ignored. Flowing scarves obstructed vision, and one study found that the male use of fashionable hard collars cut off circulation to men's carotid arteries when they turned their heads to negotiate intersections. A litany of social and cultural factors were offered as explanations as well, including age (drivers too old or too young); gender (post-pubescent boys and menstruating women); marital status (married individuals regarded as the safest, divorced the most dangerous); resident status (non-residents were associated with greater risk, in 1950 accounting for 26 percent of all auto-related deaths in São Paulo); the time of day, the day of the week, and the month of the year (greater risks were associated with night driving, Sunday driving, and holiday driving, especially during carnival); machismo; abuse of class privilege; low educational levels; and even chewing gum, an early form of distracted driving. One transit director in the early 1950s blamed accidents on Brazil's incomplete modernization and claimed the means to fully dominate the car was for Brazil to build its own automobiles in its own factories. Nations with their own automotive industry, he claimed, had fewer accidents.[21] Some such explanations seem preposterous in hindsight, but others may have been more perceptive than they were taken for at the time. One study that was considered in Brazil in 1926 claimed that a large majority of automotive accidents could be avoided if all drivers had perfect or corrected vision. Today, about two-thirds of individuals in developed nations wear corrective lenses of varying prescriptions; in 1920s Rio, the percentage was close to zero, especially among males under the age of forty who made up most of the city's drivers. It seems probable that a good number of those operating cars did not have optimal vision for driving at any speed.[22]

[21] *A Noite*, Feb. 14, 1951, 9.
[22] A sample of causes can be gleaned from the following sources spread over five decades: Seabra Junior, *Accidentes de automóveis*, 358, 387; *Automobilismo: a revista prática do automóvel*, Oct. 1926, 19; and Jun. 1926, 26; Altieri, *Variações sobre o trânsito paulistano*, 98; *Revista de Automóveis*, Aug., 1954; Oct. 1957, 38; Jan. 1957, 51;

The sheer number of named causes (and the long list just provided is only a sampling) suggested the need for an automotive code that was far-reaching and comprehensive, which is exactly what emerged over the course of a few decades in various jurisdictions. And as new causes were identified, new laws were applied, adding to the body of automotive law. For scale, automotive law was not entirely unprecedented, but it was exceptional for its power to reach into the everyday lives of everyday citizens. Laws created to solve the problem of unintentional death potentially made criminals of all who occupied the street, those killing and those being killed. Criminal law, so it had seemed, was supposed to cause apprehension only for the common criminal – the pickpocket, burglar, assailant, rapist, and murderer – but the deadly nature of driving made it incumbent to criminalize behaviors identified as potential causes of street death and injury. Eventually, the majority of the city's active police forces, often including the military, would be brought to bear on the problem of the automobile, and this heightened the likelihood that common, law-abiding citizens would have run-ins with the new laws, "state-imposed normality," making "permanent transgression inevitable," as Lefebvre stated it.[23] Despite the myths of freedom and mobility associated with the automobile, nobody was more tightly regulated in their movement than the body behind the wheel.[24] The poor on the street, of course, had often felt the heat of the policeman's vigilance, but even the elite, who had believed themselves, if not outright above the law, then outside its direct concerns, were now targets of police suspicion, because behind the wheel they posed a greater danger to the commonweal than the average criminal.

In Rio, vehicular law was well established years before the appearance of the automobile. Sections of the city ordinances dealing with carts, cabs, wagons, and streetcars ran for many paragraphs, which provided automotive law significant precedents. All vehicles were to be registered, and all – even handcarts – were required to display license plates. The city administered driver's license (*título de habilitição*) exams to those who

---

Feb. 1957, 40; Jul. 1957, 44; *Quatro Rodas*, Jul. 1961, 8; Sep. 1961, 23, 26; Dec. 1966, 59; Borges, *Segurança de trânsito*, 7–9.

[23] Lefebvre, *Production of Space*, 23.

[24] C. Emsley, "'Mother, What Did Policeman Do When There Weren't Any Motors?': The Law, the Police and the Regulation of Motor Traffic in England, 1900–1939." *Historical Journal* 36 (1993): 368, 374–75. Matthew Paterson, *Automobile Politics: Ecology and Cultural Political Economy* (Cambridge: Cambridge University Press, 2007), 142.

engaged "blood traction," the Portuguese term for animal traction. There were speed limits measured not in modern units of distance per unit of time but in nature's gaits: walks, trots, lopes, and gallops. Other than policemen, neither mounted persons nor vehicles pulled by animal traction could travel the city's streets faster than the "half trot," and wagons and carts could move no faster than a horse's walk. Infractions of the vehicular law resulted in fines and impoundments, and a surprising number carried jail sentences, including underage driving, driving without a license, and speeding.[25]

Nearly all of the pre-automotive laws that defined moving violations applied to men engaged in the business of transport – that is, working men. Even in the rare cases of luxury coaches, penalties applied to drivers and not owners. Like many street laws, they fell largely on the lower classes. However, while a number of general rules applied to all people in the street, including prohibitions against shouting, cursing, carrying weapons, and running about unclothed, there were no prohibitions or regulations imposed on the movements of pedestrians. Pedestrians moved as they pleased, and in any accident involving a pedestrian and a vehicle, the pedestrian was never judged at fault. Without commandments, there could be no sin. By contrast, to run down a pedestrian with a horse or vehicle could result in significant jail time. Pedestrians could loiter and could move as fast, as slow, and in what direction they pleased, including the wrong way on one-way streets, a tradition that would shape the city's first automotive laws.

With the arrival and early growth of the automobile, legislation began to flow from Assembly Street, although with a hesitancy driven by both uncertainty and opposition. Many of the first regulations were old vehicular laws confidently reapplied to the car, as if it were a vehicle like any other. Automobiles had to be registered, the proof of which was displayed with a new series of license plates. Unlike in the United States, where there was some opposition to the registration and licensing of vehicles as an invasion of privacy,[26] Rio's precedents made this a natural development. In fact, drivers seemed to embrace the license plate in particular as one more way to express status on the street. The plates of official cars were

[25] Intendencia Municipal, "Codigo de Posturas," published in *Diário de Notícas*, Feb. 15, 1890, 2 and Feb. 16, 1890, 4. See also correspondence and legislation in AGCRJ, Cod. 375, 58-1-22, folhas 3, 10, 107.
[26] James J. Flink, *America Adopts the Automobile, 1895–1910* (Cambridge, MA: MIT Press, 1970), 169.

white (later bronze and then the colors of the national flag), carrying the
coat of arms of the ministry or department to which it belonged and thus
displaying the passenger's official position in the city. Such plates were so
coveted that they were counterfeited for decades as they offered parking
and other privileges. The city's other plates carried prefixes: "A" for
aluguel (rent) was assigned to common taxi cabs; "G" for *garagem*, was
for cabs of a better class that one had to hire directly from a local garage
but which one might drive oneself; "L" referring to luxury, was for the
best class of vehicles that could be hired, along with a chauffeur, by
the hour or day; "F" identified freight vehicles, which mostly consisted
of trucks; and "P," the most common designation, stood for passenger
vehicles. Particularly in the "P" prefix, what determined plate status was
the low ordinal value of the number itself. Plates in Rio and other cities
were issued sequentially, from P-1, and license plates became the private
possession of the owner: they could be transferred from car to car over
many generations, and they could also be sold. Passenger cars with low
numbers carried a great deal of status. Low numbered plates were bought
and sold as freely marketed goods, as were numbers that were considered
lucky or unusual, such as 2222 or 8888. By the mid 1950s, of Rio's 70,000
passenger vehicles, seven of the ten lowest plates were attached to
Cadillacs, and one local magazine claimed that the bottom ten plates
were worth at least 1 million *cruzeiros* each. In Rio, Dr. Darciano
Goulart got the city's first number 1, which he only sold forty years later
to Alberto Pittigliani, who used it on a succession of four Cadillacs.
Pittigliani's only regret was the large number of offers he had to turn
down daily, for he claimed the plate was the primary object of his affection
and that he would never sell it. Although the prefixes were dropped early,
only in 1968, due to the growing number of cars, was the ordinal system
replaced, a development that upset the low-plate holders. The director of
transit at the time tried to appease them by offering what amounted to
vanity plates, usually a low number prefaced by letters representing the
driver's initials, but the status and monetary value of the Brazilian license
plate disappeared abruptly with the innovation.[27]

---

[27] Jorge Americano, *São Paulo nesse tempo (1915–1930)*, 80; *Quatro Rodas*, Aug. 1960, 3;
Malcolm Forest, *Automóveis de São Paulo: Memória fotográfica de pessoas, automóveis
e localidades do Estado de São Paulo* (São Paulo: Arquivo do Estado, 2002), 49; *Revista
de Automóveis*, Jun. 1954, 25–28; Altieri, Variacoes sobre o transito paulistano, 23;
Celso Franco, *Eu na contramão: Os bastidores do trânsito carioca nas memorias do seu
ex diretor* (Rio de Janeiro: Topbook, 1997), 314.

Many agreed that speed was a major factor in the number and severity of automotive-caused accidents, but there was resistance to establishing limits. The major advantage of the car, some argued, was its speed, and any limitation nullified its utility and pushed drivers back to the horse age. Others argued that limits were an infringement on the basic right of movement and that drivers alone should determine the safe speed, depending on conditions.[28] One of the difficulties of dealing with velocity derived from the terms that would be used to express it. The gait of horses was no longer useful. In Paris, initially cars were not supposed to exceed the speed of a walking pedestrian, but this did not hold. The car's speed, because of its great potential to cover ground on open roads, to conquer linear space, would come to be expressed in miles or kilometers per hour, which in the city complicated rather than simplified the issue. Nobody could visualize what 50 kilometers per hour looked like, whereas 14 meters per second, the same speed, had units more expressive of reality. São Paulo led in March 1903, just before New York City, by setting a speed limit of 12 kilometers per hour in the downtown and 20 elsewhere. São Paulo would pass no other automotive laws – due to the power of the chauffeur lobby and a liberal belief in the rights of property owners – until February 1920, after five years of legislative debate.[29] In 1907, Rio's first published speed limits were 10 kilometers per hour in the city, 20 in the suburbs, and 30 beyond the city limits. Already by 1918, Rio raised the general city speed limit to 30 kilometers per hour, but held the limit downtown, which encompassed just twenty-four named streets, to 20 kilometers per hour.[30]

Because many blamed accidents on incompetent drivers, legislators reapplied laws that had required teamsters to carry a license to those who now drove vehicles powered by motors. In fact, until at least the early 1920s, it was the same piece of paper, and each examiner had to fill in the blank corresponding to the kind of vehicle one was licensed to drive, in the case of a car, a vehicle "by explosion," as opposed to "blood traction."[31] Prospective drivers had to be twenty-one or older to hold

[28] *Revista de Automóveis*, Nov. 1911, 51.
[29] Sávio, *A modernidade sobre rodas*, 98–99. *O Estado de São Paulo*, Mar. 1, 1903; New York adopted William Phelps Eno's rules, which could fit on a small card, in November of 1903, a few months after São Paulo. See "Rules of the Road," *New York Times*, Nov. 15, 1903, 13.
[30] Regulamento de veículos, 1907, AGCRJ, código 375, 58-1-22, folha 246; *Jornal do Brasil*, Jul. 12, 1907, 3. Seabra Junior, *Accidentes de automóveis*, 77.
[31] "Carteira de habilidade de Eduardo Emiliano da Fonseca Hermes," Mar. 2, 1923, Instituto Histórico e Geográfico Brasileiro, DL 1470.014.

a license as the city felt eighteen, the standard elsewhere, was too young. Drivers had to pass a new test for automotive drivers that consisted of both oral and practical components. Two examiners questioned the candidate, each for ten minutes, on the law, the mechanical parts of the automobile, and the general circulation of the city, including the names and one-way directions of individual streets. Both examiners were also to evaluate the candidate's driving, making sure he showed calmness, perceptive vision, and prudence. The price of a license, 100$000 *reis*, was high, and so was the failure rate. In 1912, 534 individuals passed their driver's exam while 636 failed. That same year, Casa Humbert, Rio's first driving school, opened.[32]

Initially, Rio's legislators published significant penalties for drivers involved in accidents, especially those involving pedestrians. Such penalties were to create disincentives for the kind of driving that produced accidents, but penalties were applied to the consequences of the crime, not its causes. A dangerously negligent driver who caused a minor accident, where "no blood was spilled," was to be sentenced to 15–60 days in jail. If an accident incapacitated a victim for more than thirty days, the driver was sentenced to 2–6 months in jail. For accidents that resulted in permanent injury, disability, amputation, or deformity, the sentence was 2–4 years. And in cases of death, drivers could spend 3–6 years in prison. Hence, for the same driving behavior, a driver might receive a range of punishments based not on his driving but on its consequences. These harsh penalties, which were also an inheritance from earlier laws, contributed to the high rates of fleeing the scene.[33] However, already by the early 1920s, incarceration penalties were reduced and eventually eliminated. Drivers continued to be charged and fined for various moving infractions, but increasingly, the police and authorities were willing to accept that many traffic incidents were acts of God and hence without culprits. Newspapers, for a time, resisted this transition. One, in a daily accident report, complained of the increasing numbers of auto-pedestrian accidents in which the police ruled the cases "casual" or accidental, exonerating drivers on the spot. "This is how it is now: chauffeurs run people down and kill them, and the police absolve the drivers, determining every case to be accidental," and they offered a couple of cases to substantiate their point.[34] Marco Sávio notes that

---

[32] *Revista de Automóveis*, Apr. 1913, 569; *Revista de Automóveis*, Mar./Apr. 1912, 262.
[33] Seabra Junior, *Accidentes de automóveis*, viii, 415.   [34] *O Imparcial*, Jan. 4, 1921, 4.

likewise in São Paulo by the mid-1920s judges began to accept that all driving was dangerous, and, particularly when two cars were involved rather than pedestrians, were reticent to sentence either party, a sort of drive at your own risk legal environment.[35] Moreover, as drivers became increasingly victims of their own movement, the dangers of automobility became a collective concern where everyone, not just the lowly pedestrian, was at risk. That perceived reality was further impetus to creating ever finer grained legislation focused not so much on guilt and punishment but on the reduction of the risk of accidental violence.

A DRIVER'S CODE: FEDERAL LEGISLATION, 1941

Despite the accumulation of automotive law, catastrophes increased. In part due to the tendency to blame outsiders, there was a growing interest in creating a uniform national code so that all cities would have the same rules, signals, and speed limits. It had long been assumed that a large percentage of accidents were caused by out-of-towners and foreign drivers who did not know local laws and customs. One newspaper took seriously a proposal first made in Germany that every city ought to require that visiting motorists, before being allowed to enter the city, hire a local "urban pilot," a professional chauffeur familiar with local streets and rules to drive them around.[36] Municipal laws, at least in large cities, were in reality quite similar, although signs and signals might differ, but some held out hope that if a universal automotive code were imposed across the nation, visiting drivers would at least find familiar rules and signals. US automotive interests attempted a similar centralization in the United States largely because they wanted to limit what restrictions municipalities could place on the car, but this was effectively resisted, and automotive law in the US remained the purview of local governments.[37] In Brazil, Joel Wolfe describes how the desire to nationalize and rationalize automotive law culminated in Rio's 1939 Transit Week, sponsored by both the federal government and the Touring Club of Brazil, in which "officials from nearly every state spoke of the need to

---

[35] *Annuário de Automobilismo* (São Paulo: Automóvel Clube, 1929), 156, 165. Sávio, *A modernidade sobre rodas*, 121–25, examines a case in which a minor, riding on the hood of a car, is killed in a two vehicle crash in which both drivers, one himself a minor, are found negligent, which cross-canceled all guilt.

[36] *Jornal do Brasil*, Jul. 1, 1928, 16.   [37] Flink, *America Adopts the Automobile*, 166.

decrease traffic fatalities in the cities, particularly accidents between motor vehicles and pedestrians." After forty years of the automobile, officials claimed that they wanted to finally make it possible for "people and machines to coexist."[38]

Centralization was effectively accomplished in late 1941 under the Vargas administration with a National Transit Code that superseded nearly all former civic legislation. For Vargas, this was part of a larger project to centralize Brazil's governance; the nation since the end of the Empire had become one of the world's most federalized countries, each state retaining substantial constitutional powers. The 1941 code was not so much an innovation as a codification and organization of existing automotive law. Despite running for some seventy pages, including an appendix of signage standards, and listing more than 600 specific regulations, there was not much that could be called substantively innovative other than centralization itself. Some states attempted to maintain a measure of legislative prerogative, but the federal code stated emphatically that federal law took precedence in all cases. The new code was an organized reiteration of existing law, although it did attempt to universalize even the most minute details, such as the meaning of various police whistles: two short tweets meant "stop," three said "turn on your lights," one long whistle signaled "slow down." However, the National Transit Code, despite the rhetoric of safety that initiated its creation, rather than express a tougher moral and regulatory stance, in fact betrayed the growing leniency toward the car and its driver. Earlier legislation often articulated a level of moral anger and outrage at those who drove dangerously and caused accidents, and the penalties listed earlier, which included jail time, reinforced those emotions. The 1941 code is by comparison dispassionate. The car's dangers are accepted rather than challenged, and the penalties for acting dangerously and causing injury are significantly reduced from earlier decades. If there was any novelty here, the code's leniency was a step backward for those who felt stiffer penalties would get better results, but it reflected the leniency that had come to dominate local laws as well.

Speed itself had become more acceptable. Speed limits in the city, which went from a half trot in 1900 to rarely more than 20 kilometers per hour in the 1920s, were raised to 50 in the downtown and 60 on major avenues, such as Rio Branco. Speeds that had been horrifying to many residents in

[38] Joel Wolfe, *Autos and Progress: The Brazilian Search for Modernity* (New York, NY: Oxford University Press, 2010), 103–04.

the recent past would become the norm. And as speed limits went up, the penalties for exceeding them declined. In 1918, the penalty for excessive speed in Rio was 40–120 *milreis*, variable based on by how much the limit had been exceeded. Two decades later, the National Transit Code set the maximum national penalty for any speeding violation at 50 *milreis*, despite considerable price inflation in the economy in the intervening decades, 6 percent as an annual average just in the 1930s.[39] Now, one could legally drive more than twice as fast as one could two decades before, and the penalty for exceeding the limit now cost less than half as much. And while in 1918 you could convert your fine, if you could not afford it, into prison time, after 1941, there were no automotive infractions for which jail was the penalty. Now, if you killed or maimed someone by your own negligence, the penalty was never more than the confiscation of your license. Licenses could be confiscated for a period of no more than twelve months for negligently killing or injuring another, fleeing an accident, or driving drunk. There were no stiffer penalties. If there is a prejudice in the 1941 legislation, it is against bus drivers who had become the new scapegoats, who were blamed, unfairly, for the majority of the city's street disasters. Buses in many cities were required to have governors on their motors, to cap their maximum speed, and the highest monetary penalty in the new code, 1,000 *milreis*, was imposed on bus drivers who destroyed or modified their governors.[40]

For the first time the new code redefined the nature of the street on a national scale, a process that had already run its course in the cities. By the mid-twenties in Rio, the debate about the place of non-vehicles in the street, namely pedestrians, had come to a head. Already, most non-vehicular activities downtown, such as peddling, gathering, and loitering, had been outlawed and were in decline, but many pedestrians still laid equal claim to the street for their own movement. *O Paiz* in 1928 spoke for the rights of pedestrians and noted that the city's regulations stated that the "street belongs to the pedestrian." But already such a claim was

---

[39] "Estatísticas do Século XX," Instituto Brasileiro de Geografia e Estatística, Ministério do Planajamento, Orçamento e Gestão, www.ibge.gov.br/home/presidencia/noticias/2909 2003estatisticasecxxhtml.shtm (accessed Mar. 10, 2014).

[40] Código Nacional de Trânsito, Decreto-Lei n. 3,651, Sep. 25, 1941, is available on Brazil's Senado Federal website, Portal Legislação, http://legis.senado.gov.br/legislacao/ListaTe xtoIntegral.action?id=13505 (accessed Mar. 17, 2014). See also República dos Estados Unidos do Brasil, *Coleção das leis de 1941, Vol. 5: Atos do poder executivo, decretos-leis de Julho a Setembro* (Rio de Janeiro: Imprensa Nacional, 1941), 335–405. For laws and penalties in 1918, see Seabra Junior, *Accidentes de automóveis*, 358.

itself nostalgic rather than actual. The pedestrian's right to the street was poorly enforced, often unrecognized, and hence only asserted with increasing risk. When the journalist Gomes Leite was run down and killed on Avenida do Mangue in 1926, a magazine representing the interest of chauffeurs blamed him, the pedestrian, for his own death for not carefully looking before stepping into "one of the streets *almost* reserved for vehicles" (emphasis mine). Rio's 1925 building code defined the *logradouro* not generally as public space any longer, where many activities were welcome, but as the place reserved for transit. The 1941 National Code, then, codified the street bed as automotive space, lumping much of the *logradouro* into a single legal category now referred to as *vias públicas* (public thoroughfares). At that point, the legal distinctions between highway, road, and street, which had been obvious for centuries, disappeared.

The National Code also stated that any other public use of the street, be it for festival, procession, or protest, would need to secure the permission of local authorities, which would not be granted if the event did not justify the blocking of automotive traffic. And as a further disincentive to traditional street events, clubs, associations, and religious groups requesting the use of the street for such events had to pay for the entire cost of the police assigned to monitor the event and of the signage to reroute the traffic. There would be no more room for spontaneity. Significantly, the code also nationalized the legality of storing one's car on the public commons. By naming those places and conditions in which cars could not park, it opened up much of the *logradouro* to the free, sanctioned storage of private property. As a result, cars began to even more fully occupy curb-sides, squares, medians, and even sidewalks. The code ostensibly sought to regulate the car, but it also served to legitimize the conquests the motorists had already secured.[41]

EMASCULATED AGENTS OF ENFORCEMENT

Already in 1914, *Fon Fon* pointed out that while automotive laws accumulated, crashes, injuries, and deaths on the city's streets continued to increase.[42] Some would later observe that Rio had many of the same automotive regulations as New York City and Stockholm yet still

---

[41] "E o direito do pedestre?," *O Paiz*, Jul. 8, 1928; *Voz do Chauffeur*, Jun. 28, 1926, 3 (italics mine); Alfred Agache, *Cidade do Rio de Janeiro: Extensão, remodelação, e embelezamento* (Paris: Foyer Brasilien, 1930), appendix, xlviii.

[42] *Fon Fon*, Mar. 21, 1914.

experienced the automobile's rising slaughter. Setting aside for now that Brazilians often underestimated the deadliness of the car in developed nations, such comparisons led them to identify the lack of enforcement as the primary cause of the law's failure. From about 1910, the city made efforts to create, train, and empower various policing forces to discipline the car and its drivers. The police, as elsewhere, directed traffic, manned signals, blew whistles, confiscated licenses, issued warnings, chased perpetrators, impounded vehicles, and soon made hundreds of thousands of traffic citations annually. The traffic cop, in his black, wool uniform, became the street's ubiquitous authority figure, and law enforcement on the city's streets, as elsewhere, shifted emphasis from thwarting petty crime and quelling public disorder to penalizing irregular movements and illegal motions. Yet even with the emblems and tools of authority, the police struggled to impose compliance. What Rio's police lacked was social and technological status. Enforcement of the law is a contest about what can be done in particular spaces and who can do them, and the policeman's low social status had always compromised his effective power, particularly in dealing with the upper classes. The traffic policeman, who did not have a patrol car, was a mere pedestrian in a world of emboldened drivers.

Rio's ancient vehicle inspectors had regulated the movement, registration, and weights of wagons and carts well before the car. They had been expected to regulate the car as well, but it became obvious that the internal combustion engine had made the street's new vehicles different animals entirely. In 1907, to better respond to cars and their growth, the Inspectorate of Vehicles (Inspetoria de Veículos) was enlarged, made its own unit, and given an independent director.[43] In 1911, automotive interests were calling for the creation of a specially outfitted traffic police, to be trained abroad – one magazine joking that the additional cost of such a force could be paid for by savings in gasoline in the ambulance corps. In 1914, the police chief empowered the Civil Guard, the municipal police force, to become more directly involved in the regulation of traffic. But many complained that the police were understaffed, did not know what they were doing, and were often so small, sick, and rachitic in body they commanded no respect from motorists in their ample, speeding cars. One recommended that Brazil's police ought to be tall, strong, and imposing, as was required of officers in Copenhagen, Berlin, and Buenos Aires; Washington Luís, as mayor of São Paulo, set a height minimum of 1.8 meters for traffic police and insisted they be light skinned, all to enhance

---

[43] *Jornal do Brasil*, Jan. 11, 1907, 3.

their authority.[44] Police forces saw more reforms in Rio, and the Inspectorate of Vehicles was remade into the Directory of the Transit Service (DST) in the early 1920s and served as Rio de Janeiro's motor vehicle department and traffic enforcement office for almost fifty years. By the late 1920s, even the military police were assigned to help enforce traffic laws, although only temporarily; in the 1930s, specific traffic guards units were formed; and by the late 1940s, some cities, including Rio, had created civilian volunteer units who used unmarked cars and had the power to issue citations. The military police were put back on traffic in the mid-1950s, but the total numbers of traffic cops were insufficient for the growing number of cars in a sprawling city. If traffic enforcement was miserable in the central city, it was reportedly non-existent in many suburbs.[45] Impunity reigned everywhere, and it was sometimes institutionalized: in 1935, members of the Chauffeur's Union driving within the state of Rio de Janeiro were granted preemptive amnesty for their first three moving violations.[46]

Speed, frequently named as a common cause of death and injury, was a case in point. Complaints about speeding and resulting accidents are legion. Police on foot found it nearly impossible to punish speeders in cars. One problem with enforcing speed limits was that policemen had no means to measure the speed of a vehicle. Even when they did cite drivers for speeding, they had no proof, nor could they say by how much the driver exceeded the limit. Unlike with horses and mules whose gait could be observed, there was no quick method to judge a vehicle's speed. In Rio, speedometers were required equipment in cars by the mid-teens, and they helped drivers to know how fast they were going, but they did nothing for the poor policeman standing street-side. In the late 1910s, city officials considered requiring the installation of mechanical speed governors on passenger cars, but nothing came of it because motorists and chauffeurs united in opposition. Two less intrusive metrics for enforcement were

---

44 "Theórias de Castro Honório," *Fon Fon*, Sep. 17, 1910; *Revista de Automóveis*, Oct. 1911, 14–15; *Revista de Automóveis*, Nov. 1911, 58; "Inspectoria ...," Apr. 18, 1914, GIFI 6c520, ANRJ; "Amaro José Caetano to Secretary of the Police," Jan. 31, 1914, GIFI 6c520, ANRJ; *Correio da Manhã*, Mar. 6, 1920; *Ultima Hora*, Nov. 18, 1929; "Problemas de Tráfego no Rio de Janeiro: O Tráfego da Avenida Rio Branco," *Revista Municipal de Engenharia*, Jul. 1937, 238; Americano, *São Paulo nesse tempo*, 77–78.

45 McShane, *Down the Asphalt Path*, 184–85, notes the creation of traffic police in Philadelphia and New York before 1910; *Veja*, May 14, 1975, 40; "A 'PM' sabe apitar," *Revista de Automóveis*, May 1954, 4–7.

46 *A Noite*, Apr. 11, 1935, 2.

proposed. One involved two traffic cops standing at a known distance from each other on the street and using a stopwatch to time vehicles as they passed. With a quick calculation, they could accurately determine the car's speed, but it was not quick enough to apprehend the car and driver. The other technique involved photography, presumably measuring the length of the car's blurred image and dividing by the shutter speed, but such photos would have taken hours to develop and would not have retained a legible image of the driver or the license plate.[47]

There were calls to give the police vehicles so that they could both pace and chase offenders, to fight poison with poison, as it was promoted. Police supporters also insisted that police cars be more powerful than other cars, which would be achieved in part by permitting them to run with unmuffled exhausts. And to give the policeman a car was not just to give him speed; the car would also give him status. But rank-and-file traffic officers would not get police cars for decades, if ever.[48] A few did receive motorcycles in the 1920s, but too few. Motorcycles never carried the car's social and spatial status, or its protective capacity. One cartoon showed the ridiculousness of the police chasing a runaway vehicle, guns drawn, while riding in a streetcar whose tracks did not follow the perpetrator's flight path. Many drivers got away with speeding because they were going too fast to be caught or identified. In fact, speeders were not generally stopped at all. For decades, from the early 1920s to the 1950s, the police published infractions in the newspapers for all to see, but rather than shaming the perpetrators by publishing their names, they only listed license plates. These long, daily lists only advertised police impotence in catching and fining motorists who broke the law.

During the car's first couple of decades, speeding was among the more common ticketed transgressions, accounting for a third to a half of the citations, but over the years, speeding citations declined. By the late 1940s, there were only two or three speeding tickets per day compared to hundreds of tickets given for illegal parking, running signals, going the wrong way, nonworking tail lights, excessive exhaust, or inappropriate use of the horn.[49] The numbers suggest the police had essentially given up on enforcing speed limits, and ticketing generally was in decline. In 1935, Rio's

[47] *O Estado de São Paulo*, Jan. 13, 1915, 4; *O Estado de São Paulo*, Jul. 8, 1921, 4; Seabra Junior, *Accidentes de automóveis*, 77, 82, 90–91, 102–03.
[48] *Jornal do Brasil*, Jan. 1, 1915, 13. *Vida Policial*, Apr. 11, 1925, 32.
[49] See issues from the *Gazeta de Notícias* in the early 1920s where such infractions were published two or three times per week. In the 1940s, they were still being published in the *Correio da Manhã*.

police served 101,454 traffic tickets; in 1960, only 63,381, despite the fact that there were almost nine times as many cars as in 1935. And the weight of the infractions moved significantly away from speeding. In 1960, there were 21,469 citations for passing where prohibited, 6,889 for going the wrong way on one-way streets, and 8,349 for not yielding to vehicles and pedestrians, but only 543 speeding tickets.[50] In São Paulo, which ticketed more heavily than Rio, speeding tickets only accounted for 2 percent of all tickets in the years surrounding 1950, and during one study, out of 13,543 traffic citations in a week, only 13 were for speeding. The majority were parking tickets.[51] In 1961, a reporter claimed that the sky was the actual speed limit in Rio, and that among pedestrians, there were two categories: "the quick and the dead."[52]

Drivers openly flouted automotive law. One automotive magazine half-seriously encouraged its driving readers to flee if they saw a cop, pay bribes if caught, and take morbid pride in the fact that their neighbors refer to them as Deadly Joe, Mass Killer, or Pedal to the Metal.[53] Some drivers in Rio took pride in the claim that they, not Americans, had invented a switch that turned off the light illuminating their rear license plate, in case of an accident. Speed was the power to evade responsibility and ignore police authority by leaving the lawman literally in the dust and, if necessary, run him down as well. In one incident in 1928, the driver of automobile number 4,896 "came precipitously up Rua dos Arcos in search of a victim." He found one in sixty-year-old Salvador Marzulo, a newspaper vendor, whose body the collision sent tumbling up the street some distance. The driver accelerated away from the scene only to find a policeman, João Alves dos Santos, aged twenty-six, standing in the middle of the street to prevent his escape. Rather than slow and concede, the driver sped up and ran down the officer as well. Both victims were taken to the Posto Central to treat their head and general injuries. The police were so powerless in such situations that ridiculous solutions were suggested as remedy. One cartoon advertised automotive tires with the car's license plate number embedded in the treads. That way, if

[50] *O Imparcial*, Nov. 16, 1937; "Brasil: Quem não é 'vivo,' morre," *Quatro Rodas*, Nov. 1961, 22–23, 26.

[51] Altiéri, *Variações sobre o transito paulistano*, 116

[52] "Brasil: Quem não é 'vivo,' morre," *Quatro Rodas*, Nov. 1961, 22–23; *Revista de Automóveis*, Jan. 1959, 23.

[53] *Revista de Automóveis*, Jan. 1957, 51; in Portuguese, the terms were *Zé da Morte*, *Mata Quatro*, and *Pé-na-Tábua*. See also "Como Iamos Dizendo," *Revista de Automóveis*, Feb. 1957, 40.

a pedestrian were run down, the identity of his or her assailant would be imprinted as a contusion on the body. A police magazine suggested that every model of car have its own unique horn as this would help police identify, by sound, at least what kind of vehicle had been involved. More seriously, *Revista de Automóveis* published short visual tests consisting of photographs of the rear ends of various car models. Could their readers, they asked, accurately identify a vehicle's make and model from behind? If so, and the test served to educate them, then they could help the police identify the culprit in yet another hit-and-run accident.[54]

Further evidence of law enforcement's impotence were the diminishing support and declining budgets of the Directory of Transit (DST) whose task it was to license cars, police street traffic, and collect moving and parking penalties. When the first director of the DST moved into his offices on Tiradentes Square, the appointments were quite stately; the building formerly served as the Ministry of Justice. The location was in many ways ideal as the square formed something of a crossroads in the city for cars, streetcars, and buses. The square was indeed one of the busiest automotive spaces and it experienced a fair share of Rio's automotive and pedestrian accidents. From the DST's windows, one could experience the city's broader traffic problems in microcosm. One observer commented in 1925 that trying to cross the traffic at Tiradentes Square carried the same risk as jumping off Urca Mountain, a notorious spot for suicides.[55] The DST itself may have seen as much interior traffic as any building in the city. Thousands of chauffeurs, drivers, and expediting agents (*despachantes*) stood in lines each week to renew registrations, settle tickets, and apply for driver's licenses; the building became filled with yellowing piles of paper, some spilling into the bathrooms. Maintenance of the building was so neglected that by the 1950s the façade was falling away. The edifice was commonly referred to as a ruin. By the early 1960s, the building had no water other than what was pumped in by fire truck. When that was unavailable, the occupants went without water, and toilets went unflushed. During the long years in which he ran the office, Edgar Estrela used the building's lobby to park his Cadillac, license plate 2–22-22, which obstructed patrons.[56] The department's budget declined as a share of the city's total budget,

---

[54] *A Manhã*, Nov. 20, 1928, 1; *Revista de Automóveis*, Aug. 1955, 42; *Annuário de Automobilismo*, 1929, 106. *Vida Policial*, Apr. 11, 1925, 26; "Auto-Teste," *Revista de Automóveis*, Jul. 1954.

[55] *Vida Policial*, Jul. 25, 1925, 3.   [56] Franco, *Eu na contramão*, 663.

and the staff declined in absolute numbers, all while car registrations increased sometimes by as many as 100 per day. The technical section, which installed signs and painted lines, at one time had thirty-six employees. In 1952, only twelve remained to cover tens of thousands of streets, street signs, and manual signals in the entire metropolis, an area exceeding 1,100 square kilometers. Hence, the technical staff, perforce, had to focus their attention exclusively on the downtown. By 1963, the department employed 550 traffic guards, but as 350 of them worked desk jobs, some 85 percent of the city's assigned street posts were unmanned. Although the then current director, Stélio de Morais, an architect and urban planner, had an official car, the entire department had only eight total vehicles engaged in law enforcement: one functioning tow truck and seven motorcycles. Nearly all of the revenue from citations went to the city's general treasury despite directors seeking a portion to help fund their responsibilities.[57] The department staff and police were also accused of corruption. Just before the department would be renamed and reorganized in new facilities in the late 1960s, Director Celso Franco himself admitted that his officers took bribes, which he justified by their low pay. Staff in the Tiradentes office, for a small fee, could make citations disappear. When the city finally renovated the building's failed pipes, plumbers found the drains plugged with pulpy citations that had been flushed down the toilets.[58]

EVERYWHERE A SIGN: MARKING UP THE COMMONS

The DST, during the Vargas administration, rejected the view that traffic accidents in Rio were epidemic. In addition to blaming pedestrians, officials faulted the streets, which were too narrow and poorly engineered for modern traffic. What the city really needed, they argued, was more public

---

[57] "O Serviço de Trânsito Não Existe: Não Daria para Controlar as Bicicleticas da Cidade," *Tribuna da Imprensa*, without date, but probably Nov. 1952, newspaper clipping in Serviço de Comunicações, Departamento Federal de Segurança Pública, 1951, ANRJ, BR.AN.RIO, VV.O.JTA, MJ.3334; "Trânsito no Rio: Um Pardieiro contra a Cidade," *Quatro Rodas*, Jul. 1963, 42–47; "Limpeza do Trânsito não Começou em Casa," *Quatro Rodas*, Sep. 1964, 90–92.

[58] Franco, *Eu na contramão*, 266, 407. Of course, not all directors were corrupt, and there is substantial paperwork showing their diligence. António Oliveira Quito in the mid-1950s went after chauffeurs driving for city and federal agencies that had numerous unresolved tickets. See Diretor do Servico de Transito, Antonio Oliveira Quito to Diretor do Departamento de Administração do Ministério da Justica, Jul. 18, 1955, BR.AN.RIO, VV.o.PES, RDI.2127, ANRJ.

space: more streets, wider streets, more lanes, more and larger parking lots, and a system of urban highways with connecting tunnels and viaducts.[59] The engineers the city hired continued to prioritize speed and flow, rather than safety. Their motto was that cars should be speeded up "by any means." Speed limits were maligned as misguided safety measures. The engineer Aldo Mário de Azevedo in 1938 argued that slowing down cars did not make streets safer because it only encouraged more people to walk in the streets. His most salient solution to traffic safety eliminated the category of pedestrian altogether by presuming to put every Brazilian theoretically in a car – more social utopian engineering than traffic engineering.[60]

Engineers, with few opportunities to redesign Rio's streets, had to make the best use of existing public thoroughfares until the 1960s, when the city finally began constructing substantial urban highways. They were forced to prioritize the regulation of existing street space for the benefit of car movement, and they did so with traffic signs, traffic signals, and traffic lanes. Signage, flashing lights, and white paint were visual indicators of the street's now dominant role as automotive corridor, and the street was transformed from a space that had been largely unmarked to one that was visually overwhelmed by the signs and markers that tried to dictate modern movement. From colonial times, legislation itself had been ceremoniously posted in public spaces, prominent places such as Assembly Street and Praça 15, but never with this kind of permanence, ubiquity, and repetitive monotony. Although the adoption of signage and signals was rather slow in coming, many of Rio's streets would eventually become forests of posted signs and valleys of painted pavement.

Rio's streets before the car were remarkably bereft of signage. Other than the occasional one-way sign, indicated by a small plate mounted on the wall of a building, conspicuous only because it had no competing signage, one would have been hard pressed to find much else in the way of posted rules for movement. Few shops and businesses had even advertising signage before the latter half of the nineteenth century. People were so familiar with their streets they did not need signs to tell them what each office, shop, or café offered, what a street was called, or which way to go

---

[59] "Para que existe e qual o fim da Inspectoria de Veiculos?" *A Rua*, Dec. 28, 1922, 1.

[60] "Algumas indicações para a solução do problema do congestionamento," *Revista Municipal de Engenharia*, May 1939, 326. Aldo Mário de Azevedo, *O serviço de prevenção contra accidentes: Trabalho apresentado á Sociedade "Amigos da Cidade" em 9 de março de 1938* (São Paulo: n.p., 1938), 6.

to get anywhere. In the early nineteenth century, the iconography of city streets shows entire blocks and popular squares without a single visible commercial or civic sign. Even by 1900, with commercial signs increasing in size and number, other than the one-way signs, there were no traffic signs or signals before the appearance of the car.

Traffic signage was still a long time coming. Signals arrived first. The city's first traffic signals were hand signals used by motorists. *Auto-Propulsão* opined in 1915 that most traffic accidents occurred when drivers stopped or turned without signaling their intent. If drivers would engage in this simple manual courtesy, accidents, it claimed, "would be forever avoided on the streets of our very lively traffic."[61] By 1920, the number of hand signals had become a topic worthy of ridicule, and one illustrator produced an invention to mount on top of one's car, the Manual Signaler, that sported seven hands and as many signals, including a couple of obscene gestures.[62] Rio's first and only mechanical traffic signal in 1917 failed in part because it was designed for the speed of pedestrians, . The words "stop" and "go" printed on the indicating arms were so small that drivers could not see or distinguish them with sufficient time to respond. A moving vehicle needed considerable space to come to a stop, and one observer noted that a driver required binoculars to see a stop signal early enough to do any good. Because it was useless, it was removed.

Much of the opposition to signals and signage was aesthetic. The city had built a most beautiful avenue, and now the city was cluttering the views and façades with ugly, gangly contraptions.[63] But the need was great, so signals returned in the early 1920s – their utility assumed by their widespread adoption in the United States and Europe. The aesthetic liabilities of signals and signage continued to be raised. In 1928, *Revista da Semana* published a short photo essay of Rio's varied signaling devices. Some were quite primitive, squat cylinders of stone set in the middle of intersections that served to remind drivers to keep to the right and to not cut corners when making left turns. Residents referred to these as either cakes or blocks of cheese, and the many clips and gouges in their margins demonstrated how often driver's got it wrong. In one case, on Pasteur Street, the traffic "cake" was removed because it had "hit" and destroyed so many cars. Having the same function, the silent policeman, as it was known in the US, looked like a tall mile marker or small obelisk,

---

[61] *Auto-Propulsão*, May 1, 1915.   [62] *Fon Fon*, May 29, 1920.
[63] *Auto Federal*, Mar. 15, 1917, 14.

sometimes marked with lights. Rio's citizens referred to these as "Tombs of the Unknown Pedestrians." Somewhat more familiar were the many traffic signals at major intersections, some with dropping arms, some with whistles, and an increasing number with colored lights. All of these were operated manually by the police, and many were unique in their design and function such that drivers had to learn the peculiarities of each. One magazine compared Rio's traffic signals to a difficult game of charades: one player, the police officer, thrashed or flashed frantically to be understood while the drivers looked on keenly for – but in befuddlement about – what it was they should do. One signal on Rio Branco consisted of an elevated kiosk where the sheltered guard sat operating the long signal arms with a lever. Most signals required a policeman to stand at the base of a pole to manually change the indicators, depending on traffic demand. For police comfort, some signal controls were supplied with awnings to keep guards out of the sun and rain, but those posts without awnings were often abandoned in rainy weather – the poor officer trying to direct traffic with his arms while sheltering under a shop awning where few could see him. Although citizens mocked the hodgepodge of ugly signals, resulting in some being removed, the city tried to give traffic signals authority and honor, even christening one new signal after Tomé de Souza, Brazil's first colonial governor.[64]

Signals continued to multiply, some 600 being installed in the early 1930s. But traffic signs still remained few in number, despite similar calls for their expanded implementation. Traffic regulators placed a great deal of hope on signage.[65] The earliest visible evidence of an actual traffic sign was a plaque hung high above a busy commercial street in São Paulo in 1916; it was smaller than a license plate and less legible, and it reiterated the first rule of driving: "Keep to the Right."[66] In Rio, the first signs, rather than dealing with traffic directly, appear to have been bus stop signs. Few other signs appeared in Brazil's larger cities for decades. São Paulo had only twenty-three signs on posts in 1948, but it made a big push for more signage in the mid-1950s.[67]

---

[64] *Revista da Semana*, Feb. 11, 1928, 29. See Norton, *Fighting Traffic*, 54, for a description of the silent policeman in the United States.

[65] In *Diário Carioca*, May 6, 1930, the chief of police, Coriolano de Goes, announced the placing throughout the city of sturdy, metal, brilliant signs that would not age, but there was little follow-up that decade.

[66] "South America, Brazil, São Paulo, Business Street," photo 45,110, Library of Congress, Prints & Photographs Division.

[67] "Carta de São Paulo," *Revista de Automóveis*, Sep. 1954.

Traffic signage in Rio, other than the numerous reserved parking signs, did not really appear until the late 1960s, and much of it was reportedly short-lived.[68] Cost was always an issue, but there remained a strong aesthetic opposition to signs on the street because signs were considered unsightly. In the early 1970s, signs that had gone up the previous decade were being taken down. *Veja* reported that since most were too small to be read by speeding drivers and could not compete with all the commercial signage, all of the recently installed wood posts, which had also obstructed the sidewalk, were being recycled for housing and firewood, and the signs were being illegally repurposed as modern art to decorate living rooms.[69]

Paint, on the other hand, was welcomed – or at least preferred. Henry Barnes, the peripatetic troubleshooter who helped solve traffic problems in Denver, Baltimore, New York, and Buenos Aires, claimed that "the best traffic control device in the world was a bucket of paint."[70] For half a century, Rio's street had had no painted lines to divide opposing traffic, to allocate lanes among drivers, or to identify pedestrian crossings. Without dividing lines, the street's actual center line had long been contested in recurring battles of chicken between oncoming drivers. Without lane lines, cars tended to travel like unregulated herds of animals, which made for inefficient use of the street's full space. Lane lines were described as the comb that untangles the traffic. Barnes demonstrated that simply demarcating lanes with white paint upped a street's traffic capacity substantially. The first painted crosswalks in Rio went in around Cinelandia in 1956, and lane lines were tried in a variety of locations at about the same time. Initially there were two problems associated with the use of paint. First, it was not very visible on the city's remaining cobbled streets, nor where the streets were riddled with potholes. Second, the paints available at that time wore away, even from the best asphalt pavements, after a couple of weeks due to the traffic. Celso Franco observed that pedestrian feet, more than tires, wore away the zebra lines in the pedestrian crossings. Even when a paint that endured six to eight months was used, maintaining the "horizontal signalization," as it was called, kept scores of men employed full time. Franco claimed that during the three years of his tenure, some 65,000 square meters of lines,

---

[68] *Revista de Automóveis*, Nov. 1956, 42.   [69] *Veja*, Dec. 27, 1972, 54.

[70] Compendium of Technical Papers: Institute of Transportation Engineers, Annual Meeting, Mexico City, 1977 (Arlington, VA: Institute of Transportation Engineers, 1977), 322.

stripes, arrows, and commands were painted and repainted, with the help of new drivable machines.[71]

A SECOND CRACK AT NATIONAL LEGISLATION, 1966

The long disinterest in signage, its implementation and maintenance, the dilapidation of the city's traffic office, its budget declines, and the unwillingness to count the dead and injured, all suggest a flagging official interest in automotive safety.[72] Maybe most telling of the neglect was the failure to update Brazil's 1941 National Transit Code. For twenty-five years, a period in which Rio's fleet of vehicles grew almost ten-fold to more than 200,000 from the end of the Second World War, automotive law stagnated. By the mid-1950s, there were complaints about the outdated 1941 code, particularly in the price of traffic citations. In particular, the price of infractions could not be raised above federal limits. Tickets ranged from 27 cents to 2 dollars in penalties.[73] Again, inflation overtook what were already considered light fines in 1941. Inflation ran an average of 12 percent per year in the 1940s, 19 percent in the 1950s, and 40 percent per year in the 1960s, but the price of tickets did not change.[74] Speeding tickets already by the 1950s were such a bargain as to be laughable; one engineer suggested their purpose was merely educational, for they certainly served no penal purpose. By 1961, a speeding ticket cost the equivalent of a loaf bread. It was cheaper to park on the sidewalk and pay the fine, mere pennies, than it was to pay for legal parking. Nobody contested fines because they were so small, and if drivers failed to pay their traffic citations, it was not because the fines were expensive but because the lines to pay them at the DST office

---

[71] *Quatro Rodas*, Sep. 1961, 26; Franco, *Eu na contramão*, 250, 480, 665. See Henry A. Barnes, *The Man with the Red and Green Eyes: The Autobiography of Henry A. Barnes, Traffic Commissioner, New York City* (New York: E.P. Dutton & Co., 1965), 226–28, for the impact of paint in Buenos Aires in this period.

[72] Officials did organize occasional safety campaigns, but they were rare and had little apparent reach. *Legislação do Distrito Federal*, 1952, LEX, BNRJ, 14. "Campanha Educativa do Trânsito de 1957," DL 1368.8, Instituto Histórico e Geográfico Brasileiro; *Veja*, Dec. 27, 1972, 54.

[73] "Em Disparada," *Correio da Manhã*, Dec. 2, 1941, 4; "Traffic Law Breakers Rule Roost in Brazilian Capital," *Tri City Herald*, Apr. 20, 1956.

[74] "Estatísticas do Século XX," Instituto Brasileiro de Geografia e Estatística, Ministério do Planajamento, Orçamento e Gestão, www.ibge.gov.br/home/presidencia/noticias/2909 2003estatisticasecxxhtml.shtm (accessed Mar. 10, 2014).

were long and slow. It was easier just to wait for the next inevitable traffic ticket amnesty.[75]

Motorists, critics complained, were being coddled, so in 1957 a meeting was held at the military academy in Agulhas Negras to consider reforming the 1941 legislation. In the discussions, outdated laws and unenforced rules remained the most common explanations for both automotive deaths and traffic congestion. Conferees asked for substantial fines, including the return of jail time for those who put others' lives at risk. They even suggested posting the driver's infractions right on his or her license plate so the driver's civic faults would be apparent to all and his or her recidivism obvious to the police. Congestion, more than safety, was the primary impetus for the revision of traffic law because traffic jams had become serious, daily occurrences. The proposed revisions were outlined by 1960,[76] but little progress was made on implementing a new code until the military came to power and put legislation behind their desire to make Brazilian society orderly and Brazilian office holders honest.

The new National Code of 1966, like that of 1941, was not terribly revolutionary – only a bit longer and more detailed than what came before. Drivers still had to wear shoes, but now they were also required to keep two hands on the wheel, and hanging one's left arm out the window was prohibited. For the first time, law mandated that cars stay in their lanes, should there be lane markers, and that pedestrians restrict themselves to crosswalks when entering the street. The code also granted cities the power to create designated parking lots on the public domain and to expand on-street parking, but it also listed the spaces where parking was prohibited, such as in tunnels, on bridges, near hydrants, in crosswalks, at curb cuts, and on sidewalks. Restrictions remained on anyone partying, dancing, playing games, or parading on any street without a license from the city, and now, in addition to covering the cost of blocking the traffic, organizers of street activities also had to provide insurance against any risks or accidents associated with their events. However, the code did not require motorists to carry their own insurance policies. To the usual auto safety features in the old code, such as brakes and horns, the new code added windshield wipers, bumpers, sun visors, turn signals, and fire extinguishers. There had been discussion of requiring seat belts, which by this time had been shown to save lives, but they did not make the cut, and the US itself

---

[75] "O drama das multas." *Revista de Automóveis*, Jun. 1954, 6–9; *Revista de Automóveis*, Jan. 1955, 15; *Quatro Rodas*, Sep. 1961, 34.
[76] *Quatro Rodas*, Dec. 1960, 7–10.

would not require their installation in new cars until 1968. Another innovation of the 1966 code required that mental and physical exams for driver's licenses be renewed every four years, and every two years for drivers over sixty. Exhaust bypass valves were reiterated as illegal, suggesting they were still a problem, and horns were forbidden at night, if prolonged or successive, or if used to hurry up a slow pedestrian.[77]

The code, most remarkably, eliminated speed limits, ordering that driver's "transit at speeds compatible with safety," depending on the conditions, be they crowded, slippery, curvy, or narrow, or in the vicinity of schools, hospitals, or animals. The assumption was that otherwise the conditions were right for high velocity, although cities now were permitted to establish their own limits again. Fines for citations were priced as fractions of the official minimum monthly salary so that they would keep up with inflation. Now, serious violations could have fines that were anywhere from half to the full value of the monthly minimum salary, which many pointed out as astronomical compared to what had been in force. Some publications that had been calling for more severe fines now expressed second thoughts, and the police seemed reluctant to impose the fines due to stunned motorists' sticker shock to the new code.[78]

The National Code of 1966, particularly its substantial penalties, renewed hope for the establishment of safe, orderly streets in Rio; and the direct role of the military government, who made it happen and promised to enforce it, gave citizens some reason for optimism. On the day the legislation went into effect, *Quatro Rodas* believed that "the new Code is going to change the face of traffic in our principal cities, imposing order and safety."[79] Ten years later, *Veja* magazine, a supporter of the military's coup and its increasing authoritarian tack, laid bare the national legislation's utter failure: rather than improving traffic safety, traffic deaths increased year after year. By 1976, *Veja* reported that 25 percent of all crimes before the courts in the state of Rio were auto-

---

[77] The only drivers required to carry an insurance policy were minors, under age eighteen; the driving age was set at sixteen. The entire code can be accessed at Código Nacional de Transito, Lei no. 5.108, de 21 de Setembro de 1966, Câmara dos Deputados, Atividade Legislativa, www2.camara.leg.br/legin/fed/lei/1960-1969/lei-5108-21-setembro-1966-3 68929-publicacaooriginal-37246-pl.html (accessed Feb. 15, 2014). *Quatro Rodas*, Nov. 1965.

[78] Código Nacional de Transito, Lei no. 5.108, de 21 de Setembro de 1966, Câmara dos Deputados, Atividade Legislativa, www2.camara.leg.br/legin/fed/lei/1960-1969/lei-510 8-21-setembro-1966-368929-publicacaooriginal-37246-pl.html (accessed Feb. 15, 2014). *Quatro Rodas*, Nov. 1965, 13.

[79] "Código Novo-Dia Um," *Quatro Rodas*, Dec. 1966, 163.

related – more cases than any other category of crime – suggesting that
enforcement had become active but that conformity to the new rules
remained lax. In the city, someone died in traffic-related accidents every
three hours – a rate that murderers in the city "not even on their days of
greatest inspiration could attain."[80] The magazine listed many causes for
automotive deaths but concluded that the central issue was still impunity.
Ninety-four percent of auto-accident defendants were absolved of all
guilt, and of those few condemned, only 10 percent suffered any penalty.[81]

ASPIRING TO FIRST-WORLD ACCIDENT RATES

The subversive short story "A Night's Drive, (Parte I)" by Rubem
Fonseca, a former street cop and later a police commissioner, plays with
the presumed accidentalness of Brazil's automotive violence. Fonseca's
protagonist, an office worker successful enough to own a Jaguar and two
additional cars for his grown children, invites his family out for
a nighttime drive after dinner, as he does every evening, knowing full
well that none will respond to the invitation. The evening soap operas
keep his family at home. Into Rio's loneliest streets he prowls behind
salient chrome bumpers, looking for solitary pedestrians, preferably
men who offer the greater stalking challenge. Tonight he settles for
a woman. Slowing his car, cutting the lights, he follows, awaiting the
opportune moment, and then shoots the car between the sidewalk's trees,
hitting the woman mid-thigh and throwing her savagely against a low
garden wall. Returning home in no hurry, gratified in the fact he has never
failed to kill his victims, he checks his unmarked bumper, enters his house,
and goes tranquilly to bed. To drive his point home, Fonseca offers
a "Parte II" to the story. Here the murderer runs down another woman,
his date, who he strategically drops off a couple of blocks from her home.
Fonseca narrates the prosaic killing that automobiles present as the perfect
murder: the automobile's mobile, spatial power serves as the murder
weapon, as cover, as the getaway, and, above all, as an alibi. In Rio,
automotive deaths are so common and flight from the scene so anticipated
that even if one were caught, the assumption was automatic – it was an
accident – without the perpetrator ever having to make the claim.[82]

---

[80] "Os Crimes sem Castigo," *Veja*, Apr. 28, 1976, 50.
[81] "Os Crimes sem Castigo," *Veja*, Apr. 28, 1976, 50–51.
[82] José Rubem Fonseca, "Passeio noturno (Parte I)," in *Feliz Ano Novo: Contos*, 2nd edn.
   (São Paulo: Companhia das Letras, 1989).

Traffic deaths were of course not serial murders, but they were serial. Their consistent frequencies imposed on society an obligation to explain their intransigence. Roberto DaMatta's *Faith in God and Pedal to the Metal* explains much of Brazil's traffic "insanity" and the failures of enforcement as a result of the distinct and strengthened social hierarchies the automobile had created on the street. The powerful in their cars demanded spatial preference and social deference, particularly from pedestrians and other drivers, but more significantly, from the law and its enforcers. DaMatta acknowledges the causes typically given for traffic deaths and injuries, including recklessness, imprudence, road conditions, and mechanical failure, but deference to class drove much of a culture that seemed unwilling to fully regulate the automobile and punish its users for negligence or recklessness. DaMatta argues for a Brazilian exceptionalism, a nation of relatively high automotive violence, because driving remained the privilege of a small, powerful minority who shaped the law and then acted with impunity. He also posits a broader explanation for Brazilian automotive exceptionalism based on cultural and religious notions of fate or providence, which were powerful ideas in shaping a sense of futility in the face of death and tragedy. He suggests that, for many, death was such a powerful reality that its occurrence must be an act of God, and hence an expression of divine will. If one dies in an automotive accident, it must have been destined to be. This is to put causality on a transcendental or mystical level, reducing all deaths to a single cause. If automotive deaths were truly acts of God, then by definition nothing could be done about them. Mysticism substituted for criminal motive and human negligence. In fact, if auto-related deaths were providential, then they were events without evil. They were, unlike Fonseca's fictional murdering motorist, unpremeditated tragedies rather than crimes, and hence the response to automobile accidents was largely impassive, even by those who did not drive.[83]

However, as much as Brazilians may have believed in their own exceptionalism, some even taking a morbid pride in the reputedly notorious accident rates that made Rio "the capital of death," the experience of the car elsewhere demonstrated that Rio's case was rather more mundane than unique. As insightful as DaMatta's analyses are in explaining Brazil's automotive fatalities, the reality is that in more developed, law-abiding, and secular societies – and DaMatta, too, holds up the US – death and

---

[83] Roberto DaMatta, *Fé em Deus e pé na tábua: ou como e por que o trânsito enlouquece no Brasil* (Rio de Janeiro: Rocco, 2010), 15–16.

injury have been the daily fare of the streets and highways. Brazilian officials continued, as they had since the 1920s, to hold Europe and the United States as models of automotive order. Some, such as Senator Francisco Accioly Filho of Paraná, saw American success not in its laws and policing but in its automotive cultural evolution. Rather than pass new laws, he suggested Brazil "wait" it out; the current carnage was just a "passing" phase. Unlike in the US, he claimed, "in Brazil, the pedestrian and the vehicle have simply not had enough time to accommodate themselves to each other." Those who took a "do nothing" approach said they looked "confidently forward to the traffic of the future," which presumably meant the American reality.[84]

The majority, on the other hand, who sought safety through reform, credited better laws and policing for the advanced nations' presumed successes. In France, they observed, traffic officials punished offending drivers with a certainty that made motorists think twice about making an illegal move, and no exceptions were made for those of high social status. *Veja* reported on the substantial consequences suffered by Henry Ford II for driving drunk in Los Angeles, despite his family connections and his Lincoln Continental. In Brazil, they asserted, the nature of his name or the model of his car would have resulted in no prosecution and no penalties. In the US, they believed, traffic courts "are famous for their strictness." Yet there was irony in Brazil's holding up the US as a model of safety. *Veja* lamented that cars in Brazil had killed an estimated 53,000 persons in the previous six years, beginning in 1970. It failed to report that in the US during the same period, cars had killed 304,000, more than 50,000 persons per year. If law enforcement was more effective and equitable in a nation where almost everyone drove, it did not create a safer automotive experience. Even though per vehicle miles traveled, the US may have had a better safety record than Brazil, automobility as a system of movement was catastrophic everywhere it was introduced, and even the most advanced nations were failures in safety. Those who lamented Brazil's tragedies could only hope for automotive carnage on a North American scale. As they looked forward to a future of safe streets and efficient transportation, they refused to look back over seventy-five years of automotive history, at home or abroad, that spoke authoritatively to the problem's intransigence. Had they been able to look forward, they would have seen measurable improvements in mortality per mile,

---

[84] "Os Crimes sem Castigo," *Veja*, Apr. 28, 1976, 52, 58. "Questões de Direito," *Revista de Automóveis*, Jun. 1954, 22.

improvements that have been the results of better law enforcement, changes in the culture of driving, better engineered streets, and imposed automotive safety devices such as seat belts and air bags. But they would have also seen the car's catastrophic statistics overpower most of safety's gains. Globally today, the car kills some 1.2 million people annually, an extraordinary disaster with a century of building precedent. Brazil today is estimated to be the third largest national contributor to automotive deaths, behind China and India.[85]

João Amaral de Souza, a stalwart traffic guard of the military police who manned a signal and crosswalk on Marechal Floriano Avenue, showed what might have happened if the police had had the esprit and resources to enforce the laws with consistent dedication. For thirty-four years, Officer Amaral took responsibility for the safety of one intersection, primarily for the many students who attended the Colégio Dom Pedro II, an elite preparatory school that faced his crosswalk. Amaral became a beloved figure for his obvious concern, a man who took possession of the street and controlled the movement of pedestrians and drivers with care and courtesy. In three decades of service in the same place, he came to know everyone on the block by name: students, shopkeepers, popcorn peddlers, even cabbies and truck drivers. Drivers knew to expect him at his post, and in respect for the authority of his always impeccable uniform, slowed 100 meters before arriving. Students, with whom he engaged in friendly conversation, benefited from his taking extra precautions on days of exams when the students were more than usually distracted. When Chief of Police Geraldo de Menezes Côrtes transferred Amaral to a new post in the early 1950s, students walked 4 kilometers from the school to the presidential palace and demanded Amaral be reinstated at his old post, which Vargas agreed to do over the police chief's protest. The students celebrated on Marechal Floriano Avenue until Amaral politely requested that they stop blocking traffic and return to class. In all his years at his intersection, there were only two pedestrian accidents, one in which a car drove onto the sidewalk, injuring a student, and another in which a truck with failing brakes killed a teacher. Over the course of thirty-four years and an estimated 87 million cars passing over his crosswalk, two accidents were considered nothing less than a canonizable miracle. At Amaral's retirement in 1966, he wept as the students over whom he had watched

[85] World Health Organization, *Global Status Report on Road Safety 2015* (Geneva: World Health Organization, 2015), 2, 100, 264–65.

for a generation honored him with a citation.[86] His career demonstrated that dedicated service and law enforcement could make the streets safer for human bodies. It also showed that even with substantial traffic, the street could still be a place in which people, by communicating on shared spaces, built community. But Amaral, by all accounts, was exceptional. Most streets did not have an Officer Amaral; most intersections had no police enforcement at all. Despite Transit Director Celso Franco's gallant promise to the National Assembly in 1975 that the military government "will not permit that children be killed by cars," neither Officer Amaral's colleagues in the military police nor Colonel Franco's military appointed colleagues in the transit office proved capable of turning back the rising rates of automotive deaths and accidents.[87]

[86] "Saravá, seu Guarda," *Quatro Rodas*, Jul. 1966, 57–60.
[87] "Detran anuncia sua Operação Cidadela para livrar o Centro do inimigo automóvel," *Jornal do Brasil*, Jun. 19, 1975, 15.

6

Buyers and Regrets

Praça Onze

It is good, beyond compare; let it remain, since it's already there.

Assis Valente[1]

For much of the city's history, Rio de Janeiro had two public spaces known as *rocios*, the Rocio Grande and the Rocio Pequeno – that is, one large and one small. The term *rocio*, of ancient origin, identified a common space, often a public pasture, within or on the outskirts of a city. In Rio, as the city matured, these two spaces rose to the status of square (*praça*), and the term *rocio* fell into disuse, although the term is still applied today to the formal squares of a few Brazilian cities and more typically those of Portugal. Rio's Rocio Grande became Constitution Square in 1821 and received its current official name, Tiradentes Square, in 1890. The Rocio Pequeno was an ill-defined public space on the city's western fringe; it slumped into the sprawling São Diogo Mangue, a mangrove swamp that presented a barrier to the city's westward expansion. Unlike centrally located Rocio Grande, which came to be associated with the theater and public administration, the Rocio Pequeno was known to officials as an irregular urban tract associated with squalor, stench, and fugitives. Here, the poor built shacks near the fish and shellfish that provided their daily bread; here, the city tossed its refuse, to be carried away on the twice-daily tides or consumed by "thousands of vultures";

---

[1] Assis Valente, "Já que Está, Deixa Ficar," 1941, on Daniella Thompson, "Praça Onze in Popular Song, the Square that was and Will Be," part 2, Musica Brasiliensis, Jun. 17, 2003, http://daniellathompson.com/Texts/Praca_Onze/praca_onze.pt.2.htm (accessed Jun. 1, 2014).

and here, slaves fleeing their urban masters took refuge from their pur-
suers before they headed for the mountains.[2]

The Rocio Pequeno's sordid reputation improved after the 1808 arrival
of the Portuguese monarch. João VI took up residence in a palace in São
Cristovão, out beyond the mangroves. With landfill that extended out of
the Rocio itself, the king filled a strip of the São Diogo Mangue with a road
popularly known as the Highway of Lanterns. By royal carriage, he
returned from the city each night to the palace, rolling between posted
whale oil lamps that reflected their yellow, flickering flames on dark
waters. In the mid-nineteenth century, the city filled much of the rest of
the Mangue's wetlands to open the city's first intentional suburb, Cidade
Nova (New City). The handsome Mangue Canal, dressed in finished
stone, its margins planted with stately royal palms, also had the Rocio
as its starting place, forming one of the city's most majestic public spaces.
Finally, workers converted the Rocio's raw ground into a curbed, rectan-
gular public space with stone pavers, shade trees, and an elegant fountain
designed by the Frenchman Grandjean de Montigny. The square became
a gathering place and the launching platform for social promenades along
the beautified canal. When an 1867 map depicted the now formal square
between busy Soap and São Pedro Streets, the space had already become
one of the city's most fashionable districts. Surrounded by thriving businesses and grand, two-story homes, the Rocio formed the Cidade Nova's
cohesive center.

Just about the time the square was renamed Praça Onze de Junho
(June 11th Square), in honor of an 1865 naval victory in the Paraguayan
War, the neighborhood began to change, again. With the resurgence of
yellow fever, families took advantage of the new streetcar lines to vacate
what was still a neighborhood bordered by swampy lowlands to take up
residence in the fashionable southern beach suburbs. Large homes in
Cidade Nova were subdivided into tenements that filled with foreign,
particularly Italian and Spanish, immigrants and, after 1888, emancipated
slaves. Those who called the neighborhood home were solidly working
class, and their diverse origins would soon make Cidade Nova's surrounding hills and neighborhoods the city's most cosmopolitan space. It was

---

[2] Johann Baptist von Spix and Carl Friedrich Philipp von Martius, *Viagem pelo Brasil,
1817–1820*, vol. 1 (Belo Horizonte: Editora Itatiaia, 1981), 79. In Antônio Gonçalves
Teixeira e Sousa's, *As tardes de um pintor, o as intrigas de um jesuíta*, from 1847, it was
a place of hiding for deserting soldiers and fleeing slaves; cited in Bruno Carvalho, *Porous
City: A Cultural History of Rio de Janeiro (from the 1810s Onward)* (Liverpool: Liverpool
University Press, 2013), 25.

FIGURE 6.1 Praça Onze de Junho, c. 1935. From the 1870s, Praça Onze served as the preferred public space in a part of the city known variously as the Ghetto, Little Italy, and Little Africa. The square hosted the city's most dynamic expressions of carnival as well as the birth of samba. Within a decade of this photo, the city's urban planners reduced the square to a traffic median and destroyed its associated street life. The loss was much lamented in samba lyrics, the poor's only audible voice.
Source: Augusto Malta, "Praça 11 de Junho." Courtesy of the Acervo da Fundação Biblioteca Nacional, Brazil.

here that resident Jews engaged in small manufacturing, peddling, and publishing; they used the square as a place for socializing beyond their synagogues. It was here that gypsies chose to live. It was here, often living in shanties on the nearby hills, that former Bahian slaves came to find employment as laborers in local factories and the nearby docks. And it was here, in an area still referred to as the Mangue, that men entered the city's least expensive market for prostitution. This part of the city was variously referred to as Little Italy, the Ghetto, and Little Africa, encompassing a diverse set of neighborhoods. Praça Onze (Square 11), as it was popularly known, the area's foremost public space, served as their joint capital.

Maybe most famously, African residents, many of whom João do Rio reported, at the turn of the century, still spoke Yoruba as their common street language, engaged the square and its environs as a place for introducing their own musical styles, derived from the rhythms of their Candomblé religious practice. The square was the most important originator of the city's slang, and African words entered the popular music scene as lyrics. The city's former slaves and their descendants inserted samba into the street's existing musical diversity, which became the national song and dance. The spatial credit for this invention has been granted to Tia Ciata (Aunt Ciata, whose full name was Hilária Batista de Almeida), a migrant from Bahia who upon arriving in Rio at age twenty-two, married well, had fourteen children, and while dressed in the typical Bahian lace and layered white skirts, sold homemade treats on the streets. She also played, as is evident in her honorific title of "Aunt," an official role in the neighborhood's African religious life. It was in her home, at Visconde de Itaúna Street, 177 (formerly Soap Street), facing Praça Onze that she hosted frequent parties of African rites, festive music, and earthy dancing. It was said that she enjoyed the role of hostess so much that she invented birthdays for her friends as an excuse to entertain. In her home, Tia Ciata midwifed the birth of the first recorded song labeled as a samba, "By Telephone," which in 1917 satirized police efforts to eradicate gambling. There are other claimants to the invention of samba, which was played at parties, in homes, bars, and clubs, but all their origins fall not far from Praça Onze. The square and its connected streets appear also to have been central. The space located behind the Benjamin Constant School (which faced Praça Onze) and bordered by the Mangue Canal, was a vital gathering place for samba's early practitioners. Occupied by a public scale, around which composers and performers assembled, it formed a crossroads for both those who worked and those who played in the Cidade Nova.[3] There was a proud loyalty to the ethnic, racial, cultural, and socioeconomic spaces represented by Praça Onze. The famed Noel Rosa composed a samba in 1936 that categorically informed his girlfriend that despite her desire to move to the beach suburbs and live in a luxurious home, he, like the royal palms that led up to Praça Onze, could "not live in the sands of Copacabana." Musicians had sung about the Praça since the earliest days of recording in Brazil, even before samba.[4]

---

[3] Carvalho, *Porous City*, 137.

[4] Daniella Thompson, "Praça Onze in Popular Song," *Música Brasilensis*, http://daniella thompson.com/Texts/Praca_Onze/praca_onze.htm (accessed Sep. 5, 2008).

While the noisy cars of the rich came to dominate the traditional and aural spaces for carnival singing and dancing on Rio Branco, the popular carnival on Praça Onze, which supported the dancing bodies of the poor, was admired, even by some elite, for its maintenance of carnival's authentic past and its creative formation of carnival's vibrant present. When Alberto da Veiga Guignard sketched the square during carnival in the late 1920s, a dozen automobiles are evident, but their presence is overwhelmed by the myriad of human bodies, some linked by arm, that fill the square to every frontage and swarm the cars into submission. The impression is that the dancers hold the automobiles captive.[5]

The spatial dominance of proud bodies dancing in the square would not last. In 1930, Alfred Agache, the French urban planner who had coined the term "urbanism" and had been hired by the auto-boosting Washington Luiz administration, projected a broad highway that would knock down the buildings of fifteen linear blocks of the central city before passing right over and obliterating Praça Onze. Agache, who likened himself to a surgeon, described Rio as a living body that might soon die for lack of circulation. Praising the city for its polity and urbane friendliness, he felt that "only the most generous of blood can circulate in this organism." What kept Rio alive and moving, but just barely, were courteous citizens who made for nigh frictionless corpuscles in congested arteries. But courtesy could only go so far. What the city needed, he argued, was the effective integration of its various parts, which could only be accomplished with more and bigger streets.[6]

A coup in 1930, a long dictatorship, and a world war delayed Agache's surgical plans, but the highway he had sketched on top of Praça Onze broke ground in 1942. As with Avenida Central forty years before, homes,

---

[5] For various aspects of the long history of Praça Onze, see Evelyn F. Werneck Lima, *Avenida Presidente Vargas: Uma drástica cirurgia* (Rio de Janeiro: Prefeitura da Cidade do Rio de Janeiro, 1990), 49–53; Roberto Moura, *Tia Ciata e a Pequena África no Rio de Janeiro*, 2nd edn. (Rio de Janeiro: Prefeitura da Cidade do Rio de Janeiro, 2005); Samuel Malamud, *Recordando a Praça Onze* (Rio de Janeiro: Livraria Kosmos Editora, 1988), 17–31; and most recently Carvalho, *Porous City*. The last is particularly enlightening, using contemporary literature to understand the Cidade Nova in the city's urban mental geography. Guignard's sketch of the square, which is in a private collection, is reproduced in Malamud on page 25.

[6] Alfred Agache, *Rio de Janeiro; Extensão, remodelação, e embelezamento* (Paris: Foyer Brasilien, 1930), 5–7, 9. See also Denise Cabral Stuckenbruck, *O Rio de Janeiro em questão: O Plan Agache e o ideário reformista dos anos 20* (Rio de Janeiro: IPPUR/ UFRJ-FASE, Observatório de Políticas Urbanas e Gestão Municipal, 1996), 86–111; and Brodwyn Fischer, *A Poverty of Rights: Citizenship and Inequality in Twentieth-Century Rio de Janeiro* (Stanford, CA: Stanford University Press, 2010), 38–44.

businesses, industries, and schools, including the Benjamin Constant School, came down – more than 500 buildings in all – their residents, employees, and students banished to other parts of the city. This time, not even the churches were spared; five were razed, including the baroque São Pedro, despite hopes to trundle it out of the way on concrete rollers. Likewise, more than twenty streets and three major squares (Praça da República, Largo de São Domingos, and Largo do Capim), in addition to Praça Onze, were overlain in full or in part by the new avenue's concrete paving.

Avenida Central, at 33 meters, had been planned and built to increase the city's hygiene and beauty, lined with a coherent, stately European architecture. By contrast, not to discount latent desires for tenement clearing, the new Avenida Vargas, as it was named, was broadly built for automotive speed, spanning some 80 meters, dwarfing Mussolini's Via dell'Impero in Rome, built in 1932. At sixteen lanes, it had a higher automotive capacity than any US street or freeway until the end of the century. City residents had universally praised Avenida Vargas' predecessor, Avenida Central, as Rio's best face, its quintessential postcard to the world. In a dictatorship that censored the press and that was headed by the man for whom the new Avenue was named, few criticized Vargas Avenue's construction and final product. Yet almost nobody praised it. The press ventured rather to lament what was being lost in a general sense, and often did so not with words but more cautiously with photographs of a Rio that was passing away.[7] Even *O Malho*, which through 1943 praised the various facets of Vargas' national leadership, had nothing good or bad to say about the new Avenue but rather published a series of photographic essays about rural Brazil entitled "Far from the Avenue."[8]

Vargas was deposed in 1945, before his avenue was completed. He left Praça Onze a weedy rubble crisscrossed by the footpaths of those who sought refuge from a sixteen-lane phalanx of traffic.[9] Yet the square survived because, although now diminished in size and isolated in a sea of asphalt, it served the utilitarian function of a traffic divider, a median strip that prevented cars from plunging into the Mangue Canal.

---

[7] "Aspectos que ninguem mais verá," *Revista da Semana*, Jan. 17, 1942, 19; "Onde o Rio não mudou," *Revista da Semana*, May 1941 [special edition], 22–23; "Rio Desaparecido," *Revista da Semana*, May 30, 1942, 14.

[8] *O Malho*, Feb. 1944, 23.

[9] See "O Rio, esse desconhecido," *Revista da Semana*, Nov. 24, 1945, 11.

FIGURE 6.2 Avenida Presidente Vargas, c. 1945. Ultimately providing sixteen lanes, Vargas Avenue was among the world's largest automotive thoroughfares. Construction entailed the destruction of hundreds of buildings, a handful of churches, and many popular public spaces, including Praça Onze, Largo do Capim, Largo de São Domingos, and part of the Praça da República. Proponents justified its construction with arguments for increased traffic capacity. However, oversized for the surrounding network, many of the Avenue's lanes were converted into the city's first official parking lots.
Source: "Album do Rio de Janeiro," [binder's title], vol. 2, M. Wilford Poulsen Donation. Courtesy of the Harold B. Lee Library, Brigham Young University.

Eventually, the space would be recurbed and would have its neoclassical fountain replaced with an austere pool and a single jet of water. But other than its name, it retained none of its glory and little of its former identity. For years, a portion of Vargas Avenue was cordoned off for carnival parades, and later in 1984 the city would build the Sambadrome, a linear stadium for parading, within sight of the old Praça Onze, but as a result, carnival, street music, and dance became increasingly regimented, essentially ticketed affairs in exclusive spaces rather than the spontaneous celebration of locals who had shared a public space in common. There were other attempts to compensate for Praça Onze's loss. Just to its north, the city created two new squares, so-called, that were circumscribed by encircling clover-leaf off-ramps. The spaces, one named for a scholar of Rio's transportation history, today consist of untended vegetation surrounded by tall steel fencing and intermittent razor wire, public spaces in name that overtly exclude any public.

Praça Onze's fountain has been replaced by a monument to Zumbi, the seventeenth-century king of Brazil's largest runaway slave community. On a typical day, his bust witnesses and breathes the passage of tens of thousands of cars and buses, frequently jammed bumper to bumper despite the manifold lanes. Recently, during the days of carnival, he presided over an orderly army of portable toilets set at attention on Praça Onze to serve the needs of those who danced at the Terreirão do Samba, another ticketed event that clings to the location's identity as samba's birthplace. Outside the days of carnival and Black Awareness Day, Praça Onze remains inaccessible to the public. It stands unobtrusive in the middle of the city's traffic, and while it retains the appearance of sidewalks, not a single crosswalk along its length provides access to any who might want to stand reverently on the exact plot of a past that formed one of the nation's most celebrated origin stories.

BUYERS AND SELLERS

More cars seeking faster movement demanded more space. By the 1940s, to solve the problem of automotive circulation, officials increasingly converted three-dimensional spaces, such as public squares, colonial churches, and historic blocks, into two-dimensional surfaces that the car move upon and occupy. Squares became parking lots and roundabouts. Street spaces that had different names over their courses, identifying distinct public spaces in the minds of residents, were elided into single entities by the official deletion of all but one name.[10]

To mid-century, the growth of the automobile in Brazil was erratic, subject as it was to global depressions, world wars, fluctuating exchange rates, and the unpredictable price of coffee. During the Depression, between 1927 and 1938, the number of cars on Rio's central streets declined by 18 percent;[11] and during World War II, with fuel rationing, the only motorists who could consistently drive, other than cabbies who received gas rations, were those who installed a protuberant gasogene

---

[10] Rio de Janeiro, Distrito Federal. *Nomenclatura dos logradouros públicos da cidade do Rio de Janeiro, de acordo com a legislação vigente até 31 de Dezembro de 1944* (Rio de Janeiro: Secretaria do Prefeito, 1944) AGCRJ.

[11] C. A. Sylvester, "Adendo ao memorial apresentado pela The Rio de Janeiro Tramway, Light, and Power Co," in *Comissão Transportes Coletivos*, Feb. 14, 1939, Anexo 9, 379.

conversion kit in their rear trunk that allowed the vehicle to run on burning wood or charcoal. Yet, a sustained nationalist interest in importing ever more cars offers us a somewhat more accurate set of statistics on car growth than those available regarding automotive accidents. Ever more cars were evidence of Brazil's progress toward modernity, and the early automotive press published their best guesses as to how many cars the nation had, constantly comparing Brazil's states and cities with each other, and Brazil with other nations. As early as 1922, when Rio imported more than half of the 21,000 cars that came to Brazil that year, the city claimed bragging rights and goaded São Paulo by pointing out that it had only imported 6,300. Imports were one thing. Estimating how many cars were actually on the streets was another. In 1926, *Automobilismo* questioned US reports that Brazil had only 60,000 cars compared to Argentina's 170,000. Brazil had to have more, they insisted. With no other resource, the magazine tried to drum up the statistics by asking its readers to write in with their count of how many cars there were in their various cities. By the end of 1928, they confidently reported just over 100,000 cars in Brazil, based entirely on their reader's uneducated guesses.[12]

Later official numbers appear to have exaggerated the number of vehicles, constantly counting imports and registrations but failing to subtract cars that disappeared in the attrition of accidents, mechanical failure, and obsolescence. Still, they got the trends right. During the Juscelino Kubitschek administration (1956–1961), when Brazil began producing vehicles in plants established by Volkswagen, Overland-Willys, Ford, and General Motors,[13] the weight of the car in the Brazilian city seemed to tip a scale. In 1957, compared with the US's 62 million vehicles, Brazil had only 623,000, a mere 1 percent of the American total. But by 1965, as national production ramped up, Brazil would have 2.1 million vehicles – more than Spain, Argentina, Sweden, South Africa, or Switzerland, which "should constitute motive for merited pride among Brazilians."[14] *Quatro Rodas* boasted that Brazil was on the cusp of greatness as "civilization and progress marched forward on four wheels, daily conquering new geographic and spiritual

---

[12] *Retrospecto Commercial do Jornal do Commêrcio* (Rio de Janeiro: *Jornal do Comércio*, 1923), 168; *Automobilismo: a revista prática do automóvel*, Nov. 1926, 46, and Nov. 1928, 47.

[13] Wolfe, *Autos and Progress*, 119–22.

[14] Eduardo Fares Borges, *Segurança de trânsito* (São Paulo: Gráfica Sangirard, 1973), 21, 24.

spaces."[15] In Rio itself, based on a large urban planning study done in the mid-1960s, the Federal District had 64,000 private cars in 1957. By 1964, it had 140,000, an increase of 120 percent, or about 12 percent per year.[16] In 1967, *Quatro Rodas* unwittingly published a cartoon that was almost an exact copy of one published in 1926: in one frame labeled 1956, a crowd of pedestrians converge on a single car; in the second frame, labeled 1966, a crowd of vehicles press in on a single pedestrian.[17] Whether it was 1926 or 1966, Brazilians seemed to think that the rise and impact of the car was somehow a recent event. But in 1966, the car's dominance of the street was becoming a permanent reality. By 1976, Brazil produced nearly one million cars per year, and the street poet Paulo Teixeira de Souza versed that "the Chevrolet and the Ford, I tell you with great pride, reproduce faster than rats."[18]

Dealers sold cars under a variety of financing arrangements. While the legality of selling on installments in some Latin America nations was still in question, in Brazil loans with interest had overcome traditional Catholic proscriptions. Cabbies, who could claim their new car would contribute to their income, were considered a good financial risk and accounted for 75 percent of all passenger car purchases before 1927. Ninety percent of all cars sold in Brazil in the 1920s were financed, and only about 1 percent had to be repossessed. Loans had terms of 12–18 months, down payments of 20–33 percent, and interest rates of 8 percent. Dealers did most of the financing, and the loans rarely required a co-signer.[19] Automotive advertising was ubiquitous by the late 1910s and only grew in scale in the coming decades. Dealers enticed buyers with every possible angle. In a single issue of a single newspaper from 1925, car makers pitched efficiency ("Life is short; the car will save you time"), health ("It is better to spend your money on a Ford than on medical and pharmacy bills"), power and safety ("The soul of the Cadillac is superior and beautiful – its powerful engine can climb any hill, avoid any accident, and devour all kilometers"), leisure ("With a Ford, you can visit all the

---

[15] *Quatro Rodas*, Aug. 1960, 6; *Revista de Automóveis*, Feb. 1957, 47.

[16] Doxiadis Associates, *Guanabara: A Plan for Development* (Athens: Technikon Grapheion Doxiadē, 1965), 96.

[17] *Quatro Rodas*, Jan. 1967, 140.

[18] Paulo Teixeira de Souza, *Os loucos do volante* (Rio de Janeiro: Secretaria do Estado de Educação e Cultura, Instituto Estadual do Livro, c. 1978), 18.

[19] Tewksbury, "Automotive Market in Brazil," 23–24, 57–58, 60; US Department of Commerce, "Installment Selling of Automobiles in Latin America," 1929, 2, 5, 6, 10; "O eterno problema," *Automobilismo: a revista prática do automóvel*, Aug. 1928, 16.

beautiful sites of your city that the tourists admire"), wealth ("How much do you earn? The owner of a Ford augments his opportunities for income"), and general happiness and contentment ("Don't wait – Buy one today: the owner of a Studebaker is always satisfied.").[20]

SINGING LAMENTATIONS OVER PRAÇA ONZE

Popular voices for and against the car, by the poor and the pedestrian, can be difficult to discern in the sources. While automotive boosters and advertisers piled their voices high in nearly all the newspapers, in colorful magazines, and in the official instruments of government agencies, the poor, who made up most of the car's victims, had neither the power nor the place to make their views known. Much of what we do know or can assume comes from second-hand reports on popular behavior toward the car. For many a pedestrian, attitudes toward the automobile were aspirational. However, before aspiration, and possibly mixing with it over the years, there was a diffuse anger that flashed into occasional violence. As we saw, there were frequent reports of citizens threatening, restraining, and occasionally beating drivers who had run down pedestrians. Seemingly, however, only later, after the 1950s, did neighbors organize and act jointly to try to reduce the violence on their own streets as speeds and traffic increased. Reports of these kinds of activities are rare anywhere, but they are more common in São Paulo than in Rio. Middle class families who saw massive traffic increases and deaths on their streets went to authorities to demand traffic control devices, to reduce the number of cars and the number of accidents. In poorer neighborhoods, there were incidents in which residents placed barriers or dug trenches in the middle of the street. In such cases, the city might be persuaded to install more signs, signals, or speed bumps.[21]

One outlet for written, non-elite expression was a popular folk literature informally published, literally on a string (and hence its name, *cordel*). Being an apparent ancient tradition from the Mediterranean that persisted in Brazil's Northeast, these works consisted of self-published,

---

[20] *Jornal do Commércio*, Jul. 15, 1925.
[21] "Quem não é 'vivo,' morre," *Quatro Rodas*, Nov. 1961, 22–23; Eduardo Alcântara Vasconcelos and César Marrano Piovanni, "A sinalização de trânsito e a qualidade da vida urbana," *Revista Trânsito* 8 (1984) and 9 (1985): 158–59, 162–63, 168, 181; Eduardo Alcântara Vasconcelos, *Circular é preciso, viver não é preciso: a história do trânsito na cidade de São Paulo* (São Paulo: Annablume, FAPESP, 1999), 213–16.

single-fold pamphlets, whose covers often exhibited striking, woodcut illustrations. They were marketed in street stalls by suspending their folded bindings on strings, their bold covers facing out. Carlos Drummond de Andrade considered these the purest tangible creations of the common man's expressive spirit. The poetry addressed all kinds of themes, from the legendary backland bandits to polemical treatises and political satire. They were often fun and light-hearted in tone, and many would be set to music. Most *cordel* works have never been formally published nor have they been archived in libraries, although in recent decades efforts have been made to preserve them.

In the 1970s, the city of Rio republished a number of undated pieces, a few authored by Paulo Teixeira de Souza. Born in Rio, Souza took up the art as an adult, something to engage his imagination outside the hours he worked in various jobs as a baker, bookbinder, and janitor. Nightly, although he lived in the most distant northern suburbs, he wandered among downtown cafés and beach bars selling his verses to prospective buyers, "from professors to construction workers," he claimed.[22] His sixty-four page "Madmen at the Wheel" made a running commentary on the violence of the automobile as seen from the perspective of the street and from those who faced the car's dangers directly as passengers and pedestrians. The cover's woodcut illustration depicts, behind the wheel in traditional bandit hat, an overexcited, fiendish motorist, the subject of his poem, whom he refers to as the "asphaltonaut." The work, which might have been sung on the street, describes a series of automotive tragedies, both observed and experienced, and spares little in the way of gore: bodies smashed, contorted, trapped, burned, and unrecovered. As a testimony to the deadliness and injuriousness of the car, compared to the newspapers' formulaic repetitions, Teixeira de Souza offers flesh and blood narratives of a carnage that occasionally descends into a pornography of violence.

The reckless drivers who perform the savagery can nary escape it themselves. In the poem's first incident on Vargas Avenue, which appears to be based on an actual event, the driver of a tourist bus leaps onto a curb and kills four pedestrians. The driver jumps from the vehicle and flees on foot, but a speeding car runs him down and kills him instantly. The driver of that car also takes flight; he accelerates and zigzags through traffic only to crash into the rear of a truck. And then more cars pile on: a Dodge Dart hits the crashed vehicles and lands upside down, and then an Opel,

---

[22] Candace Slater, *Stories on a String: The Brazilian Literatura de Cordel* (Berkeley, CA: University of California Press, 1982), 260.

a Jaguar, and a Variant entangle themselves in the growing heap. When the fire department finally arrives, a callous witness urges them to set the whole grisly pileup on fire and be done with it. Slowly, emergency workers extricate the "Johns and Marias," living and dead, from their smashed containers. All but one driver in the accident dies. The survivor, in the Jaguar, loses both legs and an arm. The toll is ten dead with many more injured, and is reported in the next day's papers.[23]

The impression de Souza makes is that death on the street is so common, so widespread, and so mundane that most everyone is beyond anger by this point. The citizens suffer from an appalling futility, including police and fireman. When cars tumble down steep hills or plunge into the Mangue Canal, the firemen fail to show up for days to recover bodies, as if hoping some other agency would do it first. De Souza describes the demoralization of seeing the deceased occupants of a car neglected day after day, half submerged, partially decomposed, and being consumed by crabs. From the perspective of the pedestrian street, class is an explanation. De Souza blames much of the toll on wealthy car owners, and their children, driving under the influence, not of alcohol, the poor man's drug, but of marijuana, cocaine, and LSD, mood-altering substances supplied by the *favela* to the middle and upper classes.

Teixeira de Souza also narrates his own near-death experiences. He and a friend, Jorge, hire a cab to take them to see the Mangueira School perform in carnival. In the only case where his own anger gets full expression, de Souza writes of the "bastard" cabby who goes the wrong way up a one-way street and hits a *lotaçao*, a small private bus, head on. The cabby died. De Souza was thrown through the fabric roof of the car. And "to this day, my friend Jorge is ruined." In another cab ride from Caxias to the Santos Dumont airport, he suffers so many frights that he drops the whole idea of flying and orders the driver to take him home. On the return, the cabby rolls the car in a sharp corner. Four strong young men, for a fee, flip the cab back right-side up, and they continue their journey. On arrival, when the driver shows the nerve to still demand his fare, de Souza sics his dog on him. Death and injury are personal, and he describes, still in verse, numerous acquaintances who have died or who have suffered severe injuries requiring them to be screwed back together as

---

[23] By 1950, Vargas Avenue was being referred to as a cemetery, "a constant nightmare" for pedestrians; see *O Malho*, Apr. 1950, 20. But it was also one of the spaces where cars could achieve the highest velocities in the central city, which placed drivers themselves at increasingly greater risk.

if they too were machines. De Souza, in a manner more visceral than the elite critics discussed later in this chapter, emphasizes how the car not only destroys bodies but families and relationships. He addresses more than once a concern for making a widow of his "beautiful black wife." She daily sends her man off to work with a kiss and a warning to climb to the tiled roofs if a Volkswagen Beetle should threaten his safety. Every time he survives a particularly harrowing experience, he makes offerings to all the appropriate Christian saints and African divinities. The voice of a Teixeira de Souza, who commuted through the violence with millions of other residents, was as rare a voice as any in documenting the street's least palatable realities.[24]

The other place to look for the popular perception of the automotive street is in the lyrics of popular music, although these expressions focus on the competition for civic spaces rather than on the car's direct violence. The fame and reach of samba grew substantially after 1920 with the help of recording studios and radio stations. Samba's rhythm was so potent that by the 1930s it was being heard well beyond Brazil's borders. This was a cause for national pride, but it was also cause for some alarm in certain official circles that liked neither the music nor the message that it carried, which was predominantly one of the black, bohemian life of Rio's poorest residents. In the 1930s, and especially after 1940 when the Vargas regime created the Department of the Press and Propaganda (DIP), the national government worked in earnest to sanitize the samba and its lyrics to make it respectable for domestic and global consumption. In general, Vargas disliked samba's bold Africanness, and in particular he detested the constant recoronation of the *malandro* in samba culture. The *malandro* in song had become an almost mythic male figure, an anti-hero who represented street smarts and who managed to dress, eat, and fare well with the ladies, or give the appearance of such, without a steady paycheck and without a reputable car. He was astute and clever, without morals but not without honor, earning his daily bread and street credibility by charming women and conning fools. His idiom was to just get by – with aplomb – defiant of modernization's demand to subordinate himself to capitalist expectations and domestic stability. The street was his domain.

Vargas' political base, should he need it, was being built upon the productive working classes. His benefits and promises to the wage-

---

[24] Teixeira de Souza, *Os loucos do volante*. This was probably published in 1978, along with a number of his other poems, but its creation was before 1974, based on internal evidence.

earning laborer, and the propaganda machine he created to advertise them, were the foundations for his current and future political success. What he wanted was more men exiting the lifestyle of serial unemployment and entering the steady workforce where they would be corporatized into the national unions that he controlled. For Vargas, labor itself, which promised respectability and prosperity, became an ideology to be propagandized. So, rather than attempt to destroy samba, he sought above all to control it, to engage its popularity to promote his personal and national objectives.[25]

The existing tension between *malandragem* and *trabalhismo* (bohemianism and workerism) would take on spatial connotations when Vargas' Avenue, which represented modernity, came up against Praça Onze and its backward associations. To tear down the old streets and build new avenues was the solution to the city's architectural and cultural backwardness, for the city needed streets as modern as the cars that drove on them.[26] The car itself does not seem to form any sort of serious character in Brazil's samba lyrics. For the city's musicians, remarkably, the car appears to fall outside their direct concerns and does not much enter the music that represented their aspirations for fun and release, at least until the late 1950s, when the derivative style of the Jovem Guarda sang of cars in the vein of American rock and country singers. However, Praça Onze was already either a character in or the setting for samba lyrics by 1920. Once Praça Onze as a place came under threat in about 1940, the square took a starring role in samba's lyrics. Composers sang the square's defense even as traffic engineers obliterated it and Vargas' censors attempted to scrub its history from musical memory. Vargas could not outright ban samba nor carnival, but he sought to control when and where they took place, for how long, and, above all, what they expressed. After 1940, all song lyrics had to pass the official censor before being recorded, and each recording had the DIP's approval code printed prominently on the label, a sad development in a nation that for most of its history honored freedom of expression in art and in the press. With the square under threat, samba of a certain color was to become less audible, which was the point.

---

[25] Adalberto Paranhos, "Vozes dissonantes sob um regime de órdem-unida (música e trabalho no 'Estado Novo')" *Revista ArtCultura* (Núcleo de Estudos em História Social da Arte e da Cultura, Universidade Federal de Uberlândia) 4, no. 4 (Jan.–Jun. 2002); Daryle Williams, *Culture Wars in Brazil: The First Vargas Regime, 1930–1945* (Durham, NC: Duke University Press, 2001), 85–86.

[26] *Revista da Semana*, May 1941, 23.

In response to the news that Praça Onze was going to be overlain by asphalt, José de Assis Valente composed in 1941 what appears to be the first samba to defend the space. Despite evoking the *malandro* and toasting the consumption of *cachaça*, Brazil's potent rum, his lyrics got past the censors, and the single, which was pressed by Columbia Records, had "DIP-2-GN-60" dutifully stamped on the label. Maybe it was because Assis Valente was so transparent about his motives; one phrase in the song admitted that "samba speaks in slang because it is itself propaganda." Or, maybe his slang was just that slippery. Significantly, a lyrical form that usually emphasized festive singing and dancing as the highest good, written in devotion to fun, could also be more directly political. The first two lines of the lyrics, referring to the square, plead to authorities: "It is good, beyond compare; let it remain, since it's already there." Guitars should be allowed to sigh on the square, black girls to agitate their hips there, and that the samba schools, whose names cleverly surround the name of Praça Onze in the poem, be "saved." The lyrics conclude using a Guarani word that brands the plans to destroy the square as "idle conversation," and the last lines give notice to the government that the residents around Praça Onze know exactly what the officials are up to. "I have already heard someone say: 'Beat it, you Vagabond, and build some callouses.'" Vargas wants to put the party out of business and the partiers to work. There is no direct reference to the automobile or to the traffic congestion that the government has used to justify the destruction of the square. The square's defenders see the car as an excuse for motives that are more nefarious. They have learned to literally dance around the car, and even control it to some extent, in Praça Onze's carnivalesque corners. But they cannot dance if the city converts the dance floor to a highway.[27]

The same year, Herivelto Martins and Grande Otelo composed "Praça Onze," which became the square's enduring hymn, a dirge that still clings to future spatial hopes. But the imminent demise of the square was dispiriting; the lamentation, almost biblical.

> They are going to do away with Praça Onze
> No more will there be Samba Schools dancing,

---

[27] See "Já que Está, Deixa Ficar," by Assis Valente, 1941, on Daniella Thompson, "Praça Onze in Popular Song, the Square That Was and Will Be," part 2, Musica Brasiliensis, Jun. 17, 2003, http://daniellathompson.com/Texts/Praca_Onze/praca_onze.pt.2.htm (accessed Jun. 1, 2014). "Está bom, até demais/ Já que está, deixa ficar." The Portuguese for the relevant final lines is "Deixa dessa tereré/ Já ouvi alguém dizer:/ 'Vai andar, Seu Vagolino,/ pra criar calo no pé,' pois é."

No more
Weep tambourine
Weep everyone on the hills
Favela, Salgueiro,
Mangueira, Estação Primeira
Put away your *pandeiros*, put them away
Because the samba school will stay home
Adeus my Praça Onze, adeus.
We already know you will disappear
Take with you our fond recollections
But you will stay forever in our heart
And someday we will have a new Square
And there your past we will sing.[28]

The tone of a song could in fact move from lamentations, the jeremiad of one verse, to the promises of Jeremiah in the next: "Again you shall provide yourselves with tambourines, and go forth with the merry throng of dancers."[29] The following year, 1942, Geraldo Pereira performed a more optimistic song, "Voice of the Hill," that while conceding that Praça Onze was done for, held out that the samba schools were organizing and preparing their tambourines because "we have a place to play, so we are not going to cry."[30] He never specifically states where that place is, and the Vargas regime would not give them the usual public spaces on Avenida Rio Branco or Vargas Avenue itself. The samba schools might fragment themselves into their own neighborhoods and hills, whose narrow and often steep streets were free from cars but were too small to host the general party that had taken place on Praça Onze. A variety of other composers also sang with hope about the continuity of the samba, despite the loss of its most authentic venue, and such songs found little trouble getting past the censors.

But Herivelto Martins refused to be consoled. He composed a new song starring the famed samba character Laurindo, invented by the greatly mourned composer Noel Rosa. In lyrics, Laurindo had led innumerous samba marches. In response to the attack on the square, he charges into the hills to cheer the *favelados* into gathering their banners and their

---

[28] See "Praça Onze," by Herivelto Martins Grande Otelo, on Daniella Thompson, "Praça Onze in Popular Song," part 2, http://daniellathompson.com/Texts/Praca_Onze/pra ca_onze.pt.2.htm (accessed Jun. 1, 2014).

[29] Jeremiah 31: 4, *The Revised English Bible* (Oxford University Press and Cambridge University Press, 1989).

[30] See "Voz do Morro," by Geraldo Pereira and Moreira da Silva, on Daniella Thompson, "Praça Onze in Popular Song," part 2, http://daniellathompson.com/Texts/Praca_Onze /praca_onze.pt.2.htm (accessed Jun. 1, 2014).

instruments and forming organized ranks. But "when the samba school descended, it could not find Praça Onze, and nobody danced ever again." Laurindo, realizing there was no longer a field on which to battle, relented, blew his whistle to signal "the evolution," and ordered the demoralized participants to pile their instruments on the ground, forming a pyramid that kept "growing and growing," a reference to the government's call for donations of scrap metal, rubber, and paper that the military might use in the war effort. The song's melting down of samba's material culture held little hope for the future of samba without the square, even though his musicians continued to sing as they walked home.[31]

A few composers took to the official line, praising the new Getúlio Vargas Avenue "that would be the pride of this beautiful capital: Oh, how good, how good, how good," they repeated, without specifics. They remembered the square, the fun they had, and the girls they met there, but now it was time to grow up modern: "I have abandoned the partying, for today I am a laborer." Another song entitled "There Is More Space" claimed that the new Avenue, due to its huge dimensions, would in fact offer more ground than the carnival celebrants had ever before enjoyed, but failed to note that Vargas intended it for traffic. Such happy compositions often trailed off into nationalistic platitudes that spoke of a land blessed by Jesus, a nation that never lost a war, and that always fought on the side of the right. Perhaps the most celebratory and famed song of the period, Ary Barroso's "Brazilian Watercolor" of 1939, worked itself up in paeans to the nation, and while containing clichéd Africanisms borrowed from the street language of the Praça, emphasized, rather, the incorporated nation: "Brazil, my Brazilian Brazil," "the land of Our Lord," evergreen, full of moonlight and coconuts, "Brazil! Brazil!" The government embraced it enthusiastically because it made the nation, an abstract place that only existed in the modern imagination, the spatial locus of cultural identity. By contrast, real space, even a comparably tiny fragment of public space enjoyed by the poor, was maligned and dangerous.[32]

---

[31] See "Laurindo" by Herivelto Martins on Daniella Thompson, "Praça Onze in Popular Song," part 2, http://daniellathompson.com/Texts/Praca_Onze/praca_onze.pt.2.htm (accessed Jun. 1, 2014). "E quando a escola de samba chegou/ Na Praça Onze não encontrou/ Mais ninguém/ Não sambou."

[32] "Vem Surgindo a Avenida," by Benedito Lacerda and Gastão Vianna, 1942, and "Há mais Espaço," by Ary Monteiro, Arnaldo Passos, and Gil Lima, 1944, both on Daniella Thompson, "Praça Onze in Popular Song," part 2, http://daniellathompson.com/Texts /Praca_Onze/praca_onze.pt.2.htm (accessed Jun. 1, 2014).

Brazil, along with the Allies, won the war against Fascism in Europe. As the only nation in Latin America to send troops to battle, Brazilians had every right to celebrate the victory and their soldiers' contributions. But victory in Europe fully uncovered a paradox at home. If Getúlio Vargas' person, politics, and policies did not carry the full stench, they had the whiff of Fascism on them. What was the point of Brazilian soldiers fighting for democracy and freedom abroad when they did not enjoy them at home? In 1945, the victorious military forced Vargas to resign, and elections brought General Eurico Dutra to power. Late in that year, Herivelto Martins composed a petition, "Thank-you, Your Excellency," to Dutra seeking the return of Praça Onze to its traditional role as the place of carnival celebration and samba school parading.

> We will remain forever grateful
> If Your Excellency permits
> Our samba schools
> To return to sing and play in the Praça Onze.
> . . .
> There is no better place
> For the schools to parade

When Dutra gave the samba schools use of a portion the new, broad Vargas Avenue for the carnival of 1946, Martins followed up with "Thank-you, General." To everyone's elation, the president had given the residents space in which to parade, sing, and dance, and Martins went so far as to declare that Praça Onze, once declared dead, had been resurrected. "The entire hill knew that Praça Onze would return," the celebrants sang.[33] It was no doubt something of a poetic victory for the people, but Dutra could not give them Praça Onze. He would only give a short length of the Avenue's sixteen lanes, and he would only give it to them temporarily – for the days of carnival, and not even for the full holiday. The car now needed those lanes even for much of the days of carnival. The Square as public space was gone, its new identity an outsized median strip. Fascism had been defeated, and the dictator had been exiled from the capital, but Automobilism was stronger than Fascism, and its tyrannical rule continued to be embraced by those in power.

---

[33] "Obrigado, Excelência!" by Herivelto Martins, (Jan.) 1946, and "Obrigado, General," by Benedito Lacerda and Herivelto Martins, (Oct.) 1946, both on Daniella Thompson, "Praça Onze in Popular Song," part 3, Jun. 26, 2003, http://daniellathompson.com/Tex ts/Praca_Onze/praca_onze.pt.3.htm (accessed Jun. 3, 2014).

Sambistas have not forgotten Praça Onze. Grande Otelo, in early 1959, recorded "Carnival with Whom?" that lamented again Praça Onze's demise and asked, "With whom can we make carnival? Look around. I do not see anyone," and then explained that Colodionor had returned to the cane fields, a reference to the giving up of the bohemian life and entering the legitimate if oppressive world of labor, and that Laurindo had died, for what else could he do without carnival. Otelo sang of *saudades* of the "Carnival of '43," the last celebrated on Praça Onze as a public space – the end of an era. As a later sambista put it in 1980, the year carnival ceased to be celebrated on an increasingly congested Vargas Avenue, "Today, samba is played only on the radio ... because progress destroyed her cradle."[34]

MID-CENTURY IMMORTALS VERSUS THE AUTOMOBILE

As Joel Wolfe has asserted, for statesmen and businessmen alike, "cars, trucks, and buses became not only the tools for creating the modern Brazilian state but also the primary symbols of a modern, developed, and democratic nation."[35] Collectively, in official discourse, the automobile lay at the center of the nation's aspirations for first-world status. Likewise, for the individual who drove and the many more who aspired to the status of driver, the car represented freedom, status, leisure, and the most secure means to maintaining access to the public commons. The ideals to which many aspired were prominently modeled by developed nations and exaggerated in the most ubiquitous of advertising. Hence, the car's many boosters agreed that the problem of the car was simple: how to import more of them. Hence, they called for ever-lower import duties and for ever more roads on which to run them.[36]

Lamentations about the automobile, however, seemed to get little press, especially after the 1920s. Criticism had little space to develop within the dominant discourse. However, there were naysayers, critics, and killjoys, a few of whom went beyond the usual grousing about noise, accidents, and congestion. In some cases, the best evidence for the

---

[34] "Berços do Samba," by Henrique Cazes, 1980, on Daniella Thompson, "Praça Onze in Popular Song," part 7, Jul. 16, 2003, http://daniellathompson.com/Texts/Praca_Onze /praca_onze.pt.7.htm (accessed Jun. 6, 2014). The lyrics for "Carnaval com Quem?" run "Fazer Carnaval com quem? Olhe! Não vejo ninguem."

[35] Wolfe, *Autos and Progress*, 12.

[36] "O automóvel no Brasil," *Observador Econômico e Financeiro*, May 1937, 15–18, is a typical example of this kind of policy and infrastructural boosterism.

existence of the critics is not their own writings, which are few and hard to find, but in the vehement attacks of the boosters against them. In 1928, *Automobilismo* praised the car as the founder of the twentieth century: art had created the Renaissance and metaphysical ideas had created the nineteenth century, but it was the car that had invented modern age, making nations richer and transforming human ideas about space and time, now considered pliable realities rather than immutable constants. And that alone, they declared, was argument enough to shut up "those detractors of the car" who are helplessly "romantic and backward."[37]

Detractors of the technology found some of their strongest voices in this period. By the early 1930s, anti-technologists, such as Oswald Spengler and Lewis Mumford, had offered some of the most fully developed ideas about the costs of the expanding machine and its related systems. Many such pronouncements were romantic if not downright nostalgic for a more organic world. Others spoke of doomsday. For the conservative Spengler, the machine represented and promoted hubris, separating humans from nature and secularizing them such that they might deny even God. We loved the machine, he argued, because it obeyed our will and gave us power over nature, but it also gave us a false sense of pride that damaged human morality as it promoted nature's destruction. The rise of technology was one element in his prognostication that the West was already on the path to moral and cultural decline. For Mumford, who at first placed his hope in technology (including the car) to democratize power and productivity, mechanization came to threaten mankind's organic spontaneity and individuality, that all might be swallowed up in overwhelming systems. It was less the destruction of nature than man's alienation from nature's beauties and inspirations. But it was also the destruction of culture; Mumford asserted that to allow the car access to every street and building in the city was to give motorists the keys to destroy the city. He believed the city to be an invention equal in human import to that of language, and the city's primary role, or the measure of its success, was how well it provided opportunities for using language in conversation and dialogue. The car fragmented the city and hence the space for community.[38]

---

[37] *Automobilismo: A revista pratica do automovel*, Feb. 1928, 24.
[38] See Thomas P. Hughes, *The Human-Built World: How to Think about Technology and Culture* (Chicago, IL: University of Chicago Press, 2004), 54–61, for an analysis of the state of technological criticism in the 1930s. See also, Mumford, *Culture of Cities*, 5.

While American and European critics often emphasized technology's deleterious effects on individuality and morality, and looked back nostalgically for a simpler time, by contrast, many Brazilian thinkers lamented the impact of technology on community. Like Mumford, they saw the city as a place of community and conversation, but unlike Mumford, who often talked about community in the abstract or the community as a place to express big ideas, Brazilian writers were explicitly intimate and personal about human contact and engagement. For them, the car was less a culprit in destroying nature, dehumanizing individuality, or killing ideas than an object that prevented friends, families, and neighbors from bonding together. They seemed less concerned with a nostalgic romanticism for the past than in the possibilities for flesh and blood romance in the present. More than anything else, the car impeded human contact and human relations, and the car had made them nostalgic not so much for particular places lost or past eras remembered as for people missed, which is a more characteristic Brazilian understanding of nostalgia (*saudade*).

When the editors at *Automobilismo* condemned "those detractors of the car," they may have been specifically attacking Amadeo Amaral who had recently damned the car in an autobiography pointedly entitled *Memoirs of a Streetcar Passenger*. Some of the automobile's critics that we will examine were, like Amaral, important literary figures, formidable opponents who commanded respect among Brazil's elite and could not be outright dismissed. They too, by their cultured writings, embodied Brazil's aspirations to be accepted as a civilized nation. Amaral himself had taken chair number 15 (of which there are only forty) in the prestigious Brazilian Academy of Letters, filling the vacancy after poet Olavo Bilac's death in 1918, an automotive detractor taking the place of an early booster. The men, and eventually women, who sat in the Academy's illustrious chairs, were known as the "immortals," and when offered space to comment on the car, they frequently condemned it as not just a blunt object that killed but a knife that severed the ties that had made urban community and conviviality.

Amaral and his fellow immortals carried on an important tradition in Brazilian literature exemplified by Machado de Assis, whose cunning critiques of his own era Roberto Schwarz describes as "implacable in exposing the hypocrisy of modern man accommodating himself to conditions that are intolerable."[39] In a few withering pages, Amaral excoriated

---

[39] Cited by Larry Rohter, "After a Century, a Literary Reputation Finally Blooms," *New York Times*, Sep. 13, 2008.

the spatial, moral, and spiritual bankruptcy of driving automobiles, a diatribe and defense incited by his conscientious decision to decline a ride in the car of his neighbor, one Dr. Viegas, and take his place on the streetcar, where he considered his reasons for that decision. First, he noted that simply by personality, he had always been one not to be in a hurry. To rush would be to act contrary to his true self, to place time in priority over human concerns. Because he abhorred hurry, he had always enjoyed the company of the crowd. The car was antipathetic to both tranquility and sociality; he believed that the automobile represented little more than "velocity placed at the service of those who have nothing better to experience." In spaces, he argued, "it is the union of all who are there that leaves each individual fortified in their own identity," and he fingered the car as the destroyer of Rio's dying community and civility. Being connected, sharing spaces with the crowd, civilized the individual, while the isolating car demonstrably turned people into individual barbarians.[40]

A related theme that he and others took up was that the car further divided the classes. Class had always been a significant social division, but the car created a spatial separation on the public commons that was new and deleterious. The working pedestrian took no benefit from the car, only misery. Those who could afford a car, he claimed, were doing nothing more than "live in the permanent search for the superfluous" and for no better reason than to use speed to "flee from themselves" and set themselves apart from their neighbors. The car was the "exteriorization of our psychological center of gravity," an "infantile tendency reawakened in our mature years." In this sense, the car he described was not very different from alcoholism or drug abuse. "The car comes on the same platter as whisky, the tango, and morphine. All are means of avoiding the censurious and piercing eye of our better selves." The machine, he argued, turned humans, who have remarkable capacities for meditation, empathy, polity, and self-censorship, into mere respondents to external stimuli, an enslavement of the senses and thoughts. Most scathingly, as regards the car's spatial abuses, he damned "the automobile as the vehicle of those who do not love but only deflower the beauty of all things." His choice to ride in the streetcar permitted him to concentrate on himself and his own thoughts, upon the beauties and realities through which he passed slowly, and, above all, on all the other human beings with whom he traveled,

---

[40] Amadeu Amaral, *Memorial de um passageiro de bonde* (São Paulo: HUCITEC, 1976), 7–8; the first book edition of the memoir was published in 1938, but was obviously written before Amaral's death in 1929.

whom he referred to as "the only entities of real interest in the world." The car, by contrast, "splashes our souls about the street like water in a shaken vessel," leaving humanity unable to contemplate the beauties of places and faces. One's impressions of the world from the car became a series of superficial, fragmented photographic snapshots. Drivers could penetrate neither social nor physical reality, life's "enveloping tactilities" and "illuminating soundings." For those in cars, Amaral declared, the "virginity of the real is ever fugitive."[41]

Such pointed critiques seem to diminish in the 1930s and 1940s. Newspapers, which were increasingly beholden to automotive advertisers, still had reporters who complained about deaths and congestion, but they rarely attacked the car's reality, quavered over its apparent dehumanization, or questioned its place on the street. Not until the 1950s does one find an exceptional blast from prominent voices against national automobilism. Ironically, these opinions found space in *Revista de Automóveis*, another magazine promoting all things automotive: the latest model cars, the national auto industry, auto tourism, national oil exploration, and auto racing – subject matter wedged between the advertising of car makers, tire manufacturers, and oil companies. Unlike its namesake, a magazine published for a short period in the early teens, the new *Revista de Automóveis* did not declare that its mission was to "defend the interests of *automobilismo*."[42] It appeared in an age in which the car had few challengers. Or so its editors thought, and they let their guard down. The magazine commenced publication in May 1954, every colorful cover graced with a beautiful woman posed with a shiny car parked in front of some chunk of Rio's gorgeous scenery.

The magazine's weakness was in aspiring to literariness. From the first edition, *Revista de Automóveis* invited well-known Brazilian writers, some of them among the immortals, to open each issue, on page one, with a short essay on the topic of cars. As often as not, the guest writers addressed the automobile not with glowing praise and reverent admiration but with mild satire, stout ambivalence, or open lamentation. It was a rare opportunity for naysayers to target a pro-automotive audience with both subtle and direct challenges to the dominant car culture. They had few words, less than a page, in which to develop their invective, but they got away with it, remarkably, for nearly three years.

---

[41] Amadeu Amaral, *Memorial de um passageiro de bonde*, 9–11.
[42] See Wolfe, *Autos and Progress*, 18.

The themes raised by Amadeus Amaral of the car as the death of community, the decentering of the ego, the distraction of the mind, and the enslaver of desires remained current. Franklin de Oliveira, an editor and popular columnist who began his career in journalism at age sixteen, composed a clever essay describing a motorist who juggles three separate streams of consciousness as he drives through the city of Rio: the memories of a dark-skinned woman he once knew who smiled with her eyes but whose name he cannot remember; the commands of signs, laws, and policemen, all of which he unconsciously wills to obey; and his topographical memory, which he needs to navigate the difficult terrain of least congested options and the complicated system of one-way streets. As he reminisces about the girl and philosophizes about why it is we remember such relationships, his thoughts are interrupted with parenthetical, bolded text representing the mental demands of the car. As he submerges into the thickening, downtown traffic, the demands upon his conscious thoughts increase, and the parentheses disappear.

She and I were distractedly pure (**can one turn right when the light is red?**) when we met. In her eyes you could read the presence of a bird, exiled from imaginary spaces (**what does one do when the street has no lines?**) that is about to lite on the ground. If you know the mystery, do not hesitate (**it is prohibited to stop in tunnels and on bridges**) to explain to me this miracle of seeing someone, never encountering them again, but to keep thinking and knowing that she really stood right there. Now, we go about the world, and the wind comes, but nobody really ever encounters another. Misapprehension is general. Equivocal. (**Two brief whistles means stop.**) But everyone continues forward, without map, without north, just moving. Into limbo. Into fog. Into the estrangement of missed encounters. Praia do Flamengo, Leblon, Blom, blom. The search is useless. Always will be. (**Wrong way!**). **A sign of general panic** ... But we keep moving and we never meet each other. The arrows say: **keep moving forward.** Soon, another commands: **turn right or left.** It is obvious there is no destination. **Just pedal to the metal and faith in God.** Whatever will be, in due course, will become apparent.[43]

For Oliveira, the mechanical, trivial, and micro-managerial nature of traffic laws, some of them word for word from the 1941 National Code, implant themselves into the mind, distracting one from more pleasant or philosophical thoughts but unable to entirely take them away. The car represents not only the disaggregation of thought but also the destruction of place ("she really stood right there") and hence the disarticulation of community. There remained no ultimate destination, no place to meet the

[43] Franklin de Oliveira, "Trânsito," *Revista de Automóveis*, Aug. 1954, 1.

girls of one's dreams nor the friends of one's future. All had become movement but to nowhere meaningful in particular, and "nobody really ever encounters another" in a world where all is movement. The historian, Ary da Matta, who authored his essay the following year, concurred, suggesting that not only did the car make movement through the city's streets, avenues, and squares more complicated, causing long-time residents to get lost; it had also caused the city's residents to lose their better selves by having lost sight of each other, "without map, without compass, and without radar in this battlefield that is the traffic of Rio."[44]

In the January 1955 edition, Carlos Drummond de Andrade, who has become Brazil's most beloved poet, first notes the almost complete absence of the automobile in Brazil's national literature. But then he remembers an applicable poem by one of the nation's "leap-year" poets (*poeta bissexto*), a Brazilian term for writers whose work saw prompt publication but who produced rarely. Pedro Danta's "Song of the Pedestrian" does not challenge the car but simply pleads, with bribes and solicitations, for the clemency to cross the street without being killed. "Automobile, Automobile, don't kill me, please." The pedestrian promises to pay for gas, to never ride the streetcar again. "Just let me arrive to the other sidewalk, where my true love awaits; don't kill me automobile, because I am crossing to see my love." Again, the car comes between a man and a woman, in the imagination of Oliveira, but in the actual street for Danta. As with Oliveira, the main concern is the way that the car comes between encounters and relationships, which are now relegated to a noisy, difficult existence on the street's narrow sidewalk margin or to a cramped corner of the mind. Drummond de Andrade also concludes with a peace offering to the car, holding out hope that flesh and machine can find common ground and common goals, to serve humanity's higher aims, "to integrate mechanical civilization under the ideals of love and generous comprehension." Maybe, he holds out hope, the car, which shortens time and space, can in fact help us live mostly at a slower velocity, which will "permit us a greater consecration of the finest moments of our lives, which are not those spent in transit, but in immobility, contemplation, and peace."[45]

With her international success with the novel *Margarida la Rocque*, Dinah Silveira de Queiroz, one of Brazil's science fictions pioneers who in

---

[44] Ary da Matta, "Lição perdida," *Revista de Automóveis*, May 1955, 1.
[45] Carlos Drummond de Andrade, "O automóvel na literatura," *Revista de Automóveis*, Jan. 1955, 1.

1980 would be elected to the Academy, was one of the few women invited to address the readers of *Revista de Automóveis*. Auto dealers had for some time marketed the car to women: in 1929, the city claimed 122 "chauffeuses" registered in the city, and one newspaper dedicated space to list all of them by name.[46] Silveira de Queiroz explained that she took the leap in 1949, purchasing a small, green British model that fit her "spirit and personality." The automobile, she asserted, was the new race of centaurs, an extension of the human body and personality. "When you see a small, shy, bald man driving a Cadillac, the machine will make him think himself something spectacular, and he will despise and scorn all other creatures, particularly the 'contemptible pedestrian.'" Silveira de Queiroz confessed to being outwardly Christian and hence accepted that ostentation was a great sin. So, she bought her modest, feminine car with the royalties from *Margarida la Rocque* out of a personal desire to become rigorously independent rather than to practice any pretension. She named the car Margarida and began to take driving classes. They were a disaster. She could not, she confessed, manage the clutch; she hit dogs and cats left and right, and after having gone through a session of maneuvers that consisted mostly of avoiding obstacles, she would return home so distressed that she could not write. So she "renounced Margarida," but kept the car for the benefit of the driving men in the family. A male friend tried to console her in her failure to become a motorist, explaining that sensitive souls were simply not meant to drive. He himself had lost the woman of his dreams for lack of a car. A chauffeur had stolen her away using the automobile as a trump card to his merely verbal expressions of love and mechanically unsubstantiated proposals. Carless, he could not compete, but he, like Silveira de Queiroz, took the highest moral ground. He would not compete: "I preferred to be an unhappy soul than to become an assassin," he averred. The car, Silveira de Queiroz had intimated, was a technology unbefitting not only a woman and an artist, but a human being concerned about the welfare and lives of her fellow citizens.[47]

Three essayists, each writing in a different year, agreed that the purchase and driving of a car was a decision that ranged from stupid to immoral. Joel Silveira, the war correspondent who covered Brazil's forces in World War II, did not own a car himself, but he would accept rides from friends for whom the car had become the very center of their lives. All had

---

[46] *A Batalha*, Dec. 21, 1929, 1–2.
[47] Dinah Silveira de Queiroz, "Romance de Margarida," *Revista de Automóveis*, Jul. 1954, 2.

become slaves to its charms and hassles, and he wanted none of it. Guilherme Figueiredo, the dramatist, explained that first-time car buyers suffered its many anguishes only to forget them, like a mother forgets the painful labor of her first child. With his first car, the English taxonomy of the car's many parts taxed his memory, and he had to form a series of conflictive relationships with his car dealer, banker, oil man, gas attendant, mechanic, washerman, garagist, and traffic inspector, not to mention a dangerous, daily involvement with all the other motorists. Unlike most, Figueiredo had given up on the car. "Finally, at some point, the force of dignity causes us to sell the car for half its price and return to the honorable and free life of the pedestrian." The journalist Fernando Sabino, explained that he had gladly sold his car because of its innumerable headaches and its knack for making him feel like a criminal. He had no regrets. The car made most of his enemies and was the source of most of his worries: running out of gas in the New Tunnel; contributing to the city's congestion, for which he felt personally responsible; parking tickets; and the sound of the policeman's motorcycle that made him feel like a gangster being pursued. And then there were the car's noises that he could never reproduce in the shop but that could always be fixed for 1,000 *cruzeiros*. In Rio, his own hometown, he repeatedly got lost. In the end, he concluded, "[I]t was best to sell it," although he admitted that the moment the car was gone, almost immediately one begins to consider getting another.[48]

There were other interpretations of the car's impact on Brazil's culture. Ângelo Sangirardi Jr., a biologist whose interests in Brazil reached from the indigenous use of erotic plants to African religions, made the case that the automobile was driving not only the nation's cultural evolution toward modernism, but its actual biological evolution as well. Air pollution caused cancer and selected out the city's weakest, and the constant fight for space, on buses and in crossing the street, taught an organism to be agile and tough. The city's traffic, its potholes, horns, complicated navigation, and the accompanying cursing, made humans evolve faster and made the urban resident the strongest of the species. "Future generations in this moving, filthy city will be more evolved," and future authors on the city's progress would write of Rio's residents as being the fittest of all survivors, he prophesied. But more commonly, the essayists criticized

[48] Joel Silveira, "Conversa de automóvel," *Revista de Automóveis*, Aug. 1956, 2; Guilerme Figueiredo, "Reincidência," *Revista de Automóveis*, Aug. 1955, 1; Fernando Sabino, "Compra-se um automóvel," *Revista de Automóveis*, Nov. 1954, 1.

the city's socioeconomic evolution into increasingly divided classes in the public sphere. Rubem Braga said he wrote of cars from the "vague humanistic perspective of the curb," and directly questioned the way automobiles seemed to exacerbate the already entrenched problem of social inequality and further divided, indeed, isolated the classes from one another. He claimed that he was neither Communist nor Christian, but asked, "[W]hat are we going to do with all these rich people who get richer and all these poor people who get poorer?" The walking poor, he claimed, were too tired to get angry and took consolation from their indigent misery in their own ignorance or in the drums of the samba. The rich, by contrast, spent their time "trying to show other rich people that they were richer than other rich people." Foreigners were surprised by the number of Cadillacs they encountered in Rio's streets. Braga was simultaneously bored and scandalized by the ever-growing sorts of accessories one could have fitted to one's car – clocks, radios, blinking lights, air conditioning, and automatic transmissions with silly English marketing names such as Hydromatic, Giromatic, Overdrive, Fluidrive and "I don't know what other -matics and -drives." What astonished him most was the then current rage over painted whitewall tires, the least expensive of all automotive luxuries. "To the poor man who waits at the bus stop an hour in the hot sun or pouring rain, splashed with mud from one of these shiny, honking monsters (which never has a second to lose in its terrible urgency to arrive somewhere where its passengers plan to do nothing of consequence), must find some consolation indeed if the car at the very least had whitewall tires." Brazil, he concludes, was becoming unbalanced, and only its ability to focus on such trivialities kept it from tipping into social chaos and violence. The car was the precipice of social dissolution. Braga's critical leftist stance on Brazil's status quo had gotten him arrested on more than one occasion during the Vargas regime, but his voice remained consistent.[49]

Joracy Camargo, elected to the Academy in 1967, argued that the car's enticements also bankrupted the poor, many of whom sacrificed rent, food, and other necessities just to keep the family in four wheels and in pretention to a social class above their reality. Just like the state, individuals could throw money at their own modernity while those matters that were the real measures of civic advancement – education, medicine, nutrition, decent housing, running water, and sewers – were neglected.

---

[49] Sangirardi, Jr. "Fatores da evolução," *Revista de Automóveis*, Sep. 1956, 1; Rubem Braga, "Banda branca," *Revista de Automóveis*, Mar. 1955, 1.

The poor's many Tin Lizzies, he observed, were fortresses to defend: if the price of fuel rose, you worked harder to pay for it; if taxes rose, you ceased registering your car. But come Sunday, without fail, the car will be filled with the family eating roast corn at Barra da Tijuca, decorated with the flags of the Flamengo soccer club at Maracanã Stadium, parked with hundreds of other beat-up cars along the beach in Ramos, or set unabashedly among the Cadillacs in Copacabana.[50]

In other cases, the writers went for the car's jugular, two of them speaking openly of its role as grim reaper. Josué Montello, elected to the Academy just months before his contribution, had the galling impertinence to retell the story of the city's first auto-pedestrian death in 1906. As first reported by Artur Azevedo, the playwright and journalist, an elderly Italian immigrant, who in the mundane act of crossing the street, had the right frontal lobe of his cranium crushed, an instant and bloody death that launched what Montello said journalists have now long since referred to as the "Battle of Rio de Janeiro" between drivers and pedestrians. Montello observed that Azevedo had warned them of the wages of the automobile's place on the street fifty years before, and they had not listened. The film historian and critic, Salvyano Cavalcanti de Paiva, wrote of his own premonitions of automotive death, suggesting readers consider their own vulnerability in the world of the car. He had grown up, he writes, much unlike his contemporaries, entirely ambivalent about the car's merits, until he had his palm read and was told he would suffer a serious accident in middle age. Thereafter, he avoided the car, fretted when riding in public transit, and refused to cross the street against the light, regardless of what his companions did. He tried to exorcise his demons by contemplating the death of the car rather than his own. In 1952, he composed a poem, of which only a fragment is shared here, that expresses the gratifying demise of a car in the car's own voice: "the abyss is the horizon's line, which I kiss in a diving rollover, and I shatter in glass and scrap, burning up in gushing oil engulfed in flame."[51] These were hardly the images to be desired by the magazine's promoters of automobilism.

---

[50] Joracy Camargo, "A fraco abusado," *Revista de Automóveis*, Apr. 1955, 1.
[51] Josué Montello, "Artur Azevedo e o automóvel," *Revista de Automóveis*, Sep. 1955, 1; Salvyano Cavalcanti de Paiva, "Mão do contra," *Revista de Automóveis*, Mar. 1956, 1.

Finally, weighing in was the stately Austregésilo de Athayde, a man who had served as a delegate to the UN commission that drafted the Universal Declaration of Human Rights and had been elected to the Academy of Brazilian Letters in 1951 where he would serve as president for thirty-four years. In his piece, entitled "Ford and Human Happiness," Athayde recalled an interview he had had as a young reporter with the aging Henry Ford. Ford, who was not often friendly with a press that had alternately praised him for his innovations and skewered him for his bigotry, asked Athayde if he believed the press had at all advanced human happiness in the past century, to which Athayde gave a fair defense of the press's progressive and democratic intentions, despite excesses. Athayde then turned the question back on Ford: "Has the automobile made civilization any happier?" Ford frankly replied, "No. I am certain that I have not improved human life in the sense of making it any happier ... In my view, the truly happy man is the one who is born, lives, and dies all in the same place." From the horse's mouth, Athayde raised doubt about automobilism's civilizing claims, suggesting instead that the car's role had been to dislocate humanity from place-based communities and social engagement.[52]

One wonders at what point the editors of *Revista de Automóveis* began to regret their decision to permit such an open forum on the car. Possibly, despite the open criticism, the editors still hoped the names of the nation's elite poets, novelists, essayists, and dramatists would help launch the magazine to literary and financial success by building a readership. But in essay after essay that called the car a vehicle of death and a destroyer of relationships, an object that undermined the humanity of its users and cut up the very fabric of the city, there must have been some hand wringing and second-guessing. One can imagine the sentiments of the magazine's many advertisers – automakers, dealers, insurance companies, not to mention whitewall tire makers – who were the true shapers of the magazine's success. Whatever the cause, finally, in the December 1956 issue, the editors declared tersely that "from this point on, the first page will express the opinions of the *Revista*." Literary appraisals of the car and car culture ceased, replaced by rosy editorials on auto tourism, automotive accessories, and the growing domestic production of cars and petroleum. It was the sort of boostering advertisers desired and motoring readers recognized.[53]

---

[52] Austregésilo de Athayde, "Ford e a felicidade humana," *Revista de Automóveis*, Jan. 1956, 1.
[53] *Revista de Automóveis*, Dec. 1956, 1.

A REFUGEE ON RIO'S STREETS

In August of 1941, at the beginning of the lyrical battle for Praça Onze, the author Stefan Zweig and his young wife Lotte came to live in Brazil, a half-year residence that had begun with the hope of new beginnings but which would end in their tragic double suicide. Zweig had been seeking a home since 1934, when he made what his family and friends at the time had called a rash and hasty flight from his comfortable life in Salzburg and Vienna. Zweig, an Austrian Jew who knew Europe's history better than most, had a premonition that Europe was about to descend into what he would call a murderous bestiality. His first novella, *In the Snow*, published in 1901, described an entire community of German Jews who froze to death on the road to Poland in their winter flight from pogroms. By the late 1930s, many Austrian Jews had waited too long, and with few avenues for escape, faced looting, beatings, expulsions, and finally the camps. His own beloved home in Salzburg was ransacked of its art, furniture, and treasured collection of musical scores. The books he had written, dozens of titles, were publicly burned in the streets of Vienna by his own countryman.

The Nazi horror, in the news and in letters from those who remained in Austria, followed the Zweigs wherever they sought refuge. He and Lotte first landed in London and then Bath, which while friendly, did not suit them. They took up residence in a New York City hotel, and then near the Hudson River in a house overlooking Sing Sing prison, which did little to brighten their gloom. Zweig, who both inherited and earned a sumptuously comfortable living, had been known for personally giving out charity to friends and strangers, especially struggling writers and artists. But in New York, the number of penniless German refugees who crossed his threshold for help overwhelmed his compassionate heart. With every soul he supported and consoled, the scale of the calamity made him more despondent. In part to flee these pressures and to find time to keep at his writing, Zweig and Lotte lit off for the tropics, renting a small cottage in the mountains above Rio de Janeiro. This was Zweig's third time in Brazil, a place he had come to love and that seemed to love him. Here he found enough public attention to stroke his ego and enough quiet to allow him to write. As he always had, Zweig assiduously worked on multiple projects; the small house had manuscripts in various stages of preparation, among them a psychological novel revolving around the game of chess, biographies of Balzac and Montaigne, and his own nearly finished memoir entitled *The World of Yesterday*. He also seemed to hope to find a new place – a community – that he could call home. He had tired of his rootless existence and declared, "I would like to live in a Negro hut in Brazil if I should know I could stay there."[54] On the voyage down, he and Lotte practiced Portuguese to better assimilate into their adopted nation.

Zweig may have been the most read and most translated of all authors in the interwar period, churning out short stories, plays, and novels, as well as popular biographies, all of which were read across Europe and the United States. Zweig's deeply felt humanism and pacifism informed nearly all of his work. While his prose was considered a bit old-fashioned and his narratives plot-heavy and theatrical, his keen insights into the drives and frailties of the mind made him a virtuoso in the dissection of human desires and motives. As his work had already been adapted for American films, Hollywood had proffered him offers as a studio writer. But he opted for other shores where his fame was also well established. Every time he arrived in Brazil, despite a secret memo that was supposed to exclude Jews, he was received by high state officials and treated as a celebrity. When he lectured before the immortals at the Academy of Letters in 1940, lines formed and all 2,000 seats sold out immediately.

At about the time of his arrival, he would see published one of his latest works, *Brazil: Land of the Future*. Brazil's popular classes adored it, and the Vargas regime lauded its glowing commentary and florid descriptions of Brazil's national culture and natural resources. Some wished he had given Brazil's modernizing achievements more attention, but Zweig was most impressed with the essential expressions of Brazil's simple people: civility, a garrulous sociality, and a love of life. In a world that was descending into the official practice of racial cleansing and the breeding of pure races, Brazil, Zweig argued, had long ago solved the problem of racial, ethnic, and creedal hatred, in part through miscegenation, but also by long association. In Brazil he saw a "new civilization," and a model to save the world from itself. "One who has just escaped the crazy destructiveness of Europe first greets the total absence of any hatred in public and private life as something unbelievable," he wrote.[55] The Brazilian Left panned the book, calling it a naked encomium to the Vargas regime. They did not contest his characterization of the nation as a racial paradise, a myth that was widely embraced even by radical intellectuals in the

---

[54] Cited in George Prochnik, *The Impossible Exile: Stefan Zweig at the End of the World* (New York, NY: Doubleday, 2014), 266.

[55] Stefan Zweig, *Brazil: Land of the Future*, translated by A. St. James (New York, NY: Viking Press, 1941), 8, 10.

1930s, but they accused Zweig of writing it in the government's pay, just another co-opted cog of the state's propaganda machine. Zweig did not fail to see Brazil's poverty and inequalities, nor that race shaped one's fortunes, but he, on the one hand, tried to expound on the virtuous aspects of all he saw. He once declared that "I can only write positive things; I can't attack," for to do so was to stoop to the tactics of his enemies. On the other hand, Zweig believed that illusions could be powerful in keeping hatred's reality at bay. The Brazilian belief in racial equality, while misplaced and hence perpetuating discrimination, exclusion, and exploitation, made Brazil a more peaceful and harmonious place than it would have been otherwise. The Viennese had also once believed in the myth of their own cosmopolitan tolerance, but the key to Hitler's success was to promote and disinter the reality of an underlying hatred.[56]

Rio's streets in 1941 were the spaces where the illusions of racial and social harmony were maintained, whether in festivals or in the mundane, and Rio's streets were Zweig's delight. Zweig was an inveterate walker, and on his previous visits to the city he immersed himself in Rio's streets almost daily. Leaving his residence with the intent of a quarter-hour's walk downtown, he claimed he rarely returned within four hours, "seduced" forward by the constantly changing array of homes, shops, and churches that lined the city's streets and squares. "Wandering about, an old passion of mine, developed almost into a vice for me in Rio," he wrote. He praised the city's modern avenues, such as Rio Branco, for their grandeur, but he avoided them as they had become merely "thoroughfares for traffic." It was in the narrow, colonial streets, where "automobiles did not yet roar by, or traffic lights flash on and off," that he found not only charm and interest, but the very sense of civility and community he had been looking for as a refugee. In the downtown streets, which seemed to take him back in time, he wrote that "it is extraordinary how much life there is in these narrow streets; the number of men, women, and children constantly streaming through – children, especially, everywhere, children of all colors and breed – and all amidst the tumult of color and movement which is so typical of Brazil, all under the restraining hand of its quiet kindness, the unique understanding between man and man." He claimed that none, not even foreign ladies, had any reason to fear walking in the hubbub of Rio's streets. He asserted that he had never seen anything that was vulgar or indecent on the public commons. "The various classes meet

---

[56] For these insights into Zweig's personality and philosophy, see Prochnik, *Impossible Exile*, 102–03, 322–23. The quote is also cited herein, 65.

with courtesy and affection astounding to anyone coming from Europe . . . One sees two men meeting in the street. They embrace. One would naturally suppose they are brothers or friends, one of them just returned from Europe or some long voyage. But again at the next corner one notices two more men greeting each other in a similar manner." He enjoyed that when two men conversed in the street, they did so graciously, each holding their hats in their hands for the duration of the conversation.[57]

The routines of the streets seemed to Zweig so natural and so human. At 5 AM, as if on cue, the residents left their dwellings to gather on the bay's beaches for bathing. Then, after a breakfast at home that in some cases was still delivered by peddlers, all were off to work, and Zweig marveled at the constant verbal and emotional interchange of pedestrian shoppers, laden carters, hawking greengrocers, banging carpenters, the basket makers, the butchers, and the laundresses, every house and shop at ground level open to the street such that one could observe all that took place within. In particular, he noted the busy notary who placed his desk half in his office and half on the street. Ouvidor Street, like a number of downtown streets still off-limits to cars, was still a crossroads of city life, resuming its status as the city's central social focus now that Avenida Rio Branco had become noisy with buses. Zweig observed that

every real Carioca passes through it several times a day, for it is the great promenade, the one meeting place. It is so tightly packed with people that one can hardly see an inch of pavement; it is an incessant bustle of life, with everyone chattering and rushing about, turning this thoroughfare, thanks to the absence of the infernal din of automobiles, into a continual pleasure.[58]

And little changed at night, doors and windows remaining open, their lit interiors inviting the gaze of passersby, the multitude of cafés, one at every street corner, whose never-ending communion continued late into the night.

Some of Zweig's fascination with Rio's streets may have been fostered by their contrast with what had happened on the streets of Vienna after Austria's annexation in 1938. The Nazis in effect banned Jews from the theater, public gardens, and even the city's streets during most hours of the day. Zweig had received accounts of how "one of these banished men and women – hungry for fresh air, the perfume of the past and summoned by the light of the sun – would fearfully venture out into the streets of

[57] Zweig, *Brazil: Land of the Future*, 189, 140.
[58] Zweig, *Brazil: Land of the Future*, 190–91.

Vienna, strolling down the Alserstrasse with the hope of enjoying a few moments in the sun." To walk in the street was to exercise one's rights of citizenship in a way that was in some sense more fundamental than entering the voting booth or owning property. However, if recognized, the desperate trespasser was accosted by the mob, slapped, stoned, and, should the SS arrive, potentially shot.[59] For Zweig, the juxtaposition of what was happening on the streets of his native country and those of Rio must have made the inclusiveness and fraternity of Brazil's streets all the more moving.

Zweig also wandered up into the *favelas*, unafraid to scramble up steps where the formal streets ended to enter the hillside neighborhoods, which at the time were destitute but no less safe than most streets. Brazilians of a certain class would never have thought to ascend them. As an obvious foreigner, Zweig felt welcome, which was contrary to his expectation. Residents carrying water along the narrow paths up to their homes offered him smiles, and some, despite their burdens, gave him their hand in assistance as Zweig, who was nearing sixty, negotiated slippery, clay steps. Women, some indifferently nursing their infants, greeted him as he peered into their homes. Children of all colors and ages played in the streets together. Zweig lamented that modernity too might put an end to these picturesque dwellings and communities, which in his opinion would considerably reduce the city's charms. While Agache ten years earlier had considered the *favelas* a nasty wound on the city that ought to be cauterized,[60] Zweig saw them as vibrant communities worth keeping, at least some of them. He also admired the civil utility of the city's trams, which he also feared might soon disappear. They were an open community on wheels, without doors, where citizens of all genders, ages, colors, and still all classes, sat together indiscriminately, and, when the trams were crowded, the women and children, regardless of status or color, were given priority seating while the men, in their white suits or working sleeves, clung in orderly ranks on the running boards. In the heat, the trams produced "the most refreshing breeze for the price of one cent! At the same time – as opposed to the coffin-like automobile – one can look right and left into the streets, into shops, into life itself!" He claimed that what he knew of the city of Rio was entirely due to his legs and the

---

[59] Laurent Seksik, *The Last Days*, trans. André Naffis-Sahely (London: Pushkin Press, 2013), 12–13.

[60] Denise Cabral Stuckenbruck, *O Rio de Janeiro em questão: O Plan Agache e o ideário reformista dos anos 20* (Rio de Janeiro: FASE – IPPUR/UFRJ, 1996), 86–88.

streetcar, and to replace the latter with buses, a larger version of the entombing car, would be another mistake of modernity.[61]

Zweig and Lotte came to settle in Brazil just as the southern winter ended, so they chose to rent a house in Petrópolis, Rio's summer retreat where the former emperor Pedro II had built a summer palace and the aviator Santos Dumont had constructed a chalet, all to get away from the oppressive low-land summer heat. It was a quiet existence, maybe the quietest Zweig, a man of the world, of big cities, and the streets, had ever experienced. It was good for work; with few interruptions, he drafted and revised various manu-scripts. But contact with his publishers was slow and difficult from the remote cottage. Zweig was a man used to the urbane, to movement, con-versation, parties, and cafés, and he lamented the declining number of visitors and letters. Petrópolis offered an incomparable nature, but it was isolating, and this certainly contributed to darkening bouts of depression. There are many potential explanations for the Zweigs' suicide in their Petrópolis house. Zweig, said his friends, had an almost pathological fear of aging. He worried about his appearance, his wrinkles, and his graying hair. Then there were the characteristic shocks, anxieties, and even guilt of the refugee, for whom life appeared to be an eternal sentence to homelessness without old friends and familiars. The Zweigs had left a niece, who had lived with them for a short time in New York, in the care of strangers, and they struggled to convince themselves they had done right by doing so. George Prochnik, Zweig's most recent biographer, asserts that Zweig was plagued by "the notion that uprooting translates into death by disconnection."[62] And, of course, Zweig despaired for a Europe that seemed to be sinking beyond reparation, a home to which he might never return. In early 1942, their deaths came at the nadir of the war for the Allies. Hitler had occupied France, Zweig's beloved Paris; the Japanese had attacked Pearl Harbor; and Zweig feared that Fascism would next invade South America. Brazil was already reportedly full of spies, and Vargas, who strategically temporized as long as possible, would not declare Brazil's support of the Allies until later that year, in August. For Zweig, all seemed to be despair. Even D-Day was a secret whose hopeful beachhead was still months away. Maybe, if Zweig had braved Rio's summer heat, had taken up residence on one of the colonial streets he so admired, the reality and the illusion of community on the streets, the connection of the house to the public realm, the mere presence of city people and cafés, might have parried his despondency long enough for him to

---

[61] Zweig, *Brazil: Land of the Future*, 142, 195, 198.
[62] Prochnik, *Impossible Exile*, 11, 40.

see the tide change, to hope for an eventual return to his home, friends, and acquaintances in Austria, however shattered.

The people of Petrópolis took charge of Stefan's and Lotte's bodies, which their maid had found clutching one another in their shared deathbed. Zweig's suicide note, in his trademark violet ink, expressed again his love of Brazil as a hoped for home, thanking the nation for its hospitality. Residents closed their shops, and crowds of mourners paid their respects as the Zweigs' flowered caskets moved slowly through Petrópolis' streets to their final resting place in the city cemetery. For a man without a country who seemed to come closest to recovering his sense of belonging by walking Rio's streets, the Brazilian street, a space that still knew how to be mindful and reverential when circumstance required it, offered Stefan and Lotte a last and genuine expression of community.

Despite lamentations from various corners of society, and despite Zweig's encounter with surviving remnants of the traditional street, the automobile's juggernaut was unstoppable. By the 1950s, the streets were increasingly described as not just dangerous and chaotic but dysfunctional. Traffic jams during rush hours might literally freeze up the city's overall functioning, harming commerce, labor, and various essential city services, including police and ambulances. Streets became so busy that the demands of traffic took priority over other surviving street uses. While more significant street festivals survived, although often in attenuated forms, many streets that used to shut down annually or periodically for religious processions, carnival parades, or everyday funerals, could no longer spare the space, not even for a few hours. Parking itself had become a constant crisis, angering motorists. The street's malfunction as a machine for movement placed increasing pressure on city officials to find solutions. Automotive safety took a backseat to fixing the daily drama of traffic congestion. Residents came to see congestion as the city's most pressing problem, and some officials worried the crisis was becoming existential, a threat to the city's very viability. After 1950, the city began to invest more resources and expect more results from its transit director and his staff, more of whom were professionals rather than the usual political appointees. This was especially true under the military government after 1964 that took the traffic crisis in hand as a test of its ability to impose order and efficiency in the nation's former capital. It was at this point as well that substantial public funds were spent on new highways, viaducts, tunnels, and parking structures. The city would attempt to build itself out of the problem of too little space for too many vehicles.

7

Traffic Flow versus Free Parking

Morro do Castelo

I heard the transit director was dismissed.

Dias Gomes, 1968[1]

All over the city automobiles hit one another in the search for space to
move in.

Rubem Fonseca, 2009[2]

The French Huguenots, who in 1555 first settled Rio de Janeiro's bay,
centered their colony on a fortified island which they named Villegagnon,
after their leader. Here, on cliffs that commanded the bay's entrance, the
French felt safe from local tribes and from the territorial claims, backed by
papal bull, of the Portuguese. The battles fought here between the
Protestant French and the Catholic Portuguese made the Reformation
a global conflict, and the Portuguese were forced to field two expeditions
to expel the French interlopers. The Portuguese made their first settlement
on the mainland, on a broad, defensible hill that looked down on
Villegagnon's little island. At one end of the hill, they built a fortress
that gave the hill the name of Castelo, and at the other, the Jesuits erected
a church and sprawling monastery. Castelo Hill was the city's civic center,
hosting the city's first streets, squares, and monumental buildings, including the cathedral, the governor's house and the city observatory that
marked the hour of noon each day with cannon fire. Around the hill's

---

[1] Alfredo de Freitas Dias Gomes, *O Túnel. Dias Gomes teatro*, vol. 2 (Rio de Janeiro:
Betrand Brasil, 1998), 764–65.
[2] Rubem Fonseca, "The Art of Walking the Streets of Rio de Janeiro," in *Winning the Game
and Other Stories*, translated by C. E. Landers (Dartmouth, MA: Tagus Press, 2013), 138.

base clung convents, churches, the Santa Casa Hospital, the royal armory, and the city's main square. Castelo Hill was the city's true cradle, and every foreign tourist over the next three centuries made an obligatory pilgrimage to Castelo's brow, for it was from here that the city, the bay, the islands, and the mountains could be altogether best appreciated.

As residents began to settle the marshy valley below in the early seventeenth century, shifting the city's residences and commerce downhill, Castelo experienced neglect. The bishop descended to make a new church his cathedral, and the hill's public buildings were progressively abandoned. In fact, city officials came to see Castelo not as an historical and natural landmark but as a place of poverty and neglect, an impediment to the city's circulation and hygiene. Machado de Assis wrote in 1862 that from the day Brazil became Brazil, the city's administrators had wanted to knock Castelo down. This was an exaggeration, but indeed from at least 1838, the hygienists argued that the hill had to go, to open the city to the breezes that made the Santa Casa Hospital a supposed salubrious location.[3] One of Castelo's broad shoulders would be dug away with the building of Avenida Central in 1904, to make space for the National Library. Much as in other regrades of the time, such as in Boston and Seattle, Rio's downtown hills began to come down, first piecemeal and then wholesale. Castelo's final demise began in 1921 as steam shovels and hydraulic hoses undermined the hill's foundations. Augusto Malta captured the last photos of the hill in 1921, its steep, car-free streets and unpaved squares full of children, many of them unsupervised toddlers.[4] Once evicted with their families, their homes, churches, and the monasteries, jetted at the foundations, teetered and then tumbled ignominiously to the city floor. The regrade, which was largely finished by 1929, created mountains of tailings that workers dumped into the bay. The fill from the city's former hills reclaimed a vast expanse of land from the bay, eventually reaching all the way out to Villegagnon's island situated more than a kilometer from the original shore. While city residents watched the hill come down with some interest, for there were rumors the Jesuits had

[3] Robert Elwes, Esq., *A Sketcher's Tour Round the World* (London: Hurst and Blacket, Publishers, 1854), 19.

[4] Augusto Malta, "Largo do Castelo," 1921, Acervo da Fundação Biblioteca Nacional, BN Digital, http://objdigital.bn.br/objdigital2/acervo_digital/div_iconografia/icon1402123/ic on1402123.jpg (accessed Aug. 3, 2017); and Augusto Malta, "Ladeira do Castelo," c. 1921, Acervo da Fundação Biblioteca Nacional, BN Digital, http://objdigital.bn.br/obj digital2/acervo_digital/div_iconografia/icon1381743/icon1381743.jpg (accessed Aug. 3, 2017).

hidden therein a cache of gold and jewels, neither the gouging of the hill nor the filling in of the bay were popular, and the press attacked the administration for the destruction of the city's past and present. Lima Barreto fulminated against "Philistine men of our time, educated in the hidden valleys of London or the bank offices of Wall Street" for whom the hills, like the poor, were bodies to dig and exploit. They hid their greed, he claimed, behind the name of beauty while they clogged the splendid beaches with mud. In cartoons, Castelo Hill was portrayed as bearded king Neptune, dignified but defenseless against those who undermined his throne, and the bay as a graceful mermaid under the protection of her father's impotent trident.[5]

Rio's hills fell to the shovels of hygiene and urbanism. But by 1929, with the regrade complete, fresh breezes and new plots of real estate were not as important as creating more space for the city's multiplying machines. An airport was constructed on fill that sprawled out to Villagagnon's Island. Urban planners, particularly Alfred Agache, drew up elaborate designs for other portions of the reclaimed ground that included symmetrical office towers inspired by the City Beautiful movement and a radiated public square that was to become the city's new, best face to the arriving foreigner. The city was to be zoned, after the modern fashion, and divided functions would make the city orderly. However, such plans came to nothing. The automobile's increasing demand for space superseded the aesthetic and categorizing aspirations of foreign planners and domestic architects. Rio's officials committed most of the space created by the demise of Rio's hills to the car: the cuts they dedicated to automotive parking, and the fills, which reclaimed the bay, they christened as automotive highways. The fill from the destruction of the largest hill, Santo Antonio, in the 1950s, formed the Flamengo Landfill on which they built the multi-lane, limited-access freeway, known simply as Aterro (Landfill), that connects Rio's center with its southern suburbs.[6] And the hill's former site, which was originally intended for open-air parking, is now a large open space punctuated with state-owned skyscrapers.

---

[5] See article by Roy Nash in *Brazilian American*, Oct. 14, 1922, Centennial Edition, Year 4, vol. 6, no. 155, n.p. Lima Barreto, "A revolta do mar," *Careta*, Jul. 23, 1921. See *Memória da destruição: Rio, uma história que se perdeu, 1889–1965* (Rio de Janeiro: Prefeitura da Cidade do Rio de Janeiro, Secretaria das Culturas, Arquivo da Cidade, 2002), 57–61, for cartoons.

[6] *Revista de Automoveis*, Jan. 1959, 34–38, documents the removal of the Santo Antonio Hill, which opened another parking lot, and the Aterro created with its fill.

Beneath them, one finds the most capacious underground parking in the city, for even the subterranean would be reclaimed.

For decades, much of the coveted space that had lain beneath Castelo Hill was also not built upon as planned but turned over to an informal and poorly regulated parking lot. Cars began to pile in even before demolition was complete.[7] After World War II, Castelo's former footprint, from São José Street to the back of the Santa Casa – some 60,000 square meters (15 acres) of downtown space – became the city's largest parking lot. Magazines published photographs, both aerial and ground-level, of the sea of cars that had turned proposed building lots into parking spaces.[8] Even as construction began to encumber some of the space, including federal ministries, the space maintained its status as the city's principal parking lot until 1973, some fifty years after the hill's demise. Then the city permanently committed a portion of the space to automotive storage by building a long-planned-for multi-story garage on the site. The sixteen-story concrete edifice, named for Geraldo de Menezes Côrtes, a former transit director, has what is possibly the largest footprint and the biggest interior volume of any downtown building. The garage's modernist hind-quarters, an immense wall of unglazed windows, bears down on the graceful, baroque façade of the São José church directly behind it. In addition to small shops and snack counters, the garage's main floor houses the city's intra-city bus station. The remaining floors provide 3,500 parking spaces, although the original intent was to construct 8,000.[9]

Many of Rio's residents have forgotten that their city was born on a commanding hill that had stood at this location. Menezes Côrtes himself asserted in the 1950s that the latest generation of Cariocas did not know that a hill had resided at Castelo a mere three decades before.[10] The name Castelo, however, survives. While it is officially the Menezes Côrtes Garage and Terminal, everyone refers to the massive edifice as Castelo, a name that also flies prominently on the banners of the buses that have the garage as their final destination. Castelo, once a significant place, a place of origin, whose destruction was supposed to give birth to another set of landmarks attesting to Rio's modernity, is now, under the same name, the

---

[7] "Estacionamento de automóveis," *Jornal do Brasil*, Jan. 31, 1929, 5. See *A Noite*, Aug. 26, 1952, 13, for the first efforts to regulate this lot.

[8] "Rio – uma cidade entupida," *Revista da Semana*, Jan. 10, 1949; *Revista de Automóveis*, Jun. 1954; *Manchete*, Jan. 22, 1955, 24.

[9] Franco, *Eu na contramão*, 383.

[10] "Precisamos de um departemento municipal de engenharia do tráfego," *Revista de Automóveis*, Oct. 1954.

nation's largest parking garage. By chance, the edifice rises to roughly the same height as the former hill, giving the pedestrian some sense of the scale of her past's topography. To stand on the roof of the garage today is like standing at the foundation of her erstwhile castle.[11]

By mid-century, the car had largely won the downtown battle over the street's utilities. Conquests, once complete, however, often divide the conquerors, and the spatial conflict downtown now pitted motorists who wanted to drive against motorists who wanted to park. With too many cars parked on narrow streets, many of which still had colonial dimensions, motorists could not flow; yet, for the same motorists, what was the point of flow, of driving into the city, if once one arrived, there was no place to stop and store one's car? Motorists consistently faced the aggravating paradox of both not being able to move and not being able to stop. The city struggled to prioritize and adjudicate between these competing demands and concluded that the only solution was to build more space for the car – more lanes for driving and more lots for parking.

THE PROGRESS OF CONGESTION

In November of 1949, *Life* magazine reported from Rio on "the knottiest traffic jam in history." Involving some 10,000 of Rio's then 60,000 vehicles and lasting six hours, it paralyzed the southern half of the city as well as the downtown shops and offices that relied on commuters to fill the roles of both employees and customers. A collision between a truck and a streetcar precipitated the blockages along Beira Mar Avenue and Catete Street, the only viable routes from the southern suburbs to the downtown. Vehicles over a three-mile stretch hardly moved from 8:30 AM to almost 3 PM. Many never made it to work that day, and along the route, the behavior of drivers, passengers, cabbies, and shop owners, which was reported as cordial, evidenced that commuters had developed a number of strategies to cope with traffic jams. Bus passengers descended to stretch their legs, sit on the sea wall, and engage in conversation while taking in the bay that lapped the avenue's edge. Bumper to bumper, businessmen tore out pages from their newspapers to share with their neighbor in the next lane. By noon, restaurants along the route were serving lunch to windfall customers, and one shop put out a phonograph to entertain the

---

[11] For Castelo Hill's history, see Gilmar Mascarenhas de Jesus, "Espaço, tempo e paisagem no Morro do Castelo: obsolescência e morte de um lugar," *Geo UERJ* 8 (Jul.–Dec. 2000): 67–77.

stranded motorists. Community sprang up as soon as the traffic stopped. Intermittently, thousands of drivers honked their horns in unison, more in fun, the reporter claimed, than in frustration. A traffic jam, despite its inherent aggravations, was an excusable absence from work, and some commuters forsook their buses and trams and walked back to Copacabana Beach to make of it a holiday.[12]

For most, of course, jams were not opportunities to be enjoyed, and complaints about traffic congestion, about which everyone seemed to be an expert, were voiced on the street, in letters to the editor, and in comments about local and federal politicians. In 1952, one newspaper survey of city residents identified traffic as Rio's number one problem.[13] During the city's morning and evening rush hours, congestion and delay were unfailing components of getting around the city. In November 1949, the same month as the colossal jam reported in *Life*, an editorialist described Rio Branco Avenue as a daily crawl, even with its now six lanes of one-way traffic created by the elimination of its streetlights and central refuges. To travel from one end to the other required a full 35 minutes, an average of less than half a kilometer per hour. Bus riders frequently disembarked as soon as they hit the Avenue as it was faster to walk. There was a modern irony in a broad avenue, newly reengineered for traffic, that was choked with empty buses and under-occupied cars but whose sidewalks teamed with pedestrians outpacing the traffic. The *Correio da Manhã* threw up its hands at all the foreign experts hired to solve downtown congestion, to no apparent improvement. Even Avenida Vargas, still brand new in its incomparable sixteen lanes, frequently backed up.[14]

Hence, over the course of the first half of the twentieth century, the dominant classes produced, in Lefebvre's terms, automotive streets in their thousands, refashioning the city's commons to best accommodate the flow and storage of private vehicles. However, if they materially produced and socially dominated the street, they were by no means able to make it perform to their expectations for rapid movement. They called for the removal of competitors. The pedestrian had already been sidelined, and some demanded that pedestrians be placed underground or overhead, to push them off the streets entirely. From the late 1920s, drivers demanded that not

---

[12] William W. White, "Monster Traffic Jam," *Life*, Nov. 14, 1949, 21–24.

[13] *A Noite*, Sep. 4, 1952, 2. The second-ranked problem was the cost of living.

[14] *A Noite*, Nov. 7, 1949, 5; *Correio da Manhã*, Dec. 25, 1949, 2; *Revista da Semana*, Nov. 23, 1946, 6–11. Franco, *Eu na contramão*, 274.

only horse-drawn wagons (banned from Avenida Rio Branco in 1937) and handcarts (banished downtown in 1954[15]) be removed from the street, but they also suggested that the most efficient movers, streetcars (which mostly disappeared by the late 1950s) and even buses, be removed, at least from the downtown.[16] By 1950, most of the downtown streets had become auto-motive monocultures, and in this single, simple utility, they were an admitted failure. The street remained a space of chaos. In the past, the street had been chaotic, but a functional multi-use place. The automobile had made of it a single-use, non-functional space. If the elite's impotence to govern the street was not already obvious in their inability to prevent automotive deaths and injuries, this might be explained by their general disinterest in solving a problem they believed largely harmed the pedestrian. But they did want the street to function as a rapid conveyance, to provide the space on which they could move at will, at speed, and in the direction they pleased. Every transit director at his appointment spoke with convic-tion about the power of good government to regulate, order, and manip-ulate public spaces to be functional and efficient. Celso Franco, who served in that capacity from the late 1960s, even writing about it years later, claimed that what he wanted to accomplish above all else was to show Rio's residents that traffic was something that could be dominated, that congestion was not incurable.[17] But in his case, as in nearly every other, congestion, if not worse, was certainly no better when he left office.

Those who complained about traffic congestion, even into the early 1970s, frequently worked from the nostalgic assumption that in Rio congestion was a recent phenomenon, and they pined for the previous decade when vehicles supposedly flowed freely in the streets.[18] The reality was that congestion was never a new development in the twentieth cen-tury. Already by the mid-1920s, as the stock of cars began to build in earnest after the lull of World War I, complaints of congestion during rush hours became acrimonious and consistent. A police publication asked how it was that Rio, with relatively few cars, moved more slowly than cities with many more cars. "It must be political corruption," the article concluded, because the solutions, it argued, were just so obvious. In 1927, a weekly magazine lamented that "traffic is the Carioca's eternal

---

[15] *Diário de Notícias*, Jan. 3, 1954, section 2, 3.
[16] *Revista da Semana*, May 21, 1927; *Revista Municipal de Engenharia*, Jul. 1932, 19–20.
[17] Franco, *Eu na contramão*, 216.
[18] "Velocidade em metros per hora," *Quatro Rodas*, Jan. 1962, 19, as one example of many that had no sense of traffic's history.

nightmare and the constant refrain of Rio's press." It complained that the city formed committees, named commissions, and hired foreign experts, who altogether made modifications and tried new ideas, but in the end, nothing changed, and "pedestrians now walk with greater velocity than streetcars or automobiles, except when they can't, because there are occasions in which, even on foot, we cannot accomplish locomotion," largely due to the crowding on sidewalks produced by the car.[19]

Even during the Depression, with an apparent decline in driving, complaints continued apace, and Stefan Zweig described Avenida Rio Branco just before World War II as "constantly congested by a procession of automobiles moving only a few feet at a time; it is appallingly noisy, always overcrowded." The traffic and noise, Zweig observed, had destroyed the avenue as Rio's most coveted real estate, and the best shops had departed for quieter side streets.

What was once the best street is today not much more than a street obviously designed for traffic and a thoroughfare lacking any particular character of its own. What it did have of character and dignity is lost, because today it tries only to fill the everyday needs of the time, and even so is barely up to such a standard.[20]

Only during World War II's gas rationing, when fuel was reserved for public transit, cabs, and official cars, did rush-hour traffic improve for a few short years. Not long after July 1942, when private cars were denied gasoline, automotive traffic in the city fell by 82 percent. Traffic flowed better, and everyone, mostly now taking public transit, got to his or her destination with greater speed and less aggravation than when passenger cars were in the mix, which exposed the true cause of traffic jams.[21] Engineers in particular, who would become central players in the fight for more and better automotive spaces, starkly argued that they were up against a simple law of physics: that two bodies could not occupy the same space. There were "too many cars and not enough street."[22]

As Rio's wealthier classes moved south in the late nineteenth century, initially due to the benefits of public transit, the city effected a variety of

[19] *O Paiz*, Mar. 20, 1925; *Vida Policial*, Oct. 24, 1925, 1; *Revista da Semana*, May 21, 1927.
[20] Zweig, *Brazil: Land of the Future*, 180–81.
[21] "Problemas de tráfego no Rio de Janeiro: O tráfego da Avenida Rio Branco," *Revista Municipal de Engenharia*, Jul. 1937, 238; Nelson Rodriquez, "Estudo da alteração do tráfego durante a crise de gasolina de 1942," *Revista Municipal de Engenharia*, Sep. 1942, 284. *Revista da Semana*, Sep. 16, 1944, 10.
[22] Jorge Morão, "Peritos volantes," *Revista de Automóveis*, Feb. 1955; *Veja*, Nov. 25, 1970, 56; *Veja*, May 28, 1968, 46.

projects with circulation to and from the southern beach suburbs as a priority. The issue, as it had always been in Rio, was how to get thoroughfares of traffic through steep granite mountains. The city dug two major tunnels, the so-called Túnel Velho (Old Tunnel, 1892), and the Túnel Novo (New Tunnel, 1906) so that streetcars could reach Copacabana. Likewise, the city completed the broad Beira Mar Avenue in 1907, which ran from Botofogo to the city center. As Copacabana families began to purchase cars, motorists eventually joined the streetcars in the Old and New Tunnels. This further drove suburbanization. By mid-century, Copacabana was the city's booming residential district. In the decade of the 1950s, the city center became increasingly commercial, losing one-third of its residential population in a single decade. By 1960, only 25,196 people lived downtown. By contrast, in the same decade, the southern suburbs, from Glória to Gávea, ballooned to more than a half million. Those families who could afford to live near the beach were generally the same families that could afford an automobile, and car growth followed. In 1964, there were more than 100 cars per 1,000 inhabitants in Copacabana, whereas in the northern suburbs there were fewer than 20 per 1,000 residents. Before the war, automotive infrastructure had mainly focused on the downtown, culminating in Vargas Avenue in 1944. Thereafter, the emphasis became connecting the city to its growing suburbs. At mid-century, automotive infrastructure was considered to be "already on the verge of collapse." Copacabana became the city's automotive center of gravity, and politicians, many of whom lived there, responded to their constituents' strident demand for faster movement to and from their work and play at the city's center.[23]

Mountains remained the main obstacle, and before the 1950s, all automotive traffic had to pass through the same bottleneck along Guanabara Bay. The early tunnels converged on Botofogo, and then, to reach the downtown, all cars, buses, and streetcars had to merge onto either Beira Mar Avenue or Catete Street, which together offered all of six lanes, insufficient during rush hour from the late 1940s. Hence, from the 1950s, the city's mayors and the nation's presidents invested increasingly in the creation of new automotive space. In 1947, the city began to dig the Santa Barbara Tunnel, which gave drivers a bit of a bypass around the congested downtown when the tunnel, with its four lanes, was finally completed in 1963. Likewise, the city commenced construction of the two

---

[23] Maurício de A. Abreu, *Evolução urbana do Rio de Janeiro* (Rio de Janeiro: Jorge Zahar Editor, 1987), 117, 127–29. Doxiadis, *Guanabara*, 97.

Rebouças tunnels in 1962. When completed in 1967, these added six rapid lanes, serviced by a large, elevated highway, delivering motorists from the southern suburbs to the west end of Vargas Avenue. Most significantly, the city completed the eight-lane Aterro Highway in 1965 on landfill from Santo Antonio Hill regrade. The city also continued to widen existing streets, now at the expense of sidewalks, which were often narrowed by half. The outer margins of squares were chiseled away, and trees and streetlights, planted and installed a century before, were felled to make room for additional lanes.[24]

All this new asphalt did increase the city's transit capacity but only, due to many bottlenecks, in limited segments. First, improvements – widening old streets and creating entirely new roads and tunnels – in one place were of little use if they ran into old narrow streets in another. Second, the city's fleet of automobiles kept growing. If the city created new space, new drivers filled it. Improvements to the flow of traffic attracted more drivers. Already in 1946, Edgar Estrela had stated that "any solutions to transit are transitory." While the term *induced demand* was not yet in use, he already understood the concept. If drivers found roomy highways and available parking spaces, then more drivers came. Net flow increased, but so did frustration.[25]

For most city residents, especially those living distant from the center, the automobile effectively increased everyone's workday by periods measured in hours. Those who rode buses stuck amidst the cars complained of commutes that required ever earlier risings and consumed as many as four hours of their day. The commute also killed the long-enjoyed Brazilian tradition of going home each workday for lunch, the most significant meal of the day. In Rio, this practice was already under severe threat, and commuters grumbled at having to compete with other commuters and cabbies to get home for lunch and then back to work on time. In reality the city had four rush hour periods. New apartments near or in the downtown advertised lunch at home among their amenities. The urban planning firm of Doxiadis Associates reported in 1965 that the former traffic peak that had occurred every weekday during the noon hour had all but disappeared, essentially solving itself as commuters had given up, leaving officials only the morning and evening

---

[24] "Cidade estrangulada," *Revista da Semana*, Jun. 22, 1957, 38–42. *Quatro Rodas*, Jan. 1962, 20, 22.

[25] Estrela is cited in *Careta*, Jul. 6, 1946, 17. For a summary of infrastructure changes in this period, see Maurício de A. Abreu, *Evolução urbana do Rio de Janeiro*, 126–35.

commutes to sort out.[26] Traffic changed the nature of family life, traditions, and decisions that were not directly or spatially related to the street but which depended on the street nevertheless. Hoping to reduce traffic demand, the transit director's office even promoted the delivery of milk in disposable bags to eliminate the milkman's second go at his route each afternoon to pick up empty bottles.[27]

Rio's transit directors, who were political appointees, rarely had any training in urban planning, urban transit, or traffic engineering. One director had experience with airline traffic, and a few embarked on sincere personal studies of the subject after their appointment, but the key qualification for the appointment was thick skin. Few could hack it, and tenure in the position was all too frequently measured in months. Those who tried to occupy the position quietly were criticized by citizens for doing nothing. Those who were energetic were excoriated by the newspapers for making things worse. Transit directors were the city administration's most prominent lightning rod, the focus of the anger of the driving classes who accused them of incompetence, corruption, and worse moral failings. *A Esquerda* accused Zumalá Bonoso, the director in 1928, of corruption, incompetence, grandstanding, parading with strange woman in an official car during carnival, and nepotism.[28] Edgar Estrela, the longest-serving transit director, was popularly referred to as Edgar "The Big Mess" Estrela. Directors were pilloried in letters to the editor, mocked in cartoons, and sometimes threatened with violence. One angry resident in São Paulo wondered why nobody had had the courage to put a bullet in the current director, and a director in Rio reported that his car was in fact hit by gunfire after an unpopular measure. Editorials demanded the president remove the city's transit director, and it was common for the nation's highest office to overturn unpopular traffic policies and to invite the director to submit his resignation. Some directors were described as being "devoured" by the city's traffic. The directors had to excel at stress management, and contemporaries associated directors' nervous tics or early deaths with the strain and anxiety of the assignment.[29] After 1950, directors still paid lip service to safety and were sincere in their lamentations about auto-related deaths, but the

---

[26] *Correio da Manhã*, Dec. 17, 1950, 3; *Correio da Manhã*, Mar. 13, 1955, section 3, 7, and Apr. 24, 1957, section 1, 9; Richard Morse, *From Community to Metropolis: A Biography of São Paulo* (Gainesville: University of Florida Press, 1958), 283; *Quatro Rodas*, Jan. 1962, 20; Doxiadas, *Guanabara*, 99.

[27] Franco, *Eu no contramão*, 233.   [28] *A Esquerda*, Feb. 1, 1928, 1.

[29] *A Noite*, Sep. 16, 1952, 13; *A Noite*, Aug. 2, 1952, 3.

main official focus of the agency was to solve the problem of congestion. No director was ever fired over rising mortalities. In 1970, when the new director of transit in São Paulo was asked what his agency's priorities would be, he replied that "in first place is locomotion. After that, in eighth place, will be everything else."[30]

Non-motorists, of course, continued to make use of the street in various modes of mass transit, but the growing number of passenger cars increased congestion and travel times for everyone. Streetcars remained popular through the 1940s and 1950s even while the most-traveled routes were being eliminated in part due to the complaints of motorists who erroneously branded them as congestion's major causes. Trains expanded service to bring workers into the city center from the northern suburbs; however, within the city and in the wealthier beach suburbs, rail transit essentially disappeared,[31] and the bus became the primary mode of mass transit.

As with streetcars, Rio's buses cannot be strictly categorized as public transportation, for all such services were owned and operated by private concessions. The city's streetcar lines were never owned by more than a handful of companies who divided the city into rational areas of service that did not much overlap. When the lines were consolidated under the Brazilian Traction, Light and Power Company, a Canadian-held entity commonly referred to as the Light, the centralized system remained efficient, but it struggled with maintenance issues as the city held down the price of fares to assuage working-class voters who sometimes rioted over fare increases. Streetcar fares in 1939 were the same as they had been in 1907, despite general inflation.[32] Bus companies were allowed to charge higher fares, initially serving middle-class riders who saw buses as cleaner and faster than streetcars. Significantly, distinct from streetcar companies, bus concessionaires had lower initial investments for entry; they had neither to build nor maintain tracks and electrical systems. Bus owners, like car owners, used the expanding realm of smooth asphalt pavements as a free-access commons.

The city's first bus concession was requested in 1904 by the G. Frankel Company that demanded a twenty-year exclusive right to Avenida

---

[30] *Veja*, Jan. 28, 1970, 30.
[31] The one exception was in hilly, prosperous Santa Teresa where the vintage yellow trams still serve the needs of local residents and tourists.
[32] *Atas da Comissão de Transporte Coletivo* (Rio de Janeiro: Prefeitura do Distrito Federal, 1940), 204.

Central, then under construction. The company promised to run a bus, equipped with rubber tires and seating for twenty, every three minutes – a service that pledged to be "rapid, comfortable, and satisfactory."[33] The concession seems to have been granted, but the service did not long persist. A second concession served a temporary need to carry fair-goers from downtown to the 1908 National Exhibition held in Urca. In fact, buses were not much seen on Rio's streets until the late 1920s. In 1922, there were only seven buses in the entire city.[34]

Competition by a growing number of private bus concessions expanded after 1930. By 1939, there were 755 buses, including those in the suburbs, owned and operated by 39 different entities. The largest, owned by the Light, ran 149 buses, but the average number per company was about 20. The same organized criminals who ran the city's illegal lottery also owned some of the new bus companies.[35] In 1937, after a major two-year study of the issue, the Commission for Collective Transit, appointed by Mayor Henrique Dodsworth, concluded that the private system of bus concessions was a disaster. Streetcars still carried the largest share of Rio's 500 million transit passengers. Buses only carried 70 million, but the report fingered them as the primary cause of the city's growing congestion and increasing commute times. With little central planning or coordination, buses devolved into a confusion of competing, overlapping, and shifting routes. Some bus companies changed routes weekly to increase ridership, and some constantly changed their fares, both of which left riders confused and angry.[36] The Commission argued that public transit should be considered a natural monopoly, like power or water, and hence required, for efficiency's sake, state ownership or strict regulation. It held up Buenos Aires, which in 1938 had centralized street-cars, trains, and buses into a single entity, as a model of a more effective, rational system, and one in which profitable lines could subsidize the less profitable routes reaching into new suburbs.[37] Vargas favored centraliza-tion in many forms, but during World War II, traffic tapered to almost

---

[33] G. Frankel & Cia to Lauro Muller, Dec. 10, 1904, Ministro da Indústria, Viação e Obras Públicas Comissão Construtora da Avenida Central, 4/70–4, ANRJ.

[34] Noronha Santos, *Meios de transporte*, vol. 2, 204.

[35] C. A. Sylvester, "Adendo ao memorial apresentado pela The Rio de Janeiro Tranway, Light, and Power Co.," Feb. 14, 1939, in *Comissão Transportes Coletivos*, appendix 9, 383; the table is dated Aug. 12, 1940.

[36] *Atas da Comissão de Transporte Coletivo* (Rio de Janeiro: Prefeitura do Distrito Federal, 1940), 332.

[37] *Atas da Comissão de Transporte Coletivo*, 8–9, 11, 13, 151, 204–05.

nothing due to gas rationing, making congestion a non-issue. With Vargas deposed in 1945, liberal economic policies dominated policy debates, and the now rapidly growing mass transit in Rio remained private and became increasingly non-functional in contrast to São Paulo, which purchased and consolidated all mass transit under a single, municipal entity.

And then, in Rio, mass transit only got worse. The city's adaptable residents, during the war, had begun to use private cars as an informal transit system. Private drivers in private cars packed five or more fare-paying passengers into the city, meeting the needs of transit while earning an informal income. São Paulo abolished the practice after the war,[38] but it was formalized in Rio, and the vehicles, now essentially micro-buses whose chassis were built specifically for this end in Brazil, came to be called *lotações*.[39] They grew exponentially. By 1961, the Light still ran 648 streetcars, and buses had increased to 1,541, operated by 65 separate companies, but *lotações* officially numbered 2,285. The large majority of them belonged to single, owner-operators. And there were certainly more than the official numbers reported. In a traffic census of 1958, streetcars made 15 percent of all trips but carried 36 percent of all riders. Buses made 40 percent of the trips carrying 42 percent of the riders. And *lotações* made 45 percent of all the city's transit trips but, with an average load of 19 passengers, carried only 22 percent of the city's ridership. Streetcars, buses, and *lotações* often competed for the same customers, and the supply of seats came to exceed the demand for transit. Hence, unregulated buses and *lotações*, running on most of the same routes, raced each other empty trying to capture the next fare. Residents complained about the aggressive driving, but also about how the many, prowling, empty vehicles added unnecessarily to the street's congestion and pollution.[40]

But it was still automobiles that consumed most of the city's public spaces. By 1962, when bus numbers had climbed to 2,230, the number of cars and trucks in the city had reached 146,260.[41] José Carlos Mello, who would later become the federal Secretary of Transportation, observed that in Brazil's cities, as cars and their politically powerful drivers demanded more urban space, officials often restricted public transportation, which

---

[38] See Vasconcelos, *Circular é preciso*, 70.   [39] *Quatro Rodas*, Dec. 1962, 56.

[40] Luís Ribeiro Soares, O *problema do tráfego e o transporte de passageiros* (Rio de Janeiro: Presidência da República, Conselho Nacional de Pesquisas, Instituto de Pesquisas Rodoviárias, 1962), 13, 15.

[41] Doxiadis, *Guanabara*, table 1, 9.

attracted more *lotações* and more cars. He estimated that Rio had more automobiles per bus than many of the world's major cities, which confirmed that public transit was relatively underserved and explained why Rio's traffic jammed up so frequently. The inefficient mix of vehicles caused the average speed of traffic in Rio to fall below 10 kilometers per hour. Cars, he argued, were the least efficient users of the city's scarce space, and they made futile any investment in more efficient forms, such as the bus, which could carry 160 times more people in the same space. *Lotações* and buses received most of the blame, but automobiles were the grittiest sand in the city's gears.[42] Later, in the 1960s and 1970s, the city worked to reduce both the number of buses and downtown stops and stations, reducing bus lines on Avenida Vargas from thirty-one to eighteen. Cars, on the other hand, met no such restrictions.[43]

INDISPENSABLE FREE PARKING

Transit directors had long worked to identify and eliminate the frictions to automotive movement (narrow streets, trees, pedestrians, mules, handcarts, streetcars) but even by the mid-1920s, some observed that the car's greatest obstacle was already itself, especially when parked. Parking may seem the most prosaic of street topics, but it is spatially the central issue, and not just because parked cars collectively consumed more space than did moving cars, nor because they came to form a major cause of arterial narrowing. Free parking on the commons made the car spatially possible and its ownership economically viable. Driving on streets had precedents reaching back to ancient times. Parking, the storage of a private vehicle on public space, had been universally prohibited. Until the late 1920s, drivers who parked their cars on the streets were cited not with the violation of illegal parking but with abandonment, for that is how the practice was understood.[44] The revolution in car storage on the public street was one of the automobile's chief historical breaks with the street's long past, and the invention of modern parking was as important as the internal combustion engine to the automobile's ultimate success.

---

[42] José Carlos Mello, *Planejamento dos transportes urbanos* (Rio de Janeiro: Editora Campus, 1981), 10, 12, 17.

[43] Américo Freire, *Guerra de posições na metrópole. A prefeitura e as empresas de ônibus no Rio de Janeiro (1906–1948)* (Rio de Janeiro: Fundação Getúlio Vargas, 2001), 53. São Paulo had made similar moves to reduce public transit; see Altieri, *Variações sobre o trânsito paulistano,* 67.

[44] *Correio da Manhã,* Jan. 7, 1928, 9.

Before the automobile, the storage of any private property on the street was illegal, for it was anathema to the whole idea of the street as common.[45] The exceptions proved the rule. The city permitted carts and wagons to stop briefly on the streets to deliver their wares, just as cabbies and carriages could briefly stop to load and unload passengers. The city allowed builders to store construction materials, such as lumber, bricks, and lime, on the street, but again only for brief, stated periods. Cabbies, whether their vehicles were driven by horse power or internal combustion, paid a tax for the right to station (*estacionar*) their vehicles at designated taxi stands to await customers, but they were not allowed to "abandon" them at the stand. All stationary vehicles on the street had to be tended.[46] The first relaxation of this policy came in 1917 when the city granted cabbies the right to leave their cabs unattended at the assigned taxi stands for thirty minutes during the lunch hour, if they shut off the motor, a privilege won only after the chauffeurs' union had gone on strike, crippling the city's traffic.[47]

William Phelps Eno, the pioneer of urban traffic control in the United States, defined a "live vehicle" as not one that was moving or had its motor running, but "one whose driver is present and prepared to move" it. A "dead vehicle" was not a car that would not start but "one whose driver is absent or unprepared to move" it. It was an important distinction, and well into the 1920s it is difficult to find any car or truck parked on the street in Rio without someone at the wheel or leaning on the fender to monitor it. In Portuguese, one "stationed" a live vehicle; in English, one "stood" the vehicle. Today's parked vehicle was yesterday's "dead" vehicle. And "dead," parked automobiles remained illegal for three decades in Rio.[48]

In pre-automotive Rio, carriages and horses were stored inside homes, typically in stables on the ground floor. If one had no private stable, one rented space in an urban stable, of which there were many.[49] Similarly,

---

[45] "Veículos," 1881–1890, AGCRJ, 373, 58-1-3; "Código de Posturas," in *Diário de Notícias*, Feb. 15, 1890, 2 and Feb. 16, 1890, 4; see also Seabra Junior, *Accidentes de automóveis*, 118.

[46] *Jornal do Brasil*, Jan. 4, 1925, 14.   [47] *Auto Federal*, Feb. 15, 1917, 15.

[48] William Phelps Eno, *The Story of Highway Traffic Control, 1899–1939* (n.p.: The Eno Foundation for Highway Traffic Control, Inc., 1939), 288.

[49] Louis Léger Vauthier, *Um engenheiro Frances no Brasil*, vol. 2, 2nd edn., ed. Gilberto Freyre (Rio de Janeiro: José Olýmpio, 1960), 822–84. Jean Baptiste Debret, *Viagem pitoresca e histórica ao Brasil*, Tomo 1, vol. 1 (São Paulo: Editora da Universidade de São Paulo, 1978), illustration 14, sketched a typical, ground-floor stable in a Rio home.

during the car's first decades, private automobilists had to store their automobile either in their own garage, which is what they renamed their stable now that it stored a modern machine, or on the premises of a private automotive garage, a branch of business that expanded in Rio from 14 commercial garages in 1908 to 124 in 1913, a number of them former stables. Garages, which were located centrally downtown but also in the southern suburbs, advertised their new spaces for automobile storage offering services such as repairs, refueling, and lubrication. By the early 1920s, a couple of private garages had capacities that exceeded 150 cars.[50] If you owned a car, you needed a garage, for the street was not a place you could keep it, even temporarily.

By the second decade, a car, even with fuel and maintenance, was a considerably cheaper form of transportation than a carriage: one did not have to maintain live animals nor hire multiple employees to care for, maintain, and store the car as one did the carriage and its accessories. Horses in particular were a constant cost in feed and veterinary fees. An unused car imposed few ongoing costs. This cheapness explains a good deal of the automobile's growth, outstripping the number of carriages within a decade. However, by the mid to late 1920s in Brazil, cars became even cheaper in two respects. First, in labor, because by this time cars had become not only more reliable but easier to operate; hence car owners began to drive their vehicles themselves rather than hiring a chauffeur, which was a substantial savings. Before this, chauffeurs had been de rigueur, an imitation of prior practice with carriages. Even ignoring the complex setup of preparing a carriage for movement, a car was far easier to operate than a carriage, and nearly anyone could do it, including women as car makers began to enthusiastically advertise.

But there remained a substantial barrier to self-driving. If you could not park, that is, store your private "dead" vehicle on the public street, even for a few minutes to make a purchase, let alone to put in a day's work at the office, you had to have a driver who could take you to your destination and then return your car to its legitimate garage, cruise around the streets until it was time to pick you up, or find a space curbside and tend the car dutifully. Hence, the full revolution in automobility came only with the birth of free parking. In Brazil, as elsewhere, there came a point when one was allowed, even while it was still technically illegal, to store one's car on the public domain at no cost. As a result, cars became private objects

---

[50] *Fon Fon*, Jun. 6, 1908; *Revista de Automóveis*, Oct. 1911, 22; *Auto Sport*, Dec. 1926. See also Noronha Santos, *Meios de transporte no Rio de Janeiro*, vol. 2, 97.

exempt from spatial rents. Car owners no longer needed a driver to drop them off or pick them up, but could now drive their own car to work each day and leave it unattended on public streets or squares; when they returned home, rather than hire a stable or garage, they could again store their car overnight out in front of their home, all without price. Hence, a central spatial feature in the rise of automobility was the conversion of much of the public commons into free lots for rotating private storage. This put the car within economic reach of many more drivers.

Now that one was permitted to store a vehicle on the public street for free, the automobile had more right to sit immobile on the public commons than did a pedestrian. It is hard to identify exactly when this change took place. The transition came later in Brazil than in the United States. Karl Miller, reporting from Rio in 1923, noted that in Brazil, as in much of Latin America, custom still demanded that car owners employ a chauffeur. Miller's opinion was that this was an inheritance from Brazil's aristocratic and slavocratic past, that "gentlemen don't work, don't put their hands to the wheel any more than the reigns of a carriage. Driving a car was work, the task of laborers." He had forgotten that things had not been so different in the US just a few years before. But he also noted the beginnings of unauthorized free parking, explaining that while it was illegal to leave a car "standing at the curb without anybody in it," the ordinance was becoming less seldom enforced. As free street parking became more popular, it did not become legal. In fact, into the 1930s, elite drivers, who could still afford a chauffeur and a private garage, glowered at the now mobile middle classes who, demonstrating the vulgarity of their status, parked not one but sometimes two cars in front of their homes, what the elite disparaged as "garages in the middle of the street."[51]

Yet, even wealthy car owners, given the chance, preferred to park for free on the street than pay for a space that might not be convenient to their origin or destination. Hence, already by the mid-1930s, the majority parked on the street. The garaging business declined after a couple decades of growth. It got to the point that almost nobody paid for parking, at home or at work, a reality that persisted even as free parking became

---

[51] Karl W. Miller, *South America: Continent of Opportunities. Selected Articles from Detroit News' South American Correspondence* (Detroit, MI: Evening News Association, 1925), 44, 50; Jeferson Selbach, *Muito além da praça José Bonifácio: as elites e os "outsiders" em Cachoeira do Sul, pela voz do Jornal do Povo, 1930–1945*, 2nd edn. (São Luis: Universidade Federal do Maranhão, 2010), 327.

scarce relative to growing demand. In the late 1970s, even though the city of São Paulo had begun to charge for some on-street parking with their so-called blue zones, a study found that still only 4.4 percent of the city's drivers paid for parking. At home, one-third of drivers parked in a private driveway, carport, or garage attached to their house or apartment. The remaining two-thirds parked for free on the street. And nearly everyone parked at no personal cost while at work or while shopping, confirming that Brazil too fit within an irony pointed out by Wolfgang Zuckermann that "the motorcar, superstar of the capitalist system, expects to live rent-free."[52]

The street then became a space occupied by machines almost from wall to wall, a development as important as driving in displacing former street behaviors. In 1965, the Doxiadis plan for Rio estimated that each of the city's cars needed 25 square meters to park, although modern estimates raise that unit closer to 30 square meters. Cars and motorists were space hungry indeed: many *favela* homes in the same decade occupied all of 4.5 total square meters. Free parking gave drivers substantial, largely unfettered access to public space in a city where the poorest struggled just to secure a small space in which their bodies could lie down to sleep. The middle classes, of course, had more space, but even in Copacabana, a typical indoor parking space was larger than many Copacabana living rooms. Doxiadis estimated that if each of the 1,800 families living on a typical block in Copacabana owned just one car, they would collectively consume a space more than twice the size of the whole block, an unsustainable projection without the substantial construction of more multi-level parking structures.[53] Some estimated that there were more cars in the city than there was asphalt to serve them.[54]

The solution was to park in any space to which a car could gain access. Free car storage began on the street itself, particularly along busy thoroughfares and around public squares. Eventually, every curb was fair game. There were no meters, no time limits, and for many years no "no parking" signs. However, in the downtown and in neighborhoods such as Copacabana, there was not enough curbing to meet the need. By 1950, double and sometimes triple parking became the norm, on one or both sides of the street. Photos of the period, such as of Primeiro de Março

[52] Vasconcelos, *Circular é preciso*, 202; Wolfgang Zuckermann, *The End of the Road: From World Car Crisis to Sustainable Transportation* (New York, NY: Chelsea Green, 1991), 124.
[53] Doxiadis, *Guanabara*, 180, 304.   [54] *Quatro Rodas*, Oct. 1965, 52.

Street, formerly Rio's main commercial thoroughfare, show cars on one side of the street backed up to the curb (sometimes with rear wheels on the sidewalk) so their trunks project over the sidewalk and their hoods into the traffic. Directly in front of these, on the same side of the street, a row of cars is parked parallel with the street. Then, on the other side of the street, the parallel parking was doubled, thus reducing a street with a five-lane capacity down to one or two. On many streets, it appears as if drivers felt at liberty to park anywhere as long as they did not block the streetcar rails, although even here they took liberties.[55] Various attempts were made to eliminate curb parking on the city's busiest streets, but without much success, for taking away free, convenient parking was one of the surest ways for a transit director to suffer the public's wrath.

When on-street parking proved inadequate, drivers took to other public spaces, including the sidewalks, courtyards, and the city's many squares. The 1950s' large, brooding cars formed tightly arranged agglomerations on the sidewalks, which reduced pedestrian traffic to one lane or eliminated passage entirely. In one bird's-eye photo of Nilo Peçanha Avenue, more pedestrians walk in the busy street than on the sidewalk where cars park tightly against building walls. Drivers filled gutters with rubble to make it possible for their low-clearance American vehicles to safely climb the curbs. In the gardens behind the National Library, drivers removed the park benches, which took up space they wanted for parking, and used the disassembled planks as ramps to surmount tall granite curbs.[56] Citizens complained of

> fat, wealthy drivers who hung about their offices unconcerned. There isn't a corner of the city left on which you will not find some late model hedging every path, lining all the streets, one after the other, robbing from the little man on foot, the eternal sufferer, the right to cross the street, to move, to flee from the car's fury for the sidewalk's refuge that the pedestrian can no longer use.[57]

One letter writer claimed he had traveled in more than thirty-two nations around the world, but only Brazil permitted drivers to park their cars on the public sidewalks, a practice he and others referred to as the "favelazation of the sidewalks." The practice remained illegal, yet unenforced.[58]

---

55 This photograph was exhibited in the Museu do Bonde in Santa Teresa in October 2010 without attribution. See also *Revista de Automóveis*, May 1954, 20–22.
56 *Revista de Automóveis*, May 1954, 20–22; *Jornal do Brasil*, Dec. 3, 1966, 6.
57 *O Cantagalo*, Apr. 16, 1950, 3.
58 "Carros na calçada," *Jornal do Brasil*, cited in Franco, *Eu na contramão*, 646; see also 647, 649; Valter Casseb, et al. *Um estudo sobre os problemas de estacionamento*

Officials also looked the other way when cars began parking on down-town squares, an invasion that appears to have begun in the late 1920s and that carried on uninterrupted and unchallenged for half a century. Squares had been the city's quintessential civic and social spaces, places that seemed to survive the automobile's incursions into the streets and avenues during the first decades of the century. But as the supply of on-street parking spaces could not meet demand, drivers parked their cars not just on small, unimportant, and peripheral squares, but on nearly all of them. And they did not merely occupy portions of the city's squares; they occupied them in their entirety. In the early 1950s, the press, out of curiosity more than apparent anger, published two-page photo spreads documenting car yards on what used to be public squares. The Largo da Carioca, which had been the site of famous public fountains, streetcar traffic, and the purposeful movement of pedestrian crowds, had become a sea of immobile machines. Praça XV, the former gathering space for laundresses at work and businessmen at leisure, now glinted bumper to bumper with bodies of chrome and glass. If not torn down, many sur-rounding churchyards, such as those of Santa Luzia, São Francisco de Paula, Candelaria, Rosário and others became parking lots, too.[59] The largest space in which to store a car was the Castelo Esplanade, and it was here that the word *estacionar* (to station or park) was first used in its modern sense in Rio in 1928. The papers reported on the immediate popularity of the ground cleared by the removal of Castelo Hill for parking. Since the "problem that torments those who use cars is that of parking on the central streets of the city while they do their shopping, run their errands, or go to the theater or cinema," Castelo's new bare ground was now the best place "to *leave* one's car parked."[60]

A variety of strategies emerged to ration the scarce parking spaces, some based on political power and others on the creativity of the infor-mal economy. The truly privileged parkers were those whose position provided them official cars. Even before modern parking became com-mon, official cars could station themselves for as long as they liked.

de veículos (São Paulo: Companhia de Engenharia de Tráfego, 1979), 11; *Correio da Manhã*, Jan. 10, 1970, 7; also Apr. 25, 1970 and May 28, 1970.

[59] "Onde estacionar 120,000 veículos?" *Revista da Semana*, Jun. 7, 1952, 15–22; 1950s; *Revista Municipal de Engenharia*, Oct. 12, 1955, 166. For Santa Rita, see the want ads in *Jornal do Brasil*, Aug. 17, 1954, 20. The exceptions appear to have been República and Tiradentes. Largo da Carioca was a parking lot by 1941, if not earlier.

[60] *Jornal do Brasil*, Mar. 1, 1928, 18; *Jornal do Brasil*, Jan. 31, 1929, emphasis mine. See also *Jornal do Brasil*, Jan. 10, 1929, 5.

In time, with the right license plate, one could leave one's official car anywhere on the street. The number of official cars ballooned to more than 4,000 by 1955, which did not include the numerous cars owned by the military that had the same privileges. There was a vibrant business in creating fake, official car plates, and one magazine gave instructions on how to do it, including the use of indecipherable acronyms and bogus coats of arms, which they tested on Rio's streets to great success.[61] But since there was increasingly no place to park in a first-come, first-served system, the strategy from at least 1950 was to carve out individual spaces or entire zones that were marked as exclusive for government-issued vehicles. Large areas, especially surrounding the House and the Senate, government ministries, police stations, medical posts, and others, had "no parking" signs placed around them with small signs beneath identifying who could park there. Each agency employed a local traffic cop or even its own employees to enforce the exclusions.

In addition to state employees, private individuals, businesses, and corporations followed suit seeking official concessions to have their own "no parking" signs posted in front of their shops and corporate offices, which the city granted despite the contrary dictates of the National Transit Code. Álvaro Altieri documented the number and variety of "no parking" signs in São Paulo, which included, in addition to spaces reserved for the Municipal Council and the Palace of Justice, entire curbs reserved for airlines (Panair and VASP), newspapers (*O Estado*), radio stations (Rádio Excelsior and Rádio América), and everyday businesses. In Rio, by the late 1960s, privately reserved parking spaces numbered 2,293, accounting for 32 percent of all reserved spaces. Government agencies had merely turned one form of public property into another; private businesses, however, had essentially converted public street space into private property. In all, "no parking" signs accounted for more than half of all the traffic signs in the city, suggesting that a major part of the production of street space was less about traffic flow than it was about automobile storage.[62]

On the non-elite end of car storage's spatial demands, parking created a new class of street workers: the parking guard. This "new profession"

---

[61] Seabra Junior, *Accidentes de automóveis*, 139; *Revista de Automóveis*, Apr. 1955, 40; *Quatro Rodas*, Oct. 1964, 50–53.
[62] Altieri, *Variações sobre o trânsito paulistano*, 19–21, 23; *Quatro Rodas*, Sep. 1968, 52–53. "No parking" signs made up more than half of New York City's signage as well; Barnes, *Man with the Red and Green Eyes*, 213.

was first observed in 1929 as modern parking came into its own. Without a chauffeur to watch over one's car, to make sure that it or its parts were not stolen, "when one returns to the location where one left his car, the driver will meet a smiling man or youth who will declare that with the greatest care he has watched over your vehicle," inevitably with his hand out. The profession expanded, and each parking guard, made up initially of mostly the elderly and disabled, staked out, in perpetuity, a strip of curb or parcel in a square that might be passed down to heirs or friends. The guards, who could be responsible for hundreds of cars during the day, came to wear caps and uniforms, which though often threadbare and unmatched, gave parking guards the semblance of officialdom. With the growth in parking, by 1960, the occupation employed more than 1,000 men in downtown Rio. There were no set fees for their service, and payment was notionally voluntary, offered in the form of tips. To fail to compensate them involved some risk to property, but guards complained with frequency that drivers often stiffed them.[63]

The parking guard's most important collective role was not theft prevention but the provision and expansion of parking itself. His main task was to create space by juggling cars as if they were pieces in a large puzzle. Drivers did not simply place their car under the guard's care – they turned the keys over to him. The guards then jockeyed cars around to cram in as many as possible. For those who manned parking on the curbs, they arranged cars tightly, bumper to bumper and door to door, often three deep in parallel rows and taking the sidewalk if at all possible. Those on squares and the Castelo Esplanade packed cars into tight groups, sometimes six and seven cars deep. The proficient compression of parked cars was remarkable, and all this jockeying reduced the usual 25 square meters to park a car in the city, which included space to access the parking stall, to the car's actual dimension of about 9 square meters and hence increased the city's parking capacity by a significant factor. In 1961, when police suggested prohibiting the entrusting of keys to guards due to accusations of joy riding, accidents, and theft, guards resisted because if they could not pack the cars, the number of customers they could serve decreased, as did their wages – "this diminishes the number of cars in my parking and hence means less money," as Hermogéneo Francisco, a sixty-five-year-old guard, put it. Motorists

---

[63] *Jornal do Brasil*, Jan. 10, 1929, 5; *Correio da Manhã*, Apr. 19, 1961, section 1, 3. On car theft, see *Vida Policial*, Jul. 17, 1926; "É fácil roubar automóveis," *Revista de Automóveis*, Mar. 1955.

also defied the change, stating emphatically that they had the right to entrust their keys and their cars, as any private property, to whomever they pleased.

A cartoon published in the mid-1950s depicted a motorist arriving at his downtown destination in a large car. Exiting the vehicle, he expertly folds the car's body in on itself and then places it neatly inside his briefcase. The parking guards could not perform that kind of magic, but they, more than any official policy, made it possible for more motorists to find a place to come to rest. The growth in moving cars was dependent on the growth of parking spaces in both the downtown and middle-class residential areas. The tips motorists paid, while appearing ostensibly for protection (and advertised as such by the guards) in actuality were rents for storage. The rent became increasingly valuable and the profession more competitive. In later years, as demand for parking continued to rise, this informal sector of the urban economy became increasingly contested. Competing parking providers engaged in threats and even killings to capture and control profitable parking lots, not unlike turf wars over drug territory.[64]

By mid-century, parking saturation seemed almost total, which furthered the automobile's spatial conquest and destruction of traditional street utilities. In an extensive urban planning study completed in 1977, researchers at the Center for Environmental Structure at Berkeley found that saturation was not necessary for the death of the street; if a city had just 9 percent of its unbuilt spaces occupied by parked cars, about thirty cars per acre, regardless of traffic, the street's role as public space began to fail. The authors surmised that when parking density surpassed this limit "people experience the feeling that there are too many cars ... that the environment is no longer 'theirs,' that they have no right to be there, that it is not a place for people, ... that social communion is no longer permitted or encouraged." While the study noted that that 9 percent figure was tentative, there seemed to be remarkable agreement across many places, and the authors concluded that it was among the most important patterns they had found and, hence, had "colossal implications."[65] Whether or not

[64] Jorge Mourão, "Estará bem guardada o seu carro," *Revista de Automóveis*, Aug. 1954, 16; *Correio da Manhã*, Apr. 19, 1961, section 1, 3; *Revista da Semana*, Jan. 10, 1949. Claudio Emmanuel, "Guardador de automóveis é morto com vários no Centro de Niterói," *O Fluminense*, Apr. 15, 2011. http://jornal.ofluminense.com.br/editorias/poli cia/guardador-de-automoveis-e-morto-no-centro-de-niteroi (accessed Jun. 24, 2013).

[65] Christopher Alexander, Sara Ishikawa, and Murray Silverstein, *A Pattern Language: Towns, Buildings, Construction* (New York, NY: Oxford University Press, 1977), 121–23.

Cariocas responded to parking density as did Europeans and North Americans, Rio's downtown streets experienced densities well beyond 9 percent even before the 1930s, and in some locations, such as public squares and busy commercial streets, parked cars came to effectively overlay most of the bare ground. With moving cars occupying often more than half the downtown street's space, and parked cars consuming much of the rest, street life had to disappear for lack of habitat.

MILITARY INSURGENCIES AGAINST TRAFFIC

Official solutions to the problem of parking were never as creative as those of the parking guards. Because the priority remained car flow, transit directors in fact attacked parking as one of flow's major obstacles. Edgar Estrela stated a common doctrine of traffic engineers dating from the late 1920s when he contended that "circulation is in the interest of everyone; parking is the convenience of the few."[66] They failed to see flow and storage as the equal spatial foundations on which automobility stood. Motorists, on the other hand, understood it clearly and were hence sensitive to and vehement about changes to either component, but particularly parking. Heitor Muniz's complaint about the inability to finding parking raised the existential stakes for automobility. Driving was all well and good, he said, but "in the end, drivers cannot be driving around the entire day; they need to be able to stop, at some point, somewhere."[67]

When the military ousted Vargas from office in 1946, President Eurico Gaspar Dutra replaced Edgar Estrela with a succession of new transit directors who proved ineffectual. In March 1950, Dutra appointed Major Geraldo de Menezes Côrtes, who was credited with introducing the transit office to the field of traffic engineering.[68] He began to formulate policies related to parking; his main objective was to get it out of flow's way. He ordered parking meters for all downtown parking spaces and banned parking along the curbs of twelve main thoroughfares.[69] He attacked double and triple parking in particular and boldly reclaimed many of the privileged parking spaces reserved by government agencies and private

---

[66] *A Noite*, Sep. 16, 1952, 13. US engineers also attacked parking as an obstacle to flow; see Norton, *Fighting Traffic*, 139–41.

[67] *A Noite*, Aug. 2, 1952, 3.

[68] Geraldo de Menezes Côrtes, "Precisamos de um departamento municipal de engenharia do tráfego," *Revista de Automóveis*, Oct. 1954.

[69] "Atenção, Motoristas e Pedestres!," *A Noite*, Oct. 28, 1950, 8.

businesses.[70] In December 1950, towing, threats to official parking, and particularly a controversial new schedule for cab fares resulted in presidential decree that nullified Menezes Côrtes' least popular policies and temporarily dismissed him from office.[71] He was reinstated in February, which emboldened him, but that just got him into more trouble. He barred parking around Tiradentes Palace, the exclusive parking lot of members of the National Assembly, and when he deflated the tires of one offending senator, the issue came to a head.[72] Menezes Côrtes was fired by promotion, elevated to Lieutenant Colonel. His resignation letter defended his policies and addressed his critics. It had been a year and half of "terrible and punishing battles," having been personally and violently attacked from every side by "intrigue, backwardness, incompetence, and egotism." He concluded that he stepped down with a "clear conscience, having done all possible with his limited powers," but stated emphatically that he had no desire whatsoever "to be reappointed to this sacrificial post."[73] None of his many successors over the next fifteen years, including Edgar Estrela who Vargas reappointed, dared follow his ambitious agenda. Disorder, congestion, and unregulated parking returned to their normal, chaotic state.

Only after the 1964 military coup would the city again see someone with Menezes Côrtes' audacity. The military government believed they had the technical and moral attributes to solve Brazil's political and economic problems, as they saw them, and why then not traffic, too. Immediately, they appointed a string of generals as Rio's transit directors, indicating traffic's priority. However, the brief tenures of the army generals who served before 1970 suggest that if the job was not technically over their heads, it was militarily beneath their rank. When the public accused General Hildebrando of hiding in the transit director's office and not taking the fight to the street, he responded with emphasis that he was not a common traffic cop. When General Pinto Campos stepped down, he admitted that the stress of the office had caused him to lose 6 kilos just during his short, few-week tenure. And when a disabled journalist asked Transit Director General Gomide impertinent questions about the worsening state of the traffic, the general pummeled the reporter with his

---

[70] *A Noite*, Apr. 28, 1950, 2; *A Noite*, Jul. 3, 1950, 3. "O estacionamento de automóveis," *A Noite*, Jul. 21, 1950, 1, 6; Umberto Peregrino, "Suave Violência," *A Noite*, Jul. 4, 1950, 3.

[71] *A Noite*, Dec. 24, 1950, 8; *A Noite*, Feb. 8, 1951, 3.

[72] *A Noite*, Jul. 28, 1951, 2; *A Noite*, Oct. 5, 1951, 2.   [73] *A Noite*, Oct. 20, 1951, 12.

fists.[74] No general lasted more than a few months. So, the regime looked down the military ranks and appointed two colonels who had some staying power: Américo Fontenelle from the air force and Celso Franco from the navy.[75] Both were still two full ranks above Menezes Côrtes at his appointment the previous decade, suggesting that imposing order and discipline on Rio's traffic remained an official priority despite many high-ranking military officers having decamped to the capital at Brasília to administer the nation.

Francisco Américo Fontenelle had a notorious tenure as Rio's transit director, which began in May of 1964, just weeks after the military coup. He was a full partisan of the military's takeover of the national government, and not merely from the sidelines. As the coup unfolded on April 1, he, in civilian clothing, stood directly behind soldiers lined up to defend Guanabara Palace from any counter-revolutionary action. It was not coincidental that behind him on the palace steps stood Governor Carlos Lacerda of the state of Guanabara (the former Federal District) and future Governor Roberto Costa de Abreu Sodré of São Paulo, the two men who each in turn would hire Fontenelle to lead their cities' transit departments.[76] He never towed the hard line of some of his co-militarists, and he verbally supported student protests against the new government, of which his daughter was a part, and which was their democratic right, as he saw it. He had a soft spot for well-intentioned idealism and asked his opponents if that did not, in fact, prove he was not a fascist. He would later admit his regrets that some of the ideals of the "revolution of 1964" had suffered degradation.[77]

In Fontenelle's eighteen months as Rio's transit director, it is probable that he made greater changes in the areas of traffic control, parking reform, pedestrian safety, and law enforcement than all his combined predecessors. He even secured, when Congress refused to fund him, an independent source of income for his department, something directors had sought unsuccessfully since the 1930s. Within a few months of his appointment, he was the most debated and profaned individual in all of Brazil, and his exploits were reported in American and European

---

[74] *Jornal do Brasil*, May 23, 1965, 12; Franco, *Eu na contramão*, 184; *Quatro Rodas*, Dec. 1965, 10.

[75] Technically, Franco's rank was that of Captain of Sea and War, the equivalent of colonel in other armed forces.

[76] A photo of Fontenelle standing guard at the palace was published on the coup's tenth anniversary in *Veja*, Apr. 3, 1974, 53.

[77] "Êste homem é louco?" *Realidade*, May 1967, 151.

newspapers. He was known as Colonel Fon Fon (Honk Honk) – disparagingly by his opponents, and fondly by his supporters. Even Henry Barnes, New York City's brashly innovative and plain-spoken traffic director, weighed in on Fontenelle's work, stating, maybe with a bit of envy, that such drastic measures could only be accomplished in a dictatorship.[78]

Fontenelle, whose posture made him stand taller than his actual height and whose gray, crew-cropped hair made him look more mature than his forty-four years, was described as a stern but soft-spoken man, deliberate, meticulous, and dogged in the pursuit of efficiency and order. One reporter remarked that Fontenelle had at least one advantage over his predecessor: the new director was so skinny that the stress of the job was not likely to cause weight loss. In more than his trim, upright figure, the father of five exuded military discipline: he rose early and retired early to bed, the same time every day, except Sundays when he slept in religiously until 10 AM; he had been a chain smoker, but now limited himself to a single pack a day on his cardiologist's recommendation after a mild heart attack at forty-two. He was a militant fan of the Botafogo Football Club, a trait he shared with some embarrassment, as if he considered it a rare weakness. He had a biting sense of humor, joked affably with his employees, and while highly defensive when his policies were criticized, seemed to be able to accept personal epithets and fulminations with a certain good humor. Some said his most notable physical characteristics were that he was in constant motion, he exhibited a mind for quick decisions, and he had remarkable physical energy. Lacerda, himself a former reforming firebrand journalist and doggedly ambitious reforming politician, would later say that "Fontenelle was one of the few people who combined the man of action with the formidable organizer."[79] Of his many critics, the accusations that seemed to hit the mark were that he respected his own opinions above all others and suffered the narrow focus of the technocrat who saw everything in the city in the context of traffic and parking. He enjoyed his reputation as a thorn in the conscience of the city's drivers. To the many who accused him of insanity, including a five-page feature article magazine entitled "Is This Man Crazy," he replied: "Of insanity, each of us bears a little, and each offers what they can."[80]

---

[78] "Harsh Cure Eases Rio's Traffic Ills," *New York Times*, Jul. 28, 1964; "Cars Illegally Parked in Rio Get 'Aired Out,'" *Gadsden Times*, Jan. 26, 1965.

[79] Cited in John W. F. Dulles, *Carlos Lacerda, Brazilian Crusader. Volume 2: The Years 1960–1977* (Austin, TX: University of Texas Press, 1996), 468–69.

[80] *Quatro Rodas*, Dec. 1952, 9–13; *Quatro Rodas*, Jul. 1966, 31–33; and "Êste homem é louco?" *Realidade*, May 1967, 147–52. "Violências e arbitrariedades de um Diretor de Trânsito," *Jornal do Brasil*, Jan. 22, 1966, caderno de automóveis, 1.

Fontenelle's résumé, however, was at best of only tangential utility. A former air force pilot who had flown anti-submarine missions over the Atlantic during World War II, he had studied aeronautics and air traffic control in the United States where he had become fluent in English, a smoker of American cigarettes, and a fan of western movies. Newspaper cartoonists in São Paulo typically depicted him as "Kid Confusion," a slim, hatless American cowboy, sporting six shooters, neckerchief, and spurred boots.[81] Yet, well before his appointment, he had already formed firm opinions about automotive traffic reforms in Rio. The idea that oriented much of his thinking was that before the law, all citizens, whether pedestrians or motorists, had equal rights to the street, and whether powerful or popular, deserved equal justice and equal penalties in the commission of misdemeanors or crimes. Equity before the law alone, he believed, would go far in getting the city moving.

For him, traffic in Rio was not merely a problem but a disaster that threatened the city's entire economic and cultural viability. Cars had socially and politically fragmented the city, ruined public spaces, and occupied the very sidewalks. In his eyes, the public street had become an unregulated racecourse for the reckless and private storage for the rich. Catastrophic conditions demanded drastic measures, and he took as his motto a phrase used widely by the US Army Corps of Engineers during World War II: "What is difficult, we will do immediately; the impossible will take a little longer."

Unique among recent transit directors, Fontenelle aspired to the office. That two of his relatives had been victims of auto-pedestrian accidents probably shaped his view of the pedestrian's right to the street and the need for safety reform, but he explained that it was his contrasting experiences with departments of motor vehicles in Brazil and the US that spoke to his personality as a fixer. In 1940, at the age of nineteen, when he applied for his driver's license in Rio, he was accosted by dozens of private agents who for a substantial fee steered candidates through forms and scheduled physical, mental, and driving examinations with all the right doctors, psychiatrists, and examiners, many of whom were in their pay. With their help, the paper handlers claimed the process would take only forty-five days. To Fontenelle, the method stank of corruption, and he asked why he could not acquire a license without the help of extra-official agents,

---

[81] See Acervo Folha, Folha de São Paulo, http://acervofolha.blogfolha.uol.com.br/2017/02/22/ha-50-anos-diretor-de-departamento-de-transito-murchou-pneus-de-carros-no-centro-de-sao-paulo/ (accessed Jan. 5, 2017).

especially since he had already passed his military driving exam. In the end, he went it alone, studying an old copy of the traffic code, and after sixty-two days of waiting, finally took his driving exam in his father's car. At the end of the test, his examiners told him to go the wrong way up a one-way street, as they were in a hurry to get back to the transit office, an order which he refused to obey. They gave him his license anyway. It was while standing in line to renew his registration, an annual ordeal that often took three trips and eight hours of waiting, that Fontenelle said to himself, "[S]omeday I am going to be transit director and fix this mess." When he was studying in the US in 1961, the local motor vehicle office provided him a single form, charged a small fee, gave him a driving exam on the spot, and told him his license would be ready the next day. He was sure they were being politely optimistic, but there it was, the next day. As Rio's transit director, he eliminated every hoop he could within the law to speed the process, making the experiences of licensing and registration "as American as possible." And to encourage efficiency, he cut down every interior wall at the transit office to waist height, creating cubicles so he could ensure that all his employees were serving the public every hour of their workday.[82]

To solve congestion, Fontenelle implemented radical, new policies. Among the first, he banned left turns on main arteries, a major cause of local slowing. His first critics jibed that these kinds of simplistic policies, to allow only right turns, were what you should expect from a right-wing militarist (a *direitista*), and that such a ridiculous policy would get him thrown from office. Fontenelle implemented a new system of one-way streets that took into account traffic flow data. Without left turns and with a more coherent scheme of flow, traffic improved noticeably. Within a few months Fontenelle claimed that traffic moved at an average of 27 kilometers per hour during the rush, which seemed almost miraculous.

Fontenelle came to office before the new National Traffic Code, years in gestation, would be passed. He berated the National Assembly, with whom he would have a volatile relationship, for temporizing on the issue and said the blood of every accident would pool at the Assembly's feet until it was passed.[83] Fines were so low as to have no effect. So, on his own initiative, with legal advice, he began confiscating the driver's license and impounding the car of those who committed the most serious infractions. In 1965, up to the month of November, he had seized 54,387 licenses, permanently revoking 225 belonging to the worst culprits.[84] As a form of

---

[82] *Quatro Rodas*, Mar. 1967.   [83] *Diário Carioca*, Aug. 27, 1965, 3.
[84] *Jornal do Brasil*, Jan. 22, 1966, caderno de automóveis, 1.

public shaming rather than mere enforcement, he published not just license plate numbers but the names of offenders in the daily newspapers.

At first, he was of the opinion that women should not be behind the wheel. He attempted to implement something he called Operation Makeup to reduce the number of women drivers whom he believed used their mirrors more for applying color to their faces than checking the traffic behind them, but it was dead on arrival – too many women had already taken enthusiastically to the wheel.[85] Miss Guanabara 1966, Vera Lúcia Couto, won a car as grand prize for her rise to royalty, but Fontenelle's men failed her in both her attempts to acquire a license to drive it, claiming she could not stay off the curbs. She never got to enjoy her winnings. But Fontenelle's daughter, Mirian, passed her driving exam on her second try, which meant her father had to share the family car.[86] Ever practical, he later contradicted his bias against female drivers and promoted the practice of wives driving their husbands to and from work each day, becoming in essence their chauffeurs. This, he believed, would help solve the downtown parking problem, although he failed to consider it might make traffic worse, turning the commute into two roundtrips per day rather than one.

Fontenelle's bluster was earnest. For a technocrat he demonstrated a surprisingly creative mind, offering innovative solutions that were often effective and practical, although rarely popular with the driving classes. A half century ahead of his time, he suggested congestion pricing, to charge tolls to all drivers who came within a 10-kilometer radius of the city center.[87] In reality, Fontenelle's elimination of hundreds of downtown parking spaces served the same purpose and may have been the major factor in reducing downtown traffic demand and congestion during his tenure. In October of 1965, *Quatro Rodas* reported that due to the lack of downtown parking, already "many people gave up on driving to work," returning to public transportation.[88] Sparse parking capacity was more consequential to commuter numbers than lane capacity.

Fontenelle also favored pedestrianizing a fair number of downtown streets that would serve not just as refuges from traffic but as spaces for city life and living. When on an initial tour of São Paulo in 1966, where he

---

[85] *Quatro Rodas*, Dec. 1965, 13.   [86] *Diário Carioca*, Oct. 24, 1964, 9.

[87] R. J. Smeed, *Road Pricing: The Economic and Technical Possibilities* (London: HMSO, 1964) had suggested congestion pricing to reduce demand for highways, but Fontenelle's suggestion to implement it across an entire urban center may have been original.

[88] *Quatro Rodas*, Oct. 1965, 49.

was being considered as its new transit director, he declared his work was less interested in the movement of the 350,000 who owned automobiles than in that of the 4 million residents who did not. Arriving at Direita Street, a pedestrian space not unlike Ouvidor in Rio, he asked in exultation:

Can't you see what a beautiful thing this is? Tranquil pedestrians, everything in order. I am going to remove cars from many streets, just like this one. It is necessary to give some streets back to pedestrians. The street is not supposed to be a garage. The street was made for this![89]

Indeed, it was the street as garage that became Fontenelle's main focus in Rio, for he too saw the prosaic topic of parking as the central problem of flow, both of cars and pedestrians. Among his first decrees was to eliminate all the city's reserved, private on-street parking spaces. In short order, he removed thousands of reserved parking signs. Then, he outlawed parking on many of Rio's main arteries. By eliminating what was often double and triple parking, he gained three and sometimes more functional driving lanes. The difficulty was in enforcing the new policy. Parking fines were too small, the transit service had too few police to issue them, and above all, Fontenelle had insufficient tow trucks, although he kept the few he had extremely busy. In expediency, he adopted wholesale a tactic that Menezes Côrtes had only tested and mostly threatened: to deflate the tires of illegally parked cars. He would not make examples of the few but would punish every infraction he could in daily operations. And when the air was not coming out of the tires fast enough, he issued valve-stem tools to his police, which made flattening a car's tire short work. None escaped the policy of deflation. Fontenelle carried his own tool and personally flattened offenders' tires, including those of congressmen and even diplomats who mistakenly believed their immunity included parking where they liked. When US Ambassador Lincoln Gordon's limousine's tires were deflated, this time the political left cheered him, and the right, including Brazilian officials who had suffered the same penalty, accused Fontenelle of trying to create an international incident. Fontenelle chastised the ambassador who he claimed had shamed his own nation's good name by disregarding Brazil's sovereign laws. Diplomatically, Gordon apologized, but it was reported that he was livid over the incident. Over the course of 1964, Fontenelle and his men deflated, on average, the tires of more than 24,000 cars every month. They claimed to make no distinction between foreign Cadillacs and domestic popcorn wagons.[90]

[89] *Quatro Rodas*, Oct. 1966, 28.   [90] *Quatro Rodas*, Dec. 1965, 9–10.

FIGURE 7.1 Francisco Américo Fontenelle and Operation Deflation, c. 1964. With his usual crowd of male spectators, Colonel Fontenelle, in white shirtsleeves with cigarette, lets the air out of the tires of an illegally parked 1940 Chevrolet. Impotent in the face of paltry fines and insufficient tow trucks, Fontenelle innovated as he leveraged the military government's claims of technical competence to bring order to the city's chaotic traffic. Like other transit directors, he focused his energies on solving congestion, primarily by decreeing one-way streets and eliminating obstacles, such as parked cars.
Source: Photo by Ronaldo Theobald, undated. Courtesy of the Centro de Pesquisa e Documentação de História Contemporânea do Brasil and the *Jornal do Brasil*.

The work of parking enforcement produced outrageous anecdotes about Fontenelle, some of them conceivably true. In one incident that inspired the cartoonist Millôr Fernandes to call Fontenelle "our own aboriginal Batman," Fontenelle had jumped onto the hood and climbed the windshield of the Dutch ambassador's limousine when the driver tried to evade the police. Some claimed the driver had nearly run the transit director down, which explained his presence on the hood. Fontenelle placed a policeman in the limo to make sure the driver took it to the impoundment lot, but when the driver passed in front of the embassy, he veered into the compound, declared his immunity, and had security kick the policeman off Dutch property. Fontenelle would not accept defeat. He blockaded the embassy's only vehicular exit with a squad car until he was satisfied that the proper fines had been paid. The street, he countered, was Brazilian territory that he controlled. The diplomatic corps had to agree to take the driver into custody and then, after four hours of negotiation, resolved the issue with the payment of a fine. In another case, Fontenelle returned blows on the street with an officer of the State Department who refused to move his car. And in maybe the most explosive example, the traffic police had begun to deflate the tires of two prominent congressmen but backed down when the representatives, Jamil Haddad and Rossini Lopes, showed up in person and defied them. One guard darted over to the nearby traffic office to roust Fontenelle, who was taking his brief after-noon nap. Fontenelle came running. With a crowd of people cheering him on, he began deflating the first tire without an argument. When the Honorable Mr. Haddad drew a weapon and threatened to shoot Fontenelle, the latter calmly ordered Haddad to pull the trigger. The crowd rose up and began accosting Haddad and the other politicians present, and it was only by the intervention of Fontenelle and his men that the Speaker of the House himself was not injured.[91]

Letting the air out of tires became an instant cause célèbre. For the masses who struggled to walk on sidewalks crammed with parked cars or who rode public transportation on streets choked with cars parked three deep, Fontenelle's audacity was broadly cheered. Photographs of helmeted military policeman, sometimes more than ninety at a time, kneeling at the tire valves of car after car in coordinated ranks became the nation's most visible acts of law enforcement. Fontenelle himself deflated tires – in one photo, those of a Volkswagen Beetle whose driver sits at the wheel. A crowd of men observed the event, many beaming as if they were watching their favorite football star score the game's winning goal. For the moment, the street had become a place of spectacle again, and Fontenelle an instant folk hero, a Robin Hood stealing compressed air from the rich motorist and giving public spaces back to pedestrians and users of transit. One critic wrote that Fontenelle sowed disorder in the city because during his many deflationary operations, mobs of "idle" men followed him around, applauding each occurrence while taunting respectable drivers who were shamed in front of their wives and chil-dren. The enmity between chauffeur and pedestrian was as strong as ever, and with police who actually enforced the law, there were oppor-tunities for pedestrians to cheer their enemy's social leveling by the shameful inconvenience of being made immobile. Four flat tires

---

[91] "Êste homem é louco?" *Realidade*, May 1967, 148–49; *Realidade*, Apr. 1967, 129; in Portuguese, Millôr Fernandes' phrase was "nosso Bat-Man caboclo," which might also be translated our "our redneck Batman."

constituted emasculation.[92] Fontenelle seemed to enjoy confronting the most powerful people with his enigmatic composure. After deflating all four of congressman Amando da Fonseca's tires, Fontenelle waited for him to return to his car. Fonseca, the best-dressed and most flamboyant man in the Assembly, blustered onto the scene, perspiring with anger, and demanded: "Do you know who you are talking to," a snobbish phrase so clichéd in Brazil that Fontenelle, who probably anticipated it, coolly replied, "I haven't been talking to you," and serenely strode away. On more than one occasion, he and his men deflated every tire of every car parked around the Assembly building.[93]

He was making powerful enemies, but for now he could rely on Governor Carlos Lacerda and the military's favored National Democratic Union party (UDN) to back him. His other major parking innovation which came in late 1965 was the creation of city parking lots on public spaces that were available and underutilized, particularly on Praca XV and most famously on Vargas Avenue itself. He knew he had to replace at least some of the spaces he had eliminated on the streets and sidewalks, and he continued to allow motorists to park on the public squares. Fontenelle agreed with Doxiadis Associates that Vargas Avenue was far too wide to be of any effective value to traffic flow, so he created, right in the Avenue's center lanes, large parking lots enclosed in guardrails that his enemies labeled *currais* (corrals). Fontenelle liked the term and used it himself. There was ample space here, fifty-three corrals with a total capacity of 10,000 cars, and he created some thirty other such corrals elsewhere in the city. Fontenelle, for the first time in the city's history, charged drivers for storing their cars on the public commons, "as is done in every other advanced nation of the world," as he put it. Corral parking was expensive, about half the minimum daily wage. Hence, these were cordoned spaces, with official guards in the city's pay, used exclusively by wealthy drivers. As more corrals were created, many of the unsanctioned parking guards lost stakes in their claimed parking areas and became city employees at the corrals, although the Assembly repeatedly held back their wages in order to frustrate Fontenelle's plans. But the drivers came. The fees would soon provide half of the transit office's budget, which Fontenelle used to purchase signage, signals, tow trucks, and line painting

---

[92] *Quatro Rodas*, Dec. 1965, 8–9; *Quatro Rodas*, Aug. 1964, 38–39; Aulus Plautius Macedo, *A "taxa" de estacionamento, a constituição, e a lei* (Rio de Janeiro: n.p., 1965), 21.
[93] *Quatro Rodas*, Dec. 1965, 11–12.

equipment. Many complained the lots were ugly, and that on Sundays, when they were largely empty, they became places of play, space for soccer games where shirtless men retook the streets to compete on the oily asphalt, a spectacle that Celso Franco called outrageous in this the most civilized part of the city. As some of the few public spaces protected from moving cars, citizens reoccupied them as remnants of the traditional street.[94]

Various arguments and legislative attempts were made to thwart his policies, including a congressional inquiry into the transit office itself. Then, in February 1965, the Assembly attempted to outlaw tire deflation and driver's license confiscation as penalties for illegal parking and later tried to ban any fees for parking on the public streets, but it appears such bills failed, were vetoed, or ignored, during Fontenelle's term. One legalist argued that both deflation and parking fees were unconstitutional. The first trespassed on the basic right to movement, guaranteed by Brazil's constitution; the second was an infringement on habeas corpus because one's car was essentially imprisoned inside the lot. "The street is public," he insisted, an inherent human right that was obvious to even children, and hence its use could not be taxed. The constitution, he argued, guaranteed the right to free parking.[95] Others claimed that the deflation of tires was theft, "stealing" air that belonged to the vehicle's owner. Fontenelle countered, commenting acerbically that if he had the right to tow a car, he certainly had the power to extract air from tires. "The air does not belong to anyone." And on the issue of the corrals, he suggested such expedients were only temporary until the city and private investors built sufficient off-street parking garages.

Despite the support of Lacerda and many of the popular class, military politics, which brought Fontenelle to power, would also be his demise. Some claimed that it was Fontenelle's drastic traffic policies that helped bring down his benefactor, Carlos Lacerda, and the *Diário Carioca* had advised Lacerda to dismiss Fontenelle before he faced reelection.[96] But there were larger issues at play. In elections in early October 1965, the public chastised the military and its coup by electing governors from opposing parties in five states, including in Guanabara State where Lacerda's moralistic and conservative UDN partisans, despite their frequent fights with generals, had been one of the military's primary backers.

---

[94] Franco, *Eu na contramão*, 184.   [95] Macedo, *A "taxa" de estacionamento*, 2, 6–7, 13.
[96] *Diário Carioca*, May 25, 1965, 5, claimed that the corrals in particular had caused Lacerda to lose support in electoral areas that had been his stronghold.

With Lacerda out of office, the entire administration was swept clean, and new men were appointed in their place. Due to the loss of political face, the military decreed that presidential and gubernatorial elections would thereafter be indirect, and they outlawed all political parties but two official organs. Then, even Lacerda, who had his eyes on the presidency, broke with the military. The following year, the military stripped him and other prominent politicians of their political rights, and some went into exile. Both democracy and the sham of democracy were now defunct.

Some accused Lacerda of ordering the mass deflation of tires at the end of his term as retaliation for his defeat. But Fontenelle, while ousted from office with the rest of Lacerda's staff, sidestepped the politics and continued in his unrelenting battle. He was missed almost immediately in Rio as traffic and parking returned to their oppressive normality. One commented that traffic enforcement had become polite again but was entirely ineffective, and he called for the return of Fontenelle's crass incivility. After working for a time in the conservative capitals of some Northeastern states, which had survived the opposition's electoral successes, he was appointed as the transit director for the city of São Paulo by Governor Abreu Sodré. Here his reputation preceded him. Applying many of the same policies, he improved traffic flow in parts of the city, but he also likewise made many enemies, and some of his plans seemed to make things worse in the short term, particularly for merchants around whom parking had been eliminated. Most significantly, his effort to move from the downtown the city's main bus station, which was owned in part by the city's major newspaper, brought down the wrath of the press. When bus drivers threatened to blockade the street, Fontenelle announced he would impound any stalled bus for five days and asked drivers to consider what their bosses might think of losing a week's revenue. Due to his unremitting brashness, he was pilloried in newspaper articles and ridiculed in cartoons. But if the driving classes had been formidable in Rio, they were redoubtable in São Paulo, which had become the nation's automotive capital in both production and consumption. To show how they felt, a few Paulistas specifically sought out Fontenelle's service car and let the air out of its tires. Fontenelle was characterized as not just a megalomaniac but worse, as the archenemy of the automobile itself. In an essay that attacked Fontenelle's motives, Millôr Fernandes, who is pictured in the piece behind the wheel of a car, expressed the motorist's lingering sense of vulnerability in the face of a fearless opponent who condemned the car's crimes and curtailed the motorist's privileges. "As regards traffic," Fernandes feared, "the public mentality continues to hold that the motorist is always a criminal until proven innocent. And in general, the technicians who claim to solve our traffic problem – Fontenelle as the utmost example – literally hate the automobile, which is entirely intolerable."[97]

And it was. The governor, who felt Fontenelle's traffic solutions distracted from the rest of his agenda, fired his embattled director after only fifty-seven days on the job. There were street celebrations, which included fireworks, in front of the transit office over his dismissal, and the neighborhood of Tatuapé, which claimed his traffic reforms had reduced business there by 70 percent, had an entire programmed festival to observe Fontenelle's demise.[98] And yet Fontenelle kept on fighting, writing editorials and, because he drew good ratings, appearing on the media.

Under the peculiar stresses of a personally and politically fraught career, Fontenelle's health had deteriorated. While engaged in debate on the television program *The Devil's Advocate* on the night of July 8, 1967, he died mid-interview of cardiac arrest, slumping onto a desk in front of the cameras.[99] He was forty-six. As with Henry Barnes, who would also die of a heart attack suffered on the job as New York City's transit director, Brazilians saw Fontenelle's death as occupational and described him as having "died in combat." While there was some gloating by his enemies, the reaction was largely one of sympathy, and some of his harshest critics conceded Fontenelle's integrity and earnest drive to fix what all admitted was the growing calamity of Brazil's public spaces. At his funeral, Sandra Cavalcanti noted that despite his many faults, he was ultimately unable to "flatter the powerful and forget the public good."[100] Although little remembered by any but his contemporaries, his name still graces a few streets around the nation, a bus station in Rio, and most fittingly a pedestrian bridge that spans the Aterro highway, safely connecting the downtown with the Santos Dumont Airport – for those who still walk.[101]

For nearly two decades after the end of World War II, the spatial crisis of Rio's automotive streets continued to intensify, and parking was a problem equal to if not greater than that of congestion. In 1961, the

[97] Millôr Fernandes, "Fontenelle gosta de se fazer louco," *Realidade*, Apr. 1967, 132.
[98] "Paulista festeja adeus a Fontenelle," *Correio da Manhã*, Apr. 7, 1967, section 1, 3.
[99] The sources differ on the place and circumstances of his death. The *Folha de São Paulo* reported that it was on the program *Roleta Russa* of TV Paulista, and that he collapsed while pacing back and forth.
[100] Cited in Dulles, *Carlos Lacerda, Volume 2*, 469.
[101] *Quatro Rodas*, Aug. 1967, 7; *Correio da Manhã*, Jul. 9, 1967, 1. Fontenelle died after 11 PM on July 8, 1967.

magazine *Quatro Rodas* quipped that "the verb 'to park' has no present tense," but this reflected only a narrow if annoying aspect of driver experience.[102] In reality, passenger cars sat unmoving, parked on public spaces, 95 percent of their existence, all in the present tense. The roughly half a million cars in Rio by 1970 collectively consumed 12 square kilometers sitting still. This reality reshaped the city in ways as powerful as did moving traffic.

Le Corbusier, who first visited Rio in 1929, had summed up his ideal of modernist urban planning as the "tower in the park," an urban lifestyle that included car-free, landscaped spaces at every door, spaces in which residents could relax and neighbors could build community. But he and others underestimated the car's growing spatial demands, and Jane Jacobs thirty years later acerbically described modernism's pervasive reality as the "tower in the parking lot."[103] Modernism's next evolution was the tower as the parking lot. The multi-story parking garage embodied the two great symbols of the modern world: the skyscraper and the automobile. Presumably anticipating Jacob's criticism, Le Corbusier took the idea of the elevated garage to a new scale in Rio, hoping to solve the problem of too many machines in the garden. Based on ideas inspired while making flights over the city, he drew up one of the world's first limited-access freeways, but one of rather unusual form. Cars ran in multiple lanes upon the rooftops of multi-story buildings that themselves flowed in undulating ribbons along the city's beaches and across its hills and mountains. He dedicated the upper floors, connected to the rooftops with ramps, to parking – automobiles were to never touch the ground. And he set these serpentine buildings on his characteristic pillars, making of the ground an urban garden, uninterrupted space for people and community, without cars and without streets. Such a vision embodied the ultimate production and functional separation of space.[104]

To his credit, Le Corbusier's utopian fantasy attempted to keep the car in its place, limiting its spatial impacts. The unfolding reality, however, in Rio as elsewhere, was that the car went nearly everywhere, even beyond the bounds of the street. In addition to occupying spaces initially reserved for non-automotive uses, such as sidewalks and squares, the car, as Le

---

[102] "O verbo 'estacionar' não tem presente," *Quatro Rodas*, Feb. 1961, 9.

[103] Jane Jacobs, *The Death and Life of Great American Cities* (New York, NY: Random House, 1961), 343.

[104] Adnan Morshed, "The Cultural Politics of Aerial Vision: Le Corbusier in Brazil (1929)," *Journal of Architectural Education* 55, no. 4 (2002): 204.

Corbusier envisioned, did invade the city's architecture. New parking garages often towered above neighboring office and residential buildings, suggesting car density, as much as human density, led to Rio's downtown verticalization. Likewise, most new buildings after 1950 incorporated parking in their basements, and later might occupy as much as a quarter of the floors in both residential and commercial buildings. They also deformed the city's facades. Urban buildings that had before exhibited multiple ground-level doors and windows at a human scale, spatially connecting the house with the street, now were becoming dominated by garage doors. Automotive access came to account for as much as two-thirds of street-level façades. On Rio's Tiradentes Square, most of the buildings still date to the pre-car era and have façades built to the scale and utility of human bodies. One modern building, Number 10, has one small door for humans and three large entrances for cars, a typical modern configuration. Instead of coherent and often welcoming façades, pedestrians confronted gaping holes that intermittently swallowed and disgorged vehicles. From the late 1950s, the city began to require that every new building provide parking for its residents or employees, and in 1964, Doxiadis was speaking of the application of zoning laws to the floors of buildings, basement and ground-levels dedicated to parking.[105] As you walk the neighborhoods of Copacabana and Ipanema, garages and garage doors are the dominant street-level view. Each garage required access from the street, so the pedestrian sidewalk began to do double duty as walkway and driveway. For the first time, red and yellow paint was applied to the sidewalks, to warn pedestrians they had to share. Curbs were cut and sidewalks were ramped to provide cars access to their private, interior garages.[106] By law, all such garages had to be alarmed. Too many drivers, exiting their garaged buildings, have hit pedestrians on the sidewalks. Flashing lights and ringing alarms, which seem to be going off at all times, warn pedestrians to stop and wait for the cars to make their dangerous transit across of the sidewalk.

New highways and new garages: it was all never enough, and the costs were extraordinary. One observer, referring to the Castelo Garage, built at great expense on the downtown's last, large open space, called it a "disfigured concrete monster" still not large enough to accomplish its

---

[105] Doxiadis, *Guanabara*, 304–05.
[106] "O Pedestre em São Paulo," Associação Brasileira de Pedestres (ABRASPE), www .pedestre.org.br/pedestre/noticias/pedestre-sp/?searchterm=tr%C3%A2nsito (accessed Sep. 19, 2014).

objectives. "For every driver that parks in the Menezes Côrtes Garage," he asserted, "nine others will drive to town hoping to get that space when it is vacated." But the injustices ran deeper than insufficient parking for the motoring classes. The city's massive investment in towers of parking and "tongues of concrete,"[107] an automotive infrastructure that was possibly the city's largest expenditure over the second half of the century, continued to subsidize the automotive class at the expense of the large majority of the city's residents. The ongoing automotive subsidy also explains in part why so many of Rio's citizens lacked the basic services and spaces associated with modern cities, such as public schools, clean water, sewage treatment facilities, decent housing, and accessible health care. Concrete and asphalt absorbed too large a fraction of the city's limited resources.

---

[107] "A cidade desenhada para as maquinas," *Opinião*, Dec. 4, 1972, 5.

CONCLUSION

Revolutions at the End of the Street

Brasília

The revolutionary contingent attains its ideal form not in the place of production, but in the street, where for a moment it stops being a cog in the technical machine and itself becomes a motor.

Paul Virilio[1]

Ah, young man. If not for the street, there would be nothing left.

Leia, 1995[2]

At Brasília's first anniversary as Brazil's new capital in 1961, a reporter asked the engineer Pery Rocha França what had been his most memorable experience in building a city from scratch at the center of the nation's undeveloped interior. Looking back over ceremonial groundbreakings and grand inaugurations, he related an incident from the first days of the city's actual construction, when Brasília, as he put it, was nothing more than a temporary shack on the broad savannah. Rocha França's men had spent the day bulldozing vegetation from the plateau's blood-red soil, creating the city's first strip of broken ground. At quitting time, the laborers relaxed around the shack. As one man began to make his way across the day's cleared ground, another, standing at the door of the shack, gesticulated feigned panic, shouting, "Get out of the street, child!" A common enough display of co-worker banter initiated mocking and merriment among the laborers. For Rocha França, it stirred

---

[1] Paul Virilio, *Speed and Politics: An Essay on Dromology*, translated by M. Polizzotti (New York, NY: Semiotext(e), 1986), 1.

[2] Cited in Freitas, "Townscape and Local Culture," 353. "Ah moço! Não fosse a rua, sobrava nada."

tears; the casual pronunciation of the word "street" transformed the cleared ground and the transient shed into civilization in crude microcosm. For Rocha França, a sensitive man who moonlighted as bass for the Belo Horizonte opera, the emergence of the street, in however primitive a form, emotionally endorsed the work to move the national capital out beyond the frontier.[3] The street had been civilization's quintessential civic space, and opening the first stretch was a groundbreaking that mattered, as powerful symbolically as the subsequent completion of the capital's concrete palaces and futuristic monuments. However, in this instance, there was irony in Rocha França's association of civilization and city streets – Brasília was designed and built to have no streets.

Modernism's leading architects embraced the new realities and urban design possibilities that the car introduced. The automobile and its rapid movement were now to define the city and hence required a new model for efficient civic life. Most of the designs for the automotive city of the future – Le Corbusier's Radiant City (1924), Ludwig Hilberseimer's Highrise City (1927), and Frank Lloyd Wright's Broadacre City (1932), as examples – were extravagant dreams in mobility of soaring towers and flying highways that never got beyond exuberant scale models. Indeed, Brasília's conception was the first full-scale commission to create a city from the ground up that would integrate automotive movement as a central feature. The modern city's carefully plotted lines would accommodate the automobile's rapid movements but also segregate its dangers from the places people lived and played. Modernism's intent was not to promote the traditional street's evolution as an automotive corridor, as had been happening in Rio and elsewhere, but to bring about the street's outright extinction. As Le Corbusier himself put it:

It is the street of the pedestrian of a thousand years ago, a relic of the centuries. It is an obsolete and inoperable organ. It exhausts us and is altogether disgusting! Why, then, does it still survive? These last twenty years of the automobile... have carried us to a dawn of new possibilities.[4]

In 1933, the Fourth International Conference on Modern Architecture declared the death of the street.[5]

---

[3] "Brasília: um ano depois," *Quatro Rodas*, May 1961, 39; in Portuguese, "Sai da rua, menino."

[4] Le Corbusier, et al. *Oeuvre Compléte de 1910–1929*, 5th edn. (Erlenbach-Zurich: Éditions d'Architecture, 1948), 112.

[5] For a discussion of Le Corbusier and Wright's visions, see Lawrence A. Herzog, *Return to Center: Culture, Public Space, and City Building in a Global Era* (Austin, TX: University of Texas Press, 2006), 19–22.

True to the aims of the International Style, Lúcio Costa, Brasília's designer, platted the new capital with no streets. The traditional street, he agreed, had outlived its function and had no useful place in the modern city. He steadfastly refused to use the word "street" in drawings, proposals, or plans. Hence, Brasília officially has no streets, and if the roads and highways that make that city's automotive network have numbered designations (L3 South, for example), most of Brasília's "streets," its linear public thoroughfares, have no names at all. Addresses in Brasília refer to the built environment, to sectors, quadrants, blocks, and shops or apartments. For example, a typical address – SCS, Q. 6, Bl. D, loja 15 – means South Commercial Sector, Quadrant 6, Block D, shop 15, and makes no reference to the "street" or paved access on which it is located. Most significantly, residents have found no reason to give street spaces popular names. Streets in Brasília serve no spatial purpose other than as access to someplace else. The street is merely a vector, neither a space nor a place, and hence meaningless, unworthy of a name. Brasília, in a sense, was to represent the finality of the traditional street's demise in the city of the future.

To the modernists' credit, they sought to improve the city's communal areas, to literally "re-place" the disappearing street and its functions with new spaces. Costa spatially divorced automobiles from pedestrians.[6] Cars in Brasília would run rapidly not on streets but on broad urban highways and viaducts without the interference of sidewalks, intersections, stoplights, or crosswalks. In such areas, there would be no provision for the pedestrian. In compensation, residents were allotted expansive, car-free internal blocks, *superquadras*, characterized by landscaped public areas. This was to be the new commons, a garden and a playground. Costa, following Le Corbusier, lifted private residences one full story off the ground, on concrete pillars, so that essentially all the land encompassed in the *superquadra* became integrated public space.

These seemed elegant solutions: highway speeds for motorists and a dramatic expansion of the public realm for residents. But reactions, particularly to the public spaces that replaced the streets, were mixed. While residents were supposed to live in graceful towers in lovely gardens, what they in fact inhabited was a landscape dominated by the automobile.[7] And in Brasília's case, even where cars did not pack the ground, public spaces were so out of human scale that many found them

---

[6] Costa was not the first to attempt this separation, but the first on such a scale.
[7] Jacobs, *Death and Life of Great American Cities*, 343.

alienating and refused to use them. For Clarice Lispector, Brasília was "a beach without an ocean," and she felt that standing anywhere in the new capital was to sense oneself listing with vertigo toward an encompassing abyss. "If I lived here," she declared, "I would let my hair grow down to the ground," a primitive means to enclosure and stability in an astonishingly expansive urban landscape.[8]

Brasília's bold experiment as a city without streets elicited many responses, and few were neutral. *Quatro Rodas*, a Brazilian magazine promoting domestic automotive consumption, highway construction, and auto tourism in Brazil, might predictably have found in Brasília's fast lanes an urban utopia. But the magazine described Brasília's broad thoroughfares, which lacked fronting homes and businesses, as sadly depressing. Even in a male-centered world of automobility, it asked where a man was to go and to be without the street? Brasília's "superblock" neighborhoods, by design, offered no corner bar in which to discuss football, no sidewalk café, and no linear community spaces on which to collectively parade or individually philander. In Brasília, a man was a captive in his own home, reduced to "family gatherings, canasta, and high fidelity."[9] Brasília had not improved upon the traditional street; it had annihilated it, along with most of its non-linear functions.[10]

Brasília's streetless landscape was built to replace Rio de Janeiro, the former capital, a city that by the 1950s made a perfect foil to the efficient urban machine projected by the modernists. The car had changed the city, and Rio's residents began to both pine for the past and lament the present of their city's public spaces. The 1950s were a nostalgic turning point in which Rio's residents began to reevaluate what had been lost with the car's introduction to public spaces. Three films from the period evidence these sentiments, both in their content and nostalgic sensibility. The first,

---

[8] Clarice Lispector, "Brasília: Cinco Dias," in *A legião estrangeira: Contos* (Rio de Janeiro: Editora do Autor, 1964), 162–67.

[9] "Brasília: um ano depois," *Quatro Rodas*, May 1961, 39. Jacobs, *Death and Life of Great American Cities*, 83–84, would argue the same year that modern residential planning was matriarchal.

[10] Two major works, David G. Epstein, *Brasilia: Plan and Reality* (Berkeley, CA: University of California Press, 1973) and James Holston, *The Modernist City: An Anthropological Critique of Brasilia* (Chicago, IL: University of Chicago Press, 1989), take a rather critical view of Brasília's spatial and social realities; Farés El-Dahdah, *Lúcio Costa: Brasilia's Superquadra* (Munich: Prestel Verlag, 2005), makes a more positive assessment. For the mixed responses from Brasília's residents, see Sandra Bernardes Ribeiro and Marta Litwinczik Sinoti, "A Post-Occupancy Assessment of the Neighborhood Unit," in Farés el-Dahdah, *Lucio Costa, Brasilia's Superquadra* (Munich: Prestel Verlag, 2005), 92–95.

a documentary entitled *Carioca Transit* of 1954, produced by the photographer Jean Manzon, documented the street's utter failure as a place of human movement. The competition for the street between private cars and public transportation produced absolute gridlock. The film's suggested solutions – the elimination of the streetcar and the municipalization of buses – were ineffectual, but its depiction of widespread congestion, its claim that "the greatest labor of the Carioca is just getting to work," and its expression that for the moment, the only solution was to "wait, wait, wait," were lamentably accurate, even though the film largely ignored the reality of automotive accidents and deaths.[11]

By contrast, in the other two films, directors by preference set their scenes and cameras in the city's few remaining car-free spaces where actor dialogue could be successfully recorded with the day's primitive equipment. *Black Orpheus* of 1959, which retells the Greek tragedy of Euridice set in Rio's Babilónia *favela*, shows a striking contrast between the community-filled spaces of the hillside *favela* and the car-filled spaces in which carnival's dancers compete in the city streets below. The samba schools still demand their spaces in the city, but not without contest and consequences. Fleeting shots of streets running with speeding cars and swerving buses document the street's broad transformation as an automotive corridor. Likewise, the controversial *Rio, 40 Degrees* of 1955, which Menezes Côrtes, as police chief, banned for its too gritty portrayal of city life, keeps its scenes to the car-free *favelas*, parks, landmarks, and beaches as it follows boy peddlers who make the dramatic film's narrative thread. When the film set does enter the streets of Copacabana, actors must raise their voices to be heard over the charging traffic. At their hearts, both films attempt to portray a city that was passing away while giving away only a few shocking scenes of its streets' troubled present so evident in *Carioca Transit*.

Both of the latter films end in street death and *favela* dancing. Orpheus, a streetcar driver whose own occupation is not long for the world, unintentionally kills Eurydice with the streetcar's own electric lines. A shrieking, white ambulance carries her body from the dancing crowds through brightly lit highway tunnels. After searching for her in various levels of hell, Orpheus gains admittance to the city's morgue to retrieve Eurydice's body, which lies among carnival's many other casualties,

[11] *O Transporte dos Cariocas*, directed by René Persin (Jean Manzon Films Limited, 1954), accessed Nov. 21, 2016 at História do Cinema Brasileira, www.historiadocinemabrasileiro .com.br/o-transporte-dos-cariocas.

presumably victims of the automobile. But the film concludes in the happy *favela*, where children blithely sing and dance on Babilonia's, machine-free spaces to the rising of the sun. Likewise, *Rio, 40 Degrees* concludes frenetically in fatality and celebration. A young street vendor is run down in Copacabana by a passing truck, but as his body lies in the street, the film fades to an end with the Portela samba school dancing in the carless Cabuçu *favela* to a song entitled "Memories of a Rio Gone By," whose lyrics speak of horse-drawn carriages, Castelo Hill, gas lamps, colonial fountains, and the songs of peddlers, all of which had disappeared.[12] Film, dance, death, and song are conjointly employed to memorialize and lament what had been lost on the former public commons.

As it was in the 1950s, so it remains: two of the last fragments of the public commons of Rio's pre-automotive past lie largely at the extremes of the city's topography: its seaside beaches and its mountainside *favelas*. On the car-free streets and paths of many hill shanties, one still finds strips of Rio's traditional street. Alfred Agache argued that steepness was an enemy to Rio's modernization, a city that had *favela* streets so precipitous that cars could not ascend them, and where the very pavements, where installed, slipped under the force of gravity.[13] And yet the city grew in the hills as fast as it grew in the valleys. By 1949, there were 105 named *favelas*, the home of some 34,000 households. By 2010, there were 1.4 million people (22 percent of the city's population) living in 763 *favelas*. *Favelas* display a great variety of urban traits, but in those to which cars could not gain entry, the streets, sometimes little more than stepped paths between the houses, remained spaces of common use and community. Janice Perlman, who has studied Rio's *favelas* as long as anyone, writes that her first experiences in *favelas* in the 1960s were among the happiest of her life, evoking Jane Jacob's image of the street made safe and inviting by its very bodily occupation. Perlman described Rio's slums as warm and brimming with the social capital that only strong communities could produce. "I have never felt as safe or as welcomed in any community before or since ... People took care of me as they did of

---

[12] The song, "Lembranças do Rio Antigo" or "Reliquias [Relics] do Rio Antigo," appears to have emerged in the early 1950s and to have gone through various versions of lyrics, but all dealing with Rio's past. Or they may in fact be different songs using similar but often modified lyrics. One was the winning samba of 1961. See "Histórico da Escola," Unidos do Cabuçu, http://unidosdocabucu2012.blogspot.com/p/historico.html (accessed Sep. 25, 2014).

[13] Agache, *Cidade do Rio de Janeiro*, appendix, xx; Agache recommended that no street in Rio be built with more than a 12 percent pitch.

each other." Over the decades, the streets upon which community had been constructed became increasingly dangerous, not due to cars but to organized crime, and yet she and others still argue that in the *favelas*, even as criminal nests, "there is still a life force there that is absent" in the better parts of the city. Unfortunately, the violent reality of crime, like the violent reality of automobility, consumed the street to the broad exclusion of many other uses, leaving "no place for sitting or watching the parade of life go by, for playing soccer, for recreation, for leisure," a loss of public space that killed social capital, "one of the few resources that was available, abundant, and effective in poor communities."[14]

Yet still, there were pockets where neither many cars nor significant crime had come, including *favelas* where traffickers worked to keep the violence of the drug trade and everyday street crime to a minimum as it was good for business and community relations.[15] In 1985, *Veja* magazine described the Saúde *favela* near Rio's center, which used to be something of a tourist attraction, as so poor and dilapidated that no longer would anyone care to venture up. But it still depicted its lively streets, filled by day with children playing and by night with neighbors who "protected from the automobile by the luck of topography, come together for long intimate conversations in the open air."[16] Likewise, a recent resident of the nearby Conceição *favela* portrayed with pride his neighborhood in which children's games such as marbles, jump rope, and tops – games not seen for decades on most of Rio's streets – had been passed down from one generation of children to the next over the century. His neighborhood, he declared, was a place of continuity in cultural practice, bodily presence, and collective conversation. Here too, every night, "neighbors place their dining chairs on the sidewalk and receive all passersby in front of their houses. It is a place where I know the names of my mailman (Paulo Roberto) and the bakery delivery man (Marcos) who convey letters and loaves into my very own hands," a community not unlike those described in the nineteenth century.[17]

---

[14] Janice Perlman, *Favela: Four Decades of Living on the Edge in Rio de Janeiro* (Oxford: Oxford University Press, 2010), xix, xxiii–xxiv, 192–94.

[15] See Misha Glenny, *Nemesis: One Man and the Battle for Rio* (New York, NY: Alfred A. Knopf, 2016), who documents the relative success of organized criminals maintaining security in the Rocinha *favela* and the liveliness of its streets.

[16] *Veja*, Mar. 26, 1985, 60.

[17] Antônio Agenor de Melo Barbosa, "Morro da Conceição: a geografia da cordialidade," *Vitruvius* 6, (Mar. 2006), www.vitruvius.com.br/revistas/read/minhacidade/06.068/1951 (accessed Sep. 26, 2014).

At the other topographical extreme, the beach still plays an important role as civic, public space. Although Rio's citizens bathed religiously on their beaches in the nineteenth century, a routine in which they rose early, took a brisk swim, and then returned home for breakfast, Bert Barickman has pointed out that they did not begin to spend time on the city's beaches as public spaces until after 1920.[18] There are many reasons for this change in beach utility and meaning, but one was that by that date there were already few public spaces left to gather in quiet and safety. As the city had almost no parks, as the streets were filling with traffic, and since the squares were disappearing under parked cars, the beach would become, in time, the quintessential commons in Rio. Much as Thoreau observed in his own time, when the landscape was almost entirely possessed and fenced, he, like Rio's residents, found his most secure rights to public spaces on the waterfront.[19] With significant limitations and many of the same social tensions, Rio's street culture invaded the sands to create one of the world's great beach cultures.[20] Beaches tend to more naturally segregate by class than did streets, and any Carioca who comprehends her social geography knows which blocks in Copacabana and Ipanema belong to which class of residents. Many elite have made implied claims that particular strands ought to be their exclusive playground where the underclasses are not welcome. In 2001, the state of Rio constructed the Piscinão (Big Pool), an artificial lagoon of chlorinated water located on a real beach in Ramos, a northern suburb, where the bay's water has long been too polluted for bathing. The attraction has drawn as many as 60,000 people per day from the city's dense northern sprawl, and yet many of them budget a little money for public transit so they can also frequent the same beaches as foreign tourists on the Atlantic coast. The poor, particularly in the 1980s, often showed up in force, sweeping the sands ominously to express their rights to what remained of the public commons, causing consternation and sometimes real trouble. In 1985, the irreverent band Ultraje a Rigor expressed these tensions when it recorded "We Are Going to Invade Your

---

[18] "Hábito favorecia a interação entre sexos já na década de 20," interview with Bert Barickman, *Jornal do Commércio*, Recife, Jul. 9, 2000, www2.uol.com.br/JC/_2000/09 07/cd0907n.htm (accessed Sep. 29, 2014).

[19] *The Journal of Henry David Thoreau*, vol. 5 (Boston, MA: Houghton Mifflin, 1906), 45–46.

[20] James Freeman, "Great, Good, and Divided: The Politics of Public Space in Rio de Janeiro," *Journal of Urban Affairs* 30, no. 5 (2008): 529–56, examines the current state of Rio's beaches as contested spaces. See also Bruno Carvalho, "Mapping the Urbanized Beaches of Rio de Janeiro: Modernization, Modernity and Everyday Life," *Journal of Latin American Cultural Studies: Travesia* 16, no. 3 (2007): 328–30.

Beach," which sang defiantly about the city's *favela* classes looking down
from the hills onto the beaches of the elite and descending to occupy the
sands with neither courtesy nor deference.

> We can clearly tell from here on the hill
> What happens there on your littoral
> We like all we see, but what we need is more
> From the city's mountain tops to the edge of the docks
> More than just a good tan
> We want to be by your side
> We come with neither suntan lotion nor oil
> We are what needs to be spread out ...
> Now, we are going to invade your beach ...
> If this makes you uneasy
> Then it's best that you move off
> It doesn't do any good to sneer at us
> If we like the space, we are going to stay ...
> There's no reason to get nervous
> You might even find it pleasant
> To be in our most agreeable company
> Which might in fact be good for you.[21]

The lyrics, which in translation fail to convey a cheeky, brash humor,
protest the exclusivity of the city's best public spaces. But more than being
a protest, they are a plea about the city's impoverished residents needing
space in which to be accepted as *gente*, as full citizens, a term used at
various times throughout the song.

Other remnants, although often much changed, are those downtown
streets, such as Ouvidor and a few yet narrower alleys that had been
declared off-limits to wheeled vehicles in the nineteenth century.
Although often overpowered by the tall, modern buildings that enclose
them, giving them the feel of narrow, dark canyons, many are still
popular spaces and pedestrian corridors. Yet, in addition to remnant
favelas, beaches, and colonial streets, the city has, beginning with
Paquetá in 1950, incrementally added to the city's car-free realm.
The most substantial addition came in the mid-1960s in the district
known as the Sahara (SAARA District). The Society of Friends
Adjacent to Alfândega Street was formed in 1962 by merchants, many
of Middle Eastern descent, to preserve this ethnically diverse commercial
sector. The Society stopped the proposed Via Diagonal that was

---

[21] Ultraje a Rigor, "Nós vamos invadir sua praia," by Roger Moreira, 1985, Warner Music
   Group.

projected to run from Vargas Avenue to Lapa, destroying many of the district's streets and turn-of-the-century buildings. Governor Lacerda honored their petitions; as a result the SAARA District, despite the constant threat of being consumed by parked cars,[22] became one of the largest, successful pedestrian shopping areas in the Americas. Covering some eleven streets touching eighteen square blocks, the district consists of more than 1,250 shops. On weekdays, the narrow streets fill with strolling Brazilian shoppers, the appearance of a foreign tourist being rare. On a typical holiday, the streets are packed with more bodies than would seem humanly possible, individuals moving non-lineally, in all directions at the same time, demonstrating the inborn human genius for collective movement. As commercial spaces, the district produces communities of workers and shoppers rather than residential neighborhoods, but the relationships among customers, shops, owners, and employees, are long-standing, and the district has its own festivals and celebrations of Carnival, Easter, Rosh Hashanah, Mother's Day, and Yom Kippur.[23]

Other efforts to recapture the street from the car began in Rio in 1975 during a Transit Department–backed campaign labeled Operation Citadel that added three streets to the colonial pedestrian remnant. The poet Carlos Drummond de Andrade exulted that the people began to call the street 7th of September Street by the name 7th of the Pedestrian, and he suggested that just as signs were going up to demarcate "Street for Pedestrians," signs should also go up designating "Avenue for Drivers" to promote the radical idea that not every street belonged to cars by default.[24] In 1979, the Cultural Corridor Plan created some eighteen car-free streets, whose total length exceeded 4 kilometers and whose combined area, one paper touted, was more than 123,000 square meters. It was also during this period, the early 1980s, that the city banished the car from the city's downtown public squares

---

[22] "Detran esvazia pneus e multa com radar," *Diário de Notícias*, Aug. 7, 1975, 1.

[23] Annabella Blyth, "Cristalização espacial e identidade cultural: Uma abordagem da herança urbana (o Saara, na área central da cidade do Rio de Janeiro)," 2 vol. (Master's thesis, Universidade Federal do Rio de Janeiro, 1991); Paula Ribeiro, "Saara e Praça Onze," *Revista de Estudos Judaicos* (Lisbon: Associação Portuguesa de Estudos Judaicos) 8 (2005): 6–15; Andreas Valentin, *SAARA* (Rio de Janeiro: Francisco Alves, 2010).

[24] "Operação Cidadela deixará mais de 122 mil m2 livres para pedestres no Centro," *Jornal do Brasil*, Jul. 5, 1975, 5. Elsewhere, in the same edition, the same paper measured the space at 300,000 square meters. Carlos Drummond de Andrade, "Ruas só para pedestres," *Jornal do Brasil*, Jul. 19, 1975, 5.

in order to reincorporate them into the car-free network.[25] In recent decades, officials have also created temporary street spaces for recreation on weekends and holidays, allowing citizens to assert that at least "on Sundays, the Street is ours." Blocking traffic on a few major arteries, such as the Aterro Highway, Atlantic Avenue in Copacabana, and late at night in nightlife-filled Lapa, has been extremely popular with citizens who take advantage of the space to promenade, jog, party, play soccer, and ride bikes, among a variety of other activities. In fact, the closing of Lapa's streets to traffic from 10 PM to 5 AM each Friday and Saturday night, the so-called Operation Legal Lapa that began in 2010, drew so many boisterous visitors that the city shut it down in 2013. Complaints from neighbors drive the opposition to street partying, but city officials still use automotive movement to justify giving the street back to cars.[26]

The crowds who come are testimony to the pent-up desire for such spaces in which to congregate in community. Even the ugliest public spaces can be treasured. São Paulo's infamous Minhocão (the Big Worm) is an elevated highway that continues to plague the central neighborhoods, through which it runs, with noise and exhaust. Immediately upon its construction in 1971, rents in the area fell drastically, by two-thirds in some cases, and haughty drivers enjoyed mocking and making obscene gestures at vexed residents as they sat in their second- and third-story windows and balconies. The highway was a blight. However, after the city began to close it on Sundays and after 9 PM on weeknights, the highway became a popular place for gathering. Skateboarders took to the on-ramps, families picnicked on the median, and couples came to take wedding photos. Residents, who still think the highway is loud and ugly, no longer want it razed, for without it they would have no public space at all. One resident, comparing São Paulo's public spaces unfavorably to those of other major cities, remarked that "here, there is the Minhocão. It is not perfect. But it is ours."[27]

---

[25] Augusto Ivan Pinheiro and Vicente del Rio, "Cultural Corridor: A Preservation District in Downtown Rio de Janeiro, Brazil," *Traditional Dwellings and Settlements Review* 9, no. 11 (1993): 51–64.

[26] "Ruas da Lapa deixarão de ser fechadas nos fins de semana: Operação Lapa Legal terá mudanças a partir da próxima semana," *O Globo*, Mar. 13, 2014, http://oglobo.globo .com/rio/ruas-da-lapa-deixarao-de-ser-fechadas-nos-fins-de-semana-7837432#ixzz2yK deSbdM (accessed Oct. 1, 2014). The term *legal* in Portuguese has the double connotation of legal and excellent.

[27] "Um Minhocão na Janela," *Veja*, Feb. 3, 1971, 26–27; "A Highway Doubling as a Haven: Minhocão Represents São Paulo's Crumbling but Welcoming Heart," *New York Times*, Jun. 24, 2014, B12.

Traditional claims to the street have intensified. Rio's local street carnival never disappeared entirely despite official pronouncements of its death. Ramos, after some time without dancers entering the streets, started celebrating again in 1970, inviting other neighborhoods to join them.[28] Since the military's departure, the number of neighborhood carnival groups have exploded, reaching as many as 400. Many are local but can draw thousands of celebrants. Their names, which are as audacious as those from a century ago, often express how central their demand for public space is to their survival and success. Names include *Pede Passagem* (Let Me Pass), *Pés Espalhados* (Sprawling Feet), and *Rompe e Rasga* (Break Out and Tear Up). During carnival, many dance in the streets unannounced, which means they can block motorists for hours. One elderly celebrant explained the appeal: "[O]ur lives are spent inside, in shopping malls, offices, gyms, apartment building. But I think people want to meet each other and be together. That's why real carnival for us is out here on the street." These events demonstrate the temerity with which citizens still hold to the basic claim that "the street is ours" (*a rua é nossa*), a phrase that is increasingly common in the press, in song lyrics, and in carnival itself as shorthand for expressing the public claim on the public commons, or, as another put it: "[T]he street is a piece of the world that we reconquer in order to reconnect to our community."[29] Hence streets in Rio have become places of repeated reconquests and of pursued reconnections.

Rio's upper classes have also striven to recapture or create usable civic spaces, albeit usually in semi-private forms. Shopping malls, with marble pavements, glass storefronts, and bright lights substituting for sky, dot the city's better neighborhoods. They are typically furnished with secured parking garages, evidence they are fashioned for the automotive set. Most have few pedestrian entrances. As private property, they form a pseudo-commons, the private masquerading as the public. Rio's Nova America shopping mall has one corridor that its owners call Rua do Rio (Rio's Street) which has colonial façades, rustic paving, and a classical

---

[28] "Ramos volta a fazer seu carnaval popular," *Jornal do Brasil*, Jan. 14, 1970, section 1, 10.

[29] Mônica Pimenta Velloso, *A cultura das ruas no Rio de Janeiro, 1900–1930: Mediações, linguagens e espaço* (Rio de Janeiro: Edições Casa de Rui Barbosa, 2004), 28, 31–33; João Pimentel, *Blocos: Uma história informal da carnaval de rua* (Rio de Janeiro: Prefeitura da Cidade, 2002), 18, 32 (here citing Aldir Blanc), 34–38, 66. See also Beatriz Jaguaribe, *Rio de Janeiro: Urban Life through the Eyes of the City* (New York, NY: Routledge, 2014), 105–08.

fountain. But mall space is not the *logradouro*; it is private property protected by private police. Those who enter leave their constitutional rights to free speech and peaceable assembly, long associated with the street, at the door. In fact, such restrictions are central to the mall's design, and security forces are employed to keep order but also to discourage the entrance of those individuals whose dress, status, and income are judged inappropriate.

As with the beaches, exclusive claims to the mall's corridors have not gone without challenge. Recently, young, poor citizens have invaded in excursions known as *rolezinhos*. Using social media to coordinate their occupation, poor teenagers congregate within the malls, sweeping the corridors in bodies of excited chatter. Authorities have reacted in panic: judges have imposed injunctions against *rolezinhos*, mall cops in bullet-proof jackets have used clubs and rubber bullets against the unwanted invaders, and President Dilma Rousseff called cabinet-level meetings to address the incidents. Yet unlike recent riots and demonstrations, these are not protests against the reigning social order or government corruption. The demonstators simply seek space on the dwindling public commons. Hence, *rolezinhos* are, in that sense, overt political acts "to tell society we belong to it, that we're not on the margins of it," as one female participant from the Maré *favela* complex declared. Because they want a place in Brazil's economy, they demand a place in the halls of elite consumption. When they are blocked at the doors by security, they hold their cash and their credit cards in the air to demonstrate that they do indeed have the currency that should grant them admission and membership to a barred space. Teresa Caldeira has argued that public spaces can create and perpetuate a democratic polity by forcing us into the same spaces as those who are to us strangers, different, even frightening. Sometimes it is only on the public square, the *logradouro*, that we must acknowledge not only the right of others to be there but by extension that they are one of us. Spiro Kostof observes pessimistically that the real street has come to represent "the burial place of our hopes to exorcise poverty and prejudice by confronting them daily." Rio's malls masquerading as public space fail the test of democratic utility by design.[30]

[30] "Brazil's Rolezinhos: The Kids Are All Right," *The Economist*, Jan. 25, 2014, www .economist.com/news/americas/21595011-youngsters-gathering-shopping-malls-want -attention-not-political-change-kids-are-all (accessed Oct. 5, 2014); Simon Romero, "Brazil's Latest Clash with Its Urban Youth Takes Place at the Mall," *New York Times*, Jan. 20, 2014, A7; Teresa P. R. Caldeira, *City of Walls: Crime, Segregation, and Citizenship in São Paulo* (Berkeley, CA: University of California Press, 2001), 303;

Another elite response to the decline of public space is the rise of gated communities, entire suburban developments of private streets, all walled against what is seen as an increasingly dangerous, crime-ridden city. The privatization of the street, more than the gates themselves, distinguishes the gated community from all other urban forms. Streets are privatized precisely so they can be gated, so residents can control who can be on the streets that front their houses and on their private town squares. Among the largest, what amount to private cities, are those planned and constructed by Alphaville Urbanismo, a developer that began building gated communities of luxury single family housing in São Paulo in the late 1970s. Alphaville, their first development, has 60,000 residents, 2,300 businesses, 11 schools, and 960 security guards. Lining its private streets are sports clubs, entertainment venues, and restaurants. Like elite shopping malls, Alphaville has a limited number of entrances, usually one per phase, consisting of formidable security complexes manned by guards in dark uniforms. The maids and construction workers who pass through the gates each day describe it as an experience not unlike passing security at an international airport. Raised earthen berms surround the developments, each topped with steel curtain walls, themselves topped with electrified fencing and security cameras. The walls surrounding Alphaville's multiple phases total some 40 miles in length, ranking them among a list that includes those on the US–Mexican border, the West Bank, and Belfast. They enclose an area of many square kilometers bereft of any actual public space.[31]

Alphaville Urbanismo has now introduced similar gated enclaves to many of Brazil's major cities, where lots have sold before fields, forests, and mangroves have been skinned off the terrain. Alphaville Barra da Tijuca, Phase 1, which is being constructed on a mangrove forest that fringed Rio's Jacarapaguá Lagoon, advertises, in addition to a couple of preserved natural spaces, 388 lots and 16 commercial establishments surrounding swimming pools, tennis courts, and other communal areas. Most of the houses are being built around a series of small squares, which if the neighboring gated community of Quintas do Rio sets any precedent, will be named for the very birds whose habitat is being destroyed to make space for the development.

Spiro Kostof, *The City Assembled: The Elements of Urban Form through History* (London: Thames & Hudson, 1992), 243.

[31] "Our Walled World," *The Guardian*, Nov 19, 2013, www.theguardian.com/world/ng -interactive/2013/nov/walls#saopaulo (accessed Oct. 7, 2014).

The motives that create the demand for gated communities and private streets are in part revealed in the developers' promotional materials that highlight security, the power of exclusion, and defensible walls to keep the criminal element at bay by keeping them off your street.[32] It is simplistic to label those who buy into such communities as snobbish, exclusionary, and fearful, but the gated community might be seen as the final triumph of the elite over the public spaces they have been trying to control for centuries. The car certainly helped reduce the street's utility to the lower classes, but it was not a full victory. That could only come with the street's privatization, which empowered residents to exclude nonresidents and undesirables. The car remains an essential component of the gated community. Public transportation cannot exist on private streets; hence the car is part of the cost of admission. Often, the car is the ticket in as well: a "good appearance," as Brazilians would put it, and a decent car, are frequently all one needs to get past the guards, even as an uninvited nonresident.

Setha Low has argued that in addition to the negative motives for creating gated spaces, residents are also trying to "recapture an ideal world in the face of contemporary realities." Consumers of walled spaces are looking for the community that the actual streets no longer offer, a desire shaped by the perception of an idealized past "imagined from childhood." She suggests that "the gates represent a compromise, even a defense, between the way things are and the way residents would like them to be."[33] Parents tire of their children playing in the corridors and service areas of apartment complexes. They want spaces of the idealized traditional street, and that can be accomplished only by controlling who gets into the neighborhood as well as how many cars get in and how fast they drive. The multiple squares in Alphaville Barra da Tijuca are pitched as lively, multicultural spaces where children play, adults converse, dogs cavort, and single ladies can jog without fear of being mugged and without the likelihood of being run down by strangers using one's home street as a thoroughfare to rapidly get to somewhere else.

Pedestrianizing downtown shopping areas, barring vehicles permanently or temporarily from public streets, dancing spontaneously in the streets during carnival, building shopping malls, even privatizing existing streets and constructing gated communities might all be characterized as exertions toward restoring elements of the traditional street. They do not

---

[32] Caldeira, *City of Walls*, 305.

[33] Setha M. Low, *Behind the Gates: Life, Security, and the Pursuit of Happiness in Fortress America*, 224, 230.

qualify as "recommonings" since existing streets are rarely privatized and private streets are never common. However, because these developments question the street as a space legally and effectively limited to vehicular movement, they claim, reclaim, or renegotiate urban spaces in order to enlarge their potential functions. They challenge the enclosure that the car has imposed on many of the street's potential utilities.[34] Human spaces are deserving of conservationist concern – not as idealized landscapes to be preserved along the lines of some nostalgic view of what the traditional street was a century ago, but as evolving ecologies that serve the basic needs of human individuals and human societies. Cars, trucks, and buses all have roles to play in the modern world that we have chosen to live in, but their dominance of essentially every public space in our cities has harmed the street's potential as a healthy, vibrant, useful human habitat. If we value community, open commerce, safety, quality of life, free assembly, peace and quiet, spontaneous celebration, the exchange of ideas, and resource equity, we must protect the spaces where such values can be expressed and exercised.

History is the constant reconsideration of social values. As the citizens of Rio celebrated the completion of one of their first produced streets, Avenida Central, João do Rio wrote of the Cariocas' shared passion for the street:

I love the street. This sentiment, by nature entirely intimate, . . . this love, absolute and exaggeratory, is shared by all. We are brothers and feel it similarly and equally – in cities, towns, and villages – not because we suffer the street's pains and misfortunes, her laws and her police, but because the love of the street unites us, equalizes and gathers us. It is a sentiment imperturbable and indissoluble, unique like life itself in resisting the ages and epochs. Everything else is transformed, all else varies: love, hate, egotism. Today, our smiles betray more bitterness; irony is more painful. Centuries pass, slip by, bringing us things futile and happenings notable. What persists and remains, a legacy every generation passes on ever larger, is the love of the street.[35]

Do Rio expressed his day's exalted estimation of the street emphatically, but he was wrong to assume that it could not change, that the affection could not be killed. The car transformed the street from a place of dirt to one of grit, from a place of meaning to a space in between, from a place full

---

[34] Wall, *The Commons in History*, 99, observes that while enclosure has been the general trend, recommoning, the recapture of the former commons, has been exercised by human agency with some consistency. While repurposing streets is technically not a recommoning, it is the sense of reestablishing equitable access to more users.

[35] João do Rio, *A alma encantadora das ruas*, 3.

of life to one that regularly meted out death. As a result, our affinity for public spaces has diminished; our sentiments have become ambivalent.

However, for the citizens of Rio, as much as for maybe any urban people, the street remains a beloved place, at least in their collective memory. Brazilians are genuinely nostalgic for the traditional street, and it is more than the futile longing associated with the English version of "nostalgia"; in Brazil, nostalgia, more precisely *saudade*, is something deeply felt. Cariocas are still possessive of the street, and still speak of it as "ours," a sense of possession that emerges from a lingering though suppressed longing for belonging – to the streets, to the neighborhood, and to the city. Cariocas still see glimmers of the street's past possibilities; they have not yet let go of hope for its future, and when occasion requires it, still engage in the bodily practices of the traditional street. Street love persists, even if it clings to weak and sometimes false memories. Yet that passion's reemergence has resulted in the variety of reclamations and restorations of some of Rio's former spaces – spaces that are to be made free, even if temporarily in some cases, of the car's all-powerful impositions.

J. R. McNeill has asserted that the automobile "is a strong candidate for the title of most socially and environmentally consequential technology of the twentieth century."[36] The automobile's impacts on the atmosphere and climate change, on urban development and suburban sprawl, on noise pollution, congestion, mortality, and even the imperialisms of petroleum, are broadly recognized. Future studies of the car, while not neglecting these, need to examine the car's more direct spatial consequences, what it has displaced. Approaching the car spatially exposes how limited our current solutions to the car are. Electric vehicles will reduce local air pollution and noise, as mufflers and catalytic converters did before them; and self-driving vehicles will reduce deaths and accidents, as seatbelts and airbags did before them. But they too will multiply the car and occupy more human habitats, leaving less for urban space's quintessential functions of celebration, disputation, and the construction of community, particularly in those regions where the car is just beginning its urban reign.

Rio's experience with the car in the street parallels that of many global cities. Compared to the developed West, the transformations came about a decade later and, more significantly, at a slower pace. The pace of change

---

[36] J. R. McNeill, *Something New under the Sun: An Environmental History of the Twentieth-Century World* (New York, NY: W. W. Norton, 2000), 310.

and the fact that many parts of the city remained inaccessible to the car worked to extend the city's traditional street culture well into the twentieth century, to keep the past in memory by keeping it alive in fragments. Street festivals and carnival, peddlers and street musicians declined, but they rarely disappeared. If Rio's case seems at times more poignant due to the fact that it had a highly developed street culture fostered by a climate amenable to year-round street use and the traditions of communal spaces coming from southern Europe and possibly Africa, many of the results were similar, even if on a different scale. However, a primary distinction derives from the fact that in developed nations, especially in much of the United States, a far larger percentage of citizens took advantages from car ownership, and the number of people who remained exclusively pedestrians much smaller. Rio's inequitable experience seems to have stronger peers in cities that have more recently or are currently experiencing this urban, automotive transition, particularly in Africa and South and East Asia, for what we have described is very much an ongoing and unfinished process. The ideolologies of modernization and the privileges of class remain the primary drivers of motordom, whether it be in Lagos, Mumbai, or Beijing. However, more work needs to be done. What is not well known is how this transition played out in other nations in Latin America, if and how they differed from the experience of Brazil's capital. As of yet, there are few studies of automobiles in the major cities of Latin America's other nations, large or small. Much remains to be learned about the timing, scope, resistance, and enforcement of automotive culture, and its likely there is a broad range of experiences and responses.

As an ecological space, a human habitat, the street is much degraded. There are many claims about the potential technological alternatives that may replace the street's former functions, but there are as yet no viable substitutes. Virtual communities are not real communities. At best they form communities of interest that tend to fragment society and reinforce opinions rather than foster dialogue between opposing views and classes. Social media and mobile devices may provide tools to assist in the gathering of communities of place, but they are not the gathering, nor are they the places to gather. Privatized and exclusive versions of the street also fall short in their attempts at virtualized commons. Communities require physical, public spaces to inhabit; without them, a democracy of space can at best be simulated; without them, we remain atomized, segregated, and increasingly alienated from one another. Fortunately, the street, unlike in so many other compromised spaces, is a problem with a relatively simple solution. In contrast to the dire choices faced in degraded fisheries and forests, warming climates, or any number of threatened habitats, the restoration of the street, from a space of running, oil, and blood to a place of quiet, safety, and potential community, is fairly straightforward. A simple bollard can reclaim a street; merely reducing automotive volumes and velocities can go a long way in making space for other utilities. With more equitable access and broadened utilities, the street can again evolve a multitude of meanings and utilities, some of them old, such as commerce, commemoration, courting, and community, and surely some new, yet to be invented spatial practices. We lament modernity's many costs, but the loss of the street, in Rio and in all of our central cities was a price too high. Those who could afford a car took the main benefits, but everybody has lost in the collective decision to let the car occupy our public spaces. There is no community without a space for it, and, as João do Rio testified, there is no space for it equal to the street.

Bibliography

ARCHIVES CONSULTED

Arquivo Geral da Cidade do Rio de Janeiro (AGCRJ)
Arquivo Nacional, Rio de Janeiro (ANRJ)
Biblioteca Nacional, Rio de Janeiro (BNRJ)
Biblioteca do Clube de Engenharia
Instituto Histórico e Geografico Brasileiro (IHGB)
Museu do Bonde, Rio de Janeiro
Museu Histórico Nacional
Real Gabinete Português de Leitura, Rio de Janeiro
Library of Congress, Hispanic Division, Washington DC

SERIAL PUBLICATIONS

Newspapers

A Classe Operária
Correio da Manhã
O Cruzeiro
O Diário Oficial
Estado de São Paulo
Gazeta de Notícas
A Imprensa
Jornal do Brasil
Jornal do Comércio
A Manhã
A Noite
O Paiz
A Rua

Magazines

Auto Federal
Automobilismo: A revista prática do automóvel
Auto Sport
Careta
Fon Fon
Klaxon
O Malho
Quatro Rodas
Revista de Automóveis (1911–1913)
Revista de Automóveis (1954–)
Revista da Semana
Veja
Vida Policial
Voz do Chauffeur

PRIMARY SOURCES

Adam, Paul. *Les Visages de Bresil*. Paris: P. Lafitte, 1914.
Agache, Alfred. *Rio de Janeiro; Extensão, remodelação, e embelezamento*. Paris: Foyer Brasilien, 1930.
Almeida, Renato. *Velocidade*. Rio de Janeiro: Schmidt, 1932.
Altieri, Álvaro. *Variações sobre o trânsito paulistano*. São Paulo: Sociedade "Amigos da Cidade," 1953.
Amaral, Amadeu. *Memorial de um passageiro de bonde*. São Paulo: Editora Hucitec, 1976.
Antunes Filho, M. *Manual prático do chauffeur sem mestre*, 3rd edn. Rio de Janeiro: n.p., 1946.
Aragão, Fructuoso Moniz Barreto de. *Delictos do automóvel e outros carros (sentenças)*. Rio de Janeiro: n.p., 1924.
Assistência pública e privada no Rio de Janeiro (Brasil): História e estatística, 1922. Rio de Janeiro: Typográphia do Annuário do Brasil, 1922.
Automovel Club do Brasil. *Primeira exposição de automobilismo, auto-propulsão e estradas de rodagem*. Rio de Janeiro: n.p., 1925.
Azambuja, Fernando, et al. *Leis que regem o trânsito: Código nacional de trânsito com as respectivas leis e decretos-leis modificadores, regulamento do trânsito do Estado do Rio Grande do Sul, leis federais e estaduais complementares, decretos-leis federais e estaduais complementares*. Pôrto Alegre: Livraria Sulina, 1953.
Azevedo, Aldo Mário de. *O serviço de prevenção contra accidentes: Trabalho apresentado á Sociedade "Amigos da Cidade" em 9 de março de 1938*. São Paulo: n.p., 1938.
Backheuser, Everardo. *Habitações populares*. Rio de Janeiro: Imprensa Nacional, 1906.

Barbosa, Plácido, and Cássio Barbosa de Rezende. *Os serviços de saúde pública no Brasil, especializmente na ciadade do Rio de Janeiro de 1808 a 1907*. 2 vols. Rio de Janeiro: Imprensa Nacional, 1909.

Barnes, Henry A. *The Man with the Red and Green Eyes: The Autobiography of Henry A. Barnes, Traffic Commissioner, New York City*. New York, NY: E. P. Dutton & Co., 1965.

Bell, Alured Gray. *The Beautiful Rio de Janeiro*. London: William Heinemann, 1915.

Berger, Paulo. *O Rio de ontem no cartão-postal, 1900–1930*, 2nd edn. Rio de Janeiro: Rio Arte, 1986.

Borges, Eduardo Fares. *Segurança de trânsito*. São Paulo: Sangirard, 1973.

Cabral, Victor Hugo Alencar. *Transporte, automóveis e a circulação*. Rio de Janeiro: Gráfica Laemert, 1948.

Chagas, João Pinheiro, *De bond: Alguns aspectos da civilização brasileira*. Lisbon: Livraria Moderna, 1897.

Cortés Sotelo, V. *Consejos y ejemplos relativos al tránsito en la República mexicana*. Mexico City: Tipografia Morales, 1938.

Costa, G. *Mão, contra-mão, & trânsito na capital federal para exames de motoristas: Guia para condutores de veículos*. Rio de Janeiro: Livraria para Todos, 1947.

Costa, Oswaldo Dias da. *Canção do bêco: Contos*. São Paulo: Editora Rumo, 1939.

Debret, Jean Baptiste. *Viagem pitoresca e histórica do Brasil* São Paulo: Editora da Universidade de São Paulo, 1978.

Caderno de Viagem, edited by Julio Bandeira. Rio de Janeiro: Sextante, 2006.

Dent, Hastings Charles. *A Year in Brazil with Notes on the Abolition of Slavery, the Finances of the Empire, Religion, Meteorology, Natural History, etc.* London: Kegan Paul, Trench & Co., 1886.

Departamento Nacional de Trânsito. *Acidentes de trânsito: Série histórica, 1960–83*, 2nd edn. Brasília: DENATRAN, 1984.

Dias da Costa, Oswaldo. *Canção do Beco: Contos*. São Paulo: Editora Rumo, 1939.

Directoria Geral de Hygiene e Assistência Pública. *Posto Central de Assistência: O socorro médico de urgência na via pública e em domicílio no Rio de Janeiro*. Rio de Janeiro: n.p., 1909.

Doxiadis Associates. *Guanabara; a Plan for Urban Development*. Athens: Technikon Grapheion Doxiadē, 1965.

Edmundo, Luiz. *O Rio de Janeiro do meu tempo*, 2nd edn. 5 vols. Rio de Janeiro: Conquista, 1957.

Eichner, Erich. *Cidade e arredores do Rio de Janeiro, a jóia do Brasil*. Rio de Janeiro: Livraria Kosmos Editora, E. Eichner & Cia. Ltda., 1944[?].

Elwes, Robert, Esq., *A Sketcher's Tour Round the World*. London: Hurst and Blacket, Publishers, 1854.

Ermakoff, George. *Juan Gutiérrez: Imagens do Rio de Janeiro, 1892–1896*. Rio de Janeiro: Marca da Agua, 2001.

Rio de Janeiro 1900–1930: Uma crônica fotográfica. Rio de Janeiro: G. Ermakoff Casa Editorial, 2003.

Rio de Janeiro, 1840–1900: Uma crônica fotográfica. Rio de Janeiro: G. Ermakoff Casa Editorial, 2006.

Rio de Janeiro, 1930–1960: Uma crônica fotográfica. Rio de Janeiro: G. Ermakoff Casa Editorial, 2008.

Augusto Malta e o Rio de Janeiro: 1903–1936. Rio de Janeiro: G. Ermakoff Casa Editorial, 2009.

Paisagem do Rio de Janeiro – Aquarelas, desenhos e gravuras dos artistas viajantes, 1790–1890. Rio de Janeiro: G. Ermakoff Casa Editorial, 2011.

Ewbank, Thomas. *Life in Brazil.* New York, NY: Harper & Brothers, 1856.

Ferrez, Gilberto. *A fotografia no Brasil, 1840–1900.* Rio de Janeiro: FUNART, 1985.

The Brazil of Eduard Hildebrandt. Rio de Janeiro: Distribuidora Record de Serviços de Imprensa, 1989.

Ferrez, Marc. *Avenida Central: 8 de Março 1903, 15 de Novembro 1906.* Paris: Erhard, n.d.

O Brasil de Marc Ferrez. São Paulo: Instituto Moreira Salles, 2005.

Fonseca, José Rubem. *Feliz Ano Novo: Contos,* 2nd edn. São Paulo: Companhia das Letras 1989.

Franck, Harry A. *Working North from Patagonia.* New York, NY: The Century Co., 1921.

Freyre, Gilberto. *The Mansions and the Shanties.* New York, NY: Knopf, 1963.

Guerra, Domingos Martins. *Os morros do Castelo e Santo Antonio são uteis ou nocivos a saúde publica? Durante o desmoronamento destes morros correria a cidade algum perigo?* Rio de Janeiro: Faculdade de Medicina do Rio de Janeiro, 1852.

Gutman, João, and Eugenio Gutman. *Mappa portátil e guia das ruas da cidade do Rio de Janeiro e de seus subúrbios,* 12th edn. Rio de Janeiro: n.p., 1931.

Isto é o Rio de Janeiro! 105 flagrantes da capital. São Paulo: Edições Melhoramentos, 1955.

Jacobs, Jane. *The Death and Life of Great American Cities.* New York, NY: Random House, 1961.

Kidder, Daniel P. and James C. Fletcher, *Brazil and the Brazilians, Portrayed in Historical and Descriptive Sketches.* Philadelphia, PA: Childs & Peterson, 1857.

Kipling, Rudyard. *Brazilian Sketches.* New York, NY: Doubleday, 1940 (original edn. 1927).

Le Corbusier, et al. *Oeuvre Compléte de 1910–1929,* 5th edn. Erlenbach-Zurich: Éditions d'Architecture, 1948.

Lima Barreto, Afonso Henriques de. *Toda Crônica,* 2 vols., edited by R. Beatriz and R. Valenca. Rio de Janeiro: AGIR Editora, 2004.

Macedo, Aulus Plautius. *A "taxa" de estacionamento, a constituição e a lei.* Rio de Janeiro: n.p., 1965.

Machado, Antônio Alcântara. *Novelas Paulistanas: Brás, Bexiga e Barra Funda, Laranja-da-China, Mana Maria, Contos avulsos.* Rio de Janeiro: José Olympio Editora, 1961.

Maurois, André. *Rio de Janeiro.* Paris: F. Nathan, 1951.

Memória da destruição: Rio – uma história que se perdeu (1889–1965). Rio de Janeiro: Arquivo da Cidade, 2002.

Miller, Edgard A. *Guia para motiristas e pedestres: Regras e regulamentos*. Rio de Janeiro: Freitas Bastos, 1959.

Monteiro Lobato, José Bento. *How Henry Ford Is Regarded in Brazil*. Rio de Janeiro: n.p., 1926.

O choque das raças: Ou, o Presidente Negro; romance americano do anno de 2228. Rio de Janeiro: Companhia Editoria Nacional, 1926.

Morais, Stélio de. *Um seminário sôbre a epidemiologia, e contrôle e a prevenção dos acidentes de tráfego*. Rio de Janeiro: Instituto de Pesquisa Rodoviárias, 1966.

Mumford, Lewis. *The Culture of Cities*. New York, NY: Harcourt, Brace and Company, 1938.

Netto, Costa. *Relatório*. São Paulo: Directoria do Serviço de Trânsito, 1936.

Pederneiras, Raul. *Scenas da vida carioca: Caricaturas de Raul*. Rio de Janeiro: Jornal do Brasil, 1924.

Pimenta, José Augusto de Mattos. *Para a remodelação do Rio de Janeiro: Discursos pronuniciados no Rotary Club do Rio de Janeiro*. Rio de Janeiro: Rotary Club, 1926.

Pimentel, Antonio Martins de Azevedo. *Quaes os melhoramentos hygiênicos que devem ser introduzidos no Rio de Janeiro para tornar esta cidade mais saudável*. Rio de Janeiro: Imprensa Nacional, 1895.

Quintana, Mário. *A rua dos cataventos*. Porto Alegre: Livraria do Globo, 1940.

Ribeyrolles, Charles. *Brazil pittoresco. Album de vistas, panoramas, paisagens, monumentos, costumes etc ... photographiados por Victor Frond*, vol. 2. Paris: Lemercier, 1861.

Rio de Janeiro. *Secretaria Municipal de Obras e Serviços Públicos. As ruas do Rio, 31 de outubro de 1917 a 30 de setembro de 1977*. Rio de Janeiro: Departamento Geral de Edificações, 1977–1979.

Rio de Janeiro, Distrito Federal. *Indicador de logradouros do Distrito Federal*. Rio de Janeiro: Imprensa Nacional, 1942.

Nomenclatura dos logradouros públicos da cidade do Rio de Janeiro, de acordo com a legislacão vigente até 31 de Dezembro de 1944. Rio de Janeiro: Secretaria do Prefeito, 1944.

Rio, João do. *A alma encantadora das ruas*. Rio de Janeiro: Prefeitura da Cidade do Rio de Janeiro, 1995 [original edn. 1908].

Sanson, Maria Lucia David de, et al. *O Rio de Janeiro do fotógrafo Leuzinger, 1869–1870*. Rio de Janeiro: Sextante Artes, 1998.

Santos, Fernando Agenor de Noronha. *Meios de transporte no Rio de Janeiro: História e legislação*. 2 vols. Rio de Janeiro: Typografia do Jornal do Comércio, 1934.

Seabra Júnior, Gregório Garcia. *Accidentes de automoveis: Delictos profissionaes dos automobilistas, doctrina, jurisprudência, legislação*. Rio de Janeiro: L. Ribeiro & Maurillo, 1918.

Silva, Francisco de Oliveira e. *Das indenizações por acidentes nas ruas e nas estradas: Automovel, bonde, estrada de ferro e energia elétrica*. São Paulo: Saraiva, 1940.

Souza, Paulo Teixeira de. *Os loucos do volante*. Rio de Janeiro: Secretaria do Estado de Educação e Cultura, Instituto Estadual do Livro, c. 1978.

Tewksbury, Howard H. *The Automotive Market in Brazil*. Washington, DC: US Department of Commerce, 1930.

Thompson, Daniella. "Praça Onze in Popular Song: The Square That Was and Will Be." *Música Brasiliensis*. http://daniellathompson.com/Texts/Praca_On ze/praca_onze.htm (accessed Dec. 2014).

Thoreau, Henry David. *The Journal of Henry David Thoreau*, vol. 5, Boston, MA: Houghton Mifflin, 1906.

Vieira, José. *O bota abaixo*. Rio de Janeiro: Selma Editora, n.d. [c. 1904].

Zweig, Stefan. *Brazil: Land of the Future*, translated by A. St. James. New York, NY: Viking Press, 1941.

SECONDARY SOURCES

Abath, Guilherme Montenegro. *Epidemiologia dos acidentes de trânsito ocorridos no Recife; no período de 1961–1971*. Recife: G. M. Abath, 1973.

Abreu, Martha Campos. *O império do divino: Festas religiosas e cultura popular no Rio de Janeiro, 1830–1900*. Rio de Janeiro: Nova Fronteira, 1999.

Abreu, Maurício de Almeida. "Reconstruindo uma história esquecida: Origem e expansão inicial das favelas do Rio de Janeiro." *Espaço e Debates* 14, no. 37 (1994): 34–46.

Abreu, Maurício de Almeida. *Evolução urbana do Rio de Janeiro*. Rio de Janeiro: IPLANRIO/J. Zahar, Editor, 1987.

Alexander, Christopher, Sara Ishikawa, and Murray Silverstein. *A Pattern Language: Towns, Buildings, Construction*. New York, NY: Oxford University Press, 1977.

Americano, Jorge. *São Paulo naquele tempo (1895–1915)*. São Paulo: Saraiva, 1957.

Andreatta, Verena. *Cidades quadradas, paraísos circulares: Os planos urbanísticos do Rio de Janeiro no século XIX*. Rio de Janeiro: Mauad X, 2006.

Appleyard, Donald. *Livable Streets*. Berkeley, CA: University of California Press, 1980.

Araújo, Achilles Ribeiro de. *A assistência médica hospitalar no Rio de Janeiro no século XIX*. Rio de Janeiro: Ministério da Educação e Cultura, Conselho Federal de Cultura, 1982.

Araújo, Rosa Maria Barboza de. *A vocação do prazer: A cidade e a família no Rio de Janeiro Republicano*. Rio de Janeiro: Rocco, 1993.

Baldwin, Peter C. *Domesticating the Street: The Reform of Public Space in Hartford, 1850–1930*. Columbus, OH: Ohio State University Press, 1999.

Benchimol, Jaime Larry. *Pereira Passos: Um Haussmann tropical: A renovação urbana da cidade do Rio de Janeiro no início do século XX*. Rio de Janeiro: Secretaria Municipal de Cultura, 1992.

Berger, Paulo. *Dicionário histórico das ruas do Rio de Janeiro: I e II regiões administrativas – Centro.* Rio de Janeiro: Gráfica Olímpica Editora, 1974.

Blanke, David. *Hell on Wheels: The Promise and Peril of America's Car Culture, 1900–1940.* Lawrence, KS: University of Kansas Press, 2007.

Blyth, Annabella. "Cristalização espacial e identidade cultural: Uma abordagem da herança urbana (o Saara, na área central da cidade do Rio de Janeiro)," 2 vol. Master's thesis, Universidade Federal do Rio de Janeiro, 1991.

Bonham, Jennifer. "Transport: Disciplining the Body that Travels." In *Against Automobility*, edited by Steffen Bohm, et al., 57–74. Oxford: Blackwell, 2006.

Brandão, Carlos Rodriguez. *A cultura na rua.* Campinas: Papirus Editora, 1989.

Brill, Michael. "Transformation, Nostalgia, and Illusion in Public Life and Public Place." In *Public Places and Spaces*, edited by Irwin Altman and Ervin H. Zube, 7–29. New York, NY: Plenum Press, 1989.

Brown-May, Andrew. *Melbourne Street Life: The Itinerary of Our Days.* Kew, Australia: Australian Scholarly Publishing /Arcadia and Museum Victoria, 1998.

Caldeira, Teresa P. R. *City of Walls: Crime, Segregation, and Citizenship in São Paulo.* Berkeley, CA: University of California Press, 2001.

Carvalho, Aurelia Maria Pinheiro de. *Sinais do Rio: A trajetória do Detran e de seus antecessores.* Rio de Janeiro: Governo do Estado do Rio de Janeiro, Secretaria de Estado de Segurança Pública, DETRAN, 2004.

Carvalho, Bruno. "Mapping the Urbanized Beaches of Rio de Janeiro: Modernization, Modernity and Everyday Life." *Journal of Latin American Cultural Studies: Travesia*, 16, no. 3 (2007): 325–39.

——— *Porous City: A Cultural History of Rio de Janeiro (from the 1810s Onward).* Liverpool: Liverpool University Press, 2013.

Casseb, Valter, et al. *Um estudo sobre os problemas de estacionamento de veículos.* São Paulo: Companhia de Engenharia de Tráfego, 1979.

Cavalcanti, Nireu. *O Rio de Janeiro Setecentista: A vida e a construção da cidade da invasão francesa ate a chegada da corte.* Rio de Janeiro: Jorge Zahar Editor, 2004.

Chalhoub, Sidney. *Trabalho, lar, e botequim: O cotidiano dos trabalhadores no Rio de Janeiro da belle époque.* São Paulo: Editora Brasiliense, 1986.

——— *Cidade febril: Cortiço e epidemias na corte imperial.* São Paulo: Companhia das Letras, 1996.

Chasteen, John Charles. "The Prehistory of Samba: Carnival Dancing in Rio de Janeiro, 1840–1917." *Journal of Latin American Studies* 28, no. 1. (Feb. 1996): 29–47.

Chazkel, Amy, *Laws of Chance: Brazil's Clandestine Lottery and the Making of Urban Public Life.* Durham, NC: Duke University Press, 2011.

Coaracy, Vivaldo. *Memórias da cidade do Rio de Janeiro.* Rio de Janeiro: José Olympio, 1955.

Cohen, Alberto A., and Samuel Gorberg. *Rio de Janeiro: O cotidiano carioca no início do século XX = Daily Life at the Start of the Twentieth Century.* Rio de Janeiro: A. A. Cohen Editora, 2007.

Cooper, Donald B. "Brazil's Long Fight against Epidemic Disease, 1849–1917, with Special Emphasis on Yellow Fever." *Bulletin of the New York Academy of Medicine* 51, no. 5 (May 1975): 672–96.

Correa, J. Pedro. *20 anos de lições de trânsito no Brasil.* Curitiba: Infolio, 2009.

Cronon, William. *Nature's Metropolis: Chicago and the Great West.* New York, NY: W. W. Norton & Co., 1991.

Curtis, James R. "Praças, Place, and Public Life in Urban Brazil." *Geographical Review* 90, no. 4 (Oct. 2000): 475–92.

DaMatta, Roberto. *A casa & a rua: Espaço, cidadania, mulher, e morte no Brasil.* São Paulo: Editora Brasiliense, 1985.

DaMatta, Roberto, et al. *Fé em Deus e pé na tábua: Ou, como e por que o trânsito enlouquece no Brasil.* Rio de Janeiro: Rocco, 2010.

Delson, Roberta Marx. *New Towns for Colonial Brazil: Spatial and Social Planning in the Eighteenth Century.* Ann Arbor, MI: Department of Geography, Syracuse University, 1979.

Downes, Richard. "Autos over Rails: How US Business Supplanted the British in Brazil." *Journal of Latin American Studies* 24, no. 3 (Oct. 1992): 551–83.

Dulles, John W. F. *Carlos Lacerda, Brazilian Crusader. Volume 2: The Years 1960–1977.* Austin, TX: University of Texas Press, 1996.

Dunlop, Charles. *Os meios de transporte do Rio de Janeiro antigo.* Rio de Janeiro: Serviço de Documentação, 1972.

El-Dahdah, Farés. *Lúcio Costa: Brasilia's Superquadra.* Munich: Prestel Verlag, 2005.

Epstein, David G. *Brasilia: Plan and Reality.* Berkeley, CA: University of California Press, 1973.

Evenson, Norma. *Two Brazilian Capitals: Architecture and Urbanism in Rio de Janeiro and Brasilia.* New Haven, CT: Yale University Press, 1973.

Flink, James J. *America Adopts the Automobile, 1895–1910.* Cambridge, MA: MIT Press, 1970.

The Automobile Age. Cambridge, MA: MIT Press, 1988.

Forest, Malcolm. *Automóveis de São Paulo: Memória fotográfica de pessoas, automóveis e localidades do Estado de São Paulo.* São Paulo: Arquivo do Estado, 2002.

Franco, Celso. *Eu na contramão: Os bastidores do trânsito carioca nas memorias do seu ex diretor.* Rio de Janeiro: Topbook, 1997.

Trânsito como eu o entendo: A ciência da mobilidade humana. Rio de Janeiro: E-papers, 2008.

Frank, Zephyr, and Whitney Berry. "The Slave Market in Rio de Janeiro circa 1869: Context, Movement and Social Experience." *Journal of Latin American Geography* 9, no. 3 (2010): 85–110.

Freeman, James. "Great, Good, and Divided: The Politics of Public Space in Rio de Janeiro." *Journal of Urban Affairs* 30, no. 5 (2008): 529–56.

Frehse, Fraya. *O tempo das ruas na São Paulo de fins do Império.* São Paulo: Edusp, 2005.

Freire, Américo. *Guerra de posições na metrópole: a prefeitura e as empresas de ônibus no Rio de Janeiro (1906–1948).* Rio de Janeiro: Fundação Getúlio Vargas, 2001.

Freitas, José Francisco Bernardino. "Townscape and Local Culture: The Use of Streets in Low-income Residential Areas in Vitória, Brazil." PhD diss., University of London, 1995.

Gerson, Brasil. *História das ruas do Rio de Janeiro*. Rio de Janeiro: Souza, 1954.

Gibson, Hugh. *Rio*. Garden City, NY: Doubleday, Doran & Company, Inc., 1937.

Glenny, Misha. *Nemesis: One Man and the Battle for Rio*. New York, NY: Alfred A. Knopf, 2016.

Gomes, Danilo. *Uma rua chamada Ouvidor*. Rio de Janeiro: Prefeitura da Cidade do Rio de Janeiro, Secretaria Municipal de Educação e Cultura: Fundação Rio, 1980.

Graham, Sarah Lauderdale. *House and Street: The Domestic World of Servants and Masters in Nineteenth-Century Rio de Janeiro*. Austin, TX: University of Texas Press, 1988.

Guldi, Jo, and David Armitage. *The History Manifesto*. Cambridge: Cambridge University Press, 2014.

Gunn, Simon. "People and the Car: The Expansion of Automobility in Urban Britain, c. 1955 –70." *Social History* 38, no. 2 (2013): 220–37.

Harlan, David. *The Degradation of American History*. Chicago, IL: University of Chicago Press, 1997.

Herzog, Lawrence. *Return to the Center: Culture, Public Space, and City Building in a Global Era*. Austin, TX: University of Texas Press, 2006.

Holloway, Thomas. *Policing Rio de Janeiro: Repression and Resistance in a 19th-Century City*. Stanford, CA: Stanford University Press, 1993.

Holston, James. *The Modernist City: An Anthropological Critique of Brasilia*. Chicago, IL: University of Chicago Press, 1989.

Jaguaribe, Beatriz. *Rio de Janeiro: Urban Life through the Eyes of the City*. New York, NY: Routledge, 2014.

Jain, Angela, and Massimo Moraglio. "Struggling for the Use of Urban Streets: Preliminary (Historical) Comparison between European and Indian Cities." *International Journal of the Commons* 8, no. 2 (Aug. 2014): 513–30.

James, Preston E. "Rio de Janeiro and São Paulo." *Geographical Review* 23, no. 2 (Apr. 1933): 271–98.

Karasch, Mary. *Slave Life in Rio de Janeiro*. Princeton, NJ: Princeton University Press, 1987.

Keller, Lisa. *Triumph of Order: Democracy and Public Space in New York and London*. New York, NY: Columbia University Press, 2009.

Klein, Herbert S. "The Colored Freedmen in Brazilian Slave Society." *Journal of Social History* 3 (Fall 1969): 30–52.

African Slavery in Latin America and the Caribbean. New York, NY: Oxford University Press, 1986.

Kostof, Spiro. *The City Assembled: The Elements of Urban Form through History*. London: Thames & Hudson, 1992.

Lefebvre, Henri. *The Production of Space*. Cambridge, MA: Blackwell, 1991.

Lima, Evelyn F. Werneck. *Avenida Presidente Vargas: Uma drástica cirurgia*. Rio de Janeiro: Secretaria Municipal de Cultura, 1990.

Lima, Herman. *História da caricatura no Brasil*. Rio de Janeiro: J. Olympio Editora, 1963.

Low. Setha M. *On the Plaza: The Politics of Public Space and Culture*. Austin, TX: University of Texas Press, 2000.

Macedo, Joaquim Manuel de. *Mémorias da Rua do Ouvidor*. São Paulo: Companhia Editora Nacional, 1952.

Magnani, José Guilherme Cantor. *Festa no pedaço: Cultura popular e lazer na cidade*. São Paulo: Editora Brasiliense, 1984.

Malamud, Samuel. *Recordando a Praça Onze*. Rio de Janeiro: Livraria Kosmos Editora, 1988.

McDowall, Duncan. *The Light: Brazilian Traction, Light and Power Company Limited, 1889–1930*. Toronto: University of Toronto Press, 1988.

McNeill, J. R. *Something New under the Sun: An Environmental History of the Twentieth-Century World*. New York, NY: W. W. Norton, 2000.

McShane, Clay. *Down the Asphalt Path: The Automobile and the American City*. New York, NY: Columbia University Press, 1994.

Meade, Teresa. *"Civilizing" Rio: Reform and Resistance in a Brazilian City*. University Park, PA: Pennsylvania State University Press, 1997.

Miller, Shawn W. "Stilt-root Subsistence: Colonial Mangrove Conservation and Brazil's Free Poor." *Hispanic American Historical Review* 83, no. 2 (May 2003): 223–53.

   An Environmental History of Latin America. New York, NY: Cambridge University Press, 2007.

Mitchell, Don. *The Right to the City: Social Justice and the Fight for Public Space*. New York, NY: The Guilford Press, 2003.

Mom, Gijs. *Atlantic Automobilism: Emergence and Persistence of the Car, 1895–1940*. New York, NY: Berghahn Books, 2015.

Moraglio, Massimo. "Knights of Death: Introducing Bicycles and Motor Vehicles to Turin, 1890–1907." *Technology and Culture* 56, no. 2 (Apr. 2015): 370–93.

Moran, Joe. "Imagining the Street in Post-war Britain." *Urban History* 39, no. 1 (2012): 166–86.

Moreira, Fernando Diniz. "Shaping Cities, Building a Nation: Alfred Agache and the Dream of Modern Urbanism in Brazil (1920–1950)." PhD diss., University of Pennsylvania, 2004.

Morel, Marco. "A política nas ruas: Os espaços públicos na cidade imperial do Rio de Janeiro [1820–1840]." *Estudos Ibero-Americanos* (Porto Alegre) 24, no. 1 (June 1998): 59–73.

   As transformações dos espaços públicos – imprensa, atores políticos e sociabilidades na cidade imperial (1820–1840). São Paulo: Editora Hucitec, 2005.

Morse, Richard M. *From Community to Metropolis: A Biography of São Paulo*. Gainesville, FL: University of Florida Press, 1958.

Morshed, Adnan. "The Cultural Politics of Aerial Vision: Le Corbusier in Brazil (1929)." *Journal of Architectural Education* 55, no. 4 (2002): 201–10.

Morton, Timothy. *Ecology without Nature: Rethinking Environmental Aesthetics*. Cambridge, MA: Harvard University Press, 2007.

Nasaw, David. *Children of the City: At Work and at Play.* New York, NY: Oxford University Press, 1986.

Needell, Jeffrey. "Rio de Janeiro and Buenos Aires: Public Space and Public Consciousness in Fin-de-Siècle Latin America." *Comparative Studies in Society and History* 37, no. 3 (Jul. 1995): 519–40.

A Tropical Belle Epoque: Elite Culture and Society in Turn-of-the-Century Rio de Janeiro. New York, NY: Cambridge University Press, 1987.

Norton, Peter D. *Fighting Traffic: The Dawn of the Motor Age in the American City.* Cambridge, MA: MIT Press, 2008.

O'Donnell, Julia. *De olho na rua: A cidade de João do Rio.* Rio de Janeiro: Zahar, 2008.

Packer, Jeremy. *Mobility without Mayhem: Safety, Cars, and Citizenship.* Durham, NC: Duke University Press, 2008.

Paterson, Matthew. *Automobile Politics: Ecology and Cultural Political Economy.* New York, NY: Cambridge University Press, 2007.

Pereira, Sonia Gomes. "A reforma urbana de Pereira Passos e a construção da identidade carioca." PhD diss., Universidade Federal do Rio de Janeiro, 1991.

Perlman, Janice. *Favela: Four Decades of Living on the Edge in Rio de Janeiro.* New York, NY: Oxford University Press, 2010.

Pimentel, João. *Blocos: Uma história informal do carnaval de rua.* Rio de Janeiro: Relume Dumara, 2002.

Pinto, Fernanda Mousse. "A invenção da Cidade Nova do Rio de Janeiro: Agentes, personagens e planos." Master's thesis, Universidade Federal do Rio de Janeiro, 2007.

Pinto, Maria Novaes. "A cidade do Rio de Janeiro: Evolução física e humana." *Revista Brasileira de Geographia* 27, no. 2 (Apr./June 1965): 191–232.

Prochnik, George. *The Impossible Exile: Stefan Zweig at the End of the World.* New York, NY: Doubleday, 2014.

Reis Filho, and Nestor Goulart. *Contribução ao estudo da evolução urbana do Brasil, 1500–1720.* São Paulo: Livraria Pioneira, 1968.

Ribeiro, Paula. "Saara e Praça Onze." *Revista de Estudos Judaicos* (Lisbon: Associação Portuguesa de Estudos Judaicos) 8 (2005): 6–15.

Ribeiro, Sandra Bernardes, and Marta Litwinczik Sinoti, "A Post-Occupancy Assessment of the Neighborhood Unit." In *Lucio Costa, Brasilia's Superquadra,* edited by Farés el-Dahdah, 92–95. Munich: Prestel Verlag, 2005.

Robert, Karen Joyce. "*The Argentine Babel: Space, Politics and Culture in the Growth of Buenos Aires, 1856–1890.*" PhD diss., University of Michigan, 1997.

Rocha, Oswaldo Porto. *A era das demolições: Cidade do Rio de Janeiro, 1870–1920.* 2nd edn. Rio de Janeiro: Prefeitura da Cidade do Rio de Janeiro, 1995.

Rosaldo, Renato. "Imperialist Nostalgia." *Representations* 26, Special Issue: Memory and Counter-Memory (Spring 1989): 107–22.

Rosenthal, Anton Benjamin. "Spectacle, Fear, and Protest: A Guide to the History of Urban Public Space in Latin America." *Social Science History* 24, no. 1 (Spring 2000): 33–73.

Santucci, Jane. *Cidade rebelde: As revoltas populares no Rio de Janeiro no início do século XX*. Rio de Janeiro: Casa da Palavra, 2008.

Sávio, Marco Antônio Cornacioni. *A modernidade sobre rodas: Tecnologia automotiva, cultura e sociedade*. São Paulo: EDUC, 2002.

A cidade e as máquinas: Bonde e automóveis nos primórdios da metrópole paulista, 1900–1930. São Paulo: Annablume, 2010.

Sedrez, Lise Fernanda. "'The Bay of All Beauties': State and Environment in Guanabara Bay, Rio de Janeiro, Brazil, 1875–1975." PhD diss., Stanford University, 2004.

Seksik, Laurent. *The Last Days*, translated by André Naffis-Sahely. London: Pushkin Press, 2013.

Sennett, Richard. *Flesh and Stone: The Body and the City in Western Civilization*. New York, NY: W. W. Norton, 1996.

The Fall of Public Man. New York, NY: W. W. Norton, 1992.

Sevcenko, Nicolau. *Orfeu extático na metrópole: São Paulo, sociedade e cultura nos frementes anos 20*. São Paulo: Companhia das Letras, 1992.

Shapiro, Helen. *Engines of Growth: The State and Transnational Auto Companies in Brazil*. New York, NY: Cambridge University Press, 1994.

Silva, Lucia Helena Pereira da. "A Praça Onze de Tia Ciata: A interface entre história, etnia e território." *Revista do Instituto Histórico e Geográfico do Rio de Janeiro* 14, no. 14 (2005): 143–60.

Sisson, Rachel. "Marcos históricos e configurações espaciais, um estudo de caso: Os centros do Rio de Janeiro." *Arquitetura Revista* 4, no. 2 (1986): 56–81.

Smith, David M. *Geography and Social Justice*. Oxford: Blackwell, 1994.

Soja, Edward W. *Thirdspace: Journeys to Los Angeles and Other Real and Imagined Places*. Oxford: Basil Blackwell, 1996.

Southworth, Michael, and Eran Ben-Joseph, *Streets and the Shaping of Towns and Cities*. Washington, DC: Island Press, 2003.

Sposito, Marilia Pontes. "A sociabilidade juvenil e a rua: Novos conflitos e ação coletiva na cidade." *Tempo Social* 5, nos. 1–2 (1993): 161–78.

Spreiregen, Paul. *Urban Design: The Architecture of Towns and Cities*. New York, NY: McGraw-Hill, 1965.

Stiel, Waldemar Corrêa. *História do transporte urbano no Brasil: História dos bondes e trólebus e das cidades onde eles trafegaram: "summa tranviariae brasiliensis."* São Paulo: Editora Pini, 1984.

Stuckenbruck, Denise Cabral. *O Rio de Janeiro em questao: O Plan Agache e o ideario reformista dos anos 20*. Rio de Janeiro: Observatório de Políticas Urbanas e Gestão Municipal: IPPUR/UFRJ, 1996.

Táti, Miécio. *O mundo de Machado de Assis*. Rio de Janeiro: Secretaria Municipal de Cultura, 1991.

Tinhorão, José Ramos. *Os sons que vêm da rua*, 2nd. edn. São Paulo: Editora 34, 2005.

Valentin, Andreas. *SAARA*. Rio de Janeiro: Francisco Alves, 2010.

Vasconcelos, Eduardo A. *Circular é preciso, viver não é preciso: A história do trânsito na cidade de São Paulo*. São Paulo: Annablume, FAPESP, 1999.

Velloso, Mônica Pimenta. "As tias baianas tomam conta do pedaço: Espaço e identidade cultural no Rio de Janeiro." *Estudos Históricos, Rio de Janeiro* 3, no. 6 (1990): 207–28.

A *cultura das ruas no Rio de Janeiro, 1900–1930: Mediações, linguagens e espaço.* Rio de Janeiro: Edições Casa de Rui Barbosa, 2004.

Vieira, Paulo Ernani Gadelha. *Assistência médica no Rio de Janeiro: Uma contribuição para sua história no período 1870–1967.* 2 vols. Rio de Janeiro: Centro de Memória Social Brasileira do Conjunto Universitário Candido Mendes, 1979 & 1980.

Virilio, Paul. *Speed and Politics: An Essay on Dromology.* New York, NY: Semiotext(e), 1986.

Wall, Derek. *The Commons in History.* Cambridge, MA: MIT Press, 2014.

Williams, Daryle. *Culture Wars in Brazil: The First Vargas Regime, 1930–1945.* Durham, NC: Duke University Press, 2001.

Wissenbach, Maria Cristina Cortez. "Da escravidão a liberdade: dimensões de uma privacidade possível." In *História da Vida Privada no Brasil*, vol. 3, edited by Nicolau Sevcenko, 49–130. São Paulo: Companhia das Letras, 1998.

White, Richard. *Railroaded: The Transcontinentals and the Making of Modern America.* New York, NY: W. W. Norton, 2011.

Whyte, William H. *The Social Life of Small Urban Spaces.* Washington, DC: Conservation Foundation, 1980.

Wolfe, Joel. *Autos and Progress: The Brazilian Search for Modernity.* New York, NY: Oxford University Press, 2010.

Yázigi, Eduardo. *Mundo das calçadas: Por uma política democrática de espaços públicos.* São Paulo: Humanitas, USP, Imprensa Oficial, 2000.

Zuckermann, Wolfgang, *The End of the Road: From World Car Crisis to Sustainable Transportation.* New York, NY: Chelsea Green, 1991.

Index

9 781108 447119